Roman Small Towns
in Eastern England and Beyond

edited by

A. E. Brown

Oxbow Monograph 52
1995

Published by
Oxbow Books, Park End Place, Oxford OX1 1HN

© Oxbow Books, 1995

ISBN 0 946897 90 5

This book is available direct from
Oxbow Books, Park End Place, Oxford OX1 1HN
(Phone: 01865-241249; Fax: 01865-794449)

and

The David Brown Book Company
PO Box 511, Oakville, CT 06779
(Phone: 203-945-9329; Fax: 203-945-9468)

The drawing on the cover is taken from William Stukeley,
Itinerarium Curiosum (Centuria 1, Iter V, 2nd edn 1776)
and shows the Roman small town of Great Chesterford
in Essex.

Printed in Great Britain at
The Short Run Press, Exeter

Contents

Contributors

A E Brown
Department of Adult Education,
University of Leicester,
University Road,
Leicester, LE1 7RH

Gilbert Burleigh
North Hertfordshire District Council,
Museums Resources Centre,
Burymead Road,
Hitchin,
Hertfordshire, SG5 1RT

Barry C Burnham
Saint David's University College,
University of Wales,
Lampeter,
Dyfed, SA48 7ED

Frances Condron
School of Archaeological Studies,
University of Leicester,
University Road,
Leicester, LE1 7RH

Michael Dawson
County Planning Department,
Bedfordshire County Council,
County Hall,
Cauldwell Street,
Bedford, MK42 9AP

Michael Eddy
Department of Archaeology,
University of Manchester,
Oxford Road,
Manchester, M13 9PL

Michael Gechter
Rheinisches Amt fur Bodendenkmalpflege,
Landschaftverband Rheinland,
Aussenstelle Overath,
Gut Eichthal,
51491 Overath,
Germany

David Gurney
Norfolk Landscape Archaeology,
Union House,
Gressenhall,
Dereham,
Norfolk, NR20 4DR

Anthony King
Department of History and Archaeology,
King Alfred's College,
Winchester,
Hants, SO22 4NR

Peter Liddle
Leicestershire County Council Museums,
Arts and Records Service,
96 New Walk,
Leicester, LE1 6TD

D F Mackreth
120 London Road,
Peterborough, PE2 9BY

Martin Millett
Department of Archaeology,
University of Durham,
46 Saddler Street,
Durham, DH1 3NU

Judith Plouviez
Archaeological Section,
Suffolk County Council Planning,
Shire Hall,
Bury St Edmunds,
Suffolk, IP33 2AR

Brian Simmons
Gables Cottage,
66 School Lane,
Silk Willoughby,
Sleaford,
Lincolnshire, NG34 8PH

Jeremy Taylor
Department of Archaeology,
University of Durham

John Wacher
Rosewin,
Gwinear Road,
Hayle,
Cornwall, TR27 5JQ

Ben Whitwell
3, Thorngarth Lane,
Barrow on Humber,
Humberside DN7 7AW

D R Wilson
University of Cambridge Committee
    for Aerial Photography,
Mond Building,
Free School Lane,
Cambridge, CB2 3RF

Charmian Woodfield
107 High Street,
Stony Stratford,
Bucks, MK11 1AT

1 Roman small towns, medieval small towns and markets

A E Brown

This volume is a record of a conference held at Knuston Hall during the weekend of 4–6 December 1992, under the auspices of the Department of Adult Education of the University of Leicester, to consider the Roman small towns of eastern England. At the conference the wish was expressed that the papers given should be published. Most of them are here, along with several others which were sought or offered subsequently.

The aim of the meeting was not to duplicate the recent monumental survey by Barry Burnham and John Wacher (1990) or to run through again material collected in Roger Smith's compendium of 1987 (Smith, R F, 1987). Rather the purpose was methodological – to consider some theoretical approaches which might help to advance understanding of Roman small towns (chapters 2, 4, 10); to look at practical methodologies applicable in current circumstances, in particular various methods of field survey, including aerial photography, various methods of geoprospection, fieldwalking and the analysis of metal-detected material (chapters 3, 5–9); to place our sites in the context of similar sites in the western Empire (chapters 17–18); and also to look at recent excavation results from a few selected sites and reinterpretations of some old problems (chapters 11–16). The purpose of these introductory remarks is very briefly and very selectively to introduce yet another approach, namely the possibility of comparing our Roman small towns with their medieval successors, in the hope that the recognition of similarities and differences will help to throw light on both periods.

Towards the close of the Conference one of the chairmen, John Wacher, remarked that a number of the sites which had been discussed were not in his view towns at all. Many of the contributors to this volume refer to this problem of definition and the literature clearly bears this out – Burnham and Wacher (1990) discuss a selected 54 sites; in his discussion of origins Burnham (1986) has 97; Millett's map (1990) shows 82; Smith (1987) describes no less than 148 'roadside settlements'. But modern historians have had exactly the same difficulties in deciding just what a small town was in the Middle Ages. From the standpoint of the documentary sources,

a variety of criteria has been considered in attempts to define just what places ought or ought not to be regarded as urban, for example the possession of a charter, the rate at which a place was taxed when a subsidy was levied, whether it had its own jury when the assizes were held or sent members to Parliament. In the event several modern commentators have taken the proved existence of burgage tenure, a form of free tenure involving a piece of land in a settlement which was held for a money rent and used for commercial activities of one sort or another and not as a farm, as sufficient evidence to justify the inclusion of a place in a list of medieval boroughs (Beresford & Finberg 1973). This accommodates such non-controversial places as Market Harborough in Leicestershire, founded on a green field site in the 12th century but also produces some distinct oddities such as Catesby and Thornby in Northamptonshire, small places which no one today would have thought ever possessed any urban characteristics whatever. But contemporary, medieval, tax collectors also had difficulties in deciding whether a place was to be thought of as a town or not, given the variations in size between them, and the degree to which agriculture still formed a basic activity, and there are places which were considered boroughs for one tax collection but which were regarded as ordinary villages for another, Brill in Buckinghamshire or Mountsorrel in Leicestershire, for example (*ibid*, 76, 135). There are some places, such as Daventry in Northamptonshire, which despite a substantial population, many burgage tenements, abundant tradespeople and a perfectly obvious market place, but with extensive field systems, which remained technically villages as far as royal administration was concerned to the end of the Middle Ages and beyond (Brown 1991). The question of definition is an old one, and perhaps cannot altogether be expected to give clear-cut answers, because in both periods we are dealing with a continuum, with the emphasis between trade and agriculture varying from place to place .

The market towns of medieval England might be more compact than the generally irregular ribbon-like sites of Roman Britain, and the topographical study of them has its place in defining their urban status, the existence of an obvious market place being particularly relevant, but here again a plan without adequate documentation to prove the existence of what contemporaries thought of as a town may not in itself be sufficient. Several villages have greens which on a map will look just like market places and many quite ordinary farms sat in long narrow plots with standardised frontages indistinguishable from burgage tenements. In medieval England, and the same was surely true of Roman Britain, there was no sharp distinction between town and countryside.

The development of a town was a seigneurial operation involving king, abbot or lay lord. The main motive was of course financial; Maurice Beresford (1988, 60) has clearly shown how useful the rents from stalls and burgages and the tolls from the weekly markets and annual fairs were as additions to the normal run of agricultural profits. These are motives which could have been well understood by any Roman landowner (Todd 1989). But there were other, political, factors which represent points of difference with the Roman period: the planting of boroughs outside castles was part of the process of conquest by the Normans in the same way as town creation formed part of Edward I's programme for the subjugation of Wales. The process of town creation played a part in the king's management of his barons – the crown could use the grant of a market and fair as a reward or favour. Also a borough was a thing of dignity which added lustre to lordship in rather the same way that a monastery would – a Romano-British villa owner would perhaps not have quite the same feelings about a *vicus* established on his land.

In this volume Frances Condron points to the continuance of a socially embedded economy as a factor in the economic life of Roman Britain. This must be right, and there may be parallels with medieval England in this as well, since a good deal of the movement of goods and services went on outside the market system altogether, renders in kind as a condition of holding land being common up to the 12th century and surviving to a variable degree beyond – in Norfolk the Paston family were still receiving rents in barley in the 15th century (Britnell 1988). A relatively recent suggestion would be to see many apparently financial transactions between villagers as having no money element at all, payment taking the form of meals, labour or produce of some kind, with figures in manorial accounts for services rendered tacitly representing the cash value of such services rather than actual money payments (Dyer 1989, 185). Nevertheless, one of the usefulnesses of medieval England to the student of Roman Britain is to show how an apparently low level of material culture, archaeologically determined, can go hand in hand with a degree of monetization which made markets a vital necessity for a very large number of people.

There are obvious parallels between the market towns of medieval England and the small towns of Roman Britain. That many of the Roman small towns were periodic markets seems a reasonable assumption: market places or market buildings have been identified or suggested at Braughing, Godmanchester, Irchester, Water Newton/ Chesterton and elsewhere. The place-name *Bannaventa* (Whilton Lodge, Northamptonshire), meaning 'the market on the spur of land' may well have applied to the Roman site itself rather than to the nearby hill fort (Dix & Taylor 1988). That they were places where craftsmen worked is abundantly clear from archaeology (eg Sapperton and Sandy, this volume). Some in part exhibit elements of planning in a not altogether un-medieval fashion, Hibaldstow, Towcester or *Magiovinium* (Fenny Stratford/Dropshort), and Godmanchester for example. Many have elements of the mixed agricultural and craft economy familiar from the medieval sites; other places have clear links with religious foci in the manner of such places as Bury St Edmunds in Suffolk or Walsingham in Norfolk (technically not a borough, but which had a market). This volume (eg the papers by Ben Whitwell on Lincolnshire and Peter Liddle on Leicestershire) show how detailed field survey indicates that quite a few of the Roman small towns started off as Iron Age settlements and changed their character during the Roman period, in perhaps rather the same way as many medieval small towns developed from agricultural villages. In the Middle Ages such new towns survived if they had good communications and matched the social and economic requirements of the area in which they lay – Higham Ferrers in Northamptonshire for example, which already had a market at Domesday, was turned into a borough by the earl of Derby in 1251 and developed because of its position on a main road and as the centre of a large estate, with a castle (Beresford 1957, 153–79). So in Roman Britain – native sites could develop into small towns if they fitted in with the road system and administrative requirements of the conquerors (Burnham 1986). Some, such as Baldock (Burleigh, this volume), already had a quasi-urban role, as did many of the soke or estate centres of Anglo-Saxon England.

But were the Roman small towns seigneurial in the same way as the medieval ones? Some places clearly had an official role connected with the requirements of the provincial government as functioning parts of the *cursus publicus*; there were certainly more of these than the Antonine Itinerary would suggest since neither Godmanchester, which certainly had a *mansio*, nor Great Casterton, which probably had one, are mentioned in it. The town walls discussed by Charmian Woodfield in this volume clearly indicate a deep concern by the authorities with the safety of certain roads. But elsewhere the possible association between villas and small towns, a topic alluded to several times in this volume, seems quite plausible in some cases – Sapperton or Hibaldstow in Lincolnshire for example, or Medbourne in Leicestershire. Also it is possible that some of the roadside frontages in the larger small towns were developed by the villa owners through whose estates they happened to run, as has been suggested for the Alchester road at Towcester, where agricultural land was replaced by a planned series of plots containing workshops given over mainly to ironworking in the late 2nd century (Brown *et al* 1988, 49). In this way it would have been possible for more than one villa proprietor to have a share in the development of the same small town, even one with a pronounced official bias.

However, there is also the question of the location and spacing of the Roman small towns to consider, a point raised in this volume by Martin Millett. During the Middle Ages there could be a strongly competitive element in the foundation of towns by local lords. This could lead to a situation in which quite independent towns could be made to cluster together in basically the same place, although most examples of this kind of thing are to be found in the south-west of England at such places as Totnes, Newton Abbot and Looe, outside the area covered by this volume (although an eastern example can be found at Linton in Cambridgeshire (Brown & Taylor, forthcoming)). Also trade could be switched from one town or market to another and, within a dense network, roads could rise and fall in importance in a way which probably did not happen in Roman Britain. It was probably the creation by William Malet of a borough outside the castle of Eye in Suffolk, with a Saturday market, which led to the recent decline in the value of the market at Hoxne recorded in Domesday Book. In Northamptonshire the construction of a bridge over the Cherwell by the Neville family, lords of Aynho, helped to promote the market there to the detriment of the Domesday market at Kings Sutton two miles away (Britnell 1993, 11, 16; Goodfellow 1987–8, 315). Developments of this kind are not really detectable in the archaeological record for Romano-British small towns, where a fairly even spacing along the engineered roads of the province is the norm. In this we may be seeing, as well as the hand of the imperial authorities in the provision of official installations, the way in which the *civitates* of the province worked. Perhaps the element of internal competition was not so strongly developed in them and they operated on the oligarchic principles outlined by Martin Millett (1990, 82). Gaps in the provision of markets could have been filled where the *civitas* collectively thought they ought to be – perhaps to fit in with the local *pagus* system – and not through the outcome of a process of competition between rival landowners. This need not rule out intervention by the imperial representatives, through the *civitas* authorities, to secure the provision of markets and the provision of facilities for official travellers at places which were considered to be lacking, as is known to have happened in Italy, Greece and elsewhere in the East (MacMullen 1970, 334).

But the towns formed only a part of the apparatus of buying and selling in medieval England. Medieval England was also full of market villages, basically agricultural places at which weekly markets and occasional fairs were held, all seigneurially controlled, with their establishment subject to much the same pressures as the foundation of new boroughs. As a very rough indication of their density one can point to the 98 places in Suffolk which had received market grants by 1547 (Scarfe 1972, 165); Norfolk, a rich county with few boroughs but a high population, had 138 (Dymond 1985, 152); 1200 places (some of course boroughs) received such grants between 1227 and 1350, with a peak between 1250 and 1275 (Coates 1985, Britnell 1981). In general terms the growth in markets was at its greatest when the population of England was rising; when the use of coinage was increasing; and when the development of taxation based on an assessment of moveable wealth meant that the arm of the tax collector was reaching the individual peasant directly. This meant that peasants who had hitherto been able to meet their obligations to their lords by means of their labour services now discovered that lords no longer required these but demanded their equivalent in cash as well as money to meet various fines and tallages, while at the same time they found themselves personally forced to meet the demands of royal taxation. The sale of surplus produce was one way in which they could make ends meet; the growth of the market economy had the effect of depressing their economic position (others, the kulak class, could benefit, Biddick 1987). Rather similar factors could have been at work in 2nd century Britain – it may have been enforced participation in the market system, the result of the need to acquire coin, which kept the economic status of sections of the peasantry low, while increasing the number of markets. The high cost of Romanisation could have produced strains resulting in local disturbances, a possibility referred to by Charmian Woodfield in this volume.

The necessity to sell off small agricultural surpluses to meet taxation demands was, however, only one factor behind the proliferation of markets in 12th and 13th century England. Perhaps more important was the growth in the population already referred to and the accompanying expansion of agricultural land, which created a requirement for places where small agricultural surpluses could be sold off. The population of the country at this time has been variously estimated at 4 1/2 – 6 million (Hatcher 1977: Smith, R, 1988, 190–1). The population of Roman Britain at its height has proved a still more contentious matter, with recent estimates ranging from 2.8 to 5–6 million, ie approaching the medieval total, but the most carefully reasoned current estimate is more modest, *c* 3.7 million (Millett 1990, 182–5).

Now if the population of Roman Britain had in fact been round about the lower end of the range suggested for it, then we are looking at a figure which is comparable with the current best estimates for the population of England at the time of Domesday or in the early 16th century (1.75 to 2.75 million), after the population collapse of the late medieval period (Hatcher 1977). Now for certain well-surveyed areas we may well have the

Fig 1.1 *Roman small towns and early medieval markets in Northamptonshire*

Fig 1.2 *Medieval boroughs and markets in Northamptonshire, 1086–1500 (after Goodfellow 1987–8 and Beresford & Finberg 1973, with additions)*

totality of our Roman small towns – Fig 1.1 shows the position in Northamptonshire and southern Leicestershire, which have been the subject of intensive survey for some time. This is remarkably similar to the pattern of Domesday markets for the area (including a few places which were not specifically said to have had markets, but which later acquired them and as soke centres might well have had them in 1086), and might imply a rough equivalence in population between the two periods. Fig 1.2 shows the total medieval pattern of markets for the same county down to 1500. The medieval map includes both towns ie places which had plots held by burgage tenure and which therefore were supposed to contain craftsmen and retailers, and villages with markets held periodically once a week or so. This map seems to give an impression of a far denser and more complicated apparatus of commercial activity in the medieval county than its Roman equivalent, but a number of factors have to be taken into account in interpreting maps of this sort. Not all medieval markets necessarily operated at quite the same time and there is always the possibility that a market grant might not actually have been taken up; and on the Roman side there are imponderables – no doubt there are still gaps in our knowledge of Roman small towns; new sites and new roads turn up from time to time, the chapters in this volume on Leicestershire and Norfolk for example having instances of this; rural temples have for a long time been suggested as possible market sites; there could have been markets held at fixed locations in the open countryside about which we know nothing; and villas have been suggested as focal points for marketing particularly in the later Empire when they could have taken trade away from the established small towns and acted as points for tax collection, an aspect which has received added interest recently from the excavations at Stanwick in the Nene Valley, with its abundance of coin finds (Neal 1989 and pers comm). Also it is possible that there are large sites traditionally classified as villages, which may appear in gaps off the road network which could have fulfilled a periodic market function quite satisfactorily without necessarily providing the full range of craft specialisation which the small towns on the main roads had – Kirmington in Lincolnshire, discussed in this volume, can be suggested as an example of such a site.

But while acknowledging these factors, it must remain very much an open question whether in the Roman period there had been as many as the fifty or so markets the medieval county of Northamptonshire had, or the apparent 120 or more in Lincolnshire (Fleet 1993, table on p8) or the huge totals known for Norfolk and Suffolk. These figures look like a feature characteristic of the developed Middle Ages, and reflect very high population levels as well as the opportunities the system of government gave to lords to establish such places. What seems possible however is that the number of small *towns* for the given area might be comparable; not all that many sites shown on Fig 1.2 were new, post-1086, boroughs

with burgage tenure and of those that were quite a few failed. The successful ones were those with good communications and which were able to serve a particular region of the county, quite often one which had had a Roman small town in a slightly different place; thus Brackley replaced Kings Sutton, Daventry, *Bannaventa* and Thrapston, Titchmarsh. This volume shows just how many Roman small towns are known and a comparison with their medieval successors quite often shows a rough degree of similarity in geographical spread – Peter Liddle points out how the Roman small towns of Leicestershire match region for region the medieval ones; the possible twelve Roman towns for Suffolk are matched by ten in the medieval period. So, on a regional basis, there was enough demand in both periods to support more or less the same number of local marketing, craft and retail centres but a serious question must remain about a similarity in the number of rural periodic markets, which archaeology will be well placed in the end to answer. For the medieval period, field survey has been able to identify the changes to village plans brought about by the inception of a market, and at least one village market place has been identified by excavation (Taylor 1982; Alexander 1968); it remains to be seen whether Roman Britain will produce comparable observations on any scale. All this in the end may help to produce a balanced view of some of the high population figures for Roman Britain which have appeared from time to time, as well as throwing into relief the differences in lordship and its relationship with the central authorities which existed between the two periods.

Acknowledgements
The Editor wishes to acknowledge the help of Ben Whitwell (who first suggested the idea) in setting up the conference and of Martin Millet, who commented on this chapter. Gillian Patterson and Stephanie Kneller did the necessary typing; Figs 1.1 and 1.2 were drawn by Deborah Miles of the School of Archaeological Studies, University of Leicester.

Bibliography

Alexander, J A, 1968 Clopton: the life-cycle of a Cambridgeshire village, in *East Anglian Studies* (ed L Munby), 48–70
Beresford, M, 1957, *History on the ground*
——, 1988 *New towns of the Middle Ages* (2nd ed)
——, & Finberg, H P R, 1973 *English medieval boroughs: a handlist*
Biddick, K, 1987 Missing links: taxable wealth, markets and stratification among medieval English peasants, *J Interdisciplinary Hist*, 18 (2), 277–298
Britnell, R H, 1981 The proliferation of markets in England, 1200–1349, *Econ Hist Rev*, 34, 209–221
——, 1988 The Pastons and their Norfolk, *Agricultural Hist Rev*, 36, 132–44
——, 1993 *The commercialisation of English society*

Brown, A E, Woodfield, C W, & Mynard, D C, 1983 Excavations at Towcester, Northamptonshire: the Alchester road suburb, *Northamptonshire Archaeol*, 18, 43–140

——, 1991 *Early Daventry, an essay in early landscape planning*

——, & Taylor, C C forthcoming Little Linton and the Linton landscape, *Proc Cambridge Antiq Soc*

Burnham, B C, & Wacher, J, 1990 *The 'small towns' of Roman Britain*

Coates, B E, 1985 The origin and distribution of markets and fairs in medieval Derbyshire, *Derbyshire Archaeol J*, 85, 92–3

Dix, B, & J Taylor, S, 1988 Excavations at Bannaventa (Whilton Lodge, Northants), 1970–1971, *Britannia*, 19, 299–339

Dyer, C, 1989, *Standards of living in the later Middle Ages*

Dymond, D, 1985 *The Norfolk landscape*

Fleet, P, 1993 Markets in medieval Lincolnshire, *East Midland Historian*, 3, 7–14

Goodfellow, P, 1987–8 Medieval markets in Northamptonshire, *Northamptonshire Past Present*, 7, 305–323

Hatcher, J, 1977 *Plague, population and the English economy 1348–1530*

MacMullen, R, 1970 Market days in the Roman empire, *Phoenix*, 24, 333–41

Millett, M, 1990 *The Romanisation of Britain*

Neal, D S, 1989 The Stanwick villa, Northants: an interim report on the excavations 1984–88, *Britannia*, 20, 149–68

Scarfe, N, 1992 *The Suffolk landscape*

Smith, R, 1988 Human resources, in *The countryside of medieval England* (eds G Astill & A Grant), 188–211

Smith, R F, 1987 *Roadside settlements in lowland Roman Britain*, BAR Brit Ser, 157

Taylor, C C, 1982 Medieval market grants and village morphology, *Landscape Hist*, 21–8

Todd, M, 1989 Villa and *fundus*, in *The economies of Romano-British villas* (ed K Branigan & D Miles), 14–20

2 Small towns: the British perspective

Barry C Burnham

The publication of *The 'small towns' of Roman Britain* (Burnham & Wacher 1990), though not without its detractors (Clarke 1991; Esmonde Cleary 1992), has clearly done much to rekindle interest in the importance of the 'small town' as an element in the settlement pattern of Roman Britain and to draw attention to the wealth of new information now available, much of it collected over the last thirty years or so. The present volume is itself a reflection of that renewed interest, seeking to examine the topic in depth with special reference to the East Midlands and the east of England by means of a variety of papers, some looking at broad issues, others concerned with regional studies, and yet others focused on individual sites. The purpose of this paper is to try and set the wider British perspective for the rest of the volume, by reviewing some of the significant advances in our understanding of the small towns and by noting some of the outstanding issues for future discussion.

The 1960s witnessed a significant increase in the number of small towns being excavated, a trend which reached a peak in the 1970s. This high level of activity was also accompanied by an important shift away from small-scale trenching (especially on the defences) to much larger scale, open-area excavations (primarily on the internal features). Naturally, the character and intensity of this work varied from site to site, ranging from limited rescue work (eg Alchester – Young 1975, Foreman & Rahtz 1984; Ancaster- Todd 1981; Braintree – Drury 1976, Eddy 1984; Irchester – Hall & Nickerson 1968, Windell 1984; and *Margidunum* – Todd 1969), through detailed examinations of individual building complexes (eg the temple and bathing facilities at Bath – Cunliffe 1969, 1976, Cunliffe & Davenport 1985; the Bays Meadow complex at Droitwich – Freezer 1979; and the temples' precinct at Springhead – Penn 1960, 1961, 1963, 1968), to large-scale rescue excavations at one or more locations in the plan (eg Alcester-Booth 1980, Frere 1986, 393–5; Baldock – Stead & Rigby 1986; Braughing – Partridge 1978, 1980, 1981, Potter & Trow 1988; Hibaldstow – Smith 1987, 188–98; Neatham – Millett & Graham 1986; Towcester – Lambrick *et al* 1980, Brown *et al* 1983; and Wanborough-Anderson & Wacher 1980).

The information so derived was further enhanced by regular aerial reconnaissance, most notably by the Cambridge Committee for Aerial Photography (see for example St Joseph 1966; Wilson 1975 and this volume; Frere & St Joseph 1983, 166–81). This proved a welcome bonus to excavation at some sites (eg Corbridge, Kenchester and Mildenhall), while elsewhere it supplied virtually the only evidence (eg Brough-on-Fosse, Chesterton-on-Fosse). Its potential has been amply demonstrated by C Stanley's photographs of Alchester (Stanley 1979) and D Mackreth's work at Water Newton (Mackreth 1979 and this volume; Frere, Rivet & Sitwell 1987, plan v). To this we might also add the increasing use of geophysical survey as a prospecting tool, the results of which are best illustrated by work at Baldock (Stead & Rigby 1986, now updated by Gil Burleigh, this volume).

Such intensified activity inevitably led to an immense increase in the quantity and the quality of the data at our disposal and, not surprisingly, stimulated several general syntheses of the evidence and a wide range of new ideas and approaches. The first such synthesis was an article by M Todd in *Britannia*, published in 1970. This sought 'to outline the state of our knowledge and to define some of the main problems', by summarising the evidence under several headings which were to set the agenda for much later research – viz the sites themselves, size, planning and buildings, the relationship with the countryside, and industry. Todd also recognised the considerable diversity amongst the sites hitherto included within the umbrella term 'small towns', though he remained somewhat restrictive on the criteria for urban status by emphasising features which would be recognisable by a Roman from another province.

This preliminary synthesis was soon followed by a conference specifically devoted to the small towns, held in Oxford in 1975, the proceedings of which were subsequently published as an edited volume by W Rodwell & T Rowley (1975). This contained several general articles and a series of individual site summaries, which together attempted to address various issues of importance to the debate about the small towns. It also included some new approaches which were to find echoes in the future, most notably in the papers by Rivet (on classification), Webster (on the small towns without defences), and Rodwell (on a regional case study of Trinovantian towns). Lurking behind all these contributions, however, lay an unresolved issue concerning the initial criteria for inclusion as a 'small town'.

The publication of Rodwell and Rowley's volume coincided with that of two other significant books, one on the *Towns of Roman Britain* by J Wacher (1974), the other on *Oppida* edited by B Cunliffe and T Rowley (1976). Together they provoked a semantic debate on what constituted a 'town', which was to linger on throughout the 1970s. In hindsight it is easy to see that this wasted a lot of time and energy, but it did at least help to focus our attention on the nature of the archaeological evidence and the problems of analysing it in terms of recognisable urban indicators, such as settlement morphology and function. Another dimension of this debate which enjoyed a brief, if somewhat undistinguished, floruit in the 1970s, was the attempt by J Alexander (1975) and M Millett (1975) to identify imposed and indigenous forms of urbanism.

The 1970s also witnessed the popularity of various spatial and locational models, especially that of geographical central place theory. Not surprisingly, therefore, several attempts were made, most notably by I Hodder (eg Hodder & Hassall 1971; Hodder 1972; 1975), to apply such models to explaining the origins and development of the small towns. More sophisticated models were even used in an attempt to equate the distribution of Savernake Ware with the predicted market area around the small town at Mildenhall (Hodder 1974). In general, however, the results did not meet with any widespread acceptance.

This high level of interest in the small towns was maintained throughout the 1980s, stimulated by the publication of several important excavation volumes, among them works on Baldock (Stead & Rigby 1986), Bath (Cunliffe & Davenport 1985), Braughing (Partridge 1981; Potter & Trow 1988), Chelmsford (Drury 1988; Wickenden 1992), Great Dunmow (Wickenden 1988), Ilchester (Leach 1982), Kelvedon (Rodwell 1987), Little Chester (Dool *et al* 1986) and Neatham (Millett & Graham 1986). These can be supplemented by various shorter reports or reassessments of earlier work published in local journals and elsewhere on such sites as Carlisle (McCarthy 1984; McCarthy *et al* 1982), Catterick (Wilson 1984), Cave's Inn (Lucas 1981), Dorchester-on-Thames (Frere 1985), Frilford (Hingley 1985), Horncastle (Field & Hurst 1983), Kenchester (Wilmott 1980), Sea Mills (Ellis 1987) and Wilderspool (Petch 1987).

There have also been several general works of synthesis on urban issues, which have contributed much to the small town debate. These include :(i) the regional case study of *Urban settlements in the West Midlands* by J Crickmore (1984b), which concentrated on such themes as classification, origins and development, and function; (ii) the gazetteer of *Roadside settlements in lowland*

Roman Britain by R F Smith (1987), which addressed the issues of origins, growth and decline, land division and economy, and cemeteries; (iii) the survey of *Extramural areas outside Romano-British towns* by S Esmonde Cleary (1987). To these can be added my own research on the small towns, which addressed such themes as origins, settlement morphology, and the range of internal buildings (Burnham 1986; 1988; 1989). All this has now been supplemented by the publication of a volume specifically directed at *The 'small towns' of Roman Britain* (Burnham & Wacher 1990), which covers some 54 of the better known sites alongside general chapters on origins and development, morphology and function.

It should be obvious that much of this research has been concerned with the small towns or related urban issues in relative isolation. It is thus important to record that the last decade or so has witnessed a shift in emphasis, with an upsurge of interest in the ancient economy amongst ancient historians and archaeologists alike, building on the foundations laid by Finley *et al* (eg Finley 1973; Duncan-Jones 1974; Garnsey, Hopkins & Whittaker 1983; Garnsey & Saller 1987; Greene 1986; and Fulford 1989). As far as towns are concerned, this has raised important issues about their changing economic role and the relationship between town and country, topics which have been addressed by various authors including M Fulford (1982), M Millett (1982), and R F Smith (1987). Much of the discussion has been concerned with the problem of quantifying the relative importance of agriculture and craft-specialisation within the settlement hierarchy, to which M Todd (1989, 17) has added another dimension, with his suggestion that some rural townships served as estate villages and thus enjoyed a close relationship with nearby villas.

Increasingly, however, such issues are being overtaken by a debate about the relative roles of the large and small towns, a topic which has received a recent airing in M Millett's *The Romanization of Britain* (1990), drawing upon arguments first set out by Reece (1980). This draws a contrast between the apparent economic stagnation of the cities in the 3rd/4th centuries and the economic prosperity of many small towns in what had previously been the blank areas close to the *civitas* borders. The implications of this debate have yet to be worked out, but there is already a danger that too sharp a distinction is being drawn much as happened with the semantic debate of the 1970s (Esmonde Cleary 1989, 64–85; Fulford 1992, 308–9). Even so, this discussion of towns, large and small, within wider contexts, beyond the more parcelled approach of the 1970s, is one of the important trends of the last decade, not least because it raises important questions about the nature and definition of 'small towns', their regional distribution, and their relative importance through time.

From this brief review it should be clear that a considerable amount of research and synthesis has been done in recent years across a wide range of issues. It remains, therefore, to outline what seem to be some of the most significant advances in our understanding and some of the associated problems.

(1) The **first** significant point is that we continue to discover new sites, which underlines the major shortcomings in our understanding of the nature and distribution of small towns. Recent examples include Cowbridge, probably identifiable with the 'Bovium' of the *Antonine Itinerary* (Parkhouse 1981; 1982), and the new importance attached to Frilford, where a religious complex has long been known (Bradford & Goodchild 1939; Hingley 1985). Regional surveys also have an alarming tendency to 'discover' new sites based largely on a scatter of occupation debris, as for example in Essex (Rodwell 1975), Lincolnshire (May 1976) and Northamptonshire (RCHM(E) 1979, figs 11 and 12); and before we are tempted to dismiss these as large agricultural villages, we should recall the results of the excavations at Ashton, which have revealed a surprising level of specialised ironworking in connection with the strip buildings in their associated compounds or yards (Hadman & Upex 1975; 1977; 1979; Dix 1983).

(2) **Second**, we now possess a better understanding of the class of small towns without defences (Webster 1975). In this sphere, significant advances have been made as a result of the excavations at such sites as Ashton (just discussed), Baldock (Stead & Rigby 1986; Burleigh 1982; Selkirk 1983), Hibaldstow (Smith 1987, 188–98), Sapperton (Simmons 1976; 1985 and this volume; Oetgen 1986; 1987) and Tiddington (Palmer 1981; 1983). These have helped to demonstrate the complexity of the settlement hierarchy, as well as the wide range of sites hitherto called 'small towns'. The picture remains far from perfect, however, because insufficient work has yet been done at the growing number of sites which tend to be located away from the main roads of the province.

(3) **Third**, we have acquired a much clearer understanding of internal morphology, upon which there is now quite a literature (for a brief review, see Burnham 1988; 1989). The following features stand out:

a) The relative importance of a developed internal street system in contrast with simple ribbon developments along the road frontages; compare Water Newton (Mackreth 1979, fig 11) with Braintree (Drury 1976, fig 49) and Hibaldstow (Smith 1987, fig 2). In this context, analysis has shown that very few small towns exhibit any trace of deliberate planning comparable with the cities. Instead, the majority were little more than ribbon developments throughout their history, strung out along the frontages of a single through road or at the junction of two or more through routes. As need arose within such sites, however, side streets and lanes could be added between the buildings and enclosures, to provide access to land and buildings away from the frontages; this inevitably led to the development of an irregular network of internal streets, which seems to be a distinguishing feature of the more developed urban centres.

b) The presence at some sites of a developed central core and some degree of zonation within the plan; examples include the official or public buildings at Water Newton (Mackreth 1979, fig 11), the market place at Godmanchester (Green 1975, fig 10) and the temple complex at Frilford (Hingley 1985, fig 3).

c) The surprisingly restricted range of building types at the majority of sites, beyond the everyday domestic and workshop accommodation, and in particular the relative scarcity of any buildings of more sophisticated design and size; compare the relative range at developed sites like Braughing (Partridge 1975, fig 4) with that of ribbon developments like Cave's Inn (Lucas 1981) and *Margidunum* (Todd 1969). In this context, it is clear that buildings of simple design predominated at the majority of sites throughout their history, with a progressive shift from timber to stone/stone-founded buildings from the mid to late 2nd century onwards. By contrast, Romanised buildings, in the form of official *mansiones*, larger private houses and temples are far less common, and few small towns possessed more than one or two such complexes. Not surprisingly, large public buildings and amenities are rare. Equally important is the fact that most of the Romanised buildings developed away from the central area of the sites, reflecting their secondary importance to the plan and the settlement's function.

d) The growing evidence for land-division and property boundaries within the sites; e g Ilchester (Leach 1982, figs 35 and 51) and Hibaldstow (Smith 1987, figs 2 and 3). These often take the form of compounds with associated buildings.

e) The relative importance of these enclosed compounds *vis à vis* the narrow-fronted strip buildings found elsewhere along the frontages: compare Dragonby (May 1970, figs 4 and 6) and Corbridge (Bishop & Dore 1988, fig 5) respectively.

f) The nature of the defended circuit, especially the contrast between defences which enclose only a strategic strongpoint (cf Mancetter and Wall – Webster 1971, figs 20–21), and those which seem to be designed to protect both the official dimension and a suitable urban core (cf Kenchester – Wilmott 1980, fig 6).

g) The continuing importance of the extra-mural areas once the defences were provided (Esmonde Cleary 1987).

h) The relative importance of large organised cemeteries around a site, in contrast to isolated burials (cf Esmonde Cleary 1985).

(4) **Fourth**, we now possess an increasingly clear idea of the functional dimension. This has been an area of con-

siderable debate in recent years, with much of the discussion revolving around the problem of quantifying the level of dependence on agriculture or more specialised activities (Fulford 1982). Even so, the increasing evidence has emphasised a number of points:

a) The importance of agriculture at most sites; this is emphasised by the presence of field systems/enclosures at sites like Braintree (Drury 1976, fig 49) and Brampton (Edwards 1977, fig 100), by the recognition of buildings within distinctive farm compounds/cultivation plots at sites like Dragonby (cf Hingley 1989, ch 4), and by the widespread discovery of agricultural implements.

b) The relative importance of economic activities, emphasised by the increasing number of identified shops/workshops, often in the form of characteristic strip buildings (cf Burnham 1989, 41–4) and by the wide range of specialists attested in the archaeological record (Smith 1987, ch 3). The presence of a market place has also been suggested by the discovery of characteristic open spaces at such sites as Alcester (Wilson 1973, 288) and Godmanchester (Green 1975, 204).

 Despite all this, however, we remain very unsure about the relative importance of these activities at individual sites and about the degree of economic interaction between town and country through time (Burnham & Wacher 1990, ch 5). It is clear, nevertheless, that much depends upon the relative importance of the strip building at individual sites as evidence for the presence of shops, workshops and specialised activities. In this context, it has long been argued that strip buildings were the predominant building type within the small towns, even from an early date; but where the details can be assessed in the early stages and in the less well-developed roadside settlements, they always seem to exist alongside a range of other domestic buildings, arranged in more spacious plots of agricultural character. Such an early admixture of building types is well attested at Godmanchester, where the commercial aspects tended to increase with time, suggesting a progressive shift from village to small town status (Green 1975; 1977). This may well be the normal trend at the more important sites.

c) The significance of official/military functions at a growing number of sites; this is emphasised by the discovery of new *mansiones* at towns like Chelmsford (Drury 1988) and Wanborough (Phillips & Walters 1977) and by the identification of some small defended sites as probable *burgi* (for those along Watling Street, see Webster 1971). In all cases, these functions seem to be imposed upon settlements closely associated with the main roads of the province.

d) The recognition of an increasing number of sites where the primary function was either religious or industrial; eg the 140 pottery kilns at Brampton (Knowles 1977) and the temple precinct and amphitheatre at Frilford (Hingley 1985).

(5) **Fifth**, there has been a growing realisation that the term 'small town' has become a catch-all category, subsuming a very wide variety of nucleated sites between one person's town and another's village. This has led to the recognition of different categories within the small town continuum, usually based on the classification published by Rivet in 1975. An alternative threefold scheme, based on a range of structural and functional indicators, is suggested here:

a) *Upper order settlements*, covering all the sites traditionally identified as newly elevated cities in the 3rd and 4th centuries or as minor towns with developed economic functions. They can all be shown to share in some or all of the following features:- 1) an internal street network; 2) urban core defences; 3) distinctive zones in the plan; 4) a broad range of building types; 5) a broad range of workshop industries and craft-specialists; 6) large organised cemeteries. Examples in this category include Water Newton (Frere, Rivet & Sitwell 1987, plan v), Ilchester (Fig 2.1; Burnham & Wacher 1990, fig 12), Braughing (Partridge 1975, fig 4) and Alcester (Frere 1986, fig 17).

b) *Middle order settlements*, embracing a range of sites which served specialised functions. They tend to be characterised by distinctive official or religious buildings, strongpoint defences or large scale industrial activities. These are sometimes found in association with features already identified in the upper order (eg a street network), but lower down the scale they tend to be associated with ribbon developments, an increasing agricultural emphasis and the absence of any degree of zonation in the plan. They include: (1) spas and religious centres, eg Springhead (Fig 2.2; Harker 1980, fig 12.1) and Frilford (Hingley 1985, fig 3); (2) specialist extractive or manufacturing sites, eg Charterhouse – lead (Wilson 1971, fig 12), Brampton – pottery and metalworking (Fig 2.3; Knowles 1977, fig 1), and Middlewich – salt and iron (Petch 1987, fig 33); (3) roadside settlements with imposed official/military functions, eg Mancetter and Wall (Webster 1971, figs 20–21).

c) *Lower order settlements*, characterised by the absence of defences, specialised functions and buildings of any degree of sophistication. In other respects they share many of the features already outlined for the middle order sites, including ribbon developments and an increasing agricultural emphasis. Examples in this category include Hibaldstow (Smith 1987, figs 2 and 3), Braintree (Drury 1976, fig 49) and Dragonby (May 1970). Many merge imperceptibly with the sites traditionally identified as villages (Fig 2.4), such as Chisenbury Warren, Fotheringhay

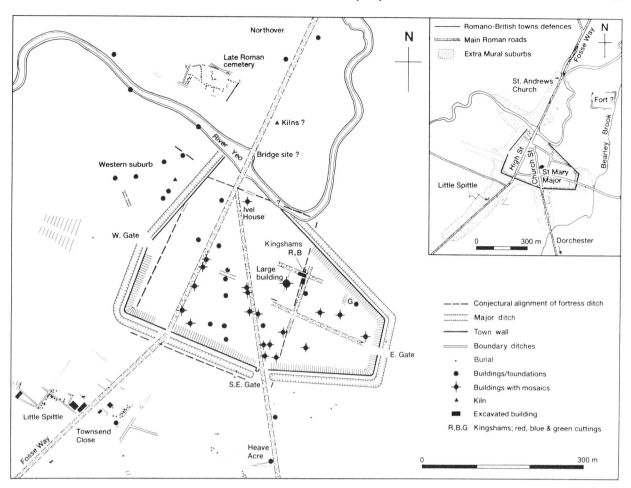

Fig 2.1 Ilchester

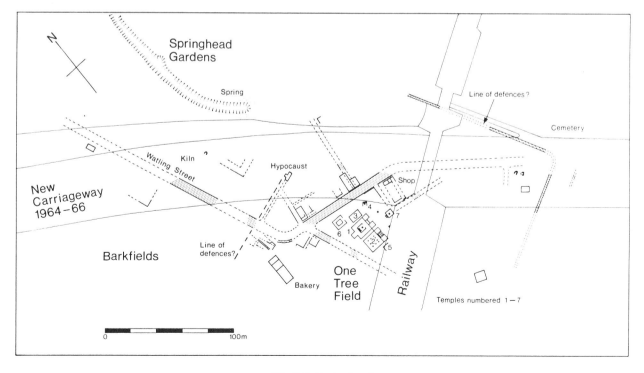

Fig 2.2 Springhead

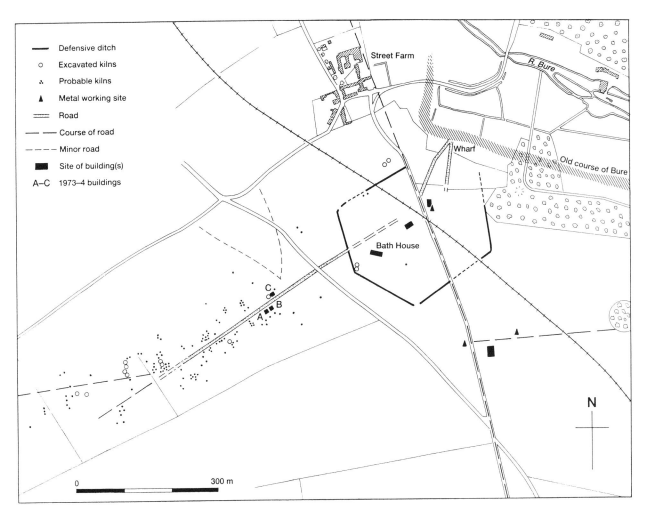

Fig 2.3 *Brampton*

(Taylor 1983, figs 29 and 30) and Catsgore (Leech 1982). Such sites still remain very poorly known, though they are crucial to our wider understanding of the distribution of 'small towns' or 'local centres' as they are defined by Hingley (1989).

(6) **Sixth**, we have a greater awareness of the complexity of urban origins, especially among the small towns of south and east Britain, to counterbalance the oft-quoted view that all the sites had military origins (cf Burnham 1986). Particular importance inevitably attaches to those sites which have been shown to develop out of pre-existing later Iron Age settlements, as was clearly the case at Baldock, where part of the internal street network pre-dated the conquest (Stead & Rigby 1986, 84–5) and at Braughing, with its extensive pre-Roman occupation and evidence for coin production (Partridge 1981). Equally interesting are those sites with evidence for a pre-existing religious function, as the recent excavations at Harlow (Bartlett 1988) and perhaps also Bath (Cunliffe 1988, 1) demonstrate. Elsewhere, greater attention has been di-

rected at the importance of the communications network and the associated *cursus publicus* in determining which civilian sites outlived their parent forts.

(7) **Seventh**, we are beginning to discern broad trends in the development of the small towns spanning the 1st to 4th centuries. The following stand out:

a) The relatively slow development at most sites before the end of the 1st century; the exceptions tend either to be sites with pre-Roman origins like Bath, where the monumental buildings were under construction between 65 and 75 (Cunliffe 1969, 129; Blagg 1979), or settlements with specialised functions like Middlewich, where early brine extraction has been dated to the 80s (Petch 1987, 202–8).

b) The much more pronounced pattern of development visible at many sites in the 2nd century; this takes the form of (i) sustained growth along the roads and a greater level of organisation in the street layouts, (ii) intensified economic activity, in the form of characteristic strip buildings and specialised produc-

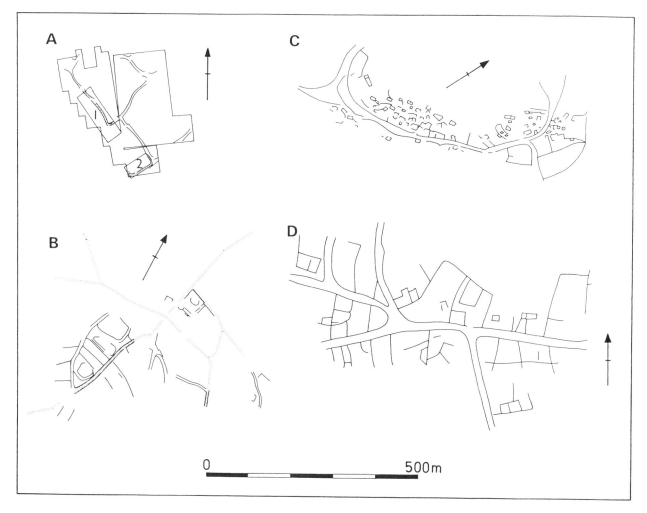

Fig 2.4 *Comparative plans of some 'village' settlements: A, Dragonby; B, Kirmington; C, Chisenbury Warren; D, Hacconby Fen*

tion, and (iii) the development of official functions in the form of official *mansiones*. This trend is clearly recognisable at a whole range of sites including Alcester (Booth 1980, 7), Ashton (Hadman & Upex 1977; Dix 1983), Chelmsford (Drury 1988), Godmanchester (Green 1975, 201–2), Irchester (R C H M(E) 1979, 91), Kenchester (Wilmott 1980, 123–5), Wanborough (Anderson & Wacher 1980, 117) and Water Newton (Burnham & Wacher 1990, 83). Such evidence runs counter to Millett's view that the small towns only really developed in the later 3rd and 4th centuries, when the cities are supposed to have stagnated (1990, ch 7).

c) The provision of earthwork defences at a handful of sites in the later 2nd/early 3rd century, contemporary with developments at most provincial cities (cf Crickmore 1984a).

d) The progressive replacement of timber structures by stone buildings in the course of the 2nd to 3rd centuries, as was the case at Alcester (Booth 1980, 12–13), Catterick (Wacher 1971), Ilchester (Leach 1982, 24–30, 65–82) and Water Newton (Taylor & Richmond 1958, 139–40; 1959, 117–18). In the process, it is clear that the strip building became the predominant building type at the best-known sites.

e) The progressive differentiation in the course of the 3rd/4th centuries of those small towns with pronounced economic and official functions, at the expense of lesser roadside settlements/villages. This is clearly seen in (i) the provision of stone defences at the most important sites, enclosing a significant proportion of the occupied area, (ii) the continued upkeep of public and religious buildings, (iii) the increased numbers of strip buildings associated with specialised production, and (iv) the concentrations of villas around likely market centres. Such trends are variously represented at upper order sites like Water Newton (Mackreth 1979, fig 11) and Ilchester (Burnham & Wacher 1990, fig 12), where there are good grounds for believing that the published plans provide a fair representation of the town's later morphology. The same seems to be true of the 3rd and 4th century plans at Corbridge (Bishop & Dore 1988, fig 3) and Catterick (Wacher 1971, fig 24).

Such evidence provides a measure of support for Millett's thesis that the small towns became increasingly important as commercial centres in the late Roman period, and that they reached the peak of their prosperity at that date, but this picture must be qualified by the realisation that not all small towns participated in the process; indeed, some sites certainly went into decline during the 3rd century, among them Kelvedon (Eddy 1982, 17 and 20; Rodwell 1987, 136) and Staines (Crouch 1978, 180; Rankov 1982, 393), while other roadside settlements became little more than defended strongpoints, as was the case at Cave's Inn and *Margidunum* (Todd 1969).

f) The provision of distinctive strongpoint defences at a growing number of small towns in the later 3rd/ early 4th century, most of them located at the heart of straggling settlements along the main roads of the province and often devoid of clear evidence for internal structures. The best known sequence lay along Watling Street between Whilton Lodge and Redhill (Webster 1971), but they are also found on Ermine Street and the Fosse Way (eg Ancaster, Dorn and Thorpe).

g) The increasing evidence for the abandonment of previously occupied areas/buildings in the course of the 4th century. This has been recognised, for example, at Braintree (Drury 1976, 46 and 125), Chelmsford (Drury 1975, 165), Harlow (France & Gobel 1985, 48; Bartlett 1988, 3) and Scole (Rogerson 1977, 120–1), suggesting that the processes of change which engulfed the towns in the 5th century were already affecting some sites at an earlier date.

(8) **Eighth**, and finally, we have a clearer idea of what happened to the small towns in the post-Roman period (for a general review of the period, see Esmonde Cleary 1989). In the past, considerable importance was attached to apparent cases of continuity into the 5th/6th centuries, as for example at Carlisle (Bede, *Vita Sancti Cuthberti*, 4), Dorchester-on Thames (Frere 1962, 121–8; Rowley 1974) and, most recently of all, Bath (Cunliffe & Davenport 1985, 66–75). Elsewhere, continuity has been argued on the basis of the presence/absence of Anglo-Saxon *grubenhauser* and cemeteries, as for example at Heybridge (Drury & Wickenden 1982) and Great Chesterford (Brinson 1963, 86–8). The real issue, however, is not so much continuity in the sense of continued occupation, but continuity in the sense of the continued existence of traditional socio-economic and institutional patterns along Roman or quasi-Roman lines; the former can often be demonstrated in some form, but there are to my mind few, if any, examples of the latter. This is hardly surprising, because the cessation of Roman control in 409 effectively ended the *raison d'etre* for most, if not all, the small towns. The speed of the resulting decline in the 5th century still needs considerable clarification, but for many it is likely to have been rapid; Bath is probably one of the few exceptions which proves the rule.

Summary

Much of what has been said above is inevitably a subjective assessment, but hopefully it has demonstrated some of the advances which have been made in the last few decades. Numerous issues have not been resolved, however, while others have received inadequate attention. In concluding, I would draw attention to the following areas which might form a focus for future discussion:

1) The problem of definition and the absence of any commonly agreed list of 'small towns', which makes it very difficult to talk with any confidence about the 'urban network';

2) The continuing bias in the quantity and quality of the evidence at our disposal, with far too little work being directed at the less well known, undefended settlements away from the provincial roads;

3) The absence in the past of any clearly-defined research priorities and related excavation strategies for investigating small towns in their wider regional context;

4) The need for more detailed research into:
   – regional variations in the character and distribution of the small towns, not least where there seem to be gaps;
   – the relationships between small towns and their hinterlands, not least in terms of their economic interdependence;
   – the relationships between the small towns and their larger urban counterparts, not least because of the current debate on their changing roles through time;
   – the morphology of sites, especially in terms of how they were originally laid out and how subsequent developments were managed;
   – intra- and extra-site variations in the distribution of artefactual and environmental material;

5) The need for greater comparison with continental small towns, given the wealth of material which has been synthesised in recent years.

Bibliography

Alexander, J, 1975 The development of urban communities: the evidence from Cambridge and Great Chesterford, in *The 'small towns' of Roman Britain* (eds W Rodwell & T Rowley), BAR Brit Ser, 15, 103–109

Anderson, A S, & Wacher, J S, 1980 Excavations at Wanborough, Wiltshire: an interim report, *Britannia*, 11, 115–126

Bartlett, R, 1988 The Harlow Celtic temple, *Curr Archaeol*, 112, 163–66

Bishop, M C, & Dore, J N, 1988 *Corbridge: excavations of the Roman fort and town 1947–1980*

Blagg, T F C, 1979 The date of the temple of Sulis Minerva at Bath, *Britannia*, 10, 101–107

Booth, P M, 1980 *Roman Alcester,* Warwickshire Museum

Bradford, J S P, & Goodchild, R G, 1939 Excavations at Frilford 1937–8, *Oxoniensia*, 4, 1–70

Brinson, J G S, 1963 Great Chesterford, in Romano-British Essex (ed M R Hull), *Victoria county hist Essex*, vol 3, 72–88

Brown, A E, Woodfield, C, & Mynard, D C, 1983 Excavations at Towcester, Northamptonshire: the Alchester Road suburb, *Northamptonshire Archaeol*, 18, 43–140

Burleigh, G, 1982 Excavations at Baldock 1980–81: an interim report, *Hertfordshire's Past*, 12, 3–18

Burnham, B C, 1986 The origins of Romano-British 'small towns', *Oxford J Archaeol*, 5, 185–203

——, 1988 The morphology of Romano-British 'small towns', *Archaeol J*, 144, 156–90

——, 1989 A survey of building types in Romano-British 'small towns', *J Brit Archaeol Ass*, 141, 35–59

——, & Wacher, J, 1990 *The 'small towns' of Roman Britain*

Clarke, S, 1991 'Small towns' and small towns, *Antiquity*, 65, 937–8

Crickmore, J, 1984a *Romano-British urban defences*, BAR Brit Ser, 126

——, 1984b *Romano-British urban settlements in the West Midlands,* BAR Brit Ser, 127

Crouch, K, 1978 New thoughts on Roman Staines, *London Archaeol*, 3, No 7, 180–6

Cunliffe, B W, 1969 *Roman Bath*, Soc Antiq Res Rep 24

——, 1976 The Roman baths at Bath: excavations 1969–75, *Britannia*, 7, 1–32

——, 1988 *The temple of Sulis Minerva at Bath Vol 2: the finds from the sacred spring*, Oxford Univ Comm Archaeol Monogr 16

——, & Davenport, P, 1985 *The temple of Sulis Minerva at Bath. Vol 1: the site*, Oxford Univ Comm Archaeol Monogr 7

——, & Rowley, T (eds), 1976 *Oppida: the beginnings of urbanisation in barbarian Europe*, BAR Suppl Ser, 11

Dix, B, 1983 Ashton Roman town, *South Midlands Archaeol*, 13, 18–20

Dool, J, Wheeler, H *et al* (eds), 1986 Roman Derby: excavations 1968–1983, *Derbyshire Archaeol J*, 105, 1–348

Drury, P J, 1975 Roman Chelmsford- *Caesaromagus*, in *The 'small towns' of Roman Britain* (eds W Rodwell & T Rowley), BAR Brit Ser, 15, 159–173

——, 1976 Braintree: excavations and research 1971–1976 and an archaeological gazetteer, *Essex Archaeol Hist*, 8, 1–143

——, 1988 *The mansio and other sites in the south-eastern sector of Caesaromagus*, C B A Res Rep 66

——, & Wickenden, N P, 1982 An early Saxon settlement within the Romano British small town at Heybridge, Essex, *Medieval Archaeol*, 26, 1–40

Duncan-Jones, R, 1974 *The economy of the Roman Empire*

Eddy, M, 1982 *Kelvedon: the origins and development of a Roman small town*, Essex County Council Occasional Paper 3

——, 1984 Excavations on the Braintree Earthworks 1976 and 1979, *Essex Archaeol J*, 15, 36–53

Edwards, D, 1977 The air photographs collection of the Norfolk Archaeological Unit: second report, *E Anglian Archaeol*, 5, 225–37

Ellis, P, 1987 Sea Mills, Bristol: the 1965–68 excavations in the Roman town of *Abonae, Trans Bristol Gloucestershire Archaeol Soc*, 105, 15–108

Esmonde Cleary, S E, 1985 The quick and the dead: suburbs, cemeteries, and the town, in *Roman urban topography in Britain and the Western Empire* (eds F Grew & B Hobley), CBA Res Rep 59, 74–77

——, 1987 *Extra-mural areas of Romano-British towns*, BAR Brit Ser, 169

——, 1989 *The ending of Roman Britain*

——, 1992 Small towns past and future, *Britannia*, 23, 341–4

Field, N, & Hurst, H, 1983 Roman Horncastle, *Lincolnshire Hist Archaeol*, 18, 47–88

Finley, M I, 1973 *The ancient economy*

Foreman, M, & Rahtz, S, 1984 Excavations at Faccenda Chicken Farm, near Alchester, 1983, *Oxoniensia*, 49, 24–46

France, N E, & Gobel, B M, 1985 *The Romano-British temple at Harlow*, West Essex Archaeol Group

Freezer, D F, 1979 *From saltings to spa town. The archaeology of Droitwich*

Frere, S S, 1962 Excavations at Dorchester on Thames 1962, *Archaeol J*, 119, 114–49

——, 1985 Excavations at Dorchester-on-Thames 1963, *Archaeol J*, 141, 91–174

—— (ed), 1986 Roman Britain in 1985, *Britannia*, 17, 364–427

——, Rivet, A L F, & Sitwell, N H H (eds), 1987 *Tabula Imperii Romani: Britannia Septentrionalis*

——, & St Joseph, J K S, 1983 *Roman Britain from the air*

Fulford, M G, 1982 Town and country in Roman Britain – a parasitical relationship? in *The Romano-British countryside* (ed D Miles), BAR Brit Ser, 103, 403–19

——, 1989 The economy of Roman Britain, in *Research on Roman Britain 1960–89* (ed M Todd), Britannia Monogr 11, 175–201

——, 1992 Review of Millett 1990, *Archaeol J*, 148, 307–9

Garnsey, P, Hopkins, K, & Whittaker, C R, 1983 *Trade in the ancient economy*

——, & Saller, R, 1987 *The Roman Empire: economy, society and culture*

Green, H J M, 1975 Roman Godmanchester, in *The 'small towns' of Roman Britain* (eds W Rodwell & T Rowley), BAR Brit Ser, 15, 183–210

——, 1977 *Godmanchester*, Oleander Press

Greene, K T, 1986 *The archaeology of the Roman economy*

Hadman, J, & Upex, S, 1975 The Roman settlement at Ashton near Oundle, *Durobrivae, a review of Nene Valley archaeology*, 3, 12–155

——, 1977 Ashton 1976, *Durobrivae, a review of Nene Valley archaeology*, 5, 6–9

——, 1979 Ashton 1977–8, *Durobrivae, a review of Nene Valley archaeology,* 7, 29–30

Hall, D N, & Nickerson, N, 1968 Excavations at Irchester 1962–3, *Archaeol J*, 124, 65–99

Harker, S R, 1980 Springhead – a brief re-appraisal, in *Temples, churches and religion in Roman Britain* (ed W Rodwell), BAR Brit Ser, 77 (i + ii), 285–288

Hingley, R, 1985 Location, function and status: a Romano-British 'religious complex' at the Noah's Ark Inn, Frilford (Oxfordshire), *Oxford J Archaeol*, 4, 201–14

——, 1989 *Rural settlement in Roman Britain*

Hodder, I, 1972 Locational models and the study of Romano-British settlement, in *Models in archaeology* (ed D L Clarke), 887–909

——, 1974 The distribution of Savernake Ware, *Wiltshire Archaeol Mag*, 69, 67–84

——, 1975 The spatial distribution of Romano-British small towns, in *The 'small towns' of Roman Britain* (eds W Rodwell & T Rowley), BAR Brit Ser, 15, 67– 74

——, & Hassall, M W C, 1971 The non-random spacing of Romano-British walled towns, *Man*, 6, 391–407

Knowles, A K, 1977 The Roman settlement at Brampton, Norfolk: interim report, *Britannia*, 8, 209–21

Lambrick, G, *et multi alii*, 1980 Excavations in Park Street, Towcester, *Northamptonshire Archaeol*, 15, 35–118

Leach, P, 1982 *Ilchester vol 1: excavations 1974–1975*, Western Archaeol Trust

Leech, R H, 1982 *Excavations at Catsgore 1970–1973: a Romano British village*, Western Archaeol Trust

Lucas, J, 1981 *Tripontium*, third interim report, *Trans Birmingham Archaeol Soc*, 91, 25–54

McCarthy, M R, 1984 Roman Carlisle, in *Settlement and society in the Roman North* (ed P R Wilson *et al*), 65–74

——, Padley, T G, & Henig, M, 1982 Excavations and finds from The Lanes, Carlisle, *Britannia*, 13, 79–90

Mackreth, D, 1979 Durobrivae, *Durobrivae, a review of Nene valley archaeology*, 7, 19–21

May, J, 1970 Dragonby: an interim report on excavations on an Iron Age and Romano-British site near Scunthorpe, Lincs, 1964–69, *Antiq J*, 50, 222–45

——, 1976 The growth of settlements in the later Iron Age in Lincolnshire, in *Oppida: the beginnings of urbanisation in barbarian Europe* (eds B Cunliffe & T Rowley), BAR Suppl Ser, 11, 163–180

Miles, D (ed), 1982 *The Romano-British countryside: studies in rural settlement and economy*, BAR Brit Ser, 103 (i + ii)

Millett, M, 1975 Recent work on the Romano-British settlement at Neatham, Hampshire, *Britannia*, 6, 213–16

——, 1982 Town and country: a review of some material evidence, in *The Romano-British countryside: studies in rural settlement and economy* (ed D Miles), BAR Brit Ser, 103, 421–431

——, 1990 *The Romanization of Britain: an essay in archaeological interpretation*

——, and Graham, D, 1986 *Excavations on the Romano-British small town at Neatham, Hampshire, 1969–1979*, Hampshire Field Club Monogr 3

Oetgen, J M, 1986 Sapperton Roman town, *Archaeol in Lincolnshire 1985–86*, 10–12

——, 1987 Sapperton Roman town, *Archaeol in Lincolnshire 1986–87*, 13–15

Palmer, N, 1981 Tiddington Roman settlement: an interim report, *West Midlands Archaeol News Sheet*, 24, 17–24

——, 1983 Tiddington Roman settlement: second interim report, *West Midlands Archaeol News Sheet*, 26, 37–47

Parkhouse, J, 1981 Excavations in Cowbridge, *Annual Report, Glamorgan-Gwent Archaeol Trust 1980–81*, 15–26

——, 1982 Excavations in Cowbridge, *Annual Report, Glamorgan-Gwent Archaeol Trust 1981–82*, 7–21

Partridge, C R, 1975 Braughing, in *The 'small towns' of Roman Britain* (eds W Rodwell & T Rowley), BAR Brit Ser, 15, 139–157

——, 1978 Excavations and fieldwork at Braughing 1968–73, *Hertfordshire Archaeol*, 5, 22–108

——, 1980 Excavations at Puckeridge and Braughing 1975–9, *Hertfordshire Archaeol*, 7, 28–132

——, 1981 *Skeleton Green: a late Iron Age and Romano-British site*, Britannia Monogr 2

Penn, W S, 1960 Excavation of Temple 1, Site C1, *Archaeol Cantiana*, 73, 1–61

——, 1961 Springhead: Temples 3 and 4, *Archaeol Cantiana*, 74, 113–40

——, 1963 Temples 2 and 5, *Archaeol Cantiana*, 77, 110–32

——, 1968 Springhead: Temple 6 / gateway, *Archaeol Cantiana*, 82, 105–23

Petch, D F, 1987 The Roman period, in *Victoria county hist Cheshire*, vol 1, 115–236

Phillips, B, & Walters, B, 1977 A *mansio* at Lower Wanborough, Wiltshire, *Britannia*, 8, 223–27

Potter, T W, & Trow, S D, 1988 Puckeridge-Braughing, Herts: the Ermine Street excavations, 1971–1972, *Hertfordshire Archaeol*, 10, 1–191

R C H M(E), 1979, *An inventory of archaeological sites in Central Northamptonshire*

Rankov, N B (ed), 1982 Roman Britain in 1981, *Britannia*, 13, 328–395

Reece, R, 1980 Town and country: the end of Roman Britain, *World Archaeol*, 12, 77– 92

Rivet, A L F, 1975 Summing up: the classification of minor towns and related settlements, in *The 'small towns' of Roman Britain* (eds W Rodwell & T Rowley), BAR Brit Ser, 15, 111–14

Rodwell, K, 1987 *The prehistoric and Roman settlement at Kelvedon, Essex*, CBA Res Rep 63

——, 1975 Trinovantian towns and their setting: a case study, in *The 'small towns' of Roman Britain* (eds W Rodwell & T Rowley), BAR Brit Ser, 15, 85–101

——, & Rowley, T (eds), 1975 *The 'small towns' of Roman Britain*, BAR Brit Ser, 15

Rogerson, A, 1977 Excavation at Scole, 1973, *E Anglian Archaeol*, 5, 97–224

Rowley, R T, 1974 Early Saxon settlement in Dorchester, in *Anglo-Saxon settlement and landscape* (ed R T Rowley), BAR Brit Ser, 6, 42–50

St Joseph, J K S, 1966 The contribution of aerial photography, in *The civitas capitals of Roman Britain* (ed J S Wacher), 21–30

Selkirk, A, 1983 Baldock, *Curr Archaeol*, 86, 70–74

Simmons, B B, 1976 Sapperton, an interim report, *Lincolnshire Hist Archaeol*, 11, 5–11

——, 1985 Sapperton, *Archaeol in Lincolnshire 1984–5*, 16–20

Smith, R F, 1987 *Roadside settlements in lowland Roman Britain*, BAR Brit Ser, 157

Stanley, C, 1979 Thames Valley, *Aerial Archaeol*, 4, 105–6

Stead, I M, & Rigby, V, 1986 *Baldock: the excavation of a Roman and pre-Roman settlement, 1968–1972*, Britannia Monogr 7

Taylor, C C, 1983 *Village and farmstead: a history of rural settlement in England*

Taylor, M V, & Richmond, I A (eds), 1958 Roman Britain in 1957, *J Roman Stud*, 48, 130–149

—— (eds), 1959 Roman Britain in 1958, *J Roman Stud*, 49, 102–35

Todd, M, 1969 The Roman settlement at *Margidunum* : the

excavation of 1966–8, *Trans Thoroton Soc Nottinghamshire*, 73, 6–104

——, 1970 The small towns of Roman Britain, *Britannia*, 1, 114–30

——, 1981 *The Roman town at Ancaster, Lincolnshire: the excavations of 1955–1971*

——, 1989 *Villa* and *fundus*, in *The economies of Romano-British villas* (eds K Branigan and D Miles), 14–20

Wacher, J, 1971 Yorkshire towns in the 4th century, in *Soldier and civilian in Roman Yorkshire* (ed R M Butler), 165–177

——, 1974 *The towns of Roman Britain*

Webster, G, 1971 A Roman system of fortified posts along Watling Street, Britain, in *Roman frontier studies 1967*, 38–45

——, 1975 Small towns without defences, in *The 'small towns' of Roman Britain* (eds W Rodwell & T Rowley), BAR Brit Ser, 15, 53–66

Wickenden, N P, 1988 *Excavations at Great Dunmow, Essex: a Romano-British small town in the Trinovantian civitas*, E Anglian Archaeol, 41

——, 1992 *The temple and other sites in the north-eastern sector of Caesaromagus*, CBA Res Rep 75

Wilmott, A, 1980 Kenchester (*Magnis*): a reconsideration, *Trans Woolhope Natur Field Club*, 43, 117–133

Wilson, D R (ed), 1971 Roman Britain in 1970, *Britannia*, 2, 242–88

—— (ed), 1973 Roman Britain in 1972, *Britannia*, 4, 270–323

——, 1975 The 'small towns' of Roman Britain from the air, in *The 'small towns' of Roman Britain* (eds W Rodwell & T Rowley), BAR Brit Ser, 15, 9–49

Wilson, P R, 1984 Recent work at Catterick, in *Settlement and society in the Roman north* (eds P R Wilson *et al*), 75–82

——, Jones, R F J, & Evans D M (eds), 1984 *Settlement and society in the Roman north*

Windell, D, 1984 Irchester Roman town: excavations 1981–82, *Northamptonshire Archaeol*, 19, 31–51

Young, C J, 1975 The defences of Alchester, *Oxoniensia*, 40, 136–170

3   The aerial view

D R Wilson

The regional studies contained in this volume make clear that two of the most powerful tools for identifying settlements with a claim to be regarded as Roman 'small towns' are aerial reconnaissance and fieldwalking. Aerial reconnaissance is admittedly unhelpful in establishing the full extent of settlement, but it has the advantage of usually indicating something of the character and anatomy of the archaeological remains observed. By this means it is possible to trace the Roman roads on which most 'small towns' lie and to recognise characteristic features such as defensive circuits, street networks, buildings with stone foundations and the presence of wells, cesspits and rubbish pits. In favourable conditions it may also be possible to detect timber buildings and inhumation cemeteries. In addition, aerial photography may reveal the existence of a nearby or underlying Roman fort to which the settlement may initially have been related.

The individual sites mentioned below are further documented in the bibliography following this paper.

Main roads

Roman roads are important in this context because it is difficult to imagine any settlement with pretensions to calling itself a town being able to operate without good communications. Sometimes detailed examination of the course of a known road will lead to identification of a likely 'small town', and sometimes identification of a new 'small town' will prompt the subsequent tracing of the relevant road(s). The contribution of aerial photography is not, however, limited to establishing the former existence of a road on the line from A to B; it can also pin down the exact course of that road within or adjacent to a given settlement. The major Roman roads, such as Ermine Street, the Foss Way and Watling Street, are followed by modern roads for much of their length, but it would be a mistake to believe that the modern highway accurately reproduced the Roman line at every point. The siting of Roman settlements along these and other roads should be analysed in relation to the verified course of the Roman road, not by blind reference to its modern successor. Thus, at Whilton Lodge (Northants) the Ro-

man course of Watling Street runs relatively close to the south-west defences of *Bannaventa*, whereas the modern A5 follows a different line virtually bisecting the settlement. At Brough and Thorpe (both in Notts), by contrast, the A45 follows the Foss Way closely within the limits of their respective defensive circuits, but at Thorpe it diverges northwards the moment it passes the north-east gate. At Chesterton (Cambs) the line of Ermine Street is marked by a clear causeway on a straight line through *Durobrivae*, from which the A1 swings away westwards just before it reaches the town's south-east gate and to which it does not return for another 18 km, just the other side of Great Casterton (Leics).

Defences

The possession of defences was once seen as the criterion by which Roman settlements in Britain could be identified as towns, whether large or small. It was one of the contributions of the 1975 Oxford conference (Rodwell & Rowley 1975) to make clear that undefended settlements could be every bit as large and often as important as many of those that did receive defences. Furthermore, the defensive circuits seldom enclosed more than a convenient fraction of the total area already settled, so that a walled town might come to lie at the centre of a much larger undefended settlement. We can now see that defences were reserved for 'small towns' of special importance to the provincial government, certainly including those that were relatively large and successful, but also others whose sole claim to fame was that they lay at appropriate intervals along certain strategic roads.

'Small towns' with defences may, therefore, be in a minority, especially if we exclude (as air-photographers effectively must) all examples covered by modern towns and villages. Where defences are present, however, aerial observation is of great value in drawing attention to them and plotting their course. At a few places, as at Ancaster (Lincs) and Great Casterton, both on Ermine Street, part of the circuit is still marked by visible surface relief: at both these settlements a great 4th century ditch can still be seen going round nearly half the defended area, though the accompanying town wall with its projecting bastions fails to offer any clear sign to aerial observers. At Irchester (Northants) much of the defensive circuit is marked by earthen banks, assumed to cover the remains of its walls, but in the southern half of the west side cropmarks confirm the line of the town-wall, in two straight lengths meeting at a slight angle. There is no sign here of external bastions. It is doubtful how far the accompanying ditches are genuinely visible on air-photographs (*pace* RCHM(E) 1979); the clearest linear mark in the appropriate place happens to be on the line of a former field boundary and cannot be safely attributed to a Roman feature. At Chesterton the defences of *Durobrivae* have been ploughed over but are still capable of being followed on the ground in terms of low relief. On the south-west side of the settlement the line of the town wall is also shown with sufficient clarity by cropmarks to establish not only that there were shallow rectangular towers or bastions at regular intervals along it, but that their foundations were separate from those of the curtain and therefore structurally secondary (Pl 3.1).

Elsewhere in our region there is no appreciable relief at the surface, and knowledge of the course and composition of similar defences comes primarily from the evidence of air photographs. At Great Chesterford (Essex) the south-west side of the walled settlement is defined by cropmarks, not of the wall itself, but of its four-metre-wide robber trench. At Thorpe the story told by aerial photography is particularly complex: on the same site are seen two successive and overlapping rectangular enclosures, one (of the earlier 2nd century) bounded by a rampart and ditch, the other (of the early 4th century) defended by a wall with no bank fronted by two ditches. This is not to mention a double-ditched military fortlet of 1st century date, which preceded them both. The 4th century wall had sharp (not rounded) corners, but no visible bastions.

Other defended settlements have yielded cropmarks solely of their ditch systems. At Brampton a single ditch 5–7 m wide encloses a hexagonal area of about 6 ha at an important crossroads in north-east Norfolk. At Brough on Foss a close-set double ditch encloses 6.5 ha in a rough rectangle; a further ditch on the west side is set far enough out to suggest that there were two phases on this side, implying either a reduction or an expansion of the defended area. Without knowing why it was done, we can hardly say which alternative is correct, though in general terms a reduction seems more probable. At Whilton Lodge there were three ditches, enclosing 5 ha. The innermost ditch is difficult to trace from the air because the corresponding cropmarks are broken and confused; this is apparently because the ditch itself was deliberately filled with turf and clay when the defences were remodelled, possibly in the early 4th century.

It is reasonable to suppose that the areas enclosed by the defensive systems described above bore some relationship to the contemporary pattern of settlement, but that relationship is unlikely to have been simple. While it is probably safe to infer that a large defended area is an index of prosperity, it is much less safe to argue that a small defended area or an absence of defences altogether indicates the opposite. A balance will have had to be struck between the desire to protect as much of the settlement as possible and the cost of doing so. Any peculiarities of shape, nevertheless, are likely to reflect the disposition of the facilities to be protected, whether public installations or the houses of local worthies who were paying for the work.

The elongated polygonal outline seen at Chesterton, often likened to a kite or a coffin, is typical of prosperous roadside settlements. The length is determined by the density of ribbon development along the immediate frontage of the highway, while the width results from local expansion at a nucleus taking shape near the centre of the settlement. A superficially similar outline is to be seen at Thorpe, in the field crossed by the Foss Way immediately north-east of the 'small town' previously described. Here a polygonal ditched enclosure was provisionally identified, after exploratory excavation, as an annexe attached to the 1st century fortlet, with which it agreed more or less in date. In 1975 the present writer put forward an alternative hypothesis, that this was an early phase of civilian settlement, but this suggestion paid too little attention to the context and timetable involved. It would have implied that a settlement developed here beside the fortlet sufficiently substantial to justify enclosure by the ditch seen on air photographs, apparently still within the 1st century. While this might seem improbable, we should remember that there was native settlement already on the site before the Roman troops arrived, so further development was not starting from nothing. But then it has to be supposed that this thriving settlement expanded or was transferred to the site of the abandoned fortlet, where a new earthwork defence was thrown up in the first half of the 2nd century. This new site was no doubt more attractive because closer to the river Trent and to the bridge which gave the place its name *Ad Pontem*, but the postulated sequence of events remains implausible unless (or until) substantiated by further evidence. It is better to accept that the polygonal enclosure goes with the fortlet, while noting that it was imposed on an area of existing native settlement, and at the same time not excluding some civilian settlement along the Foss Way in the post-military phase.

The kite-shaped plan is not in fact common in the region, most defended settlements tending towards rectangular plans or more regular polygons. The main settlement at Thorpe displays in an extreme form a fairly general tendency for roadside settlements (or any rate their defences) to lie mostly on one side of the road and not the other. This is seen also at Whilton Lodge, and less strikingly at Ancaster, Brough, Great Casterton and even Chesterton, and is in contrast to the shape of settlements at Brampton and Great Chesterford, where the

Pl 3.1 South-east half of the town of Durobrivae at Chesterton (Cambs), showing negative cropmarks of Ermine Street with its buildings, yards and side streets, and of the town wall with one very clear (and other less clear) bastions. 19 July 1981. Photo : Cambridge University Collection of Air Photographs

defended area lies more symmetrically about a major road junction, and at Irchester, where the defended area is sited away from the highway altogether.

Streets

Towns contain streets and buildings. The streets are revealed on air photographs by negative cropmarks over their road metalling and by positive cropmarks over their side ditches. When ditches are absent and metalling either never provided or subsequently removed, streets can only be detected as reserved strips between areas of visible settlement (marked by ditches and pits of various kinds).

The most developed street network is to be found, as we should expect, at Britain's largest 'small town', Chesterton (Pl 3.1, and Mackreth, p 148). The primary road is Ermine Street. Off this run not only metalled yards and alleys, but a number of side streets serving the back-lands. These conform to no predetermined plan but must have grown up organically in response to successive needs. It is noteworthy that the straight line of the Roman road from Irchester leading directly to the south-

west gate is not continued within the defended area; the principal internal street leading from this gate does not even connect directly with Ermine Street. In this it contrasts with another main street that emerges through the town wall on the west, possibly by means of an otherwise invisible postern. By-pass roads skirt the walls on both sides of the town, that to the north confined by the presence of the river Nene, that to the south diverging more widely. On the far side of the Nene the presence of several streets, partly shown by metalling, partly by side ditches, emphasizes the importance of Normangate Field at Castor (Cambs) as the nucleus of extensive suburban settlement. (In this context it should be noted that most of Margary's road 250 towards Milton Park and the whole of road 251 towards a possible wharf on the Nene are illusory, being no more than medieval headlands.)

Irchester provides an interesting contrast to Chesterton in that there is no through road to provide a starting point. There is nevertheless a central spine from which other streets branch off at various angles. None of these leads directly to a gate through the town wall. We can say this, despite being ignorant of the exact position of any of the gates, because every street that approaches the defences at a plausible position makes a sharp turn or dogleg as it does so, as if providing access to the gate were the result of second thoughts.

A network of metalled streets is the most obvious feature of civilian settlements that override two of the military forts of the region. At Kirmington (Humberside) an assumed fort of about 3.4 ha is apparently sandwiched between a flourishing Iron Age settlement and an equally flourishing Roman one (see Whitwell below, p 100). Metalled streets belonging to the latter cross the military defences in a straggling irregular pattern; there are also lanes bounded by ditches that probably belong to the pre-Roman phase, but the pattern is confused and it is by no means clear that some of these lanes do not actually form part of the later street network. At Pakenham (Suffolk) the identification of a 4–ha fort is more certainly established, on the south-west side of Ixworth village. Air photographs display its triple ditch system and some of its internal streets, but superimposed on both of these are the streets of a subsequent civilian settlement. This sequence has now been confirmed by excavation (see Plouviez below, p 69), but is implicit in the layout of the second phase which distorts the previous pattern into a form incompatible with military planning. (A similar development is known at Newton Kyme in N Yorks: see Frere & St Joseph 1983, 112.) A street leading out of the south-east gate connects with a Roman road going north-westwards into Ixworth. In the other direction, for what it is worth (perhaps not a great deal), the same road appears to be heading directly for Street Farm, Norton, by way of Stanton Street, a combination of names that suggests a possible alternative route for Margary's road 330.

By far the most regular street layout to be found in the region, but without any sign of road metalling, is also found at a military site, in the settlement revealed by aerial photography outside the west and east gates of the Saxon Shore fort at Brancaster. Here a grid of streets, mostly at right angles, is defined by boundary ditches of the house plots that continuously border their length. It is possible that this unusual regularity is to be attributed to military influence, but, if so, it must derive from a predecessor of the Saxon Shore fort, whose foundation is reckoned to be a century later than the earliest phase of civilian settlement encountered by excavation. A similar conclusion can be derived from study of the overall plan: both parts of the civilian settlement are on the same alignment, which differs from that of the fort. The suspicion that the Saxon Shore fort was superimposed on a pre-existing settlement is reinforced by seeing short lengths of ditch on the civilian alignment in several places near the centre of the fort.

Amongst the smaller settlements metalled streets are quite rare. At Brough there is one metalled street each side of the Foss Way, but that on the north-west side connects with a ditch-defined street like those at Brancaster. Something similar is seen, though less clearly, even in the much larger settlement at Great Chesterford.

There three main roads meet in a junction at the centre of the town; metalled yards run back from the north-south road and unmetalled streets appear to lead away from some of them. At Thorpe one metalled road runs out through the south-east gate and a metalled street runs nearly parallel to it; various metalled yards can be seen along the Foss Way frontage both inside and outside the walls. Unmetalled streets bounded by ditches occur at Ashton (Northants) and Littleborough (Notts).

Buildings

Buildings with stone foundations, provided they lie beneath a suitable crop, can be expected to show up on air photographs relatively often, whereas those wholly of timber will appear only seldom. From this it follows that far more is known in detail about the density of settlement in 'small towns' sited close to sources of building stone than in those at a greater distance. At the same time, it should be remembered that timber buildings had a place even in areas where good stone was abundant, so apparently blank areas in towns should be treated with caution and not automatically assumed to be completely empty. This is especially true if a street is present, for we should hardly expect streets to have been constructed to serve areas that were actually empty of habitations.

At Chesterton we can see that within the defended area the frontage of Ermine Street was crowded with buildings throughout its length. Such few gaps as appear to exist were quite possibly filled with timber structures. The impression is given that the buildings were mostly just simple strip-houses, though it is difficult to trace individual plans with any certainty. On the side streets there was room for larger houses, some of which presented their long sides (instead of their ends) to the street, but the frontages are still fairly crowded. Wholly exceptional is the great courtyard-complex measuring *c* 22 × 36 m, variously interpreted as a *mansio* (official posting-house and inn) or as a kind of *forum* (civic centre). Some timber buildings were sufficiently substantial to be detected on air photographs, perhaps stores rather than dwellings, but others (less substantial) almost certainly existed. Outside the walls there are few certain traces of actual buildings except in Normangate Field, and even there only one of the structures known from excavation was clearly visible on air photographs.

At Irchester the evidence of air photographs extends and supplements the results obtained in the excavations of 1878–9. The spinal street was well built up, the more substantial houses lying on the west side. The Romano-Celtic temple uncovered by Baker on the north side of the street leading towards the east gate survives more completely than his excavation records show, and two statue or column bases stand in the front member of the ambulatory. A number of circular or octagonal foundations elsewhere in the walled area may indicate other religious buildings. There are signs of stone foundations along most of the length of most of the streets, and once again we should allow for the additional presence of timber buildings. At Thorpe the south-east side of the Foss Way was packed with buildings having stone foundations, but the greater part of the defended area gives little sign of having been anything but empty. This appearance must surely be deceptive, for why else would a street have been provided or so large an area have been defended at all?

In East Anglia the appearance of Roman 'small towns' is quite different: buildings with stone foundations are extremely rare, timber buildings are seldom actually visible and the main signs of occupation are pits and ditches. At Great Chesterford, for example, one building with stone foundations was recognised from cropmarks by Stukeley in the early 18th century, but exploratory excavation at the north end of the town in 1948–9 found only one other. Timber buildings on the same site were indicated by floors of clay or gravel and by associated rubbish pits, wells and cess pits; only the pits would have shown from the air, as they do in other parts of the town. At Wixoe (Suffolk) a single house with stone foundations is visible; at Brampton, Brancaster and Pakenham

there is none. The same is true further north at Littleborough and Old Winteringham (Humberside). Only at Kirmington are buildings to be seen and they are of timber, both perhaps 20 m long; although similar in size to large early Saxon halls, they show none of the distinctive signs of Saxon building and are best understood, until further evidence is forthcoming, as belonging to the Roman settlement.

Pits and ditches

Before returning to the cropmarks of cesspits, wells and rubbish pits, it is worth briefly looking at those of graves, a form of pit that is rarely recognised in this context, though inhumation cemeteries must have existed on the margins of virtually all the settlements with which we are concerned. At defended settlements the zone lying just outside the defences became the obvious burial area, once they were constructed, and cemeteries in this position have been located by excavation at Ancaster and Great Chesterford. So far only Chesterton appears to have furnished comparable cropmark evidence; a ditched enclosure beside the southern by-pass road, close to the Billing

Pl 3.2 An undefended settlement is disclosed by abundant cropmarks of large pits beside the river Stour near Wixoe (Suffolk). A single building with stone foundations lies beside the road junction (top, left of centre). The site is disturbed by shallow gravel digging to right of centre. 24 June 1976. Photo: Cambridge University Collection of Air Photographs

Pl 3.3 *The line of Ermine Street approaching the Humber at Old Winteringham (Humberside) is marked by negative cropmarks of its carriageway and by positive cropmarks of its well spaced side ditches. A branch leads to the left at the bottom of the picture, and the shoreline is just visible, top left. A group of ditched enclosures to the right of Ermine Street apparently respect the road, whereas others are crossed by it. 5 July 1975. Photo: Cambridge University Collection of Air Photographs*

Brook, can be seen to be full of graves in orderly rows on a more or less east-west orientation. It is possible that other inhumation cemeteries existed along the same road, but cropmarks there have not yet been seen with sufficient clarity to make this sure. Elsewhere, the cropmarks of graves do not seem to have been noticed but should certainly be looked for; while strongly implying the proximity of settlement, they also help to define its limits.

Cesspits, wells and rubbish pits, if they occur in some abundance, are a positive index of settlement, and one that is particularly valuable when other indications, such as streets and buildings, are absent. While often found associated with ditches in various ways, pits on their own are quite capable of making a sufficiently distinctive pattern to draw attention to a given site, provided cropmarks are seen with real clarity. At Wixoe there are slight traces of two streets, but it is the abundant large pits that identify a substantial area of settlement (Pl 3.2). Similarly, at Pakenham, while the realigned streets in the fort provide the vital clue that elucidates the succession of settlement, it is the distribution of pits both inside and

outside the fort that establishes its extent and apparent continuity over a very large area. At defended settlements the presence of pits outside the defences is a clear reminder that the defensive circuit need not contain more than a proportion of the settled area; obvious examples are at Brampton, Brough, Great Chesterford, Whilton Lodge and possibly Thorpe (if the pits there are not pre-Roman).

When pits are accompanied by ditches, a more coherent pattern often emerges, defining small land parcels (presumably house plots) separated by lanes or streets, as remarked above for Ashton, Brancaster, Brough, Great Chesterford and Littleborough. This is in contrast to the groups of overlapping enclosures found, for example, at Old Winteringham, where there is little sign of order apart from the fact that certain enclosures respect a reserved strip each side of Ermine Street (Pl 3.3).

'Small towns' and forts

It is well known that many 'small towns' owe their position to a pre-existing fort. Often they will have developed directly from a *vicus* outside the gates of the fort and this may be suspected when the remains of fort and town are found to lie side by side, as at Ancaster and Great Casterton (Pl 3.4). Elsewhere the important factors may have been the existence of the road network, originally built to provide lines of communication between the forts, and the logic of the forts' own spacing, at intervals of something like a day's journey. There are certainly a number of places where the site of an abandoned fort was taken over for civilian settlement, as indicated by aerial archaeology at Kirmington and Pakenham and by excavation at Thorpe (all discussed above).

At some other 'small towns' an early military presence has been suspected from peculiarities of planning in the subsequent civilian layout. At Great Chesterford, for example, Rodwell has drawn attention to the puzzling way that the roads from Braughing and Colchester meet near the centre of the town; this road junction has no particular meaning in the context of the walled town, but would make a great deal of sense if it marked the site of the south gate of a pre-existing military installation. A military ditch of early Flavian date had been discovered outside the north gate of the town in 1948; although the

excavator had believed that the corresponding rampart had stood on the *north* side of this ditch, the evidence was slight and not necessarily conclusive, so this could have formed the north side of what was seemingly a very large fort. Rodwell completed the plan of this fort (or vexillation fortress) by reference to faint marks seen on air photographs; these must be discounted as either spurious or too faint for confidence, but the basic concept remains attractive and has been confirmed by excavation of the fort's east defences, which lay on a line just outside the town wall. At Irchester, too, a Roman fort has been suggested to lie beneath the north half of the walled area, but on different grounds. As far as they can be determined from surface inspection, both the west and east defences of the town appear to change their alignment by 5°–8° somewhere near the middle of each side, suggesting that the southern part of the town might have been in origin an extension of a primary fortification in the north half. This primary fortification is tentatively identified as an early fort. This suggestion is also attractive, though it does depend on the assumption that the town wall follows an uncomplicated line directly beneath the banks that seem to mark its course, which is less than certain. Once again, however, we must demur when the

Pl 3.4 Cropmarks of a Claudian military fort can be seen outside the town defences, which partly survive as earthworks, at Great Casterton (Leics). 8 July 1959. Photo: Cambridge University Collection of Air Photographs

evidence of air photographs is adduced in support of the hypothesis. A band of dark tone can sometimes be seen on air photographs crossing the walled area on the line that would have been taken by south defences of the putative fort. This has been described as traces of what may have been a ditch, but that is not what it really looks like; the edges of the mark are soft and blurred, unlike those of a buried ditch but very similar to those of a grubbed out hedgerow. Such a hedgerow did formerly exist along this line.

Conclusions

Aerial photography is one of several methods of exploration that can be applied to the discovery and subsequent investigation of Roman 'small towns' and the rural landscape into which they fitted. In optimum conditions (which, however, occur only seldom and briefly) it can reveal a great deal about the extent, anatomy and sometimes the history of such sites, as noted above. The results of aerial photography, however spectacular or however understated, will nevertheless be understood to best advantage when they are integrated with those derived from other techniques: fieldwalking, topographical, geophysical and geochemical surveys, and exploratory excavation. The following bibliography, therefore, which brings up to date that given in Wilson (1975), contains references both to aerial reconnaissance and to other kinds of fieldwork.

Bibliography

A. *Sites*: (i) aerial photography; (ii) excavation and survey

Ancaster	(i) – ; (ii) Hawkes 1946; Todd 1975, 1981.
Ashton	(i) – ; (ii) Hadman & Upex 1972, 1975, 1977, 1979; Dix 1983; Frere 1984–6.
Brampton	(i) Edwards 1977; (ii) Green 1977; Knowles 1977; Frere 1977, 1983–7; Goodburn 1978–9; Grew 1980–1.
Brancaster	(i) Edwards 1976; St Joseph 1977; (ii) Hinchliffe & Green 1985.
Brough on Foss	(i) St Joseph 1953, 1961, 1965, 1966; Wilson 1975; Whimster 1989 (South Collingham); (ii) Walters 1910.
Chesterton/Castor	(i) Margary 1935; St Joseph 1953, 1958, 1961, 1965, 1966, 1969, 1973; Wilson 1975; Mackreth 1979; Frere & St Joseph 1983; (ii) Artis 1828; Taylor 1926; Taylor & Richmond 1958; Taylor & Wilson 1962; Wilson 1963, 1964, 1969–72, 1974; RCHM(E) 1969; Dannell & Wild, 1971, 1974; Dannell 1974; Wild 1976; and see Mackreth, below.
Great Casterton	(i) St Joseph 1961; (ii) Corder 1951, 1954, 1961; Todd 1968.

Great Chesterford	(i) St Joseph 1953; Rodwell 1972; Wilson 1975; ii) Stukeley 1724; Neville 1847, 1855, 1860; Brinson 1949, 1950, 1963; Rodwell 1975; Collins 1980.
Irchester	(i) St Joseph 1953, 1965, 1966; Wilson 1975; RCHM(E) 1979; Frere & St Joseph 1983; Maxwell & Wilson 1987; (ii) Baker 1879; Haverfield 1902; Hall & Nickerson 1968; Knight 1968; Rankov 1982; Windell 1984; Frere 1985.
Kirmington	(i) Riley 1977; St Joseph 1977; Frere & St Joseph 1983; (ii) Hemblade & Cooper 1989; and see Whitwell, below.
Littleborough	(i) St Joseph 1969, 1977; (ii) Stukeley 1724; Walters 1910.
Old Winteringham	(i) Riley 1974; (ii) Stead 1976; Whitwell 1983; and see Whitwell, below.
Pakenham	(i) Wilson 1975 (Ixworth); St Joseph 1977 (Ixworth); Frere & St Joseph 1983 (Ixworth); (ii) see Plouviez, below.
Thorpe	(i) St Joseph 1953, 1958, 1966; Wilson 1975; (ii) Walters 1910; Oswald 1939; Taylor & Wilson 1961; Wilson 1964, 1966; Inskeep 1966.
Whilton Lodge	(i) St Joseph 1971; Wilson 1975; (ii) Haverfield 1902; Dix & Taylor 1988.
Wixoe	(i) St Joseph 1977; (ii) Rodwell 1975; and see Plouviez, below.

B. *References*

Artis, E T, 1828 *The Durobrivae of Antoninus*

Baker, R S, 1879 Roman exploration at Irchester, *Rep Pap Associated Architect Socs*, 15, 49–59

Brinson, J G S, 1949 Great Chesterford, *Archaeol Newsl*, 1 (10), 12–13

——, 1950 Roman Essex Society excavations during 1949, *ibid*, 2 (9), 146–8

——, 1963 Great Chesterford, *Victoria County Hist Essex*, Vol 3, 72–87

Collins, A, 1980 Great Chesterford, in Excavations in Essex 1979 (ed M R Eddy), *Essex Archaeol Hist*, 12, 42–3

Corder, P, 1951 *The Roman town and villa at Great Casterton, Rutland: first interim report*

——, 1954 *The Roman town and villa at Great Casterton, Rutland: second interim report*.

——, 1961 *The Roman town and villa at Great Casterton, Rutland: third report*

Dannell, G, 1974 Roman industry in Normangate Field, Castor, *Durobrivae, a review of Nene valley archaeology*, 2, 7–9

——, & Wild, J P, 1969 Castor, in Archaeology in Northamptonshire 1967–68 (ed A E Brown), *Bull Northamptonshire Fed Archaeol Socs*, 3, 7–9

——, 1971 Castor, Normangate Field August – September 1970, in Archaeology in Northamptonshire 1970 (ed A E Brown), *ibid*, 5, 12–15

——, 1974 Castor, Normangate Field, in Archaeology in Northamptonshire 1973 (ed A E Brown), *Northamptonshire Archaeol*, 9, 86–8

——, 1976 Castor, Normangate Field, in Archaeology in Northamptonshire 1975 (ed A E Brown), *Northamptonshire Archaeol*, 11, 186–91

Dix, B, 1983 Ashton Roman town, *South Midlands Archaeol*, 13, 18–20

Dix, B, & Taylor, S, 1988 Excavations at *Bannaventa* (Whilton Lodge, Northants), 1970–71, *Britannia*, 19, 299–339

Edwards, D, 1976 The air photographs collection of the Norfolk Archaeological Unit, *E Anglian Archaeol*, 2, 251–69

——, 1977 The air photography collection of the Norfolk Archaeological Unit: second report, *ibid*, 5, 225–37

Frere, S S, 1977 Roman Britain in 1976, *Britannia*, 8, 356–425

——, 1983 Roman Britain in 1982, *ibid*, 14, 280–335

——, 1984 Roman Britain in 1983, *ibid*, 15, 266–332

——, 1985 Roman Britain in 1984, *ibid*, 16, 252–316

——, 1986 Roman Britain in 1985, *ibid*, 17, 364–427

——, 1987 Roman Britain in 1986, *ibid*, 18, 302–59

Frere, S S, & St Joseph, J K S, 1983 *Roman Britain from the air*

Goodburn, R, 1978 Roman Britain in 1977, *Britannia*, 9, 404–72

——, 1979 Roman Britain in 1978, *ibid*, 10, 268–338

Green, C, 1977 Excavations in the Roman kiln field at Brampton, 1973–4, *E Anglian Archaeol*, 5, 31–95

Grew, F O, 1980 Roman Britain in 1979, *Britannia*, 11, 346–402

——, 1981 Roman Britain in 1980, *ibid*, 12, 314–68

Hadman, J, & Upex, S, 1972 Ashton, in Archaeology in Northamptonshire 1971 (ed A E Brown), *Bull Northamptonshire Fed Archaeol Socs*, 7, 12

——, 1975 The Roman settlement at Ashton near Oundle, *Durobrivae, a review of Nene valley archaeology*, 3, 12–15

——, 1977 Ashton, 1976, *ibid*, 5, 6–9

——, 1979 Ashton 1977–78, *ibid*, 7, 29–30

Hall, D N, & Nickerson, N, 1968 Excavations at Irchester 1962–63, *Archaeol J*, 124 (1967), 65–99

Haverfield, F, 1902 Romano-British Northamptonshire, in *Victoria county hist Northampton,* 1, 157–222

Hawkes, C F C, 1947 Roman Ancaster, Horncastle and Caistor, *Archaeol J,* 103 (1946), 17–25

Hemblade, M, & Cooper, R, 1989 Recent surveys of the major Roman settlement of Kirmington, *Lincolnshire Hist Archaeol,* 24, 57

Hinchliffe, J, & Green, C S, 1985 Excavations at Brancaster 1974 and 1977, *E Anglian Archaeol*, 23, 1–240

Inskeep, R R, 1966 Excavations at *Ad Pontem*, Thorpe parish, Notts, *Trans Thoroton Soc Nottinghamshire,* 69 (1965), 19–39

Knight, J K, 1968 Excavations at the Roman town of Irchester, 1962–63, *Archaeol J*, 124 (1967), 100–28

Knowles, A K, 1977 The Roman settlement at Brampton, Norfolk: interim report, *Britannia*, 8, 209–21

Mackreth, D, 1979 Durobrivae, *Durobrivae, a review of Nene valley archaeology*, 7, 19–21

Margary, I V, 1935 Roman roads near *Durobrivae* (Castor, Northants), *Antiq J*, 15, 113–18

Maxwell, G S, & Wilson, D R, 1987 Air reconnaissance in Roman Britain 1977–84, *Britannia*, 18, 1–48

Neville, R C 1847 *Antiqua explorata*, Saffron Walden

——, 1855 Notices of certain shafts containing remains of the Roman period discovered at the Roman station at Chesterford, *Essex Archaeol J*, 12, 109–25

——, 1860 Account of recent discoveries of Roman remains

at Great Chesterford, Essex, *ibid*, 17, 117–27

Oswald, A, 1939 Excavations at *Ad Pontem, Trans Thoroton Soc Nottinghamshire*, 42 (1938), 1–14

Rankov, N B, 1982 Roman Britain in 1981, *Britannia*, 13, 328–95

Riley, D N, 1974 The end of Ermine Street at the South Shore of the Humber, *Britannia*, 5, 375–7

——, 1977 Roman defended sites at Kirmington, S Humberside, and Farnsfield, Notts, recently found from the air, *ibid*, 8, 189–92

Rodwell, W, 1972 The Roman fort at Great Chesterford, Essex, *Britannia*, 3, 290–3

——, 1975 Trinovantian towns and their setting, in *The 'small towns' of Roman Britain* (eds W Rodwell & T Rowley), BAR Brit Ser, 15, 85–101

——, & Rowley T (eds), 1975 *The 'small towns' of Roman Britain*, BAR Brit Ser, 15

RCHM(E), 1969 *Peterborough New Town: a survey of the antiquities in the area of development*

——, 1979 *An inventory of the historical monuments in the County of Northampton, Vol 2, Archaeological sites in North Northamptonshire*

St Joseph, J K, 1953 Air reconnaissance of southern Britain, *J Roman Stud,* 43, 81–97

——, 1958 Air reconnaissance in Britain, 1955–7, *ibid*, 48, 86–101

——, 1961 Air reconnaissance in Britain, 1958–1960, *ibid*, 51, 119–35

——, 1965 Air reconnaissance in Britain, 1961–64, *ibid*, 55, 74–89

——, 1966 The towns of Roman Britain: the contribution of aerial reconnaissance, in *The civitas capitals of Roman Britain* (ed J S Wacher), 21–30

——, 1969 Air reconnaissance in Britain, 1965–68, *J Roman Stud* 59, 104–28

——, 1971 Air reconnaissance: recent results, 24, *Antiquity*, 40, 140–1

——, 1973 Air reconnaissance in Britain, 1969–72, *J Roman Stud,*
63, 214–46

——, 1977 Air reconnaissance in Roman Britain, 1973–76, *ibid*, 67, 125–61

Stead, I M, 1976 *Excavations at Winterton Roman villa and other Roman sites in North Lincolnshire 1958–1967*

Stukeley, W, 1724 *Itinerarium curiosum*

Taylor, M V, 1926 Romano-British Huntingdonshire, in *Victoria county hist Huntingdon*, 1, 228–48

——, & Richmond, I A, 1958 Roman Britain in 1957, *J Roman Stud*, 48, 130–49

——, & Wilson, D R, 1961 Roman Britain in 1960, *ibid*, 51, 157–91

——, 1962 Roman Britain in 1961, *ibid*, 52, 160–90

Todd, M, 1968 *The Roman fort at Great Casterton, Rutland*

——, 1975 *Margidunum* and Ancaster, in *The 'small towns' of Roman Britain* (eds W Rodwell & T Rowley), BAR Brit Ser, 15, 211–23

——, 1981 *The Roman town at Ancaster, Lincolnshire: the excavations of 1955–71*

Wacher, J S (ed), 1966 *The civitas capitals of Roman Britain*

Walters, H B, 1910 Romano-British Nottinghamshire, in *Victoria county hist Nottingham*, 2, 1–36

Whimster, R P, 1989 *The emerging past: air photography*

and the buried landscape

Whitwell, J B, 1983 Old Winteringham, *Lincolnshire Hist Archaeol*, 18, 103–4

Wild, J P, 1976, A Roman farm at Castor, *Durobrivae, a review of Nene valley archaeology,* 4, 26–7

Wilson, D R, 1963 Roman Britain in 1962, *J Roman Stud*, 53, 125

——, 1964 Roman Britain in 1963, *ibid*, 54, 152–77

——, 1966 Roman Britain in 1965, *ibid*, 56, 196–217

——, 1967 Roman Britain in 1966, *ibid*, 57, 174–202

——, 1968 Roman Britain in 1967, *ibid*, 58, 176–206

——, 1969 Roman Britain in 1968, *ibid*, 59, 198–234

——, 1970 Roman Britain in 1969, *Britannia*, 1, 268–305

——, 1971 Roman Britain in 1970, *ibid*, 2, 242–88

——, 1972 Roman Britain in 1971, *ibid*, 3, 298–351

——, 1973 Roman Britain in 1972, *ibid*, 4, 270–323

——, 1974 Roman Britain in 1973, *ibid*, 5, 396–460

——, 1975 The 'small towns' of Roman Britain from the air, in *The 'small towns' of Roman Britain* (eds W Rodwell & T Rowley), BAR Brit Ser, 15, 9–49

Windell, D, 1984 Irchester Roman town: excavations 1981–82, *Northamptonshire Archaeol*, 19, 31–51

4   Strategies for Roman small towns

Martin Millett

Introduction

In this paper I wish to look at some of the prospects for developing our ideas about the roles of so-called Small Town[1] sites within Roman Britain, without, I hope falling into the trap of suggesting that there is any single prescription for future progress in research. With the publication of the recent survey by Burnham and Wacher (1990) we have the opportunity to enter a new era of understanding based on the sound foundations of the synthesis they have provided for a good number of the sites. Nevertheless, there remain a whole series of unanswered and even unasked questions which should form an agenda for the future. In the present state of research, however, the danger lies in becoming trapped by a belief that work already completed defines the only legitimate approach to these sites. I suspect that the most interesting results in the next few years will come from the application of fresh ideas from the new generation of research students, even if some of their approaches appear alien or even naive and unsophisticated when they are first introduced (cf Scott 1993). For this reason, although I shall offer one or two directions and thoughts for future research I do not intend to provide an exclusive shopping list of new research questions; a diversity of approach is the key to future progress.

Strategy and definition

At the risk of stating the obvious it is worth observing that the definition of any refined research strategy presupposes a secure knowledge of the object under study. Without this no worthwhile results can be produced. With this in mind I can see two connected barriers blocking our way forward in the study of these sites. First there does not yet seem to be a satisfactory consensus over what constitutes a Small Town. Most seem to have been assigned to the category because they are *not* members of other easily defined groups. Second in our attempts to grapple with the problems of definition we remain over concerned about the question of which sites (if any) have distinctively urban characteristics.

The discussion at the conference seems to confirm my suspicion that sites are grouped together and classed as Small Towns because we know neither what they were nor how they functioned, and not because we have any clear and rational understanding of the ways in which they might have functioned within the Romano-British landscape. This itself would not be too serious a problem if it were generally recognised as a research issue which still needed to be investigated. However, although the question of definition has been widely debated since the 1970s (see Todd 1971; Rodwell & Rowley 1975; Millett 1976a), the approach to its resolution has been simply to attempt a classification of sites. Thus in the latest study Burnham and Wacher (1990) have subdivided the sites into categories like Potential Cities, Minor Towns, Specialised Religious Sites, Specialised Industrial Sites, Minor Defended Settlements and Undefended Settlements. In doing this they were constrained by the limitations of the available archaeological evidence and thus relied primarily on morphology and assumed functions for their categorisation.

The problem of establishing what the individual sites were and how each functioned within Roman Britain is in danger of being confused with classification. Attributing a site to a grouping and labelling it (*classification*) is not the same as understanding its potentially diverse roles (*explanation*). We do not, for instance, understand any more about Kenchester because it has been described as a Potential City. This confusion of classification with explanation is not restricted to the study of Small Towns (or even Roman Britain) but in this particular instance it has had the effect of a dead hand on research.

In Roman studies in general classifications too often isolate sites from the remainder of the settlement pattern, dealing with them out of context and isolating particular differences rather than common patterns. I believe for instance that this is reflected in Burnham and Wacher's (1990) characterisation of sites as specialised religious or industrial centres. Particular characteristics are of course important for understanding individual sites but they are less useful for establishing roles within the overall settlement system. It is probable that my own comments about the Small Towns (Millett 1990, 147–51) are flawed but an approach which relates a growth in their importance to changes in balance within the economies and administrative structures of the *civitates* is surely soundly based. I would challenge those who believe that the greatest relative importance of Small Towns was not in the late Roman period to collate the evidence and present an alternative holistic explanation.

Past approaches to site classification are also very closely associated with the question of how far particular sites possessed characteristics which might be considered urban. I fear we cannot escape the underlying issue that a demonstration of machismo has become associated with excavators' attempts to prove the urban character of their sites. I can justifiably be accused of this in the context of my discussion of the site at Neatham (Millett & Graham 1986, chapter 8). The desire to classify a site (preferably as urban, and thus in some way more important) has obscured the issue of what the site was and how it may have functioned. This is especially problematic as I am now far from convinced that the concept of urbanism has validity outside the confines of a particular society; what might be considered a town in one context may not be in another and checklists of urban characteristics (such as that devised by Childe) obscure the point that the definition of a town is culturally constructed and should thus be expected to vary. This is especially important within the Roman Empire as different provinces clearly did not share a cultural unity. The problem we have been grappling with has perhaps been wrongly framed. It should not be 'Are these sites urban?', but 'What constitutes urbanism in this particular society at this period?'

Some may object to these points with the rejoinder that urbanism in the Roman world is well understood and a classification of the British sites in relation to this norm is an important part of the process of understanding Britain in relation to other, arguably better known provinces. The reply to this criticism lies in two areas. First, although there is a reasonably clearly understood legally-based definition of Roman urbanism which is widely used and can be reasonably applied to Britain, it does not help with the problem of the Small Towns. These are defined only in the sense of not falling into one of the principal categories of administrative centre conveniently called public towns (*municipium, colonia* or *civitas* capital). Similar Small Town sites are found widely across the whole Empire but are equally ill-understood. Perhaps because they were originally local centres (using the useful terminology of Hingley 1989) their administrative status was largely irrelevant to their characteristics as settlement sites. In this sense the importance of understanding them through archaeology is increased because they are almost universally problematical. Secondly, it is becoming clear that the characteristics of even the public towns are poorly understood. Current research is doing much to question what constituted Roman

urbanism behind the veneer of the public buildings (Cornell 1993; Dobinson 1992; Lomas 1993). This work illustrates that even towns within the central provinces were highly variable in layout and function and certainly did not always comprise densely occupied and carefully planned settlements as is often assumed. The question of how all towns in the Roman world operated is thus of serious importance; a question for future investigation and not a closed book. Their characteristics will clearly not be resolved simply by the subdividing and labelling of sites in an increasing number of decreasingly common 'types'.

Sites in context

The first stage of an alternative approach should start from the basic evidence available without making rigid assumptions about what the sites mean. We need to draw the net widely and look at how the whole landscape might have functioned during the period with which we are concerned. Small Towns cannot be understood on their own but need to be seen in relation to the other contemporaneous features in the landscape. They should also be viewed in relation to a full range of different social and economic functions, not simply the politically dominant administrative structure. I would outline three areas where we might make some fairly rapid progress with this type of investigation. Moving from the provincial to the regional scale, and then to the individual site I shall discuss the following themes:

(1) the investigation of site interrelationships
(2) the study of site distribution
(3) the investigation of a settlement's character

Site interrelationships

In Britain we have a strong tradition of landscape study but all too often the examination of settlements is concerned only with individual site types, villas, *civitas* capitals etc. It is surely time that we developed the landscape tradition so that emphasis is placed on investigating the context of different sites. In addition we need to look not only at the statics of the settlement system but also at the dynamics of the flows of people and goods between them. Although such aims are not necessarily fully achievable they do provide a direction for future effort and a context within which to place the artefact and ecofact studies which have blossomed in recent decades (cf Millett 1991). All too often these studies have achieved a high technical standard but have not been closely integrated into the broader archaeological discussion. Those writing syntheses have ignored them whilst the authors of specialist reports have remained ignorant of the most recent interpretative debates.

In examining artefact distributions and the supply of agricultural goods it is important not to begin from the assumption that there will be differences between types of site. Although current syntheses are pregnant with assumptions about towns as centres of distribution and villas as centres of consumption we have precious little evidence on which to base such beliefs. The role of a *civitas* capital as a political centre with religious functions and access to the Roman road network does not necessarily mean that it was economically or productively more important than other local centres be they small towns, villas, forts or religious sanctuaries. Until we have used archaeological evidence to explore economic relationships between sites with fewer firmly held beliefs colouring our interpretations we are unlikely to move beyond some of the present barriers. Basic questions about whether distributions of goods really were based on towns and the extent to which they varied between site types have hardly yet been asked. It might be suggested that the only proper way by which to classify the sites under study is through an assessment of whether or not they acted as local regional distribution centres.

One of the more interesting potential areas for investigation lies in the relationship, long ago mentioned by Todd (1971), between a number of Small Town sites and individual closely adjacent villas. A similar pattern has been noted in Gaul (Drinkwater 1985), but as far as I am aware not a single project has attempted to look at such sites together in their landscapes and investigate the possibilities of tenurial links between them through an analysis of topography, artefacts and ecofacts (cf Millett 1990, 150). The suggestion by Don Mackreth at the conference that a provincial administrator who controlled an assumed Imperial Estate was the owner of the extensive and opulent villa at Castor adjacent to the Small Town at Water Newton (Mackreth 1984 and this volume) ignores this observed general regularity of association between site types. It also follows the old but doubtful logic that the most magnificent in Roman Britain must always have been the property of officials or outsiders. This is a view which I would strongly dispute.

Site distribution

One of the most obvious characteristics about the Small Towns is their ubiquity. Whilst we cannot of course be certain that all were the same, a very large number of them have been identified in both Britain and adjacent parts of Gaul and Germany (King and Gechter, this volume). This lends some weight to the notion that they served as important local foci, perhaps fulfilling a range of functions which need not all have been economic. Without making the detailed assumptions which underpinned Hodder's influential spatial studies of the distribution of walled towns (Hodder & Hassall 1971; Hodder 1975 – discussed in Millett 1976b; 1986) it does seem worthwhile to look at the patterns of site distribution more closely. In doing this we do not need to accept the tenets of Central Place Theory, which are now generally

agreed to be too modernising in their character and too deterministic in their scope (Grant 1986). Nevertheless where we have reliable information on the size and distribution of sites we should examine them to see whether comprehensible regularities emerge. Any such patterns will need to be carefully considered, and not simply interpreted by reference to supposedly universal models.

Such good quality information was presented at the conference and has kindly been made available to me for parts of the East Midlands and East Anglia. Within this area we have information about sixty-one sites (Fig 4.1, Table 4.1). These data are probably not complete since in areas like Leicestershire sustained fieldwork has increased the numbers of identified sites in recent years. Nonetheless the evidence clearly suggests that an evenly distributed pattern of Small Towns was emerging through the Roman period. This is illustrated by simply measuring the distance of each town to its nearest neighbouring Small Town or Public Town. I have measured this to the nearest km as the crow flies. A more accurate and more realistic assessment might be produced by taking account of the roads and topography and making the measurements using a Geographical Information System. However my simple data (Fig 4.2, Table 4.1) show that the vast majority of the sites are spaced at around 15km, meaning that most of the region lay within a day's return journey of a Small Town. This density and regularity would seem to confirm that these sites served vital functions for much of the population.

The sizes of the sites shown on Fig 4.1 are not so easily measured and data were only available for just over half the sites (Table 4.1). We need to be a little cautious in our use of this information most of which is derived from surface fieldwork. Not only is it difficult to distinguish areas which were occupied from those which were simply used for the disposal of rubbish but the nature of the sites also makes them difficult to measure accurately. At sites like Shiptonthorpe (Taylor, this volume) the evidence shows that agricultural zones and cemeteries were interspersed with settlement areas so gross site size is easy to overestimate. Similar factors may explain the huge area recorded for sites like Water Newton. This problem is particularly important if we wish to make comparisons with more densely occupied Public Towns or arrive at reliable population estimates. Nevertheless Figure 4.3 shows that the majority of the sites were in the range 10–30 ha which overlaps with the smallest of the Public Towns (Millett 1990, illus 62). The smallest were only equal in size to some farmsteads highlighting the danger of being over enthusiastic in identifying sites as Small Towns. When we remember that we are dealing with only part of the province's settlement system it is obvious that despite the proliferation of Small Towns Britain remained dominated by the very small number of very large centres like London. Although there was a wide and closely spaced distribution of local centres a strongly integrated economy was probably not fully de-

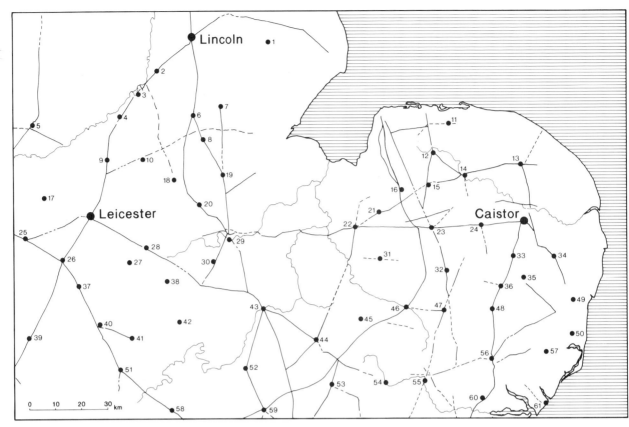

Fig 4.1 *Map showing the distribution of Small Towns in parts of the East Midlands and East Anglia. For site identifications see Table 4.1. (Drawn by Yvonne Beadnell)*

Table 4.1 *List of sites shown on Figure 4.1 together with details of their estimated size (where available) and the distance to their nearest neighbouring Small Town or Public Town.*

Map no.	Site	Estimated size (ha)	Nearest Neighbour (km)	Map no.	Site	Estimated size (ha)	Nearest Neighbour (km)
1	Horncastle	2.5	29	34	Ditchingham		14
2	Brough		11	35	Needham		9
3	East Stoke		11	36	Scole		9
4	East Bridgeford		11	37	Caves Inn	13	11
5	Littlechester		25	38	Kettering	23	15
6	Ancaster	28	9	39	Chesterton	3.2	28
7	Sleaford	25	11	40	Whilton Lodge	5	14
8	Sapperton	4	9	41	Duston		14
9	Willoughby	20	14	42	Irchester	20	16
10	Goadby Marwood	25	14	43	Godmanchester	10.9	23
11	Walsingham		13	44	Cambridge	10.1	16
12	Dunton		11	45	Exning	10	18
13	Brampton		21	46	Icklingham	17	15
14	Billingford		15	47	Pakenham	19	15
15	Kempstone		11	48	Stoke Ash	7	9
16	Narford		11	49	Wehaston	15	12
17	Ravenstone		11	50	Kodishall	8	12
18	Thistleton	33	14	51	Towcester	28	13
19	Bourne		14	52	Sandy		16
20	Great Casterton	7	14	53	Great Chesterford	14.5	20
21	Fincham		11	54	Wixoe	12	15
22	Denver		11	55	Long Melford	24	15
23	Saham Toney		16	56	Coddenham	40	15
24	Wicklewood		16	57	Hacheston	30	12
25	Mancetter	35	16	58	Dropshort		24
26	High Cross	12	11	59	Baldock		17
27	Market Harborough		9	60	Chapel St Mary	10	15
28	Medbourne	60	9	61	Felixtowe	18	18
29	Water Newton	110	11		Lincoln	39	19
30	Ashton	21	11		Leicester	42	19
31	Hockwold		15		Caistor	14	14
32	Brettenham		15				
33	Long Stratton		9	Mean (Small Towns only)		20.83	14.20
				Standard Deviation		19.61	4.52

veloped. If it had been we would expect far less distinction between the largest towns and those of average size.

Finally we may note that there is no close relationship between the size of a Small Town and the distance to its nearest neighbour. If the settlement pattern were simply a result of locational factors we might predict that larger sites would develop where there was least competition from adjacent centres, in which case site size would tend to be larger for sites further apart. Figure 4.4 shows that this is not the case as the bulk of the sites cluster together and there is no evidence of any linear pattern on the graph. The sizes to which the sites grew was thus presumably a result of more complex factors which surely deserve closer investigation.

What this evidence makes abundantly clear is the need to collect further detailed regional data from Britain and other provinces. It would be useful to ascertain how far these patterns were regional and to what extent they reflect general characteristics which underpinned settlement within the north-western Roman provinces. The latter perhaps resulted from such factors as social and economic organisation and limitations on communication speeds.

The remarkably even distribution patterns seem to me to raise important questions about the nature of society within these regions of Britain. Indeed they bring to mind the issue of whether we are seeing an indigenous form of urbanism which I tentatively suggested in an earlier discussion (Millett 1976a). This is a point to which I will return towards the end of this paper.

Site character

However before we can make progress in considering the meaning of these patterns of distribution we need far more evidence about the nature of the sites with which we are dealing. (This applies equally to the public towns, villas and rural settlements). One of our greatest challenges as archaeologists is to move beyond the very small samples of excavated evidence to make broader sense of whole sites. The largest excavated samples rarely represent more than one or two per cent of a single site and this has generally been selected for excavation as a result of haphazard factors. Even were we to have a sample of this size selected on a statistically random basis it would only be reliably representative if the site were unusually homogenous. To judge this we would need further evidence about the site as a whole.

This does not mean that I support the view that we cannot conclude anything until we have more data. Indeed, one of the great achievements of Burnham and Wacher's study (1990) is that it brings together and makes sense of the piecemeal and inadequate excavated evidence from a wide variety of sites. Nevertheless even such synthesis leaves us with only a very limited picture of most sites so that it is very difficult to establish the extent to which they were heavily occupied, let alone

what was the balance and range of their functions. Even where we have excellent and carefully plotted aerial photographic evidence from sites like Water Newton (Mackreth 1979 and this volume) we have remarkably little understanding of what the different elements identified were or how they functioned. This methodological point itself leads me to doubt the extent to which the functional groupings of the Small Towns used by Burnham and Wacher (1990) can be relied upon.

One answer to this problem lies in the application of a variety of surface survey techniques which enable us not only to map the archaeology more accurately (Keay *et al* 1991) but also to achieve some closer understanding of the functions of different elements of a site. On a modest scale this approach has proved very effective at the Small Town site of Shiptonthorpe in East Yorkshire where intensive survey has been combined with limited excavation to produce a fuller understanding of a significant part of a settlement which lies at the smaller end of the spectrum of sites. This work is presented in more detail in Jeremy Taylor's contribution to this volume (pp 39–51).

Taylor's work is only a first step in this direction but it does illustrate the potential and surely shows that similar integrated surface studies could pay significant dividends on larger sites. It seems remarkable that although we have the means to produce such surveys they are not being used for the large scale investigation of a number of the sites under discussion which are easily accessible on agricultural land. In some respects there can be no case for any further excavation on Small Town sites until we have a better understanding of them through surface work. This does not mean we should overlook the problems of such survey, especially as it is clearly much easier to make sense of a small and simple site than one which comprises a multitude of superimposed structures over a large area. Nevertheless it should be possible to begin to test ideas about the extent of intensive occupation and agricultural areas even in the most complex sites since progress along these lines has already been made in Mediterranean cities (Keay *et al* 1991).

Conclusions – an indigenous urbanism?

In a deservedly widely ignored paper (Millett 1976a) I suggested that Small Towns represented a native form of urbanism in Roman Britain. Although that paper did not develop the issue at all fully, I think it remains valid to see the character of these sites as a result of native response to the Roman presence. The character of individual sites was not determined by the imposition of any Roman template and is thus the result of native responses to changed circumstances most likely stimulated by Roman control. As some of these centres developed as extensive settlements, and presumably served a large proportion of the province's population without significant imposed constraints, I would argue that they pro-

34 *Martin Millett*

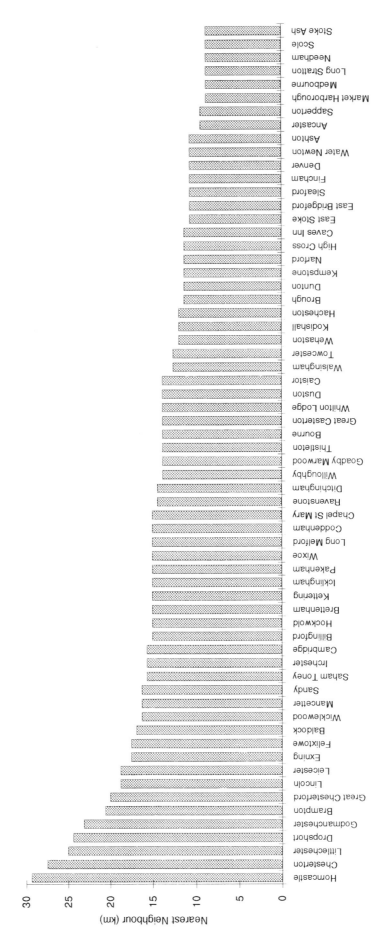

Fig. 4.2 *Graph showing the distance of each Small Town and Public Town shown in Figure 1 to its nearest neighbouring site. For data see Table 4.1. (Generated by author using Excel 4.0)*

Fig 4.3 *Graph showing the estimated size of Small Towns and Public Towns shown on Figure 1. For data see Table 4.1. (Generated by author using Excel 4.0)*

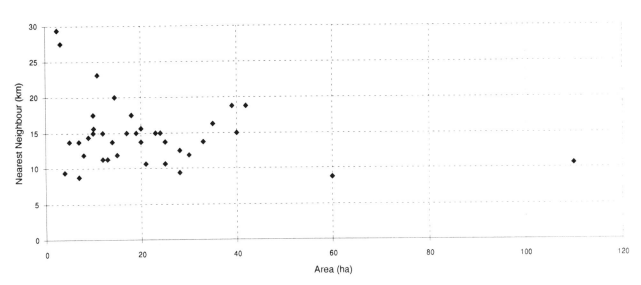

Fig 4.4 *Graph showing the relationship between estimated size and distance to nearest neighbour. For data see Table 4.1. (Generated by author using Excel 4.0)*

vide one of the best indices of native development within the Roman provinces. In this sense it is very interesting to note the contrasts between the often monumentalised sites of southern Gaul discussed by Tony King (this volume, p 185–192) and those of northern Gaul and Lower Germany which share more in common with those in Britain (Hiddink 1991).

This theme of native character highlights one of the points which has recently emerged from my own excavations at Shiptonthorpe. Near the centre of this small settlement lay an apparently functional waterhole in the angle between a side street and the principal road (Taylor, this vol Fig 5.9). This prosaic feature, which appeared to have acted as a communal watering place for stock, emerged on excavation to have been a focal place for carefully structured ritual activity. The analysis of its contents is not yet complete but it is clear that a number of animal and infant burials focused upon it, whilst a range of other items was carefully placed within it. Such a religious focus should not occasion surprise on a Romano-British site for anyone with an open mind must be aware that behind the comfortably familiar and seemingly rational economic façade of Roman Britain there lurk a range of unfamiliar features which, despite the writings of Anne Ross (1967), we are only slowly beginning to appreciate let alone understand (see for instance Scott & Poulton 1993; cf Hill 1989).

This religious focus raises the question of the relative importance of the different functions of this apparently agricultural site. Rationalist, western archaeologists are too much inclined to think about urbanism in terms of the economics, seeing rituals as at most peripheral. At the extreme even sites like Bath, which were self-evidently religious centres, are too often seen only as variants of the 'normal' economically functioning town.

However, if one looks both at the religious aspects of the major public towns and the rituals involved in their foundation (cf Salway 1985) it is clear that in the Roman mind the sacred was often prominent. Equally a recently published paper concerned with the Small Towns of Gallia Belgica and Lower Germany observed 'The fact that cult places are found in nearly every rural centre, and that they are often large complexes with several sanctuaries raises the question of the relative importance of the cult function' (Hiddink 1991, 218).

This leads me to the question of how far sites like Shiptonthorpe, representing as they do the native extreme of formalised religious practice, might have been important as sacred centres within the landscape. This is not to say that they were primarily religious sites – although they might have been – but it does emphasize how important it is to try to think ourselves out of the comfortable certainty that Roman Britain was somehow rational and similar to the twentieth century. One aspect of this must be to reintegrate religious evidence into our understanding of Roman provincial society for it is probable that its segregation and omission from most explanations is solely a result of our own peculiarly secular society. If we can accept this and go on to try to investigate more subtly what different things happened at the various sites within the landscape (including Small Towns) we might approach a clearer view of Roman Britain.

Acknowledgements
I am most grateful to Tony Brown, Peter Liddle, Jude Plouviez, Brian Simmons, Jeremy Taylor, and Ben Whitwell who kindly provided data which are incorporated in Table 4.1. Jeremy Taylor has also kindly commented upon an earlier draft of this paper. Ideas discussed

have been stimulated by the recent work of Eleanor Scott and J D Hill and have benefitted from critical scrutiny at a seminar at IPP in Amsterdam organised by Nico Roymans and Jan Slofstra.

Note

1. Although I do not like this term I hope I will be permitted to use it as a shorthand throughout this paper. The problems in its use in many ways exemplify the problems I am attempting to explore.

Bibliography

Burnham, B C, & Wacher, J S, 1990 *The 'small towns' of Roman Britain*

Cornell, T, 1993 *Urban society in Roman Italy*, unpublished paper presented to the Classical Association Conference, Durham, 9 April 1993

Dobinson, C, 1992 *Studies in Romano-British urban structure*, Cambridge University PhD thesis

Drinkwater, J, 1985 Urbanisation in the three Gauls: some observations, in *Roman urban topography in Britain and the western Empire* (eds F Grew & B Hobley), CBA Res Rep 59, 49–55

Grant, E (ed), 1986 *Central places, archaeology and history*, Sheffield, Department of Archaeology and Prehistory

Hiddink, H A, 1991 Rural centres in the Roman settlement system of Northern Gallia Belgica and Germania Inferior, in *Images of the past: studies on ancient societies in northwest Europe* (eds N Roymans & F Theuws), Amsterdam: Instituut voor Pre- en Protohistorische Archeologie, 201–34

Hill, J D, 1989 Re-thinking the Iron Age, *Scottish Archaeol Rev*, 6, 16–23

Hingley, R, 1989 *Rural settlement in Roman Britain*

Hodder, I, 1975 The spatial distribution of Romano-British small towns, in *The 'small towns' of Roman Britain* (eds W Rodwell & T Rowley), BAR Brit Ser, 15, 67–74

——, & Hassall, M W C, 1971 The non-random spacing of Romano-British walled towns, *Man*, 6, 391–407

Keay, S J, Creighton, J, & Jordan, D, 1991 Sampling ancient towns, *Oxford J Archaeol*, 10(3), 371–83

Lomas, K, 1993 *The Italian city: urbanisation in southern Italy*, unpublished paper presented to the Classical Association Conference, Durham, 8 April 1993

Mackreth, D F, 1979 Durobrivae, *Durobrivae: a review of Nene Valley archaeology*, 7, 19–21

——, 1984 Castor, *Durobrivae: a review of Nene Valley archaeology*, 9, 22–25

Millett, M, 1976a The native towns of Roman Britain, *Curr Archaeol*, 52, 134–38

——, 1976b Review of W Rodwell & T Rowley (eds), *The 'small towns' of Roman Britain*, 1975, *Bull Univ London Inst Archaeol*, 14, 212–13

——, 1986 Central places in a decentralised Roman Britain, in *Central places, archaeology and history* (ed E Grant), 45–48

——, 1990 *The Romanization of Britain*

——, 1991 Roman towns and their territories: an archaeological perspective, in *City and countryside in the ancient world* (eds J Rich & A Wallace-Hadrill), 169–90

——, & Graham, D, 1986 *Excavations on the Romano-British small town at Neatham, Hampshire, 1969–79*

Rodwell, W, & Rowley, R (eds), 1975 *The 'small towns' of Roman Britain*, BAR Brit Ser, 15

Ross, A, 1967 *Pagan Celtic Britain*

Salway, P, 1985 Geography and the growth of towns, with special reference to Britain, in *Roman urban topography in Britain and the western empire* (eds F Grew & B Hobley), CBA Res Rep 59, 67–73

Scott, E (ed), 1993 *Theoretical Roman archaeology: first conference proceedings*

——, & Poulton, R, 1993 The hoarding, deposition and use of pewter in Roman Britain, in *Theoretical Roman archaeology: first conference proceedings* (ed E Scott)

Todd, M, 1971 The small towns of Roman Britain, *Britannia*, 1, 114–30

5 Surveying small towns: the Romano-British roadside settlement at Shiptonthorpe, East Yorkshire

Jeremy Taylor

Introduction

The 2nd–4th century AD site at Shiptonthorpe lies midway between the roughly contemporaneous settlements at Brough-on-Humber and York. It is at present under study as part of a survey of the Holme-on-Spalding Moor area by Durham University Department of Archaeology, Hull City Museums, and the East Riding Archaeological Society.

Shiptonthorpe has been recognised for some years as a major settlement in the Roman period but no attempt had been made to assess either its size or status. Fieldwork in the surrounding area since 1983 identified the site as a focal point of the Roman settlement system and suggested that it could cover up to 20 hectares, falling into the category generally known as 'small towns'.

On the strength of this a programme was set up under the auspices of Durham University Department of Archaeology to assess the value of a series of commonly used surface analysis techniques when studying the morphology and chronology of a Romano-British small town within the landscape.

Shiptonthorpe: landscape and setting

The Roman road from Brough (*Petuaria Parisiorum*) to York (*Eburacum*) runs between two distinctly different geographical regions. To the east lies the escarpment of the Yorkshire Wolds with its characteristic shallow well drained calcareous silty soils over chalk on slopes and crests and deep, non-calcareous silty soils in the valley bottoms. To the west are the low lying agriculturally marginal soils of West Humberside with their complex microtopography, which have been subject to flooding until recent times. The Roman road runs along the eastern fringe of the low lying area following the slightly higher sandy ridges undulating to the west of a major band of Jurassic and Cretaceous clays between Market Weighton and Pocklington. The settlement area at Shiptonthorpe lies on one of these low sandy ridges between two now canalised waterways; the River Foulness and Fox Beck.

Recent survey in the low lying sandy and glacio-fluvial soils to the south west (Halkon 1987; Millett & Halkon 1988) has shown that in the late Iron Age at least, the area now known as Walling Fen was estuarine (see Fig 5.1). Settlement in that region also appeared to show a marked preference for the drier sandy hilltops, particularly those close to the various river channels which are frequent across this area. Much of this region was thus

> 'on the margins of an estuarine creek system with easy access to the rest of the Humber drainage basin *via* the river system' (Millett & Halkon 1988, 41).

Through the application of the techniques outlined in this survey it is hoped that the relationship of the settlement to the road and riverine system will become better understood in order to place the site at Shiptonthorpe within its regional context. The survey was also initially designed to assess three basic questions about the settlement itself. First, the overall extent of the intensively occupied area. Second, the chronological development of the settlement and last, its morphology and internal organisation. In this way the survey was intended to briefly characterise the nature of settlement at Shiptonthorpe and provide a context for the excavations.

Fieldwalking and pottery analysis

In the course of the Holme-on-Spalding Moor survey Fields Two and Three (see Fig 5.2) were grid walked to determine the distribution and extent of ceramics in the ploughsoil. Field Two, walked in 1984, was divided into a series of squares approximately 25 × 25 metres. Field Three, walked in 1985 by a different team, was divided into rectangles 30 × 10 metres on an east-west axis. Though these differences in time, team and method cause problems in the comparison of the two areas the material recovered allowed a simple study of the pottery by fabric, sherd count, weight and average sherd weight.

The material was divided into known fabric groups so that distinct chronological and functional types could be plotted to identify possible spatial variation over the area

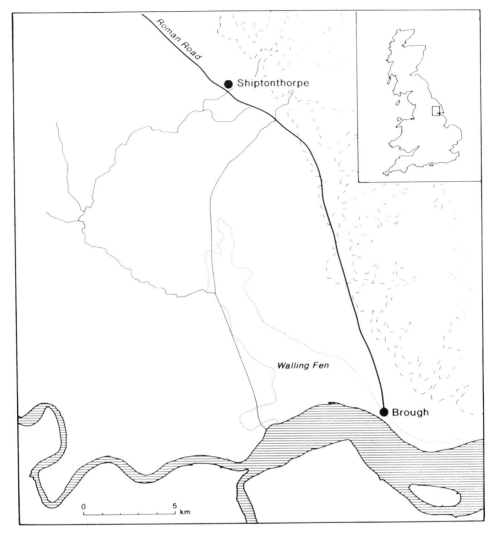

Fig. 5.1 *Regional location of the Shiptonthorpe settlement*

covered. In recording both sherd numbers and weights the two distributions could be compared to determine the consistency of the plot produced (Fig 5.3a & b).

The pottery was quantified by fabric group and recorded on pottery summary sheets. Nine major fabrics were identified from the Shiptonthorpe material along with a number of other rarer fabrics grouped together for statistical presentation as group J. The more diagnostic fabrics were then dated approximately using a range of published descriptions for the area (especially Gillam 1968; Evans 1985 and Halkon 1987).

Chronological study

Five common, datable non-local fabrics were present among the assemblage and could be placed into a broad chronological framework:

i)   Samian – 1st to late 2nd/early 3rd centuries (Hartley 1969, 235–52).
ii) Crambeck Parchment Ware – mid to late 4th century (Evans 1985, 324).

iii) 'Huntcliffe' Ware – late 4th century.
iv) Lower Nene Valley Colour-coated Ware – late 2nd to 4th century (Howe *et al* 1989).
v)   Dressel 20 amphora – late 1st to late 2nd century (Peacock & Williams 1986).

As well as these, fabric C, identified as a local product from the Hasholme Hall Area (see Hicks & Wilson 1975) has been dated to the mid-3rd to mid-4th centuries (Evans 1985, 242) on the basis of the Trentholme Drive excavation at York (Wenham 1968).

On the basis of this evidence the datable fabrics were divided into two broad categories:

i)   Early fabrics – Samian and Dressel 20 amphorae.
ii) Late Fabrics – Crambeck Parchment and 'Huntcliffe' Wares.

It was felt that to include Lower Nene Valley Ware or fabric C, the so-called 'Dales Ware' type (Halkon 1987) would create too great a possibility of overlap in the chronology of the two groups and so these were excluded from the analysis. The distribution of early and late fab-

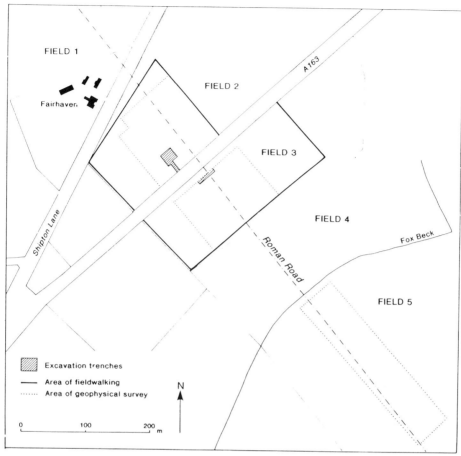

Fig. 5.2 *Shiptonthorpe survey areas*

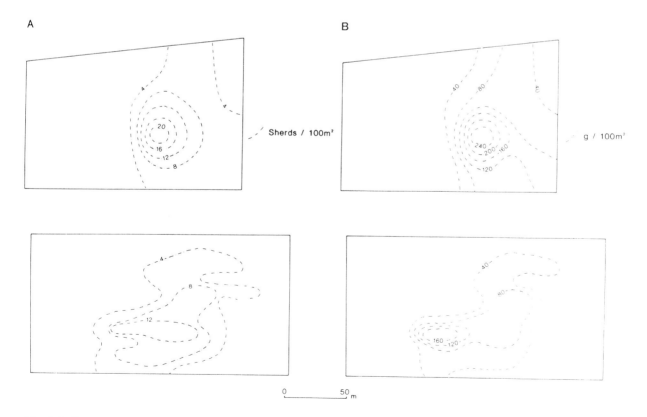

Fig. 5.3 *Shiptonthorpe: contour plot showing the distribution of all Roman pottery by (a) sherd count and (b) weight*

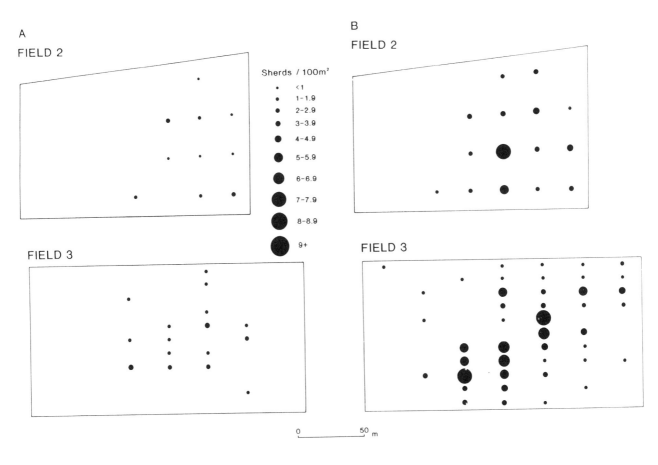

Fig. 5.4 *Shiptonthorpe: the distribution by sherd count of (a) earlier and (b) later Roman pottery*

rics was then plotted (Fig 5.4a & b). Despite the low levels of early pottery it is still possible to recognise the remarkable consistency between the two plots although during analysis it was noted that amphorae were found only in Field Two and that Crambeck Parchment Ware came predominantly from Field Three (Fig 5.5). The levels at which they occurred however were too small to make firm statements about any possible shift in settlement emphasis.

Functional analysis

Initially the functional analysis of the pottery from the two fields centred around the study of four broad categories of material:

i)   Fine wares – Samian and Lower Nene Valley Colour-coat (Fabrics F and G).
ii)   Coarse wares – Fabrics A, B, C and D.
iii) Dressel 20 amphora – Fabric E.
iv)   Mortaria – Fabric H.

On studying the material however, the quantities of Dressel 20 amphorae and Fabric H mortaria were considered too low for their distribution to be worth plotting

(although all the Dressel 20 sherds came from immediately to the north of the A163 road in the area of the main excavation trench). Figure 5.6a and b, therefore, shows the distribution of the two remaining categories; fine wares and coarse wares for Fields Two and Three. Again it can be seen that though the fine wares are rare their distribution is very similar to that for coarse wares. Both categories' distributions correlate strongly to the overall distribution plot.

Discussion

The simple analyses outlined above seem to show little divergence from the overall pottery distribution by either date or functional category. This may seem to indicate that there is little functional or temporal variation across the study area at Shiptonthorpe. There are, however, a number of reasons to doubt this which are discussed in conjunction with the information from the rest of the survey below.

Phosphate and magnetic susceptibility survey

The joint soil phosphate and magnetic susceptibility sur-

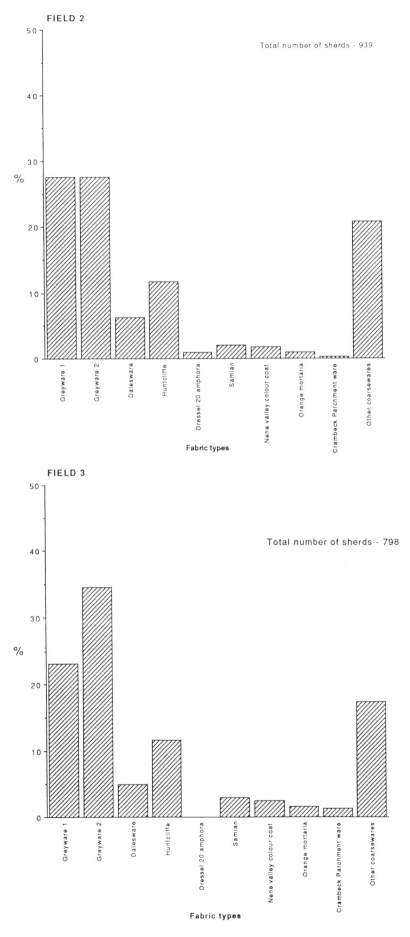

Fig. 5.5 *Shiptonthorpe: percentage frequency of the main pottery fabric groups in Fields Two and Three*

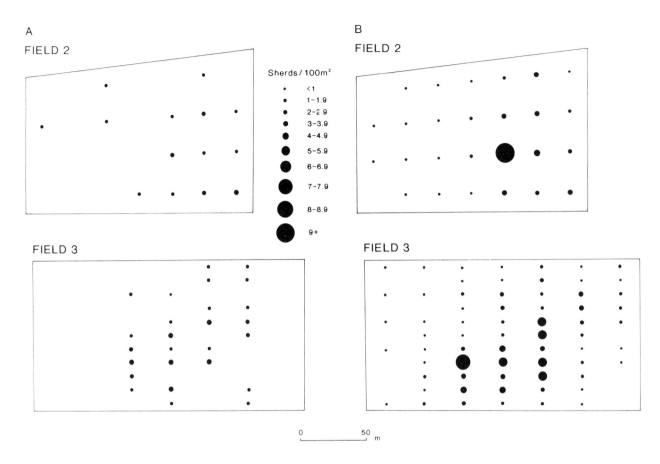

Fig. 5.6 *Shiptonthorpe: the distribution by sherd count of (a) fine wares and (b) coarse wares in Fields Two and Three*

vey represents a key element in the attempt to interpret the nature of settlement at Shiptonthorpe. It has long been noted that both techniques have the ability to identify anthropogenically altered soil horizons (sometimes referred to as anthrosols) by the enhanced levels of each in formerly intensively occupied areas (eg Arrhenius 1929; Wild 1950; Cook & Heizer 1965; Provan 1971; Le Bourgne 1960; Tite & Mullins 1971 and Tite 1972). The precise processes by which a concentration in human activity is linked to this enhancement are not well understood and still constitute a major hindrance to interpretation.

At Shiptonthorpe the critical question was how to interpret intra-site spatial variation in the two data sets in terms of varying activity across the site. Thankfully a number of recent studies have attempted to tackle the complex connection between past human behaviour and changing soil properties (eg Bakkevig 1980; Clark 1983; Conway 1983; Eidt 1984; Craddock *et al* 1985; Gurney 1985; Gaffney & Gaffney 1986; Freij 1988; Nunez & Vinberg 1990 and Challands 1992). The information obtained from these was linked to some simple experiments carried out during the course of the survey to help to produce a provisional interpretative scheme for the phosphate and magnetic susceptibility results.

Survey design and analysis

At present two surveys have been completed at Shiptonthorpe covering 60m × 35m in Field Two and 120m × 100m in Field Three (see Fig 5.2) with the rest of Field Two to be sampled in the near future. At the outset both the samples for soil phosphates and magnetic susceptibility were taken from the same cores using a 60cm long auger in order to reduce the survey time and to allow direct comparisons of the results. The sampling interval in the main survey (Field Three) was set at 10m as a compromise between speed and quality of spatial resolution. Phosphate data in particular tend to show a high level of localised variability largely of non-anthropogenic origin which could affect the reliability of individual samples (cf Walker 1992). To counteract this three sub-samples were taken from each sample point and their scores combined to smooth out any such bias.

Coring allowed samples to be taken directly from the top of the surviving archaeological deposits at a consistent depth thus helping to circumvent some of the inferential problems encountered when surveying from the modern ploughed surface. Although the sampling procedure was slowed somewhat coring meant that reading variations could be ascribed to archaeological causes more confidently.

Once taken the samples were air dried and sieved through a 2mm mesh to remove stones and any other debris. The samples were then split into two for phosphate and magnetic susceptibility analysis. The magnetic susceptibility samples were accurately weighed and measured using a Bartington MS2B laboratory sensor. The phosphate samples were assessed qualitatively using the hydrochloric acid/ammonium molybdate filter paper technique outlined by Eidt (1977). A more detailed account of the methods used for the analyses and the reasons for choosing them at Shiptonthorpe are given elsewhere (Taylor 1989). The qualitative phosphate analysis, though crude, was adopted partly for its speed of operation but also because the soil pH at Shiptonthorpe (between 6.5 and 7) favoured the recovery of calcium phosphates. Initial experiments by Meece at Claydon Pike have also suggested a high degree of correlation between the spot test scores and quantitatively recorded phosphate levels.

The survey results

The data from the two techniques are plotted in Figures 5.7 and 5.8. Each is plotted against the results of the fluxgate gradiometer survey to provide a framework for comparison and interpretation, both of which are discussed further below.

The fluxgate gradiometer survey

One of the primary aims of the initial survey carried out in Field Two had been to determine the likely suitability of the area for the magnetometer survey. A series of control samples was taken away from and across the main focus of settlement activity. Sub-samples from each core were taken from the basal layers of the topsoil and the subsoil to compare the susceptibilities of the likely fills of buried features and the matrix into which they were cut. The consistently low subsoil susceptibility and the enhanced levels found in the topsoil suggested that a magnetometer survey was likely to be profitable. On the strength of this a fluxgate gradiometer survey was carried out over three hectares of Fields Two and Three. An interpretative plan of the results of the survey is illustrated in Figures 5.7 and 5.8. The intensity of stippling is linked to the strength of the anomaly recorded.

The assessment and interpretation of the overall survey

The extent of the settlement

Comparison of the magnetic susceptibility plot (Fig 5.7) and the general pottery distributions (Fig 5.3a & b) indicate that the main areas of settlement lay within approximately 60m either side of the Roman road from Brough

to Hayton. This view is broadly supported by the features recorded in the gradiometer survey although some linear boundaries do extend beyond the survey area. Fieldwalking in Fields One and Five (Fig 5.2) has broadly located the limits of the settlement along the main Roman road and suggests that the total area intensively used is approximately 10 hectares. It is possible, however, that the settlement continues to the north of Field One as the break in the surface artefact distribution is close to the modern field boundaries here. The magnetometer survey also indicates a secondary road running west from the survey in Field Three and the settlement may have extended some distance in this direction though both the pottery distribution and a small group of magnetic susceptibility samples do not seem to indicate so.

Settlement morphology and structure

In the area of the magnetometer survey a reasonably detailed picture of the settlement's layout was achieved. The main Roman road can clearly be seen running north to south. It was bordered by ditches along most of its length in this sector and probably acted as the key determinant in the settlement's initial development. The settlement itself consists of a ribbon development of simple ditched enclosures probably stretching along a frontage of approximately 700m. There is little evidence for extension of the settlement away from the road apart from the side road in Field Three already mentioned, another side road to the west in Field Two (marked R in Fig 5.9 running in the direction of Holme-on-Spalding Moor) and a double enclosure extending east from the road in Field Two. The plot also shows a series of maculae which are possibly large pits but more likely wells or water holes similar to those discovered in the course of the 1987–1991 excavations (Millett 1992). To the west of the enclosures in Field Three runs a poorly defined area of slightly enhanced magnetometer readings which are thought to be caused by the silty sandy fill of a relict watercourse. This interpretation fits well with the topography of the settlement which appears to lie atop a low sand ridge.

The majority of features identified by the gradiometer survey give the impression of stability in the layout of the settlement at this scale. The results of the excavations however have revealed the considerable number of smaller scale changes that take place in and around an individual enclosure. It is important therefore to be very cautious of over simplistic interpretations of the settlement's development on the basis of surface survey alone. Some idea of possible larger scale change in the layout of the settlement is provided by the somewhat unusual feature running NNE to SSW through Field Three in Figure 5.9 but it is still noticeable how little the settlement appears to change on a large scale.

The somewhat uneven nature of the enclosures and the evidence of limited excavation suggest that the set-

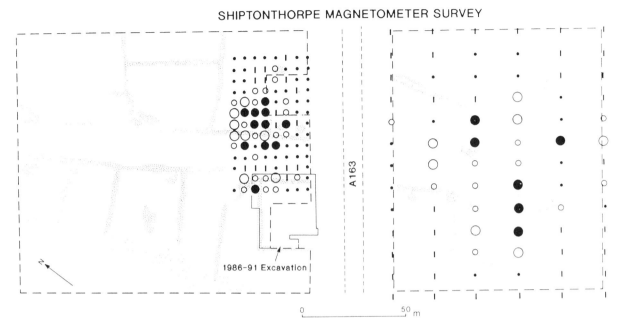

Fig. 5.7 Shiptonthorpe: comparative plot of the magnetic susceptibility and gradiometer surveys

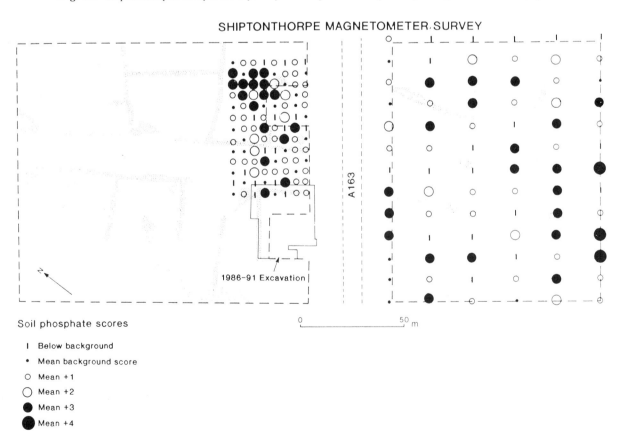

Fig. 5.8 Shiptonthorpe: comparative plot of the soil phosphate and gradiometer surveys

SHIPTONTHORPE SURVEY INTERPRETATION

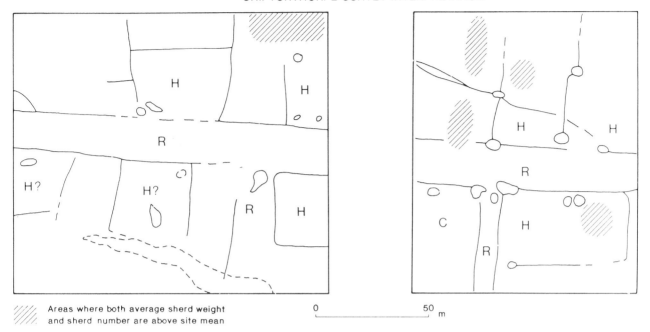

//// Areas where both average sherd weight
//// and sherd number are above site mean

0 ————— 50 m

Fig. 5.9 *Shiptonthorpe: an interpretative plan of Fields Two and Three showing areas of high surface pottery density (hachured), habitation areas (H), roads (R) and the cemetery (C). The dashed line delimits the area of a probable relict watercourse*

tlement grew in an organic manner to its full extent (in the central area examined at least) during the course of the later 2nd century. In order to assess the use and internal organisation of the settlement, however, we must combine the evidence of all four survey methods with the findings of the excavations to produce a simplified interpretative plan (Fig 5.9).

Functional organisation

The phosphate and magnetic susceptibility surveys combined with the evidence from ploughsoil artefacts were the main source of information available for classifying the functional organisation of the settlement. The problem for the survey however was, and to some extent still is, how to infer past human behaviour from changes in soil composition and unstratified artefacts. In an attempt to see whether there was a reasonable correlation between a combined phosphate/magnetic susceptibility 'fingerprint' for a particular area and its usage, samples from areas subsequently excavated or in the immediate vicinity of early excavations were compared. As well as classifying the use of these excavated areas samples taken from over the course of the main Roman road were also studied to see if they displayed any consistent phosphate/ magnetic susceptibility ratio. For comparative purposes the control samples taken well away from the likely settlement area were also plotted to show the contrast between them and those from the selected 'on-site' areas.

The results of this exercise are shown in Figure 5.10 where samples are classified as *Road, Habitation, Cemetery* and *Background* according to their provenance. The habitation samples were all taken in the eastern end of the 1987–1991 trench in Field Two before it was excavated in 1990–91 and were subdivided into two categories according to whether they were taken from inside or outside the buildings discovered. The cemetery samples were from the 1986 trench immediately south of the A163 road which contained a small group of adult and infant burials.

Although the number of samples is small and the circumstances of the exercise far from ideal the plot does appear encouraging. The habitation samples display a wide variety of scores (as might be expected of an area where a very wide range of domestic activities would have taken place) but both *Building* and *Surface* categories show consistently higher levels of magnetic susceptibility than the surrounding background scores. This suggests that, on a lithology such as Shiptonthorpe's at least habitational areas can be realistically distinguished from their surrounding landscape. The *Cemetery* ratios are also encouraging as they are consistent with what might be expected from a combined phosphate/magnetic susceptibility survey. The area, which on excavation revealed no evidence for use other than burial, would be expected to have magnetic susceptibility levels little different from the surrounding country but phosphate levels that were high from the decayed burials.

The widely dispersed scores from the *Road* samples are not so disappointing as they may at first seem. The nature of the road's usage was such that, logically, it would not necessarily have a distinctive fingerprint, a point which appears valid in the light of a re-examination of the provenance of each sample. Those road samples taken nearest to the known habitation and cemetery areas have broadly similar ratios to them. It is possible that in these areas there is a 'blurring' effect with soil from the adjacent enclosures being dispersed by, for, example, trampling, erosion or spoil clearance from ditches. The problems in interpretation that this can lead to are discussed further below but as an initial guide the results of this exercise were used in conjunction with the magnetometer survey and pottery data to identify changing functional patterns across the settlement (see Fig 5.9).

The schematic plan illustrated in Figure 5.9 shows the probable location of habitation *loci* within the framework of the results of the magnetometer survey. The H symbols were placed where magnetic susceptibility levels rose above 40 cgs (the *Buildings* category in Figure 5.10) based on the results of the samples from the main trench in Field Two. Samples from this area that fell in the 20–35 cgs range (the *Surfaces* category) came from within the excavated settlement enclosure but away from the sequence of buildings discovered. Question marks were used in the area outside the present phosphate/magnetic susceptibility survey to indicate further probable habitations. Their interpretation was based on an assessment of the strength of contrast in anomalies from the magnetometer survey (which can be linked to magnetic susceptibility levels) and the presence of concentrations of maculae (probably water sources) within enclosures. This interpretation produces a total of eight habitation *loci* within the surveyed area. If this density is repeated across the full extent of the settlement at Shiptonthorpe then there would be approximately 24 habitation areas in all.

The enclosures left blank in Figure 5.9 are likely to have been for ancillary purposes such as the corralling of animals or intensive arable farming and there is as yet no evidence for the use of furnaces in industrial or craft production at Shiptonthorpe. Initial results from the botanical survey from the excavations show that brassicas were very common (Moynihan 1987). The poor drainage of the area in the Roman period and the absence of cereal chaff from excavated samples may suggest that some of these enclosures were used for vegetable growing rather than cereal cultivation. The faunal evidence so far studied implies a reliance on cattle and sheep rather than pigs or fowl but there is no evidence yet for production for export of these animals (Mainland pers comm). It must be remembered however that the total biological assemblage from Shiptonthorpe comes from the very limited area so far excavated and may represent no more than the activities being carried out in those specific enclosures, a common problem when attempting to interpret the economy of a complex settlement from such a small sample.

Using the pottery from surface collection for interpreting the varied use and status of parts of the settlement is a complex issue which there is insufficient space to discuss here. Useful discussions of the varied processes involved in the disturbance and exposure of buried artefacts are available in Haselgrove *et al* 1985; Schofield 1989, 1991; Boismier 1989 and Yorston *et al* 1990 for example. At Shiptonthorpe simple analysis of the finds did not appear to show any marked functional or chronological patterning and it might be suggested that this implies a stability and lack of differentiation between habitation areas in the settlement. If the pottery distributions are compared with the habitation areas identified by the magnetic susceptibility survey however we can see that sherd peaks by both weight and number (and thus also average weight) do not correspond closely to the habitation areas. This is indicated in Figure 5.9 where hachuring shows the highest average sherd weight where both sherd counts and weights were above the median for the survey area. In this way the hachured zones show where both methods of quantification show the highest densities of pottery.

A preliminary study of the ceramics from these grid squares shows that by both functional and chronological criteria they are highly consistent with each other and the overall site distribution (see Fig 5.5). There are a number of possible explanations for this related to depositional, post-depositional and recovery factors but the interpretation at present is that they probably relate to recently ploughed out middens. This can help to explain the consistently undifferentiated composition of the high density groups as well as their loose juxtaposition with the habitation areas identified in the magnetic susceptibility survey.

The absence of high density, high average sherd weight scatters in the northern half of Field Two is likely to be related to the shallower depth of ploughsoil found there. In this area wind deflation, probably during the early and middle parts of this century, has led to subsequent serious plough damage of all surviving superficial archaeological deposits leaving only more substantial soil cut features intact. Trial excavation and augering in Field Two has confirmed that this problem becomes more severe the further north one goes. Any localised densities of sherds in this area will have been in the ploughsoil for some considerable time and probably too severely fragmented and dispersed to be easily recognisable.

Recent work on the density and sherd size range of ceramics found in the better preserved layers in the 1987–1991 trench appears to indicate that contexts related to the buildings and their immediate surroundings have low sherd densities (Eastaugh pers comm). The primary silts of ditches (beyond the depth of modern ploughing and thus not represented in the ploughsoil) and certain surface deposits in open areas away from the buildings do have high densities and sherd weights. The latter, not easily discernible to the eye from surrounding

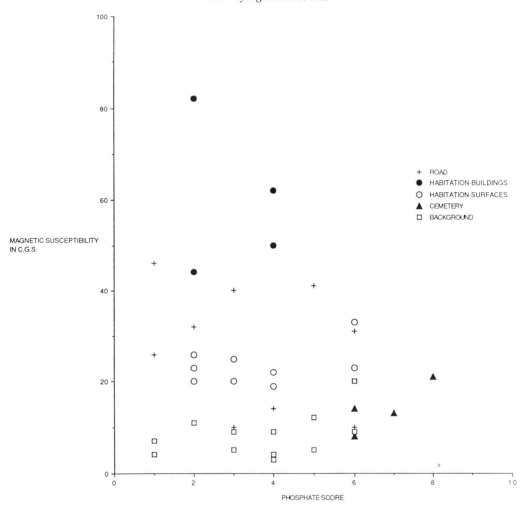

Fig. 5.10 Shiptonthorpe: soil phosphate and magnetic susceptibility scores for samples from classified contexts

layers, may represent the basal levels of once upstanding features and commonly contain a wide range of small artefacts and debris. It is at present too early to say whether these contexts (probably middens and/or abandonment deposits) act as the main reservoirs for the majority of sherds found through fieldwalking at Shiptonthorpe. It is hoped however that the continued combined study of excavated and fieldwalked material linked to some relatively simple conceptual models for the derivation of ploughsoil assemblages will help us to considerably advance their interpretation.

If the main surface artefact concentrations at Shiptonthope are mostly related to recently ploughed out middens then they have important implications for interpretation. First, the fieldwalked material at Shiptonthorpe will largely be derived from secondary depositional contexts (cf Haselgrove 1985) and thus be of limited use in trying to interpret localised variation in function but can be used to differentiate between areas of dumping and clearance. Ploughsoil pottery derived largely from abandonment layers (the *de-facto* deposition described by Schiffer 1976) will largely represent the functional and

depositional patterning apparent at the site shortly before its abandonment at the end of the Roman period. This difficulty in differentiating between the wide range of depositional factors responsible for the composition and distribution is still a key part of continuing work at Shiptonthorpe.

What does appear clear, however, is that the surface distribution of ceramics at Shiptonthorpe should not be used to indicate the presence of former buildings but rather some of the main surface depositional areas probably related to middening in the vicinity of houses. They may thus represent an amalgam of the range of refuse of all dates and types in use around particular buildings. They are not very useful for identifying different functional zones within the settlement, a role better served by the combination of magnetic susceptibility, soil phosphate, gradiometer and excavation data.

Back to earth: limitations of the survey

Perhaps inevitably this paper has tended to concentrate on some of the problems related to the use and interpretation of field survey data for the assessment of settlements the size of Shiptonthorpe. The complex issues behind each survey technique cannot be adequately dealt with here but it is to be hoped that the work in progress at Shiptonthorpe will show the benefits to be gained from a broader analytical approach to the study of these sites within their local and regional context. The issues discussed here, some of the key problems associated with inferences based on field survey, are intended not to discourage but to encourage more rigorous and integrated analysis of the structure, development and function of these still poorly understood sites.

The key problem with all the survey techniques used in this case study is that they produce a data base which is essentially a palimpsest of the total archaeological record at Shiptonthorpe. The magnetic susceptibility/phosphate samples record the sum of a wide range of processes that have taken place in that immediate area, not necessarily just the behaviour we are seeking to study. Similarly the ploughsoil artefact collections represent the continually changing end product of a complex series of depositional, post-depositional and recovery factors which all have to be better understood if we are to understand their link to past human behaviour.

Many possible examples of inferential problems could be cited, but for the purposes of illustration three cases are given here. First, the survey interpretation at Shiptonthorpe is at present a rather static one as it lacks the chronological resolution achievable by excavation. Although the survey can identify probable habitational *loci* within the settlement the pottery collected from the surface cannot be used to date their occupation securely. The possibility that the majority of the ploughsoil ceramics at Shiptonthorpe is derived from secondary contexts means that it may well be of limited use for both chronological and functional purposes. Thus it is difficult to identify changes in use for areas within the settlement and to establish the contemporaneity or otherwise of each inhabited area. Even if the estimate of a total of 24 inhabited areas at Shiptonthorpe is accurate it is impossible at present to suggest how many were in use during any particular period within the settlement's history.

A second problem encountered with the survey is the shifting nature of activity *loci*. At Shiptonthorpe the evidence from survey and the trial excavations to date suggests that particular areas can change in use but that the focus of activity tends to remain broadly in one place. On settlements where activity is less structured or bounded, however, the already poor resolution of much survey data could be further blurred until it became impossible to recognise distinctive zones within the palimpsest of information recorded. Little is known of the level at which this will tend to happen but it is obviously a more severe problem on complex sites with a long occupational history.

A final point to consider is the range of information that is not easily identifiable from the survey techniques outlined above alone. If we wish to study the relationship of settlements such as Shiptonthorpe with their agricultural base and local environment then it is important to integrate the survey with zoological and botanical sampling schemes, usually as part of limited trial excavations. At Shiptonthorpe the little information available to date from such a regime has still been of invaluable and complementary help in interpreting the economic structure of the settlement. Similarly, small scale excavation has added invaluable insights into some of the social and ritual practices carried out which are largely invisible to the coarse view of field survey (Millett 1992).

These considerations may appear to play down the role of geoprospection and fieldwalking but are intended rather to highlight the complementary nature of information available from other sources. The techniques described above are best utilised as only a part of the overall strategy for investigating large settlements.

Surveying small towns: summary and prospects

This paper has attempted to outline one way in which relatively complex large scale settlements can be studied, whilst trying to make some of the more immediate pitfalls apparent. It is necessarily a brief account of work still in the process of completion but despite its weaknesses it could provide a very useful and comparatively efficient way of analysing a scale of settlement which is poorly served by limited excavation or fieldwalking alone. Although inferences based on the battery of techniques used at Shiptonthorpe are often simplistic they allow us to study large parts or even the entirety of a settlement. Thus a small town's overall structure and development can be understood, helping us to move away from the problems inherent in interpreting such large scale settlements from often very limited excavations. At Shiptonthorpe, less than two per cent of the total probable area of the settlement has been excavated and analysis of the situation elsewhere suggests this is not uncommon (eg Burnham & Wacher 1990; Millett & Graham 1986). In the current and probable future financial situation this is not likely to improve considerably. Furthermore, these excavations are often carried out for rescue purposes and their location may be of limited value for better understanding the wider context of the settlement.

A further considerable advantage of an integrated survey based approach is that it can be used to draw attention away from the biases that have inevitably come from a site oriented excavation based methodology. Projects founded on material from fieldwalking and excavation tend to concentrate research on to artefactually or structurally rich areas and often ignore those that are less obviously responsive. Some of the techniques above can and should be used to help interpret these formerly blank areas based on theory and methodology not handicapped by the overworked and limited concept of the 'site' (cf Haselgove 1985; Gaffney & Tingle 1984 and

Dunnell 1992). If both surface survey in archaeology and the study of Roman small towns are to develop then they need to be employed and assessed critically. Roman small towns do not simply exist as easily classifiable types, each has a separate and often very individual history and should be studied with this in mind.

Given the diversity in range and development of small towns in this period, survey has one more final advantage. Integrated survey linked to limited excavation allows us to study a number of these settlements along with their surrounding landscapes relatively quickly. Thus we can assess their status and development within their local context and concentrate on achieving a better understanding of a poorly understood level of settlement agglomeration in Roman Britain, which can then be compared with the results of similar work on higher order centres elsewhere (eg Fulford 1984 and Dobinson 1990).

Bibliography

Arrhenius, O, 1929 Die phosphatfrage, *Zeitschrift fur Pflanzenernahrung, Dungung und Bodenkunde*, 14, 185–194

Bakkevig, S, 1980 Phosphate analysis in archaeology – problems and recent progress, *Norwegian Archaeol Rev*, 13, 73–100

Boismier, W A, 1989 Recognising and controlling for cultivation induced patterning in surface artefact distributions, in *Computer applications and quantitative methods in archaeology 1989* (eds S Rahtz & J Richards), BAR Int Ser , 548, 133– 145

Burnham, B C, & Wacher, J, 1990 *The 'small towns' of Roman Britain*

Challands, A, 1992 Field magnetic susceptibility measures for prospection and excavation, in *Geoprospection in the archaeological landscape* (ed G Spoerry), Oxbow Monogr 18, 33–41

Clark, A J, 1983 The testimony of the topsoil, in *The impact of aerial reconnaissance on archaeology* (ed G S Maxwell), C B A Res Rep 49, 128–135

Conway, J S, 1983 An investigation of soil phosphorous distribution within occupation deposits from a Romano-British hut group, *J Archaeol Sci*, 10, 117– 128

Cook, S F, & Heizer, R F, 1965 *Studies on the chemical analysis of archaeological sites*, University of California Publications in Anthropology 2, UCLA, 1–102

Craddock, P T, Gurney, D, Pryor, F, & Hughes, M J, 1985 The application of phosphate analysis to the location and interpretation of archaeological sites, *Archaeol J*, 142, 361–376

Dobinson, C, 1990 Aldborough Roman town. Unpublished paper presented to conference on *The Romans from the Tees to the Tyne*, Cleveland County Archaeology Section Day School

Dunnell, R C, 1992 The notion site, in *Space, time, and archaeological landscapes* (eds J Rossignol & L Wandsnider)

Eidt, R C, 1977 Detection and examination of anthrosols by phosphate analysis, *Science*, 197, 1327–1333

——, 1984 *Advances in abandoned settlement analysis. Application to prehistoric anthrosols in Columbia, South America*, The Center for Latin America, University of Wisconsin, Madison

Evans, J, 1985 *Aspects of later Roman pottery assemblages in Northern England*, unpublished PhD thesis, University of Bradford

Freij, H, 1988 Some attempts to relate ancient land use to soil properties by means of statistics, in *Multivariate archaeology: numerical approaches in Scandinavian archaeology* (ed T Madsen), Aarhus University Press

Fulford, M J, 1984 *Silchester: excavations on the defences 1974–80*, Britannia Monogr 5

Gaffney, C F, & Gaffney, V L, 1986 From Boeotia to Berkshire: an integrated approach to geophysics and rural field survey, *Prospezioni Archaeologiche*, 10, 65–70

——, & Tingle, M, 1984 The tyranny of the site: method and theory in field survey, *Scottish Archaeol Rev*, 3, 134–140

Gillam, J P, 1968 *Types of Roman coarse pottery vessels in Northern Britain*

Gurney, D A, 1985 Geophysical and geochemical analysis of subsoil features, in FMM Pryor, CAI French, D R Crowther, D Gurney, G Simpson & M Taylor, *Archaeology and environment in the Lower Welland Valley*, E Anglian Archaeol 27, 38–41

Halkon, A P M, 1987 *Aspects of the Romano-British landscape around Holme-on-Spalding Moor, East Yorkshire*, unpublished MA thesis, University of Durham

Hartley, B R, 1969 Samian ware or *terra sigillata*, in R G Collingwood & I A Richmond, *The archaeology of Roman Britain*, 235–251

Haselgrove, C C, 1985 Inference from ploughsoil artefact samples, in *Archaeology from the ploughsoil* (eds C C Haselgrove, M Millett & I Smith), 7–30

——, Millett, M, & Smith, I, (eds) 1985 *Archaeology from the ploughsoil. Studies in the collection and interpretation of field survey data*

Hicks, J D, & Wilson, J A, 1975 The Romano-British kilns at Hasholme, *E Riding Archaeologist*, 2, 49–70

Howe, M D, Perrin, J R, & Mackreth, D F, 1980 *Roman pottery from the Nene Valley: a guide*, Peterborough City Museum Occasional Paper 2

Le Bourgne, E, 1960 Influence du feu sur les propiétés magnetiques du sol et granite, *Annales de Géophysique*, 16, 159–195

Millett, M, 1992 Excavation and survey at Shiptonthorpe, East Yorkshire, 1991, *University of Durham & University of Newcastle upon Tyne Archaeol Rep 1991*, 29– 33

——, & Graham, D, 1986 *Excavations on the Romano-British small town at Neatham, Hampshire 1969–1979*, Hampshire Field Club Monogr 3

——, & Halkon, A P M, 1988 Landscape and economy: recent fieldwork and excavation around Holme-on-Spalding Moor, in *Recent research in Roman Yorkshire* (eds J Price & P R Wilson), BAR Brit Ser, 193, 37–47

Moynihan, S J, 1987 *An environmental survey of the Shiptonthorpe site and the surrounding area*, unpublished BA honours dissertation, University of Durham

Nunez, M, & Vinberg, A, 1990 Determination of anthropic soil phosphate on Aland, *Norwegian Archaeol Rev*, 23, 93–104

Peacock, D P S, & Williams, D F, 1986 *Amphorae and the Roman economy*

Provan, D M J, 1971 Soil phosphate analysis as a tool in archaeology, *Norwegian Archaeol Rev*, 4, 37–50

Schiffer, M B, 1976 *Behavioural archaeology*

Schofield, A J, 1989 Understanding early medieval pottery distributions: cautionary tales and their implications for further research, *Antiquity*, 63, 460–70

——— (ed), 1991 *Interpreting artefact scatters: contributions to ploughzone archaeology*, Oxbow Monogr 4

Taylor, J, 1989 *An integrated survey of the Romano-British settlement at Shiptonthorpe, East Yorkshire*, unpublished BA honours dissertation, University of Durham

Tite, M S, 1972 *Methods of physical examination in archaeology*

———, & Mullins, C, 1971 Enhancement of the magnetic susceptibility of soils on archaeological sites, *Archaeometry*, 13, 209–219

Walker, R, 1992 Phosphate survey: method and meaning, in *Geoprospection in the archaeological landscape* (ed P Spoerry), Oxbow Monogr 18, 61–73

Wenham, L P, 1968 *The Romano-British cemetery at Trentholme Drive, York*, Ministry of Public Building and Works Archaeol Rep 5

Wild, A, 1950 The retention of phosphate by soil, *J Soil Sci*, 1, 221–238

Yorston, R M, Gaffney, V L, & Reynolds, P J, 1990 Simulation of artefact movement due to cultivation, *J Archaeol Sci*, 17, 67–83

6   Small towns and villages of Roman Norfolk. The evidence of surface and metal-detector finds

David Gurney

Introduction (Fig 6.1)

This paper considers some of the larger Romano-British settlements in Norfolk, sites which could, on the present evidence, be viewed as either certain or potential 'small towns', large villages or substantial rural settlements (whichever term the reader prefers). In the 'theatre' of Romano-British small towns these will be the cheapest seats and, to continue the analogy, it is a case of being behind pillars rather than having them!

The aim will also be to illustrate the potential of non-intrusive survey methods (excluding geochemical and geophysical techniques), and the value of evidence that can be recovered from the ploughsoil, with reference to some of these sites. Where necessary, excavation and cropmark evidence will also be drawn upon in order to present a fuller picture, although any conclusions must be viewed as provisional.

The sites which it could be suggested might fall into the category of small towns in Norfolk are shown on Figure 6.1. This of course does not cover the full territory occupied by the Iceni, which extended south into north Suffolk and west into the Cambridgeshire fens.

Four of these sites will be considered in a little more detail, namely Brampton, Billingford, Saham Toney and Hockwold. Figure 6.1 also shows the location of Caistor St Edmund, the *civitas* capital *Venta Icenorum* (meaning 'the market place of the Iceni').

'Shadowy' settlements

In the first paper to address the issue of small towns, Malcolm Todd described three types of settlements; those with walled areas between ten and thirty-five acres, those walled or unwalled between four and ten acres (where defended) and a third category, which he described as a 'shadowy group of scattered settlements, several of which cover, *in toto*, very large areas' (Todd 1970, 117). The extensive settlement at Hockwold cum Wilton, Norfolk, as published by Salway (1967), less understood then than it is today, was cited as the clearest example. These sites, Todd continues, 'may differ very little from the humbler walled sites'.

In Norfolk, for Todd's third category, the 'shadowy' settlements, the adjective is entirely appropriate, as so little is known about most of them, except for some where limited excavation has taken place. The surface evidence, such as it is, merely provides a tantalising glimpse of the archaeology that, hopefully, may still survive below the ploughsoil. The example cited by Todd, Hockwold, remains one of the most enigmatic, but it is only one of sixteen such sites across the county (Fig 6.1) which it could be argued might be considered as candidates for inclusion in a category of 'small town', 'minor town' or 'large village'.

These sites are indicated by very extensive scatters of pottery and metalwork, generally lacking evidence of defences, and variously with cropmarks and evidence of substantial masonry buildings, temples, baths, burials or industrial activity. Some of the sites no longer include areas where surface survey is feasible, for example Scole (Rogerson 1977), generally reckoned (in competition with Stoke Ash and Stanton, both in Suffolk) to be 'Villa Faustini' of *Iter* V of the Antonine Itinerary. This settlement is now largely built over, except for one Scheduled Area including both medieval and Roman earthworks which are soon to disappear (after excavation) under a new bypass, work on which is due to start in the course of 1993. The recent discovery of the late Roman treasure at Hoxne, only a mile or so to the east of Scole and just over the border with Suffolk, one item in which is inscribed with the name FAUSTINUS, must make one wonder if 'Villa Faustini' is anything to do with the Scole Roman settlement at all.

Collection of data

Most of the data on the surface finds from these settlements has been collected by amateur archaeologists and metal-detectorists, and this inevitably leads to great variability in the data collected. Some metal-detectorists will automatically collect at least a sample of any pottery and tile, others will when the importance of this is explained to them. Others, it would seem, are quite incapable of collecting anything that doesn't announce its existence

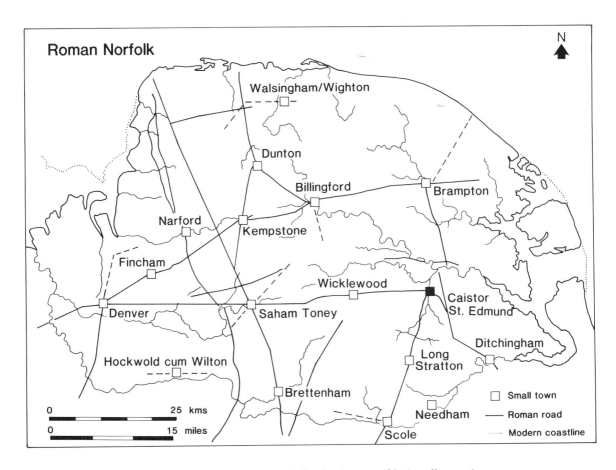

Fig 6.1 *Map of Roman Norfolk, showing possible 'small towns'*

by producing an audible signal in the headphones! This however is not to denegate the enormous amounts of time and effort put in by those who have undertaken painstaking and extremely thorough surveys of the metalwork alone on particular sites, the result of which has been an enormous input of finds data to the Norfolk Sites and Monuments Record.

The process of identifying, cataloguing and photographing this wealth of material demands considerable resources, and it is usually a constant and uphill struggle to keep up with the recording, let alone start to think about what it all means. Hopefully what we record today our successors may be able to interpret. The crucial thing is to record everything as fully as possible while we have these finds before us, probably for the only time.

Methods employed to record the locations of surface finds vary, but the most usual is to collect coins (when they occur in abundance), metal objects which to the untrained eye do not appear to be of any great significance, and any other finds (such as pottery, tile, flints) in 'collection areas' of roughly equal sizes, perhaps subdividing a large field into a number of smaller search areas. Finds of particular note (brooches, votive objects, figurines, gold coins, Iron Age coins) would usually be individually plotted.

Locations and origins (Figs 6.1–2)

Fourteen of the sites are located at important river/road junctions; Fincham and Long Stratton are the only two which are roadside settlements alone. Caister-on-Sea on the east coast (sometimes referred to as Caister-by-Yarmouth) is now certainly excluded from the list, as this site, earlier thought of as a walled civilian settlement and harbour (and referred to as such in several papers of the 1975 Oxford conference; Frere 1975, fig 1; Webster 1975, 53, fig 1) is clearly an early fort of the Saxon Shore defensive system, similar to Brancaster and Reculver. The report on the excavations of 1951–55 by Charles Green has recently been published (Darling with Gurney 1993).

Although most sites have produced some Iron Age finds, pottery, Icenian coins or metalwork, there is little clear evidence to demonstrate that most developed from pre-Roman Icenian settlements. The presence of Icenian silver coin hoards at Walsingham/Wighton and Scole is at least indicative of an early start date for those sites.

The best evidence comes perhaps from Saham Toney where coin finds suggest a small streamside native settlement (Brown 1986, fig 3), which was then succeeded by a Claudian fort (the approximate position of which is shown on Fig 6.2) and *vicus* which later developed into a substantial civilian settlement (shown hatched).

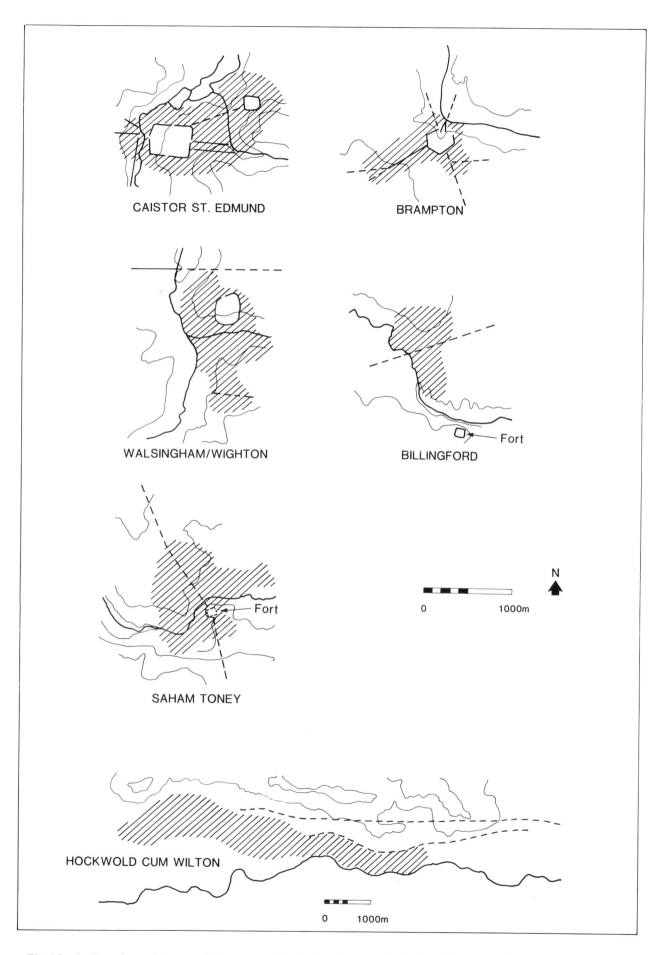

Fig 6.2 *Outline plans of five 'small towns' and Caistor St. Edmund. Scale 1:40,000, except Hockwold, 1:80,000.*

At three sites, there is good evidence for religious activity, with votive artefacts in abundance at Walsingham/Wighton, no less than two temples at Hockwold and one at Wicklewood.

There are early forts at or close to Saham Toney and Billingford. That at Saham Toney was discovered by Robin Brown's systematic fieldwalking and metal-detecting over many years, and is indicated by a scatter of Claudio-Neronian military metalwork (Brown 1986, fig 27) and Claudian irregular coins (Brown 1986, fig 4) over an area of four acres on a strategically-situated hill crest (Brown 1986, fig 1). A similar finds assemblage comes from the fort at Swanton Morley which overlooks Billingford (Fig 6.2), and these two sites will be considered further below.

Industrial activity includes Brampton (which was a major local pottery), Needham and Ditchingham (pottery kilns), Denver (salt-production) and metalworking (Brampton, Kempstone, Wicklewood).

Figure 6.2 shows the approximate extents (hatched) of the settlements at Brampton, Walsingham/Wighton, Billingford, Saham Toney and Hockwold cum Wilton. It is immediately apparent that each of these sites covers an area close to, the same as or greater than that occupied by the *civitas* capital *Venta Icenorum* at Caistor St. Edmund (which is also shown for comparison), including the defended walled area, the *temenos* of a Romano-Celtic temple to the north-east and fairly extensive suburbs.

The numismatic evidence (Fig 6.3)

One of the main categories of evidence recovered by metal-detecting is that of coin-loss, and a recent study of coins finds from Norfolk by John Davies and the late Tony Gregory (1991) has applied Richard Reece's (1987) method of distinguishing 'urban' sites from 'rural' sites by comparing the percentages of coins from the periods AD 259–294 (Reece's Phase B) and AD 330–402 (Phase D). Put simply, the suggestion is that on 'urban' sites coins of the late 3rd century equal or outnumber those of the later 4th century, while on 'rural' sites post-AD 330 coins predominate. Davies and Gregory consider the coin assemblages from the small towns/large settlements at Saham Toney, Brampton, Hockwold, Wicklewood, Walsingham/Wighton, Billingford, Brettenham and Ditchingham (see Fig 6.3). They looked at all the coin evidence for these sites collected up to 1988, so it is already time for a review, as the last five years have seen a significant expansion of the database for several of these sites. Without going into all the details, the only Norfolk site considered here which behaves like an 'urban' site is Brampton, and Billingford and Walsingham/Wighton both behave like 'rural' sites (Fig 6.3). Can it possibly be as easy as this, with sites falling neatly into urban or rural categories? This can be questioned, particularly as at one point Davies and Gregory are pre-

pared to accept Walsingham/Wighton as a 'small town / temple service area' (1991,70), even though it falls well into the 'rural' category on the Reece-type graph. This is something which does need to be looked at further; in the meantime, it is perhaps unwise to attempt to categorise Norfolk sites as 'urban' or 'rural' on the basis of coin-loss alone, and analysis of larger samples hopefully from a wider range of small town/large village sites is required. There is scope here for at least a regional, if not a national study.

Four Norfolk sites

Brampton (Fig 6.2)

Brampton is the one site in Norfolk which would almost certainly be universally accepted as a Roman small town (Burnham & Wacher 1990, 203–208), although the only discernable difference between this and other sites is the certain presence at Brampton of defences. The presence or absence of defences is, however, not a valid criterion for determining what is and what is not a small town. Surely some at least of the other sites in Norfolk must have had some form of defences in the later Roman period? The recent Norfolk Archaeological Unit excavations at Billingford revealed some not insubstantial ditches along what appears to be the southern limit of the site, and these could possibly have served a defensive purpose.

At Brampton amateur excavations and fieldwork since 1965 led by Dr Keith Knowles and metal-detecting by Mr John Pope have done much to establish the extent and nature of the site, although only small areas have been examined and the full report on these has yet to be published. An interim report (Knowles 1977) provides an outline, and a small area of the kiln field to the west has been excavated by the Norfolk Archaeological Unit and published by Green (1977).

The settlement is located at an important road-river junction. Here the northern branch of a major east-to-west Roman road (which becomes the Fen Causeway beyond Denver and which runs from north-east Norfolk to *Durobrivae*) meets a north-to-south road running north from *Venta Icenorum* to form a major crossroads adjacent to a crossing of the River Bure. It covers perhaps thirty hectares (seventy-five acres) with six hectares enclosed by a defensive ditch (but not a wall), most probably of 2nd century date. The only masonry building known is a bath-house within the defended area.

An industrial suburb to the west includes 132 known pottery kilns, with nine others elsewhere in the settlement. The excavated kilns appear to range in date from the late 1st century to the early 3rd.

Inside the defended area, timber workshops for bronze and iron-working have been found, and across the settlement area evidence for extensive iron-working is found with the remains of furnaces and large quantities of iron slag.

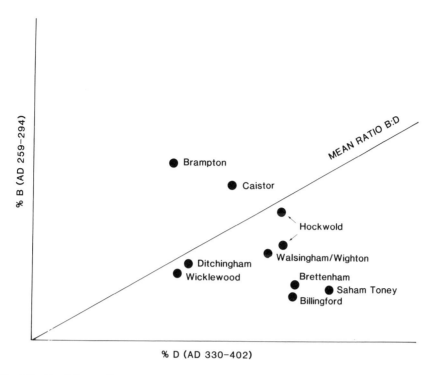

Fig 6.3 *Norfolk small towns: percentages of coins, after Davies & Gregory 1991, fig 5.*

Surface finds are extensive, but no clear patterning emerges at the present time. A number of figurines have been found at various times and it would be surprising if the settlement does not include at least one temple, and perhaps several.

There are no clear indications of pre- or post-Roman settlement on any scale, although one sunken featured building has been recorded in a pipe trench, and both Iron Age and Pagan Saxon material is present in the surface and detector collections.

The histogram of more than eleven hundred coins exhibits a peak in coin Period X (AD 259–75), and this feature links the pattern of coin-loss at Brampton with urban sites in general and, in Norfolk, with *Venta Icenorum* (Fig 6.3) and also, incidentally, the Saxon Shore forts at Brancaster and Caister-on-Sea.

Walsingham/Wighton (Figs 6.4–5)

The settlement at Walsingham/Wighton (Gregory 1986) is strategically situated at a road/river junction, and is centred around a subsidiary stream running into the River Stiffkey from the east. The settlement area includes Wighton Camp, probably of late- or sub-Roman date (see below).

Within the settlement (Fig 6.4), seven scatters of building remains have been located, and at least five of these can be interpreted as certainly the remains of substantial masonry buildings. One has clear indications of being a bath-house and one is likely to be a temple (Fig 6.4).

To the north, the line of a probable east-to-west Ro-

man road passes close to the apparent limit of this scatter. This road may well be the main east-to-west road through north Norfolk (Fig 6.1), from a junction with the

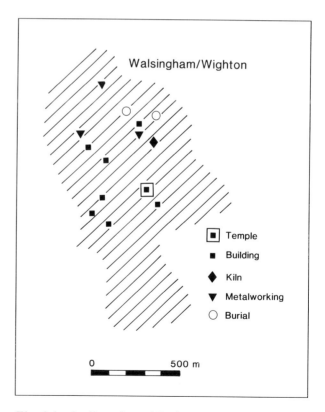

Fig 6.4 *Outline plan of Walsingham/Wighton. Scale 1:20,000.*

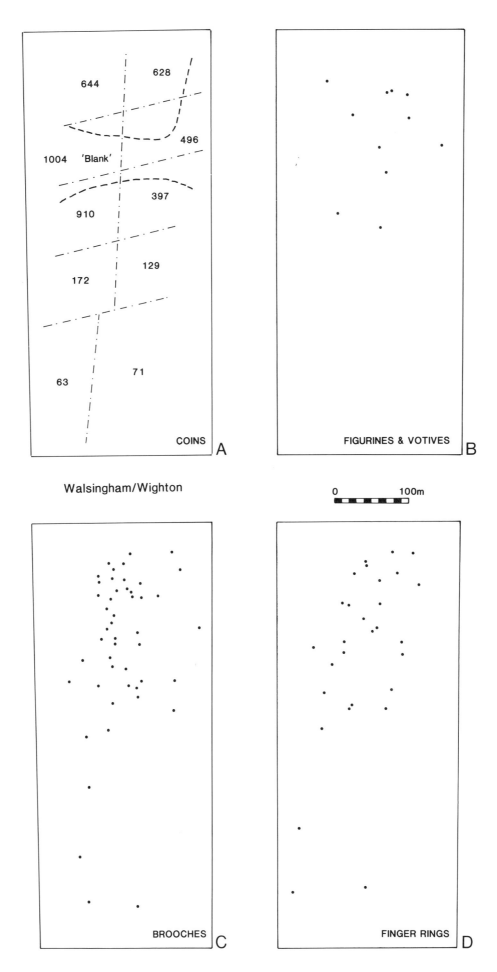

Fig 6.5 *Distributions of finds from Walsingham/Wighton. Scale 1:5000.*

Peddars Way at Fring to the west, to perhaps a destination in the Sheringham/Cromer area to the east. There is a possible second east-to-west road line to the south (Fig 6.2).

This site is probably the best-detected site in Norfolk. Many seasons of patient and well-recorded survey by David Fox have produced a staggering amount of Roman pottery, coins, metalwork and building materials spread over an area of some 84 hectares (207 acres). From the site as a whole, the metalwork includes a remarkable assemblage of more than two hundred brooches, an improbably high proportion of which are substantially complete, and a range of votive objects, including three Mercury figurines, a number of animal figurines, a votive stand, a miniature axe and fragments of votive letters. The finds also indicate industrial activity, certainly bronze-working, and probably also iron-working and pottery manufacture. Finds of special note include three silver finger-rings with inscriptions, one TOT (for the Celtic god Toutates), MER (for Mercury) and a third ? MATRIBUS TR[ANS MARINI], 'To the Matres overseas'.

It will not be a quick task to plot in detail this amount of material, but preliminary work on one of the main fields has been carried out. This has provided distribution maps of various artefact types (Fig 6.5). Because this is an area of some archaeological sensitivity, the field boundaries have been removed from Fig 6.5 so as not to reveal its precise location.

On Fig 6.5 the distributions within one area of the site are shown of votive objects (Fig 6.5B), mainly figurines, surely indicating a temple in that half of this field, the distribution of brooches (Fig 6.5C) (attempts to plot earlier and later types across the whole settlement area have so far not led to any apparent patterning), the distribution of finger rings (Fig 6.5D) and the distribution of coins (Fig 6.5A). Coins are so prolific on this site that they are not individually plotted, but divided between ten 'collection areas'. This gives some idea of the overall distribution, but it does mask one very interesting and important feature of the metalwork distribution which was very obvious to those detecting on the field, and that was a very clear 'blank' area, where very few finds were recovered, consistently, over several seasons (Fig 6.5A). This 'blank' seems to be far too wide to be, for example, a road, and it remains unexplained.

The Iron Age coins from the site include at least one and probably two dispersed Icenian silver hoards, only recognised as hoards quite recently after reconsideration of the coins found over a number of years. The pattern of Roman coin-loss for the site (Davies & Gregory 1991) provides a histogram which behaves more like a rural than an urban site (Fig 6.3).

Areas of Pagan Saxon finds occur within the 'Roman' settlement area and suggest some overlap between the areas of Pagan Saxon settlement (and possibly also burial) and that of the Roman settlement.

Wighton Camp, located and sample excavated in 1974 (Lawson 1976), in the north-east part of the settlement (Fig 6.2) has produced considerable evidence for Roman settlement, with building remains, burials, evidence of metalworking and possibly also pottery kiln debris – a grey ware waster embedded in a fragment of kiln wall. Burials include those found in excavation in 1974 to the east (five inhumations) and a recent metal-detector find to the north-west of a bronze finger-ring still encircling a bronze-stained first phalanx (from the 4th or 5th finger). The earthwork defences enclosing an oval area of just under nine hectares (twenty-two acres) with an entrance to the north-west were recorded as surviving as late as 1775, and while they are not yet conclusively dated, are probably of late Roman, sub-Roman or post-Roman date.

Linear features inside the enclosure (aligned east-to-west and north-to-south, and clearly visible on the contour survey (Lawson 1976, fig 23) could well be streets, either contemporary with the Camp or, more probably, from an earlier pre-Camp settlement street grid.

In interpreting Walsingham/Wighton, the religious component of the site appears, from the surface evidence, to be very important, and one must consider if this is basically a settlement within which there happens to be an important temple, or if the temple is the very reason for and the focus of the settlement. It is possible to think of the Roman settlement at Walsingham/Wighton as the precursor to the settlement around the Priory of Our Lady of Walsingham at Little Walsingham, which was one of the most important pilgrimage centres in medieval England. In 1511, this was described by Erasmus as 'a town maintained by scarcely anything else but the number of its visitors', and the same could well apply to a specialised Roman settlement around an important temple or shrine.

Billingford

The settlement at Billingford has been the subject of a detailed landscape study by Barrie Sharrock (unpublished), including the roadside settlement and the nearby Roman fort at Swanton Morley. The fort is dated by Robert Kenyon's analysis of the irregular Claudian and other early coins to the early Neronian period, while the amount of broken Icenian metalwork from the site (which one suspects was being recycled by the military) most probably indicates a Boudiccan or post-Boudiccan date. The relationship of the Swanton Morley fort to the civilian settlement at Billingford is clearly in need of further research, but the presence of a number of silver Icenian coins, Claudian irregular *asses* and some early metalwork on the latter may indicate an early start date. It is possible that the origin of the Billingford site might be a military presence to secure the river crossing, associated with the Swanton Morley fort (see Fig 6.2).

Roman remains were first found at Billingford in 1934,

David Gurney

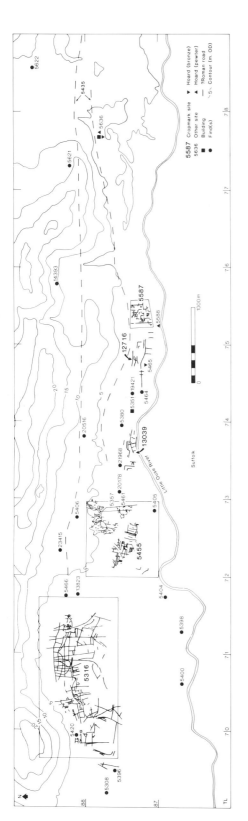

Fig 6.6 The Hockwold Fen-edge, showing the locations of sites and finds. Scale 1:50,000 .

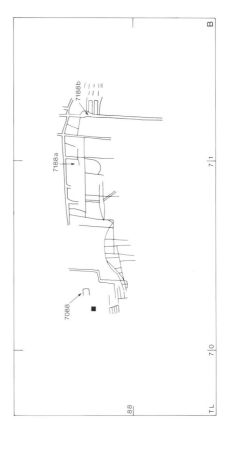

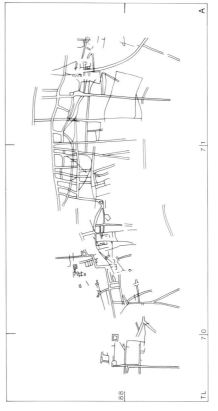

Fig 6.7 Plans of cropmarks at Hockwold, Site 5316. A after J Roman Stud, 52, B after Salway 1967. Scale 1:2000.

followed by finds between 1946 and 1951 and substantial pottery scatters found by Peter Wade-Martins in the late 1960s. There is no evidence at all for substantial buildings on the site, and presumably all the structures were of timber.

The line of the Roman road (see Fig 6.1) from Brampton to Denver (where it merges with the Fen Causeway to Peterborough) marks the centre of the settlement, its line being known from cropmarks and a possible earthwork.

Metal-detecting began on this site in 1984, by Barrie Sharrock and Pride James. The site was probably not detected prior to this date, but shortly after the first season it became subject to the attentions of less responsible detectorists. However, the early survey work and subsequently reported finds appear to give a representative and quite large sample of the surface finds.

The distribution of surface and ploughsoil finds suggests that the nucleus of the settlement is located, as might be expected, in the field bisected by the Roman road and in the area of cropmarks.

However, excavations in 1991–2 by the Norfolk Archaeological Unit in advance of gravel extraction demonstrated that the settlement extended considerably further south than anticipated, with the discovery of a number of posthole structures (of Roman or post-Roman date; the evidence is not conclusive, but perhaps favours the latter (Heather Wallis pers comm)), some substantial enclosures, and a small cemetery area. The southern limit of the settlement appears to be defined by at least two quite substantial ditches which could possibly be defensive.

A curious feature of the Billingford metalwork assemblage is what appears to be a relative absence of domestic artefacts in the metal-detector collection. From an assemblage of 926 finds, 829 are coins, 29 are brooches, four are finger-rings, five are items of harness, and the only recognisable domestic artefacts are two key handles, a nail cleaner, a spoon bowl, a tankard handle, a bronze bowl foot and a few cauldron patches. This paucity of domestic artefacts is surprising, and not easy to account for.

The total number of coins from the site now stands at just under 1500. 1075 of these were found in earlier surveys, mainly close to the road line (1032 coins), with only 43 coins from the area to the south. However, use of metal-detectors during the excavation of this area in 1991–2 (now routinely employed on all Norfolk surveys and excavations) produced 410 coins in an area masked by colluvium, which had prevented their discovery by earlier detector surveys.

The coin assemblage has been studied by John Davies who notes that the striking feature of the coins is the very low number of late 3rd century coins; only eleven coins for the period AD 259–96. This, he suggests, is far more typical of *rural* sites in Norfolk than urban sites. In coin Period X (AD 259–75), the contrast could hardly be greater, with a staggeringly low 1.6% of the assemblage at Billingford belonging to Period X, compared to 30.6% of the assemblage at Brampton.

Hockwold-cum-Wilton (Figs 6.6–10; Pls 6.I–II)

The Fen-edge in the parishes of Weeting with Broomhill and Hockwold cum Wilton has long been known as an area of rich prehistoric (Bamford 1982; Healy 1980) and Romano-British settlement (Gurney 1986), known from chance finds, fieldwalking, excavation and aerial survey. A desk-top review of the cropmarks, earthworks and surface finds in this area, primarily of the Romano-British period, has been prompted by remarkable new cropmark evidence for Hockwold from aerial survey by Derek Edwards during the drought of 1989.

The area covers a ten-kilometre length of the Norfolk Fen-edge, from Brandon to the mouth of the river valley at Blackdyke Farm, Hockwold (Fig 6.6). Here, the greensand further to the north is lacking, so the Fen peat butts directly up to the edge of the chalk with only a narrow band of skirtland or sand-hills between. It is on this narrow band below the 5 m OD contour and just above the probable ancient limit of peat Fen, that dense settlement is found. There are few sites on the adjacent chalk upland.

Figure 6.6 shows the locations of cropmark and earthwork sites, buildings, hoards and roads in this area. The three main areas of interest are Sites 5316, 5455 and 5587, where surface finds, cropmarks, survey and excavation indicate particularly dense occupation. These will be considered in turn.

Site 5316 (Salway 1967) (Fig 6.7)

Site 5316 to the west is by far the largest area of cropmarks recorded to date – forty acres. In 1961–2, areas of the cropmark complex were excavated by Peter Salway in advance of the construction of the Cut-Off Channel, which sliced through a linear band of prehistoric and Romano-British settlement unparalleled anywhere in the county. Unfortunately only three sites were excavated, the Feltwell bath-house and a saltern mound at Denver (Gurney 1986) and Salway's sites at Hockwold (Salway 1967). There are, in fact, two published plans of this part of the Hockwold complex, one in the short note in the *Journal of Roman Studies*, 52 (1962), fig 24 and the other in the excavation report (Salway 1967, fig 2); Fig 6.7 shows them both, as they do differ. Salway's Site 7088 areas included an enclosure and road with indications of a wattle-and-daub building nearby. What dating evidence there was suggested a 2nd century AD date. Site 7188a revealed a 1st century AD storage pit, a number of ditches and middle to late 2nd/early 3rd century pottery. Site 7188b examined a north-to-south road and two side roads joining it from the east. After a possible period of abandonment in the late 2nd century, areas of the site were covered with what is described as 'planking', perhaps to consolidate a patch of wet ground for the construction of timber structures (of which no clear evidence was found).

In his conclusions, Salway suggests that the excavations indicate that the area of cropmarks consisted of part of a settlement rather than a field system, and that it was occupied from around the mid-2nd century to the early 3rd century, after which the settlement was abandoned. Salway also saw Hockwold as a likely candidate for *Camboritum* of the Antonine Itinerary, but the mileages do not fit at all well and Icklingham in Suffolk is perhaps a better choice.

Sites 5357, 5455 and 5461 (Fig 6.8)

Site 5357 consists of the earthworks of the shrunken village of Hockwold with a scatter of Roman (and earlier) pottery. An earthwork survey (by Brian Cushion and Alan Davison) suggested that the southern part of these earthworks (associated with prehistoric, Iron Age and Roman sherds) should perhaps be viewed as part of the same complex as the Roman earthworks of Sites 5461 and 5455. The suspected Romano-British – medieval divide is shown as a dashed and dotted line (Fig 6.8).

Site 5455 (Ennefer's Field) contains evidence of Roman settlement and possibly a cremation cemetery. Apart from what appears to be a later trackway or drove to Site 5357 which crosses the other features diagonally, there appears to be a complex of linear features which would appear to be based upon an east-to-west road or track.

The general impression is not dissimilar to the cropmarks in Salway's area (see Fig 6.7).

Site 5587 (Leyland's Farm) (Figs 6.9–10; Pls 6.I–II)

Site 5587 at Leylands Farm, Hockwold (Gurney 1986, 49–92) was first plotted by Rainbird Clarke when he sectioned the Dark Age linear earthwork known as The Fossditch which then appeared to bisect an oval settlement area (Clarke 1955, fig 3). Subsequently the site has produced evidence of structures (Gurney 1986, 86–87), two hoards of pewter vessels (Gurney 1986, 149–153) and a structure with religious connections containing the Wilton crown and diadems; priestly headgear perhaps associated with a cult of Attis and Cybele (excavated by Charles Green in 1957; area 2).

In the early 1980s the late Tony Gregory carried out a detailed surface collection in the Crowns Field, as it is called, and some of this data has now been plotted (Fig 6.9). An approximate 25 metre grid was established, and all surface finds were collected. The actual amounts of material recovered were not enormous, but nevertheless fairly consistent patterning emerges from the distributions of coarse wares (Fig 6.9), fine wares, samian, mortaria and animal bone (not illustrated), all tending to show concentrations towards the south-east and south-west corners of the field. Evidence of metalworking seems to be rather more widespread (Fig 6.9). There are concentrations of tile (Fig 6.9), probably indicating buildings, the clearest evidence of which is a scatter of red

TL 7287   0   25m

Fig 6.8 Plan of earthworks at Hockwold, Sites 5357, 5455 and 5461. Scale 1:1000.

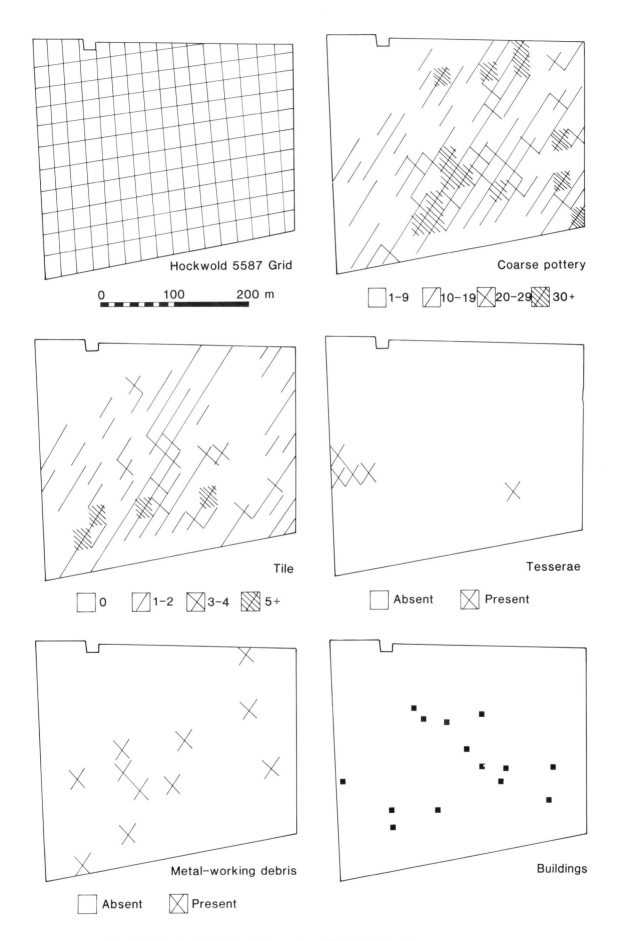

Fig 6.9 *Hockwold, Leylands Farm, Site 5587, finds distributions. Scale 1:500.*

Fig 6.10 *Hockwold, Leylands Farm, plot of cropmarks, based on photograph reference DMJ 12, 12 July 1989. Scale 1:2500.*

brick *tesserae* (Fig 6.9) across four adjacent grid squares on the western edge of the field.

Remarkable aerial photographs of 1989 (Pls 6.1–2) provide an indication of the size and layout of the settlement in this field, although it must be remembered that the settlement extends into the field to the east, now Weeting Heath Nature Reserve, where it is today only

discernable by the occasional sherd brought to the surface by the activity of moles or rabbits.

Prior to the aerial photograph of 1989 it was unclear how extensive the settlement was in this particular field, but we can now see that the whole field is covered by a series of roads or tracks, between which there are enclosures and structures (Fig 6.10).

Pl 6.1   Hockwold, Leylands Farm, cropmarks looking north (D A Edwards, 17 July 1989, photo ref TL 7587 AFJ DNU13).

Pl 6.2   Hockwold, Leylands Farm, cropmark detail looking north-west (D A Edwards, 13 July 1989, photo ref TL 7587 AER DMV12).

The soils vary between light sands and darker peat, the latter visible as tongues of peat or smaller pockets of peaty soil (Pl 6.1). The principal features on the aerial photograph are the roads or tracks (which tend to run along the sandy or gravelly ridges), and a number of structures and enclosures.

Starting with the roads, the dominant alignment appears to be that of two east-to-west roads or tracks 1 and 2 (Fig 6.10), represented by stretches of parallel roadside ditches continued in places by single ditches. In the south-east corner of the field, an alignment of single ditches (3) suggests a possible third east-to-west road, which possibly turns north (for a short distance it is double ditched) to become what appears to be a main north-to-south road (4) crossing both the east-to-west roads.

The southern east-to-west road (1) passes just south of the approximate location of Charles Green's excavation of the structure containing the Wilton crown and diadems, and in this area Green found an east-to-west trackway of rammed chalk and gravel. The published interpretation of this trackway as possibiy of fairly recent origin (Gurney 1986, 57) is now somewhat suspect in the light of the cropmark evidence, and it can now be reinterpreted as part of the southern road visible on the aerial photograph.

There is a most curious cropmark at one of the cross-roads (Pl 6.2). One can only speculate what this curious arrangement is for, but perhaps this small triangular area contained a statue or monument of some kind, situated prominently at one of the major road intersections of the settlement.

Between the roads or tracks there are linear features and alignments of postholes or post-pits which appear to indicate the presence of property boundaries, subdivisions of the larger blocks of land created by the roads (either ditched or fenced) and enclosures. Only in one area can a coherent layout be seen, and that is to the north of the site where there is a group of three interlinked enclosures. A distinctive feature of the ditch dividing the western and central enclosure is the change in alignment where the double-ditched entrance apparently ends, and this looks as though it is designed for stock control, with cattle being turned left or right through gates into either enclosure. Together, these three enclosures occupy an area of about half an acre. Such a planned system of linked enclosures suggests stock management, with the enclosures functioning as paddocks or folds.

At least six possible rectangular structures can be identified on the aerial photograph, visible as rows (or part rows) of post-pits. The buildings seem to be between 10m and 15m long and between 3m and 6m wide, but one larger structure towards the south-west corner measures around 20m × 5m and has a distinctly curved linear feature at its east end. Field survey has located a scatter of chalk and tile building debris on or very close to this spot. If one combines all the evidence of buildings in this field, including old excavations, surface finds and cropmarks, the locations for at least fourteen separate buildings can be suggested.

To summarise the evidence for Hockwold, there appears to be relatively sparse Iron Age and 1st century AD occupation, a marked increase in occupation during the 2nd and 3rd centuries, and the temple sites appear to have been the main centres of activity in the later Roman period.

In addition to the the masonry villa at Weeting there are hints of fairly substantial masonry buildings at Eastfen Drove and near Grange Farm, while at Leyland's Farm part of a possible masonry building was uncovered in 1966. At Leyland's Farm and elsewhere there are indications of timber buildings (in the form of chalk floors and occupation debris) and it seems probable that there are a very great number of such buildings within this strip of densely-occupied Fen-edge. The new cropmark evidence for Leyland's Farm probably only shows a small proportion of the roads, buildings and enclosures which must have belonged to this remarkable linear Fen-edge settlement.

The sites in the area are generally represented by pottery scatters but by few other finds, with the exception of the larger sites and/or temple sites. The absence of coins from seemingly all but the temple sites is an important and intriguing feature of the area. In this respect, the temple site at Leyland's Farm with its coins, brooches and other metalwork is unusual, but it can now be seen that this is not just an isolated religious site but perhaps an important temple area within a much larger linear settlement. The Leyland's Farm temple can now be seen in a little more of its context, and a picture is emerging of a virtually continuous band of Fen-edge settlement, with main and subsidiary roads, many timber structures, masonry buildings at intervals and the occasional temple, all spread over a distance of some 6 km.

Conclusions

To conclude, it is very difficult to even start to say what makes a Roman settlement in Norfolk a small town. Does it matter very much whether we call those settlements which stand out as being larger and, in some respects more important, small towns, minor towns, large villages or even just villages? There is really too little evidence at the present time (and there may never be enough) to allow us to establish any sort of hierarchy within this group of sites. While the presence of defences at Brampton could be held to be significant, this does not necessarily lead to any firm conclusion about its status. Is it simply a measure of economic success that Brampton acquired defences when other settlements without such extensive industrial activity (and presumably profits) did not? Is Brampton at the upper end of a widely-varying class of settlement, or is it altogether different? The present writer would argue for the former.

The surface and metal-detector evidence from Norfolk which has been briefly reviewed for some of the sites, can provide us with a great deal of information, but so far is unable to resolve any questions about the status of any particular site in the Roman period, or its relative importance compared to the others. The behaviour of the coin histogram is one area where surface finds may be able to point to significant differences between sites, and there is great scope here for further research. It may be that a fuller consideration of other categories of evidence recovered by means of fieldwalking or metal-detecting will supply some clues about the position of these sites within the hierarchy of settlement types in Roman Norfolk. There is clearly still a great deal of information to be collected, and a mass of data already collected to be worked on.

To conclude, have the last twenty-two years seen much light shed upon Malcolm Todd's 'shadowy' settlements? In Norfolk, the combination of fieldwalking and metal-detecting mainly by amateur archaeologists and the allocation of professional resources to identify and record this material has certainly moved us in the right direction, but we need to continue this process, perhaps for several decades more, before enough of those shadows are dispelled to enable us to see the picture more clearly.

Acknowledgements
This paper would not have been possible were it not for the information provided by metal-detector finds. In particular, surveys by David Fox (Walsingham/Wighton), Barrie Sharrock (Billingford), John Pope (Brampton) and Robin Brown (Saham Toney) have greatly enhanced our knowledge of these sites. The coin evidence is the work of John Davies and the late Tony Gregory. Heather Wallis and John Davies both kindly provided information about Billingford in advance of the publication of their own site and coin reports respectively. The aerial photographs were taken by Derek A Edwards who also drew Fig 6.10, working from a computer-rectified plot supplied by John Haig of the University of Bradford.

Bibliography

Bamford, H M, 1982 Beaker domestic sites in the Fen-edge and East Anglia, *E Anglian Archaeol*, 16

Brown, R A, 1986 The Iron Age and Romano-British settlement at Woodcock Hall, Saham Toney, Norfolk, *Britannia*, 17, 1–58

Burnham, B C & Wacher, J, 1990 *The 'small towns' of Roman Britain*

Clarke, R R, 1955 The Fossditch – a linear earthwork in southwest Norfolk, *Norfolk Archaeol*, 31, 178–196

Darling, M J, with Gurney, D, 1993 Caister on Sea, Norfolk; excavations by Charles Green 1951–55, *E Anglian Archaeol*, 60

Davies, J A, & Gregory, T, 1991 Coinage from a *civitas*: a survey of the Roman coins found in Norfolk and their contribution to the archaeology of the *Civitas Icenorum*, *Britannia*, 22, 65–101

Frere, S S, 1975 The origin of 'small towns', in *The 'small towns' of Roman Britain* (eds W Rodwell and T Rowley), BAR Brit Ser, 15, 4–8

Green, C, 1977 Excavations in the Roman kiln field at Brampton, 1973–4, *E Anglian Archaeol*, 5, 31–96

Gregory, T, 1986 The Iron Age and Romano-British sites at Warham and Wighton, in Gregory, T and Gurney, D, Excavations at Thornham, Warham, Wighton and Caistor St Edmund, Norfolk, *E Anglian Archaeol*, 30, 14–16

Gurney, D, 1986 Settlement, religion and industry on the Fen-edge; three Romano-British sites in Norfolk, *E Anglian Archaeol*, 31

Healy, F M A, 1980 *The Neolithic in Norfolk*, unpublished PhD thesis, University of London

Knowles, A K, 1977 Brampton, Norfolk: interim report, *Britannia*, 8, 209–222

Lawson, A J, 1976 Excavations at Whey Curd Farm, Wighton, *E Anglian Archaeol*, 2, 65–99

Reece, R, 1987 *Coinage in Roman Britain*

Rogerson, A, 1977 Excavations at Scole, 1973, *E Anglian Archaeol*, 5, 97– 224

Salway, P, 1967 Excavations at Hockwold-cum-Wilton, Norfolk, 1961–62, *Proc Cambridge Antiq Soc*, 60, 39–80

Todd, M, 1970 The small towns of Roman Britain, *Britannia*, 1, 114–130

Webster, G, 1975 Small towns without defences, in *The 'small towns' of Roman Britain* (eds W Rodwell and T Rowley), BAR Brit Ser, 15, 53–66

7 A hole in the distribution map: the characteristics of small towns in Suffolk

Judith Plouviez

Whether various Roman settlements in East Anglia can be classified as small towns remains an open question, both because of the general difficulty in defining this type of site and also because of the nature of the evidence in this region. My title refers to the map of small towns discussed by Burnham and Wacher (1990, 2) on which Suffolk can be distinguished as a large open space next to the Fens. Within this space, however, there is a normal complex range of Roman settlement types. At the top of the hierarchy I suggest that eight settlements can be described as small towns on the basis of size, location and evidence for multiple functions. So far there is no trace of defences and, as usual in East Anglia, there is far more use of timber than of stone in buildings. These factors, coupled with a shortage of published excavation data (for which I take some share of the blame!), go a long way in explaining the gaps in general distribution maps.

The eight small towns in Suffolk are, from west to east: Wixoe, Icklingham, Long Melford, Pakenham (also referred to as Ixworth in some publications), Coddenham, Felixstowe, Hacheston and Wenhaston (Fig 7.1). The southern suburbs of the very similar settlement at Scole in Norfolk also extend into Suffolk. A further group of sites – Sicklesmere, Stoke Ash, Capel St Mary, Knodishall – are very under-investigated but seem to be smaller and to produce less varied material. These are perhaps better described as 'villages'.

There have been large scale excavations at Pakenham, Coddenham and Hacheston, but little information is available from the Coddenham site. Excavation of a smaller area at Icklingham has been published (West & Plouviez 1976), as have limited investigations in Long Melford (Smedley 1961; Avent & Howlett 1980). Wixoe and Wenhaston are almost entirely known from surface finds and Felixstowe from chance discoveries in the 19th and early 20th century.

Overall sizes vary from 10 to 40 hectares (25–100 acres), most of the sites being between 15 and 30 hectares. This is larger than for any other Roman sites in the county except for some of the Fen edge complexes in the north-west which superficially resemble urban or subur-

ban sprawl but without any focus. All the sites are on certain or probable major roads and are at or near river crossings except for Felixstowe which is on the coast. At least three of them are also at junctions in the road system. Distances between the towns vary from 15 to 30 kilometres, most commonly 23 to 27 kilometres, and nowhere in Suffolk is more than about 10 miles from a town, a practical distance for a local market centre.

The basic recorded information for each of the eight small towns is given in Appendix 1 with a summary of various types of locational, chronological and functional evidence in Table 7.1. Further consideration of their origins, development and layout relies heavily on the large excavated areas at Pakenham and Hacheston.

At the time of the Conquest Suffolk was on a political and possibly cultural divide between the Belgic Trinovantes in the south and the Iceni in the north. Nowhere is there much sign of a hierarchy of Iron Age sites which includes trading or manufacturing foci. There are rather occasional high status defended sites, most notably Burgh (Martin 1988) which has a range of late Iron Age imported goods similar to those found at *Camulodunum*. Examples of Dressel 1 amphorae also turn up along the Stour valley on the southern edge of the county, again well within *Camulodunum's* sphere of influence. Several of the Roman towns, particularly in the Trinovantian area (Long Melford, Coddenham and perhaps Hacheston), do produce finds and features of Iron Age date, including a reference to 1st century hut circles at Coddenham, but there is no evidence for a continuity of function as suggested by Rodwell for the Essex towns in 1975.

Aerial photographs suggest an early Roman military presence at Coddenham and at Pakenham. At Coddenham the photographs show two phases of multiple ditched forts straddling the Colchester to Caistor by Norwich road. The hypothesis is that these most likely relate to military activity in or soon after 43 and in 61 after the Boudiccan revolt. Unfortunately the only excavations have been well outside the forts so the hypothesis re mains untested.

At Pakenham in 1985 we examined a strip across the

Judith Plouviez

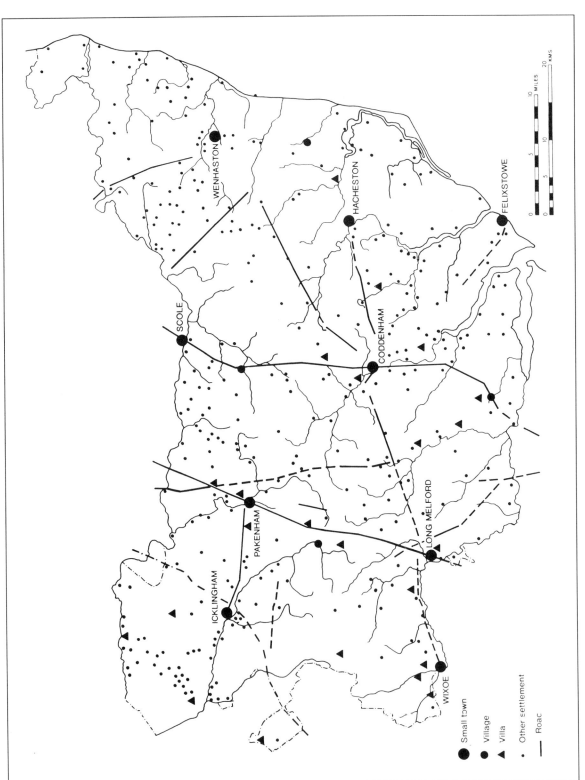

Fig 7.1 Roman settlements in Suffolk

Table 7.1

Site Name	Size (ha.)	Road Plan	Buildings Wood	Buildings Flint	Industry	Religion	Cemetery	Military	Iron Age	Saxon
Coddenham COMBRETOVIVM	40	complex	?	?	P	Y	?	1st C.	Y	C
Felixtowe	18?	linear?	–	–	–	Y	?	4th C.	–	?
Hacheston	30	complex?	2+	1	P, I	Y	Y	–	Y	P
Icklingham CAMBORITVM	17	complex	1+	3	P	Y	Y	–	–	P
Long Melford	24	linear?	–	1	–	–	?	–	Y	–
Pakenham	19	complex	8+	1	P, I, B	Y	?	1st C.	–	P
Wenhaston	15	?	–	–	–	?	–	–	–	C?
Wixoe	6+	complex?	–	1	–	?	Y	–	–	C?

Notes: Combretovium and Camboritum are the suggested Antonine Itinerary identifications for Coddenham and Icklingham (Moore 1988, 32–37).

Industries: P= pottery, I= Iron-working, B = Bronze-working.
Religion: based on artefact evidence only except at Icklingham.
Early Saxon: C = from central part of site, P = peripheral.

triple ditched fort seen on the air photographs, including a fairly central road junction (Fig 7.2). Previous speculation about the site favoured the idea that the fort, presumed to be post-Boudiccan, gave rise to a *vicus* that was conveniently visible as a series of roadside enclosures to the east of the fort; this *vicus* then expanded over the fort area after its abandonment. My equally vain hope was that there would be a flourishing late Iron Age centre, displaced by the military after Boudicca but then re-established as a town. In practice there was more late Neolithic than Iron Age activity in the excavated area. The dating of specific features and of the artefacts generally is consistent with a Neronian foundation and seems to confirm the post-Boudiccan date for the fort. Our impression of the military phase is that it was short-lived, lacking permanent buildings and with most activity around a small central area which respects the east-west road. Of the three perimeter ditches the innermost was rapidly backfilled with almost archaeologically sterile material, presumably the levelling of the rampart, but the middle and especially the outer ditch remained as visible depressions well into the 2nd or 3rd centuries, and in places were re-used and backfilled in the late 4th century. The internal military phase features were also rapidly backfilled with contemporary material. Following this orderly military withdrawal there is a good sequence of buildings in the central part of the site in exactly the same area as the military period features. The first was an 8 metre diameter circular structure, much flimsier looking than the usual Iron Age house with individual posts about 5cm across. It had a larger post setting around half the circumference and an entrance facing onto the existing road. The area was next divided up into fenced plots each about 7.5 metres wide and a rectangular building constructed in the westernmost plot, again fronting the road. Before the end of the 1st century this layout was disrupted by the introduction of the north-south road and the fences and building plans were adjusted to the remaining space. By contrast there was much less 1st century activity in the eastern half of the fort interior and none identified in the limited area examined beyond the eastern ditches; this completely rules out the idea of development from an external *vicus*. The military contribution to the process of urbanisation seems to have been the creation of half a main road system and a large open space.

At about the same time as this typical small town layout of buildings fronting onto main roads began in the centre of the town, a subsidiary north-south road was established within the fort area and another led to the east from the fort edge. The few excavated buildings along these back roads date from the mid 2nd century. All the buildings were timber, mostly post built with clay floors. The first rectangular buildings, in the central crossroads area, were about 5.5 by 11.5 metres with large clay hearths. These were replaced during the first half of the 2nd century by a larger, semi-aisled building which was 19 metres long and about 8 wide. There were several small clay hearths in the front half of this building and traces of painted plaster walls, presumably a residential area, to the rear.

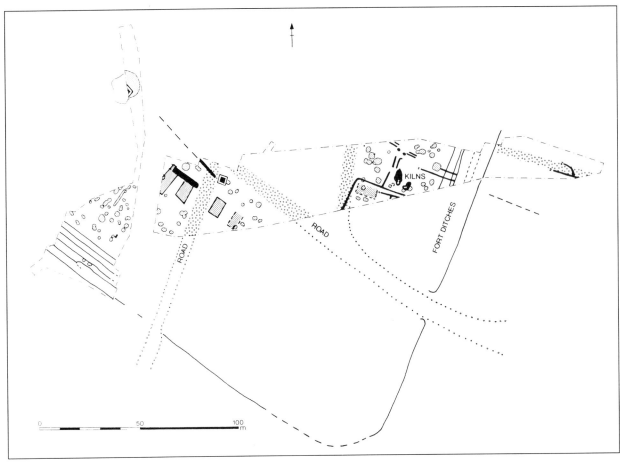

Fig 7.2 *Pakenham, Suffolk: the 1985 excavation and southern extent of the fort. Stippled features and buildings are 1st or 2nd century, solid ones are 3rd or 4th century.*

Ideally the 1973 excavation at Hacheston, which is currently being worked on for publication, should have produced a comparable sequence. Unfortunately the lowest levels in the stratified area, adjacent to and under a Roman road, were sampled in very small sections. These give us enigmatic glimpses of small boundary ditch and fence systems in the 1st century. During the 2nd and 3rd centuries the excavated road had at least two clay floored buildings fronting it; these may have been sill beam constructions (Fig 7.3). The status of the road is not clear – it is possibly a back road with a main route about 100 metres to the north.

At Pakenham the area east of the minor north-south road was used during the 3rd century for pottery production. The industry was aimed at the upper end of the market, producing colour-coated, mica-dusted and painted wares. Kilns producing the same range were identified in the 1950s about half a mile to the south-east of the fort in what was assumed to be an industrial suburb of the town. However the idea that potting should be kept outside the town does not seem to have applied at any time to the Suffolk towns – kilns are found throughout the Hacheston site from the 1st century on, and fairly close to the centres of both Coddenham and Icklingham.

As well as the kilns a new system of enclosures was established in the later Roman period at Pakenham. The small ditches cut across the minor roads and seem to be orientated on the re-cut outer ditch of the fort (Fig 7.2, solid features). Even in the central area the site of the large aisled building was cut by an early 4th century ditch and there appear to have been no further buildings on this plot. As in most of the towns there was at least one late building with flint wall foundations, which in this case had a hypocaust and was probably a bath-house. It was almost certainly supplied with water *via* a wooden pipe from a timber structure interpreted as a water tower or tank close to the crossroads. We can speculate whether these structures represent public organisation or a private concern encroaching on an area which formerly seemed to be public open space along the edge of the road.

At Hacheston one ditch cut the road and there were considerable spreads of debris over part of the road surface by the 4th century. There was also a system of field or droveway ditches on the hill to the south-east of the main urban area; preliminary assessment suggests that finds in this area are mostly 3rd and 4th century (Fig 7.3, solid features). Again we seem to be seeing a new ditched

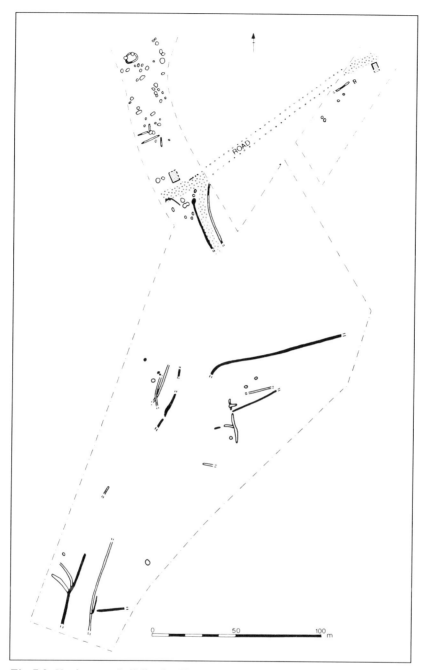

Fig 7.3 *Hacheston, Suffolk: the 1973 excavation. Stippled buildings are 1st or 2nd century, solid features are 3rd or 4th century.*

layout in and around the town, perhaps with much more widely spaced buildings.

Although the main aim was to discover the layout of the roads and buildings in these towns, the majority of excavated features from the late 1st to the mid 3rd century were pits of various shapes and sizes which were backfilled with domestic rubbish. Some contain evidence of use as latrines, perhaps the primary function of many of them. All produce useful assemblages of pottery, animal bone and so on. I find it puzzling that such pits virtually disappear sometime in the 3rd century, at much the same time as other changes in organisation at both

Pakenham and Hacheston. So far only one pit at Hacheston and a couple at Pakenham can be shown to have been dug or infilled in the late 3rd or 4th centuries. On the other hand surface debris becomes much more frequent with distinct midden areas next to buildings at Hacheston in the 3rd century. The top layer of stratified occupation debris at Hacheston could be described as a 'dark earth', as could some of the latest deposits at Pakenham. Similar material is also currently being found around Scole, where it will be sampled for comparison with the more substantial dark earths found in major Roman towns.

The recovery of large groups of coins from Hacheston and Pakenham plus the large amount of data now available after fifteen years of widespread metal detecting in Suffolk prompted study of coin loss patterns. I intended to look at the small towns against a general Suffolk norm to see whether there were any characteristics specific to them, while bearing in mind that Richard Reece's work had shown that the large towns could be distinguished as a group but that there were no clear distinctions between other types of site (Reece 1991, 104). All the coin identification data in the county's SMR files was listed on Reece's system of 21 coin periods (Table 7.2). Coin numbers for each period could then be converted to a percentage of the total and displayed in a histogram-like diagram for visual comparison. In broad terms of course the diagrams all correspond to the peaks and troughs of coin loss on British sites in general as established by Reece (1987a, 83).

Table 7.2 Coin periods used for analysis of coins from Suffolk small towns

Period 1	up to AD 41	Period 12	238 to 260
Period 2	41 to 54	Period 13	260 to 275
Period 3	54 to 68	Period 14	275 to 296
Period 4	69 to 96	Period 15	296 to 317
Period 5	96 to 117	Period 16	317 to 330
Period 6	117 to 138	Period 17	330 to 348
Period 7	138 to 161	Period 18	348 to 364
Period 8	161 to 180	Period 19	364 to 378
Period 9	180 to 192	Period 20	378 to 388
Period 10	192 to 222	Period 21	388 to 402
Period 11	222 to 238		

The total number of identifiable Roman coins recorded for the whole county now stands at 10,325. Of this figure 5,522, just over half, came from the small towns. The bulk of these (3,267) resulted from intensive search in the area of excavation and earth moving for road construction at Hacheston and Pakenham. However the totals of 831 from Wenhaston, 414 from Wixoe and 624 from Icklingham illustrate that all these sites do produce exceptionally large groups of coins (and the number of coins reported from each of these three sites is still rising rapidly). The largest non-urban site collection recorded is 333, and only twelve other sites have yet produced more than 100 coins.

It rapidly became apparent that there was more variation between sites and aggregated site totals on a geographical basis than between functional site groups. This was first observed when the coins from all non-urban sites in the east and west halves of the county were combined and compared; they were then sub-divided into smaller geographical blocks as illustrated (Fig 7.4). The critical variation is in the second half of the 4th century, after the peak in period 17 (330–348). In southern and

eastern areas of the county the proportions of these coins are low, often dropping between periods 18 (348–364) and 19 (364–378), as in areas F, G, H and I, and very low in both periods in area D. The areas closest to the British average (as illustrated by Reece 1987a, 83) are Areas A and C, although the whole county falls below the average in the final years of coin use (388–402).

If we now add the towns to the picture (Fig 7.5) we can see whether they compare to their regions as one might assume given a market centre role. Looking at the 1st and 2nd centuries there is relatively higher coin loss at Wenhaston, Hacheston and Pakenham than in their background areas (areas D, I, B) which correlates well with the apparently high levels of activity in the excavated areas at Hacheston and Pakenham. By contrast Icklingham and Wixoe are virtually non-existent in coin terms until the 3rd century.

In the 4th century most of the towns show exaggerations of both the peaks and the troughs in their regions. Wenhaston is particularly low in period 19 (364–378). Hacheston has a phenomenal peak in the 330s (actually over 50%), and again the period 19 level is even lower than adjacent areas H and I. In the west, Pakenham has a less fluctuating level than its surrounding region, whereas Icklingham and Wixoe have more exaggerated peaks and generally higher numbers from the 330s (period 17) on.

This excursion into the coin date patterns reinforces questions about the later period in the towns which need exploring against other types of evidence. The huge coin loss increase at Hacheston between 330 and 348 may well correlate with the enlarged settlement area mentioned above. The decline in the second half of the 4th century in both town and countryside in east Suffolk needs examining against a range of sites over a broader area, including Colchester where there is again a slight drop

Note on data used for Fig 7.4

Area A: TL 66–68, 76–78, 86–88. 1,099 coins from 31 sites including four large (277, 149, 133, 106) groups. Icklingham is in the centre of the area.

Area B: TL 96–97, TM 07. 388 coins from 19 sites, including one large (125) group. Pakenham is in the west of the area.

Area C: TM 16–17, 26–28. 255 coins from 17 sites, but 167 of these are from areas immediately south of Scole; remaining sample too small.

Area D: TM 36–38, 46–48, 58–59. 375 coins from 19 sites. Wenhaston is in the centre of the area.

Area E: TL 64, 74, 84–85. 266 coins from 12 sites including one large (102) group. Wixoe and Long Melford are on the south edge of the area.

Area F: TL 93–95, TM 04–05. 584 coins from 20 sites including two large (184,100) groups.

Area G: TM 13–15. 893 coins from 37 sites including two large (333 and 101) groups. Coddenham is in the north-west of the area.

Area H: TM 23–25. 592 coins from 45 sites.

Area I: TM 33–35. 342 sites from 22 sites. Hacheston and Felixstowe are in the north-west and south-west corners of the area.

Fig 7.4 *Coin histograms for nine areas of Suffolk excluding the small towns. X-axes are the coin periods as listed in Table 6.2, Y-axes are the numbers of coins as a percentage of the total.*

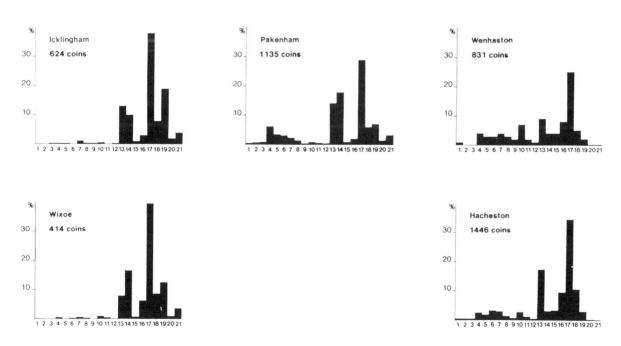

Fig 7.5 *Coin histograms for five small towns in Suffolk. The number of period 17 coins from Hacheston has been cut from 1186 to 500 so that the rest of the diagram is visible.*

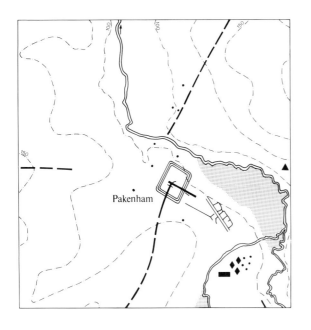

Pakenham

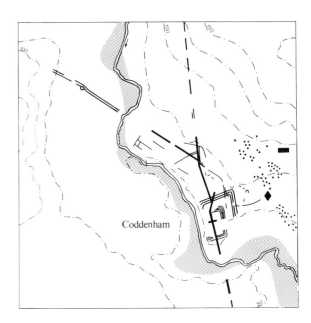

Coddenham

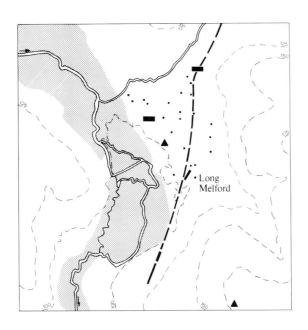

Long
Melford

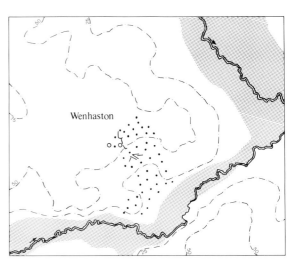

Wenhaston

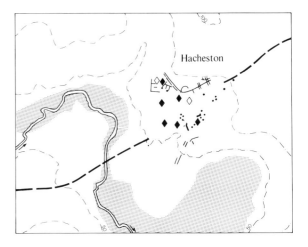

Hacheston

0   500   1000 metres
0   500   1000 yards

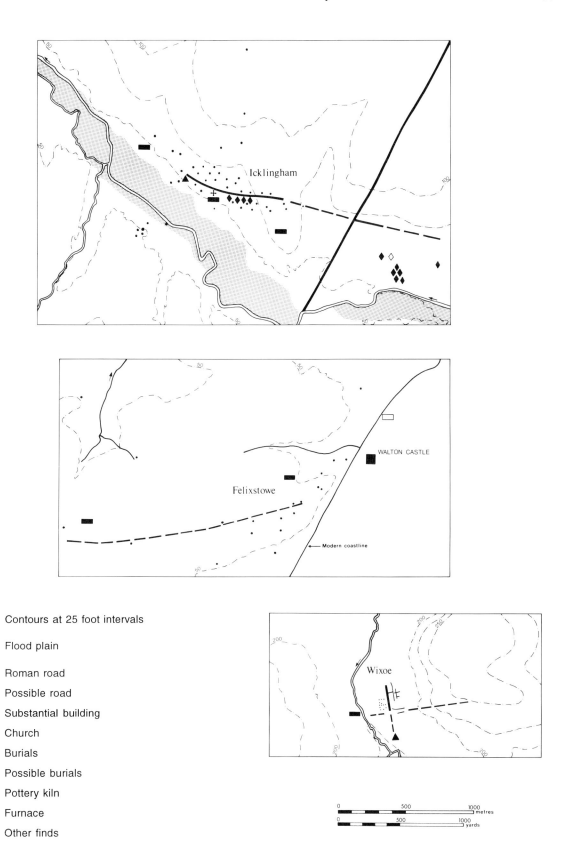

Fig 7.6 *Plans of the small towns in Suffolk showing topography, cropmark features and the distibution of finds.*

between periods 18 (348–364) and 19 (364–378) (Reece 1987b, 18).

The very different patterns at Icklingham and Wixoe pose questions about whether these really are urban centres and if so whether they are market centres in the 1st and 2nd centuries. In practice it can be argued that earlier evidence may be masked at Icklingham because of only limited investigation at one end of the settlement. The dominant function recorded at Icklingham so far is religious, a pagan temple indicated by the notorious hoard of temple bronzes and a 4th century Christian cemetery and church. At Wixoe however there is good evidence from accidental and metal detected finds that there was activity from the 1st century onwards so the low percentages of early coins is more surprising.

It seems more productive to pursue these questions about possible changes in status and function through time in the 'small towns' than to debate whether or not the term is applicable to the East Anglian sites. They were certainly a significant element in the Roman landscape and play a major part in the dissemination of at least the material aspects of 'Romanisation' to the rural population. The evidence discussed here which suggests distinct differences in their character in the later period may be related to changes taking place in the major towns in late Roman Britain. Certainly there is no hint that these sites retain any urban significance into the 5th century or beyond – the earliest English towns in Suffolk could be slightly more convincingly correlated with large villa estates than the Roman small towns.

Appendix 1

Gazetteer of small towns in Suffolk

The eight small towns are listed in alphabetical order. Key references are given but much of the information derives from material held as part of the Suffolk County Council Sites and Monuments Record.

Coddenham TM 1152

Situated at the crossing of the River Gipping by the road from Colchester to Caistor by Norwich. Roads from the east, northeast and west also converge on the site; the junction of the Colchester-Caistor road with another is visible on air photographs. First identified as an important site in the 1820s when finds included the road, a flint wall foundation and cremation burials (with one of which was a bronze mirror case showing Nero and his troops, now in the British Museum). Air photographs show two forts, presumably 1st century. Excavations in the 1950s to the north of the forts suggested a date of around 70 for the metalled Caistor road with earlier pits underneath it (West 1956, 73). More extensive excavation in 1973 to the east of the forts produced a sequence of features from the late Iron Age up to the 3rd century, including timber buildings and pottery kilns (Loughlin & Moss 1974). The area identified as part of the settlement has been greatly extended in the last twenty years by metal detecting. Much of the evidence sug-

gests diminished activity in the 4th century. Early Saxon pottery and metalwork has been found within the small town area. Coddenham is generally identified with *Combretovium*, named on the Peutinger Table and in the Antonine Itinerary *Iter* IX (Rivet & Smith 1979,170 & 313).

Felixstowe TM 3135

On the coast between the Deben and the Stour estuaries. A possible fort of the Saxon shore at Walton Castle, Felixstowe, had been completely removed by the sea by the late 18th century although lumps of masonry are still occasionally visible on the beach at very low tides. To the west of the fort finds spanning the entire Roman period have been recorded from a fairly broad area under the present town. There has been no systematic excavation but finds include building materials (tile, painted plaster), a wide range of pottery tablewares, metalwork (coins, figurines, brooches etc) and cremation and inhumation burials. It seems likely that there was a port here before the establishment of the shore fort, presumably in the 3rd century.

Hacheston TM 3156

On the north side of the River Deben, the site was first identified in observation of a service trench in 1964, followed by small scale excavations of pottery kilns and other features and then a large area excavation in 1973–74 (Blagg 1975). One Roman road identified in 1973 runs parallel to the old A12 which may also be on a Roman road line. The distribution of finds and features suggests a complex settlement plan rather than a linear roadside layout. Material includes late Iron Age coins and pottery but no structural evidence of this date. Roman timber buildings, evidence of ironworking, possibly pewter manufacture and pottery production (fine and coarse wares) are known. Just outside the main settlement area to the west a group of Roman cremation burials was found with early Saxon domestic features; an early Saxon building was also found on the south-east edge of the 1973 area.

Icklingham TL 7872

A generally linear arrangement of finds along the north side of the Lark valley, just west of the supposed course of the north-south Icknield Way. A Roman road, identified on air photographs and confirmed by excavation, runs through the settlement and towards Pakenham to the east. To the west there is an almost continuous band of Roman sites along the edge of the Fens.

Part of a building with a hypocaust and small rooms (a bath-house?) was excavated in 1877 (Prigg 1901, 72–75). At least two late Roman cemeteries, several late coin hoards and various other objects were also found in the 19th century. A group of pottery kilns producing coarse wares was identified in the 1930s. Excavation in 1974 of the area around the find spot of a large lead tank revealed a 4th century inhumation cemetery associated with a rectangular building, possibly a church, and a small tile ?baptistry. An earlier pagan temple in the vicinity was suggested. In 1981/2 a hoard of bronze masks and figurines of mid-Roman date was stolen from the settlement area. There is little evidence for activity before the 2nd century – but pottery kilns producing fine wares were established at West Stow about one mile to the east in the later 1st century (West 1990). Early Saxon settlements and burials also occur to the east and to the west but not within the Roman small town area. It is arguable that Icklingham can be identified with *Camboritum* in *Iter V* of the Antonine Itinerary although Hockwold (Norfolk) and Lackford (just south of the River Lark) have also been suggested (Rivet & Smith 1979,294).

Long Melford TL 8645

Lies on the east side of the River Stour, at a probable road junction and river crossing although only a north-south road has been located within the settlement.

Late Iron Age and Roman occupation partially underlies the southern half of the medieval settlement. Early discoveries in the 19th century showed that there were burials in fields west of the village; a further picture of the extent of Roman material was collected along a sewerage scheme in the 1950s (Smedley 1961).

Only one area on the southern edge of the settlement has been excavated (Avent & Howlett 1980) but one building (perhaps a bath house) with a tessellated floor was found in the sewerage trench in 1958. Most identified features have been pits (containing 1st and 2nd century material) or burials but recent watching briefs on small town centre developments also record later Roman deposits over the early features. Finds suggest that pre-Roman activity is likely and certainly the quantity of early Roman finds is substantial and includes imported pottery, such as Lyons ware; a first century military presence is a possibility. The only recorded early Saxon material in the vicinity is nearly a mile outside the Roman small town area.

Pakenham TL 9369

Sited on a north facing gravel terrace beside a crossing of the River Black Bourn at the intersection of a road from Long Melford to the north Norfolk coast with the Icklingham road. First identified as an area of Roman finds in the 19th century; a triple ditched fort was seen from the air in 1945. Subsequent photographs show several roads and numerous pits and ditches within and beyond the fort area. In the 1950s a record of pottery kilns and burials plus early Saxon occupation was salvaged from gravel workings at the south-east end of the settlement (Smedley & Owles 1960).

A large area excavation across the fort took place in 1985 which produced a surprising depth of surviving deposits adjacent to the central Roman road junction. Although late Iron Age coins were found in the excavated area these were most likely deposited post 60. The small town seems to have developed outwards from the centre of the fort, with several minor roads as well as the two main ones. There were traces of bronze casting in a 1st century context, several areas of iron smithing waste and pottery kilns producing predominantly 3rd century fine wares. Although no religious structures have been identified finds include a bronze letter P, a bronze mask and a fine figurine of Priapus. There is no early Saxon activity on the central part of the site but it is present in several peripheral locations.

Wenhaston TM 4275

A large area overlooking the River Blyth, identified at first in fieldwalking in 1975 and more recently supplemented by metal detecting finds. There is no evidence of settlement layout and its relationship to the road system in north-east Suffolk is uncertain. Finds range in date from late Iron Age through Roman to early Saxon and the medieval village core overlaps the Roman area.

The evidence for small town status is apparently weaker than at other sites due to a lack of excavation. However, the size of the site and the quantity and range of finds are very different from any other Roman site in the north-east quadrant of the county and are comparable to Hacheston to the south.

Wixoe TL 7043

A relatively small area on the north side of the River Stour on several possible road lines. An earthwork enclosure and Roman burials were recorded on the Essex side of the river in the early 19th century (Walford 1803). A building with flint foundations was partially uncovered in 1950 and is visible on air photographs. Photographs also show a possible crossroads with numerous pits and possible house plots along the roads. Fieldwalking and metal detecting show that there is a broad range of material; only a small proportion of the detected finds has been recorded but these include coins, brooches, figurines etc, plus late Iron Age coins and one early Saxon girdlehanger. A cremation group (pottery jar with accompanying samian dish and grey ware cup) has been found in the same area. Again the status of the site is open to debate because of the quality of the evidence.

Bibliography

Avent, R, & Howlett, T, 1980 Excavations in Roman Long Melford, 1970–1972, *Proc Suffolk Inst Archaeol*, 34, 229–249

Blagg,T, 1975 Hacheston, in *Archaeological Excavations 1974*, HMSO, 63–64

Burnham, B, & Wacher, J, 1990 *The 'small towns' of Roman Britain*

Loughlin, N, & Moss, G, 1974 *Combretovium*, Baylham House, Coddenham, in *Archaeological Excavations 1973*, HMSO, 58–59

Martin, E, 1988 Burgh: the Iron Age and Roman enclosure, *E Anglian Archaeol*, 40

Moore, I, *et al*, 1988 *The archaeology of Roman Suffolk*

Prigg, H, 1901 *Icklingham papers*

Reece, R, 1987a *Coinage in Roman Britain*

——, 1987b The Roman coins, in Crummy, N, *The coins from excavations in Colchester 1971–9*, Colchester Archaeol Rep 4, 17–23

——, 1991 *Roman coins from 140 sites in Britain*

Rivet, A, & Smith, C, 1979 *The place names of Roman Britain*

Rodwell, W, 1975 Trinovantian towns and their setting, in *The 'small towns' of Roman Britain* (eds W Rodwell & T Rowley), Brit Archaeol Rep, 15, 85–101

Smedley, N, 1961 Roman Long Melford, *Proc Suffolk Inst Archaeol*, 28, 272–289

——, & Owles, E, 1960 Some Suffolk kilns II, two kilns making colour-coated ware at Grimston End, Pakenham, *Proc Suffolk Inst Archaeol*, 28, 203–225

Walford, T, 1803 An account of a Roman military way in Essex and of antiquities found near it, *Archaeologia*, 14, 61–74

West, S, 1956 A Roman road at Baylham, Coddenham, *Antiq J*, 35, 73–75

——, 1990 West Stow: the prehistoric and Romano-British occupations, *E Anglian Archaeol*, 48

——, & Plouviez, J, 1976 The Roman site at Icklingham, *E Anglian Archaeol*, 3,63–126

8   Roman small towns in Leicestershire

Peter Liddle

In this paper the evidence for Roman small towns in the modern county of Leicestershire – or, in Roman terms, in the area around the Roman city of *Ratae Corieltauvorum* – will be examined. There is no really objective definition of a Roman small town. The lack of Roman documentary sources and of systematic modern work at many of the potential sites are considerable problems. In the end the major criterion must be the size of the site, but this should be supported by evidence of industry and trade, social or administrative functions. A summary of each site including the area that it covers can be found in Table 8.1.

For the major part of this paper the evidence for the one *civitas* capital, the nine probable and two possible small towns (Fig 8.1) will be examined before looking at the group as a whole.

Leicester (Roman name: *Ratae Corieltauvorum*) (Fig 8.2a)

This is clearly not the place for a full discussion of Roman Leicester, but merely to emphasise the features that distinguish it from the small towns. It had a rectilinear street grid, apparently laid out in the later 1st century AD. In the centre are large public buildings – a forum and basilica, a baths complex and a *macellum*. Many mosaics have been found over the years. Excavation has shown that these generally mark the sites of rich town houses (Mellor 1976). Leicester's origin lies in the Iron Age with a large area producing late Iron Age pottery and structures underlying the western part of the Roman city (Clay 1988). There was also a military presence with several finds of equipment and early timber buildings but only one short piece of ditch that is unequivocally from a fort. Defences were built in the late 2nd or 3rd century surrounding some 42 hectares (Buckley & Lucas 1987), but recent work is revealing more of the suburbs to the west, north and south. No recent opportunities have presented themselves to the east. A relatively large suburban villa is known on the west side of the city at Norfolk Street (Mellor & Lucas 1979).

The probable small towns

Witherley/Mancetter (Roman name: *Manduessedum*) (Fig 8.2b)

This settlement has been described in some detail by Burnham & Wacher (1990, 225–260). A small earthwork enclosure bisected by Watling Street has long been known and identified as the *Manduessedum* named in the Antonine Itinerary. Small excavations in 1927, in the 1950s (Oswald & Gathercole 1958) and in 1964 (Mahany 1971), showed that this probably dated to the late 3rd century (although the circuit partially coincided with an earlier ditch). Traces of 4th century buildings were noted within the defences. Subsequent excavations by Kay Hartley (1973) revealed part of the large surrounding settlement with an irregular street system and many kilns, specialising in mortaria, with others at nearby Hartshill. Keith Scott (1981) has revealed a large military establishment, probably an early legionary fortress, under Mancetter village across the River Anker. Little work has been done on the northern, Leicestershire, side of Watling Street and there are some indications that the settlement may extend some distance on this side as well. This is supported by small-scale work by Keith Scott in 1993 which appears to show a side street running north from Watling Street (K Scott, pers comm).

High Cross (Roman name: *Venonae*) (Fig 8.3a)

The site was well known as early as the 17th century. Prolific finds of Roman coins are mentioned by all the writers. The county historian Burton (who lived near the site) says 'on both sides of the way have been ploughed and digged up many ancient Romayne coynes, great square stones and bricks and other rubble of that ancient Roman building'. Ashmole in 1657 added 'At High Cross .... is the foundation (as I guess) of a Roman temple about six yards long, and four yards broad; and where they say, not long since, was a thing like a silver mace dug up'. Dugdale notes that ovens and wells had also been found and states (in a reference very worrying for fieldwalkers) 'the earth .... being of a darker colour and of such rank-

Table 8.1

| | SITE | | | HISTORY | | CHARACTER | | INDUSTRY | | | COINS | BUILDINGS | | | | ARCHAEOLOGICAL HISTORY |
	Road Junct.	River Crossing	Stream Crossing	Iron Age	Roman Military	Size	Defences	Pot Kilns	Large Scale Iron	Other Iron		Temple	High Status Buildings In	High Status Buildings Near	Strip Bldgs	
Leicester	Yes	Yes		Yes	Yes	41 ha in walls	Large	Yes		Yes	Many	Yes	Yes	Yes	Yes	Many Excavations
Witherley	Near	Yes			Yes	35+	Small				Many					Several Excavations
High Cross	Yes			Yes	Near	12	Small	Yes + Glass		Yes	Many		?	Yes		Small Excavations/ Watching Brief
Caves Inn	Prob	Yes			?Near	13+	Small			Yes	Many		On Edge		Yes	Several Excavations
Medbourne	Prob	Near	Yes	Yes		60			?	Yes	Many		On Edge			Fieldwalking/Tiny Excavations
Great Casterton	Yes	Yes		?	Yes	7 in walls	Medium	Yes	Yes		Many		Yes	Yes	Yes	Campaign of Small Excavations
Thistleton	Yes			Yes		33+	?	Near	Yes		Many	Yes	Yes	Yes	Yes	Large Excavation
Goadby Marwood	Yes		Yes			25+			Yes		Many			Yes		Watching Brief Metal Detecting
Willoughby	Prob		Yes			20+?					Many	Name	?		Yes	Small Excavations Metal Detecting
Ravenstone	?	Yes	Yes		?	9+		Yes + Tile				Circular Building			Yes	Fieldwalking Excavations Watching Brief
Market Harborough	-	Yes		Yes		7+										Casual Finds
Barrow	-	Yes		Yes		-										Tiny Excavation

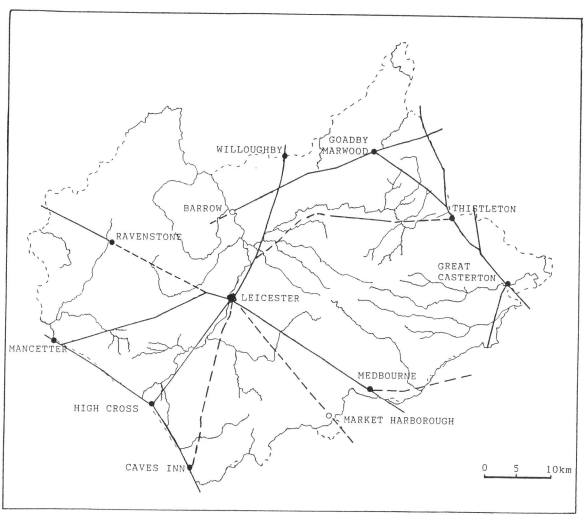

Fig 8.1 Roman towns and roads in Leicestershire

ness that much of it hath been carried by the housbandmen to further distances, like dung, to make the ground more fertile'. Early work is summarised by Pickering (1935). Widening of the A5 (Watling Street) led to excavations by Ernest Greenfield and Graham Webster (1965) and a watching brief by Jack Lucas which produced evidence of timber buildings fronting the main roads. A tessellated pavement was, apparently seen *in situ,* as were burials, but no records of their exact locations can be traced. A recent campaign of fieldwalking by the Lutterworth Archaeological Fieldwork Group has defined the shape of the scatter around the road junction, although detailed work on the material has yet to be completed. As yet, the only evidence of industry is in the form of iron slag.

Evidence of a defended area has now been produced from the air by Jim Pickering. This appears to be a small double ditched enclosure around the road junction but the full circuit is not known. A villa – at least a stone building producing tesserae – has been found by the Sapcote Fieldwork Group some 450 metres away to the east.

Caves Inn Farm (Roman name: *Tripontium*)
(Fig 8.3b)

Roman finds have been known in the vicinity of Caves Inn since the 17th century and considerable amounts of material were collected from gravel pits in the 19th and early 20th centuries (early finds summarised by Pickering 1935, 71–80). Excavations by the Rugby Archaeological Society led by Jack Lucas have produced a small (*c* 0.8 ha) rectangular defended area defined by a ditch 4.3m wide and 2.5m deep. This was bisected by Watling Street and dated to the 4th century. It lies within a considerable area on each side of the road which has produced wells, gullies, pits, timber buildings, burials and some iron slag and furnaces (Cameron & Lucas 1972). The rescue nature of the excavations has meant that, all too often, only fragmentary structures were revealed. Also, the area fronting Watling Street, where most buildings would be expected, was not threatened and, therefore, not excavated. The area has been heavily quarried so the limits of the settlement, particularly on the Leicestershire side,

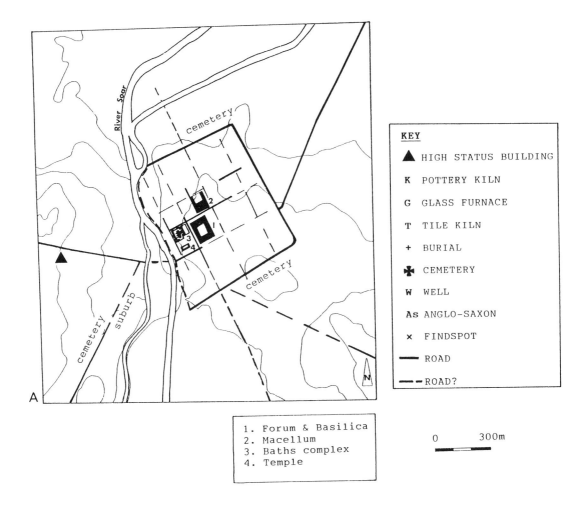

KEY

▲ HIGH STATUS BUILDING

K POTTERY KILN

G GLASS FURNACE

T TILE KILN

+ BURIAL

✸ CEMETERY

W WELL

As ANGLO-SAXON

× FINDSPOT

─── ROAD

--- ROAD?

1. Forum & Basilica
2. Macellum
3. Baths complex
4. Temple

0   300m

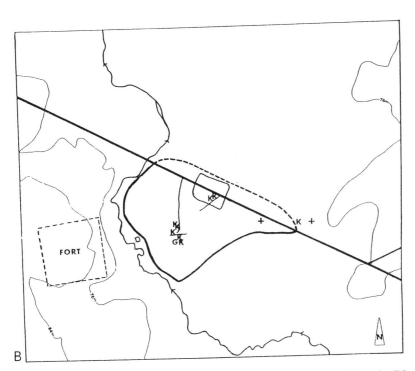

Fig 8.2 *Leicestershire: a, Leicester; b, Witherley/Mancetter*

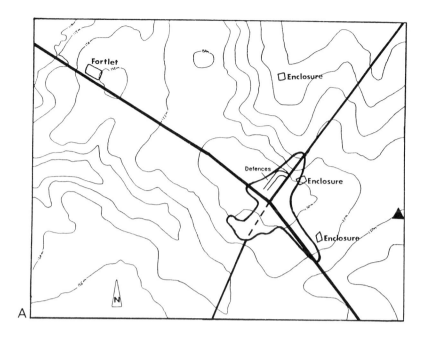

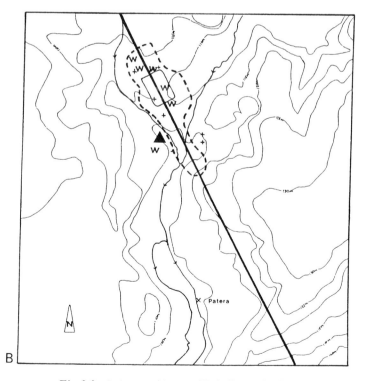

Fig 8.3 *Leicestershire: a, High Cross; b, Caves Inn*

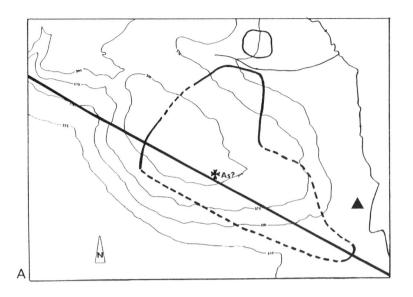

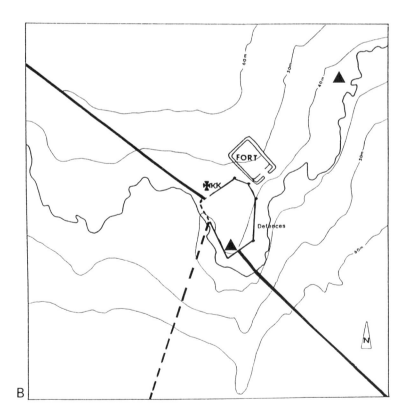

Fig 8.4 *Leicestershire: a, Medbourne; b,Great Casterton*

can probably not now be established. There is no indication of pre-Flavian occupation, although by the early 2nd century the site was intensely settled. A military skillet comes from quarries south-east of the known settlement and has been seen as evidence of a fort (Webster 1966). A stone building complex lies on the southern fringes of the settlement and has been identified as a *mansio* (Lucas, J 1981). A bath-house attached to this complex is currently being excavated (Lucas, pers comm).

Medbourne (Roman name unknown)
(Figs 8.4a and 8.7)

Around 1800 work by John Tailby of Slawston partly defined a large scatter of Roman material on Mill Hill, which produced many hundreds of coins (Nichols 1798, 717 and 1800, 540). Despite the large numbers of coins recovered, a coin list is now difficult to reconstruct as most of the coins have been lost without record. The few that can be identified range from Republican to Honorius. Recent work has produced a very large pottery scatter defining a settlement mostly along the Gartree Road, with a substantial northern extension. Sample excavation has produced evidence of stone and timber structures (none complete, but probably low status), wells, ditches, gullies, iron working hearths and inhumation burials of uncertain, but probable Anglo-Saxon, date. Iron Age and early Anglo-Saxon occupation has also been recorded. Rather poorly defined cropmarks suggest a pattern of ditched enclosures over (at least) part of the site. A high status building lies in the valley of the Medbourne Brook under the modern village. A large mosaic was found in the 18th and drawn in the 19th century (Dibden & Hill 1862). Recent work is beginning to piece together some details of the complex. A suite of rooms linked by a corridor and a possible bath-house have been recorded. Both Iron Age and Anglo-Saxon pottery have been recovered.

Recent work has also begun to define the surrounding rural settlement pattern. Six parishes to the east of the Roman small town (Medbourne, Blaston, Nevill Holt, Drayton, Bringhurst and Great Easton) have now had all their ploughed fields systematically walked. Work is now in progress in two parishes to the west (Slawston and Cranoe). It is planned to extend this work to the next three parishes which will link the area to a completed five parish survey in the Langtons, giving a block of sixteen parishes surveyed as completely as possible. The first four parishes will soon be published (Liddle, forthcoming). The Roman settlement pattern shows a succession of villas along the Welland Valley east of the town. In the uplands to the north-east are a group of 'peasant' settlements which, in contrast to the villas, all (except one) disappear during the 3rd century (Fig 8.7). The completion of the wider survey will put this into a proper context, and allow the small town to be considered in the context of a significant slice of its hinterland.

Great Casterton (Roman name unknown)
(Fig 8.4b)

Great Casterton is the other Leicestershire site considered by Burnham and Wacher (1990, 130–5). Roman defences and finds have long been known but the first modern work was carried out by University of Nottingham Summer Schools in the 1950s led by Philip Corder (1951, 1954, 1961). The earliest phase of settlement appears to be a Roman fort, immediately east of the later town (although a recent evaluation found a small amount of Iron Age pottery within the town defences). The fort was occupied from the 40s to the 80s AD (Todd 1968). The town defences enclose some 7.3 ha and were built in the late 2nd century. Corder trenched extensively within the defences but did not find any streets and he described the density of occupation as 'rather sparse'. However, only 1–2% of the interior was examined and six stone structures were revealed, while the Ermine Street frontage – where most structures would be expected – was hardly touched. Much slag was found as well as two pottery kilns producing colour-coated wares of the second half of the 2nd century to the north of the defences. A recent evaluation has produced evidence of bronze working.

The reason for the provision of defences enclosing a large proportion of this settlement in contrast to all the other Leicestershire small town sites, is quite unknown. It may be because it had a higher status, perhaps as a *pagus* centre (a subdivision of a *civitas*), or because a strategic decision had been made to defend settlements along Ermine Street. Substantial stone buildings, including a bath house, are known just inside the south gate. A large villa complex lies some 800m to the north-east.

Thistleton/Market Overton (Roman name unknown)
(Fig 8.5a)

The site was noted by early antiquaries, particularly Stukeley, who visited in 1733. Huge numbers of coins ranging from late Iron Age to late Roman have been recovered over the years (certainly several thousand). Early sources refer to 'a wall that enclosed a kind of court' said to be *c* 100 feet square and in 1910 'the foundations of a wall quite 4 feet wide showing several openings, evidently gateways, and enclosing .... about 4 acres' is mentioned (Philips 1910). Neither of these structures (if indeed they are different) can now be identified but the second sounds like a small defended area similar to Mancetter. Pottery kilns are known within a kilometre to the west.

In the 1950s Ernest Greenfield, in advance of ironstone quarrying, excavated a strip across the site. This is still unpublished and I am indebted to David Jennings for a copy of the plan of this work. Greenfield's interim report notes that he found seven stone buildings, postholes, three wells, a series of gullies, twenty three circular hearths, seventy five pits, sixty two much-used oven bases, twenty six small stone quarries and a cemetery. Clearly, this is a slice across a busy settlement where iron smelting was a major activity (Greenfield 1958).

Immediately north of this J K St Joseph photographed from the air a temple complex which was also excavated by Greenfield. The sequence apparently starts with a circular Iron Age timber building. The second phase was also circular with limestone walls and was *c* 135m in diameter with a crushed stone floor. Tessellated floors were laid before it was rebuilt as a basilican temple, some 20m x 14m with thick limestone walls. A votive object is dedicated to Veteris. Within the *temenos* a long subsidiary building with a corridor on its west side lay at right-angles to the basilica (Greenfield 1962; Lewis 1966, 84 & 93–5).

No less than twenty-nine Iron Age coins, mostly Corieltauvian silver units and half units (pers comm J May) are known from the site – by far the most from any site in Leicestershire but in line with a series of sites – mostly manifesting themselves as small towns in the Roman period – in Lincolnshire (May 1984).

Goadby Marwood (Easton parish)
(Roman name unknown) (Fig 8.5b)

This site was first noted in 1952 during ironstone quarrying. It was partly recorded by Mr Eli Coy, the quarry manager who noted 'signs of buildings' (mostly stones) , a 'plaster floor ... similar to concrete' (presumably *opus signinum*), a north-south cobbled road, an old quarry and twelve stone-lined wells. Four of these are in a south-west to north-east line and six in a south-east to north-west line and they almost certainly relate to buildings fronting the main roads through the site. 'Numerous shallow pits, roughly oval in shape .... [which] contained calcined stone and slag from the smelting of ironstone' were found in topsoil clearing and are clearly Roman bowl furnaces. Many skeletons were noted in the southern part of the site (partly published in Abbott 1956).

Since 1982 metal-detecting over the back-filled quarry has produced hundreds of Roman coins (of which well over a hundred have been identified at the Jewry Wall Museum), one Corieltauvian stater, over sixty brooches and many small finds. These include finger rings, belt fittings, dice, leather working stamps, spoons, keys, knives, bracelets, seal boxes, pendants, a votive axe, pins, weights etc. Recent fieldwork has shown that the site extends to the north-west and that an 'island' of surviving archaeology exists between old quarries.

The next hamlet to the south of Goadby is called Wycomb making this one of a group of small towns associated with the *wicham* names noted by Margaret Gelling (1967).

Willoughby on the Wolds/Wymeswold
(Roman name: *Vernemetum*) (Fig 8.6a)

Stukeley visited the site in 1722 when the area was under open field agriculture, and his observations are still the basis for our understanding of it. An area of dark soil associated with Roman material was visible on the northern (Nottinghamshire) side of the valley of the Willoughby Brook and similar evidence was visible on the south side of the valley in an area called 'Wells'. Small-scale excavations have recently been published by Gavin Kinsley (1993). These confirmed the line of the Fosse Way some way to the west of the modern A46 and produced one unequivocal rectangular timber building, and a spread of stone which may represent a robbed out stone building. Fragments of other timber buildings were also seen and a stone column fragment of 3rd–4th century date was recovered which clearly indicates a sophisticated stone building in the vicinity. A series of enclosures defined by ditches was recorded near the road. Recent metal-detecting has produced many Roman coins, brooches (mostly 1st-2nd century in date) and other small finds, including rings, pins, bracelets and strap-ends (as well as Middle/Late Anglo-Saxon material) in the southern (Leics) area. Stukeley spoke to a farmer who had ploughed up tessellated pavements but whether these were in the settlement or belong to a villa lying close by is not known (Nichols 1795, 120–1).

Ravenstone/Ibstock (Roman name unknown)
(Fig 8.6b)

This site was discovered in 1976. A single pit was noted by Arthur Hurst during the construction of a power line and 400m to the south-east Jim Pickering photographed a series of cropmarks. It took eight years of fieldwork by Arthur Hurst and the North-West Leicestershire Archaeological Fieldwork Group to fill the gap. Pottery survived poorly because of the acid nature of the soil and the site was under-estimated, leading to partial destruction by opencast mining and an associated treatment works. In 1981 three pottery kilns, producing grey ware probably of 3rd century date, a later tile kiln, a cemetery, a circular stone building, 10.5m in diameter, and a post-built rectangular building some 4m x 6m, were excavated at the west end of the site (J N Lucas 1981). In 1984 eight Roman buildings – all simple stone strip buildings – were noted in a watching brief in the central sector. Only the eastern sector remains substantially undamaged. The site is clearly aligned on a Roman road running west-north-west to east-south-east (although this was not seen in the watching brief). This has recently been traced for some 25km to join Ryknield Street and, in the other direction, must run to Leicester (Liddle & Hartley forthcoming). A rectangular cropmark north of the site coincides with a Roman pottery scatter and seems to include another pot-

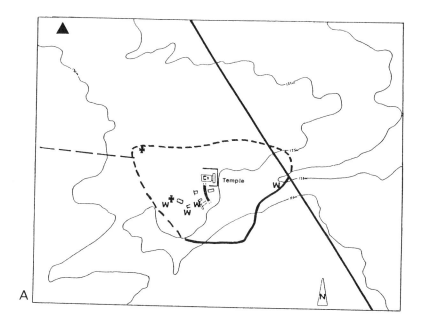

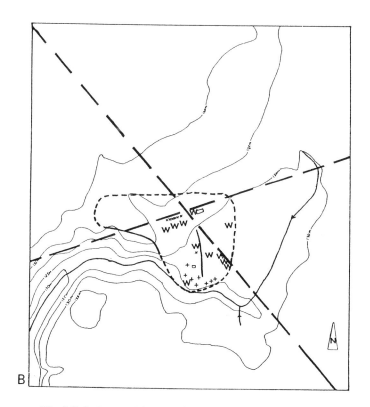

Fig 8.5 *Leicestershire: a, Thistleton; b, Goadby Marwood*

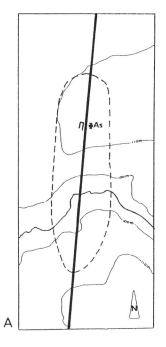

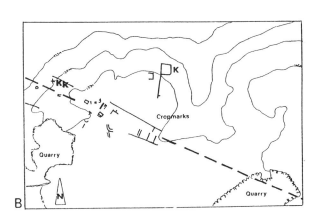

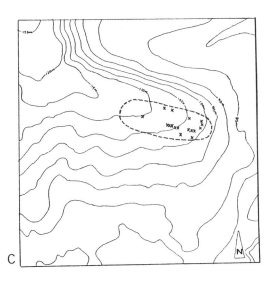

Fig 8.6 *Leicestershire: a, Willoughby; b, Ravenstone/Ibstock; c, Market Harborough*

tery kiln. The records of the late Arthur Hurst's work have been lodged with Leicestershire Museums and it is hoped to publish them with the results of the 1981 excavations.

Other possible sites
Market Harborough (Fig 8.6c)

The best candidate so far known is at The Ridgeway, Market Harborough. Querns and a few sherds of Iron Age pottery were found here in the 1930s, but it was not until houses were built in the 1950s that Roman material was found. Since then fourteen gardens have produced material including four hundred sherds and coins (mostly from an appeal to residents in the early 1980s). The coins are late 3rd and 4th century, but the pottery sequence runs from the late Iron Age to the late Roman period. Fieldwalking is impossible because the area behind the houses is permanent pasture with prominent ridge and furrow, but several sherds have been picked up there. At least seven hectares of material is indicated. The topography – on a flat topped ridge close to a river crossing with some (admittedly tenuous) indications of a Roman road – is reminiscent of the other small town sites.

Barrow-on-Soar/Quorndon

A second possibility lies north of Leicester where the Salt Way crosses the River Soar. The area alongside the river crossing is permanent pasture on each side. Much Roman pottery (over 1,600 sherds) and a few coins with some building material were recovered during gravel quarrying in the 1950s. Recently a considerable number of Roman coins and small finds has been produced by metal-detecting on a site nearby on the west bank of the River Soar in Quorndon parish. Other finds have been found in and around Barrow-on-Soar. It is still unclear whether these finds represent a large settlement or a series of small sites. It is hoped to launch a fieldwork group in Barrow and this will be a major problem to be tackled.

Others

The spacing of the sites is in general remarkably even except in the east of Leicestershire, where there is a prominent gap. Certainly the area supported an Iron Age centre at Burrough Hill – where small-scale excavation has revealed occupation well into the 4th century AD. Not enough is known to assess its Roman status. Some 10km south of Burrough a large cropmark enclosure has been recorded at Skeffington. It is almost of hill fort proportions. Metal-detecting has produced over 200 coins, over 40 brooches, steelyard weights etc. More work is required to properly assess the site (C Dawson, pers comm), but details of the finds are held in the Leicestershire Sites and Monuments Record and it is clear that the material spans the entire period from the late Iron Age to the late Roman period.

The small towns as a group
Distribution

The definite small towns (leaving out those to the northeast where the status of some sites is unclear) are, on average, 23 kilometres from Leicester but are only 15 kilometres from one another (again, not including the East Leicestershire problem area). The distribution is very similar to that of medieval market towns. Although never coinciding, there is a close correspondence between the two groups of sites. A similar function might be suspected. Although archaeologists tend to look for evidence of metal-working and pottery production to suggest an industrial element at our small towns, it should be noted that the documentary evidence from medieval towns indicates that agricultural processing, such as leather working, brewing and baking were predominant.

Table 8.1 shows the evidence from each of the settlements set out under general headings: site; history; character; industry; coins; buildings and, so that these can be assessed, archaeological history.

Siting

All the definite sites are on known Roman roads and most (and perhaps all) are at or near road junctions. Most are close to river or stream crossings where communications would be channelled.

Origin

The origin of the settlements is generally uncertain because of the lack of excavation at most of the sites. Although not yet fully published, the interims strongly suggest that Thistleton had an Iron Age origin and the temple and coin finds argue for a high status, perhaps a Corieltauvian royal centre. Elsewhere small excavations have produced Iron Age material underlying the small towns at Medbourne and High Cross. Many writers have seen Roman military activity as the origin of a large proportion of small town sites – with Great Casterton as a classic example and Mancetter/Witherley in the same category. It would be foolish to deny that this must sometimes have been the case, but it should be remembered that military establishments were sometimes placed to police existing Iron Age settlements (as at Leicester) and the discovery of some Iron Age material at Great Casterton raises some doubt even here.

Character

Our present estimates of size may well be in need of considerable revision. Recent work at Medbourne and Goadby Marwood, for example, has shown them to be bigger than previously known, while at High Cross the site has proved to be smaller. More work is clearly needed.

Defences indicate official interest in some of the set-

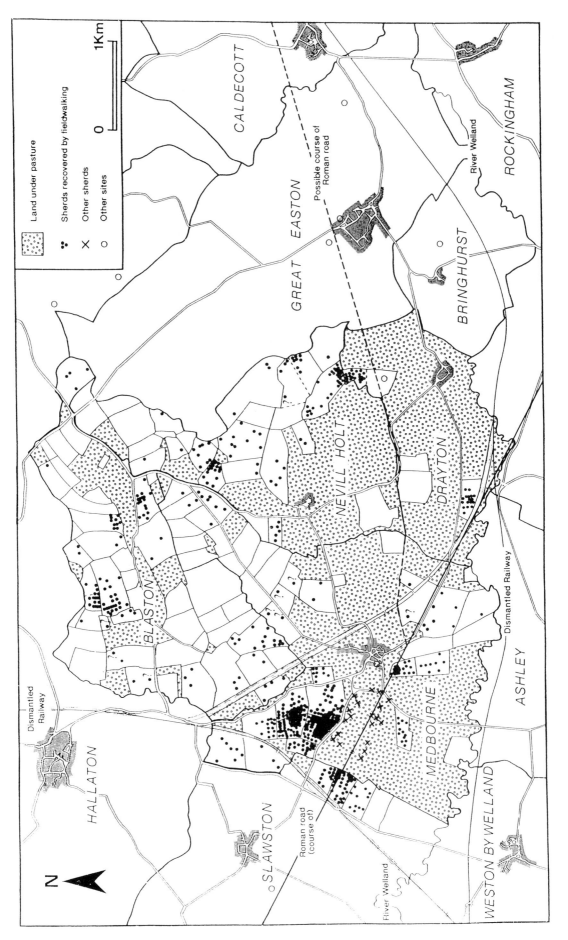

Fig 8.7 Leicestershire: Roman finds in the Medbourne survey area

tlements. The large investment in town defences at Leicester is not surprising but why Great Casterton should be singled out for town walls is more problematic. The small enclosures on Watling Street are quite different in character, defending only a tiny area within the settlement. These have been termed *burgi* by Graham Webster (1974) but resemble nothing more than secure lorry parks for traffic along the Watling Street. It may be that the series of sites along Ermine Street is an earlier, and more ambitious, version of the same thing or was designed to act as a back-stop to the coastal defences (but see Charmian Woodfield, this volume).

Industry, coins and buildings

Bearing in mind the relatively small amount of work undertaken at many of these sites, it is remarkable that virtually all produce evidence of industry, mostly pottery making and iron working, but also glass making (Mancetter), tile making (Ravenstone), bronze working (Great Casterton) and leather working, indicated by metal punches (Goadby Marwood). Commercial activity is surely indicated by the huge numbers of coins produced by these sites (literally thousands are known from some of the better documented ones). The strip buildings known at many of the sites probably fall into the same sort of context, being best interpreted as, for the most part, craft workshops. Only Thistleton, so far, has produced a temple although others will probably come to light (the site at Red Hill, Ratcliffe-on-Soar, just over the border in Nottinghamshire seems to be a small town around a temple complex). Willoughby's Roman name, *Vernemetum* (meaning Great Sacred Grove) clearly implies a religious dimension at this site.

There are few high status buildings within the settlements. Only Great Casterton has a well documented example – what sounds like a bath-house immediately inside the south gate – but a tessellated floor was seen in roadworks at High Cross in 1957 while Stukeley's tessellated pavements at Willoughby/Wymeswold may be another example. Each could be related to a *mansio*, although the most convincing example is the building on the edge of Cave's Inn excavated by Jack Lucas. The building close to the Medbourne site, in contrast, seems to be a genuinely high status ('villa-type') complex. Malcolm Todd (1973, 69) has noted the close relationship between villas and many of these settlements and has suggested that they may be peasant agricultural villages for workers on the villa estate. As indicated above I do not accept the conclusion and yet a relationship does appear to exist with many 'villas' within a few hundred metres. An alternative explanation is widely accepted to explain the creation of markets in the Middle Saxon period, which was also a period of transition between an economy embedded in social relations and a (partial) money economy. It is argued that markets were created close to estate centres where renders in kind (ale, bread, grain etc) which were originally consumed by peripatetic royal/noble households, could be sold off as a centralising society made their original function redundant. In this model the 'villas' would be the estate centres and the 'small towns' the markets. A market of this sort could then attract craftsmen. I would not put this forward as a complete explanation for the creation of small towns in the 1st century AD, but it is a model worth considering for at least some of these sites. Clearly, if this model is correct, the 'villas' would need to be earlier than the 'towns'. Only a very few have had even limited excavation. The Medbourne and Thistleton villas both have evidence of Iron Age occupation, although at neither has excavation been extensive enough to suggest whether this is likely to have been high status. At Great Casterton all the excavated buildings were late 3rd/early 4th century or later. However, there are indications that the excavated area lies on the southern fringe of a large complex and the northern area produced significantly earlier material. No other site produces even this limited information.

Clearly, more work is needed at most of the sites mentioned here. Work at Medbourne where the town site is being sampled and a large slice of the surrounding landscape is being fieldwalked offers the best chance in Leicestershire of understanding a small town in the context of its surrounding landscape.

Bibliography

Abbott, R D, 1956 Roman discoveries at Goadby Marwood, *Trans Leicestershire Archaeol Hist Soc*, 32, 17–35

Buckley, R J, & Lucas, J N, 1987 *Leicester town defences*

Burnham, B C, & Wacher, J, 1990 *The 'small towns' of Roman Britain*

Cameron, H, & Lucas, J, 1972 *Tripontium*, second interim report, *Birmingham Warwickshire Archaeol Soc Trans*, 85, 93–144

Clay, P N, 1988 *Leicester before the Romans*

Corder, P (ed), 1951 *The Roman town and villa at Great Casterton, Rutland*, by members of the summer school in Roman-British archaeology held at Great Casterton, 1950

——, 1954 *The Roman town and villa at Great Casterton, Rutland. Second interim report for the years 1951–1953*, University of Nottingham

——, 1961 *The Roman town and villa at Great Casterton, Rutland. Third report for the years 1954–1958*, University of Nottingham

Dibbin, H A, & Hill, J H, 1862 Medbourne tessellated pavement, *Trans Leicestershire Archaeol Hist Soc*, 5, 69–71

Gelling, M, 1967 English place names derived from the compound *Wicham, Medieval Archaeol*, 2, 87–114

Greenfield, E, 1958 Thistleton, in Roman Britain in 1957, *J Roman Stud*, 48, 137

——, 1962 Thistleton, in Roman Britain in 1961, *J Roman Stud*, 52, 172–3

——, & Webster, G, 1965 Excavations at High Cross 1955, *Trans Leicestershire Archaeol Hist Soc*, 40, 3–41

Hartley, K, 1973 Mancetter, Warks, in *Trans Leicestershire Archaeol Hist Soc*, 47, 72

Kinsley, A G, 1993 *Broughton Lodge – excavations on a Romano-British settlement and Anglo-Saxon cemetery at Broughton Lodge, Willoughby-on-the-Wolds, Notts*, University of Nottingham

Lewis, M J T, 1966 *Temples in Roman Britain*

Liddle, P, forthcoming A Welland Valley landscape – the Medbourne area archaeological survey

——, & Hartley, R F , forthcoming A Roman road through north-west Leicestershire, *Trans Leicestershire Archaeol Hist Soc*

Lucas, J, 1981 *Tripontium*, third interim report, *Birmingham Warwickshire Archaeol Soc Trans,* 56, 104–107

Lucas, J N, 1981 A Romano-British settlement at Ravenstone, *Trans Leicestershire Archaeol Hist Soc*, 56, 104–107

Mahany, C, 1971 Excavations in Manduessedum, 1964, *Birmingham Warwickshire Archaeol Soc Trans*, 84, 18–44

May, J, 1984 The major settlements of the later Iron Age in Lincolnshire, in *A prospect of Lincolnshire* (ed N Field & A Winter)

Mellor, J E, 1976 Roman Leicester, in C D B Ellis, *History in Leicester*

——, & Lucas, J N, 1979 The Roman villa at Norfolk St, Leicester, *Trans Leicestershire Archaeol Hist Soc*, 54, 68–70

Nichols, J, 1795 *History and antiquities of the county of Leicester*, 2, pt 1

——, 1798 *History and antiquities of the county of Leicester*, 2, pt 2

——, 1800 *History and antiquities of the county of Leicester*, 3, pt 1

Oswald, A, & Gathercole, P W, 1958 Observations and excavations at Manduessedum 1954–6, *Birmingham Warwickshire Archaeol Soc Trans*, 74, 30–52

Philips, G, 1910 Market Overton, *Rutland Magazine*, 1, 129–136, 161–7

Pickering, A J, 1935 The Roman sites of south-west Leicestershire, *Trans Leicestershire Archaeol Hist Soc*, 18, 44–85, 157–194

Scott, K, 1981 Mancetter village: a first century fort, *Birmingham Warwickshire Archaeol Soc Trans*, 91, 2–24

Todd, M 1968 *The Roman fort at Great Casterton*, University of Nottingham

——, 1973 *The Coritani*

Webster, G, 1966 A Roman bronze saucepan from Caves Inn, *Birmingham Warwickshire Archaeol Soc Trans*, 81, 143–4

——, 1974 The West Midlands in the Roman period, *Birmingham Warwickshire Archaeol Soc Trans*, 86, 49–58

9   Some Roman small towns in north Lincolnshire and south Humberside

Ben Whitwell

Introduction

This paper gives an interim report on recent fieldwork carried out on four Roman small towns north of Lincoln. The work forms part of a survey of the 26 or so small towns known in Lincolnshire and has been assisted by a grant from the Royal Archaeological Institute. Most of these sites have been briefly mentioned or discussed in Whitwell 1982 and 1992. The sites described in this article form an ill-defined group. The first three, at Owmby, Hibaldstow and Winteringham, lie approximately equidistant on Ermine Street north of Lincoln on its course to the Humber. Kirmington, on the other hand, lies on the Lincolnshire Wolds two miles or so to the east of the course of Caistor High Street, a presumed prehistoric trackway which is thought to have continued in use throughout the Roman period (Fig 9.1). Virtually all the sites described as Roman small towns in Lincolnshire are on arable land, and though quite a number of them are scheduled as Ancient Monuments, often very little is known about them beyond the approximate area from which surface finds have been recovered. Even at the few sites where there have been major campaigns of excavation, such as Hibaldstow, Ancaster and Sapperton, we are left with the basic questions about origin, function and demise of the settlements far from completely resolved.

The following section describes ongoing work at each of the four sites before turning in the final section to a general discussion.

Sites on Ermine Street

1. *Owmby* (Fig 9.2)

The course of Ermine Street itself is clear at Owmby from the aerial photographs. The modern road has veered to the east around Blacklands Wood so that a stretch of the Roman road is seen on aerial photographs lying to the west of the modern road both to the south and north of Blacklands Wood itself. The area of the Roman settlement on the western side of Ermine Street appears to coincide with the western edge of Blacklands Wood. To the north and south of the wood dark occupation soil appears to give way to

the lighter colour of the surrounding arable land, approximately in line with the western side of the wood. Though aerial photographs show a side road at right angles to Ermine Street to the south of the wood and other markings, it is on the eastern side of Ermine Street that the major part of the settlement lies, and here aerial photographs show an irregular arc of enclosures running out from Ermine Street to the south, and returning to Ermine Street at the point where the approach road to Owmby Cliff Farm branches off to the north-east.

Apart from Blacklands Wood itself, the site is totally arable and has been known for many years for the quantity of metal detected finds which have come from it. Largely on account of this, and aided by the somewhat sparse information provided by the aerial photographs, the site has been scheduled. No excavations have taken place here but fieldwalking undertaken by the writer with members of an Adult Education class, has started to define the area of settlement, particularly on the eastern side of Ermine Street. Opposite Blacklands Wood, for instance, the major area of settlement extends some 120 metres into the field with an outlying area of dense pottery scatters between 150 and 200 metres into the field. Further north, the area running north-eastwards from the corner of Blacklands Wood is the course of an old stream and here the pottery lies concentrated to either side of the filled-in course of the stream on a north-east/south-west alignment. Beyond the 200 metre mark east of Ermine Street there is a thin scatter of pottery extending to the eastern field boundary at approximately 420 metres from Ermine Street. It is in this area that a small quantity of slag and industrial material has been found in the form of fragments of burnt clay. This is too thin a scatter to point to industrial concentrations but does suggest that on this downward slope of the limestone, industrial activity was taking place. Among the few finds of pottery in this same area of possible industrial activity, a number of rims of large shelly ware storage jars have been noted. These are of types which could either be of late Iron Age or early Romano-British date. It was hoped that fieldwork in this field would give some clues to the date of the arc of enclosures observable on the

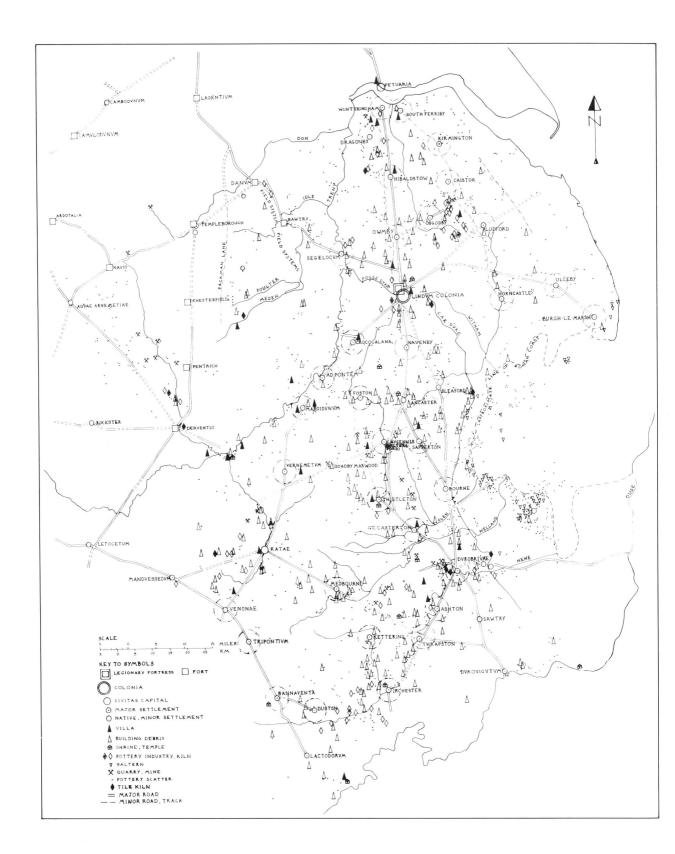

Fig 9.1 *Romano-British settlement in the East Midlands (after Whitwell 1982)*

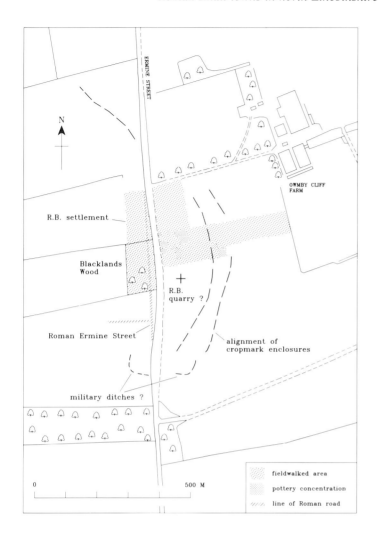

Fig 9.2 Owmby (based on an initial plot of aerial photographs)

aerial photographs. Though the fieldwork is as yet incomplete, the swathe that has been walked through the area of these enclosures suggests Roman occupation with a hint of some possible Iron Age pottery types, as noted above, to their east. One major purpose in the fieldwaking at Owmby was to try and define the area of Iron Age settlement which is hinted at by the finds of later Iron Age brooches, coins and other artefacts found by metal detectorists (Whitwell 1965, fig 4a, for mid 1st century AD brooch types and some possible military equipment). Indeed if the Iron Age coin record for Owmby is to be believed, standing as it does at well over 50, then this should be one of the most important Iron Age sites known in Lincolnshire (Whitwell 1982, 16). However since these are all metal detected finds their provenances are unknown and in some cases must remain in considerable doubt. Fieldwalking to the west of Ermine Street has concentrated on the area to the north of the wood, where some Iron Age pottery in the form of pedestal bases and one sherd from a curvilinear rouletted bowl has been found. These are similar to Iron Age pottery forms found in Phases I and II at Dragonby, near Scunthorpe, dating to the 1st century BC (May 1970, figs 7 & 8). In this area to the north of the wood,

English Heritage have undertaken some trial geophysical work. Though this has yet to be tested, it suggests a regular layout of Roman rectangular buildings and the possibility of a back lane parallel to Ermine Street and at approximately 70 to 80 metres to the west of it. Trial geophysical work in the area of Blacklands Wood has also proved promising and it is hoped that English Heritage will be able to return there in the future as this is the one area of the site which has not been intensively cultivated. Iron Age roulette-decorated pottery has also been located within Blacklands Wood, in recent clearance.

Only one possible clue as to the whereabouts of Roman military installations has been found at Owmby, on an aerial photograph of the southern end of the site. This shows rectilinear ditches with rounded corners both to the west and east of Ermine Street though not on the same alignment (Everson & Hayes 1984, fig 10). Though they are somewhat faint, the marks to the west of Ermine Street particularly do look remarkably like the double ditches of a fort enclosure. This appears to be the only photographic evidence of a possible military phase at Owmby, though, as noted above, there are a few finds of 1st century military date from the metal detected collections from the site, whose precise provenance is not known.

One final point on Owmby concerns a large dark mark, visible on aerial photographs, to the east of Ermine Street opposite Blacklands Wood, where field walking has produced Roman pottery from an area of slight depression. At Hibaldstow there is a similar large dark mark visible on the air photographs and a more pronounced depression on the ground to the east of Ermine Street. It is possible that these may represent Roman quarry pits.

2. *Hibaldstow* (Fig 9.3)

Here excavations on the western side of Ermine Street have been occasioned by proposals to widen the course of the modern road. A series of excavations in the 1970s conducted by Roger Smith (Smith 1987, 189–194) was followed in the 1980s by further work by the Humberside Archaeology Unit (not yet published). This work has defined a series of strip buildings to the west of Ermine Street and lying either side of a shallow valley, running north-west to south-east across the line of Ermine Street. The valley contains a stream which may well have formed a major source of water for the settlement. Geophysical work by English Heritage to the south of the area of excavation suggests that the settlement extended in the form of ditched enclosures for about 800 metres along the line of Ermine Street. Though these remain to a large extent untested, one of them was investigated by Roger Smith and found to have a timber building within it. Other large anomalies found within the enclosures might possibly represent well pits since this area lay on the limestone plateau at some distance from the water source provided by the stream.

The site was first mentioned by Abraham de la Pryme in his diaries in 1697. He says that the main area of settlement lay between two springs called Castletown and Jenny Stanney and refers to a tradition that there had been an old city here. The spring of Jenny Stanney accounts for the stream which ran in the shallow valley mentioned above, and the Castletown spring lies to the south in a fold of the limestone escarpment and is now piped virtually all the way across the area of Roman settlement. Both springs rise well to the west of Ermine Street and ran across its course. It appears that remains of the buildings survived above ground in the late 19th century when they were recorded as making a playground for the local children. It is also recorded that cartfuls of stone were taken away from the site at about this time (Dudley 1949, 159). From the evidence of the excavations occupation on the site seems to have started in the later 1st century at the earliest and continued through into the 4th century, though, as one might expect, it lasted longer in some buildings than in others. One of the buildings excavated on the north side of the valley appears to have been burnt down during the 4th century, whereas one of those buildings on its south side appears to have had a further period of use, when a metalled surface was

laid over the top of the remains of the building perhaps during the late 4th or early 5th century.

Fieldwork by the writer, again with the assistance of an Adult Education class, concentrated on the east side of Ermine Street and defined an area of occupation at some distance from the strip settlement, which lined the west and east sides of Ermine Street. Here, at the southeast corner of Castlehill field, there was evidence of buildings in the form of stone, tile and tesserae. Also considerable quantities of slag and much burnt tile which, although not in the form of wasters, suggests the possibility of tile production in the vicinity. It is hoped that at some stage in the future it may be possible to check these preliminary results with geophysical survey. Further east along Manton Lane the remains of a villa were fieldwalked. This had first been disturbed by the laying of the railway in 1868. Its perimeter ditches and area of buildings were defined by a geophysical survey carried out ahead of a British Gas pipeline. Fieldwalking defined an area of tesserae adjacent to the railway which clearly had destroyed part of the main buildings of the villa. Alongside the perimeter ditch of the villa in the field to the west, two late Roman burials were discovered. However the main gain in our knowledge of the settlement at Hibaldstow comes from the field to the east of Ermine Street and adjacent to and east of the stream which ran through the shallow valley. Here a small amount of Iron Age pottery, in the form of pedestal bases as discovered at Owmby, and also of pagan Anglo-Saxon pottery has been found. Though the amount of material so far is small, these discoveries do suggest both a pre-Roman settlement close to the Roman 'small town' and also some form of occupation, however transitory, in the post-Roman period. At this stage nothing can be said about the size or status of either the pre – or post-Roman phases at Hibaldstow, or their relationship to the 'small town'. Knowledge of early Anglo-Saxon settlement in this area has tended to be confined to sites along the limestone escarpment immediately west of Middle Street (Fig 9.3). So the discovery of Anglo-Saxon pottery adjacent to Ermine Street is of particular interest.

Unlike Owmby there have not been large quantities of metal detected finds recorded and there is no evidence of an early Roman military phase.

3. *Winteringham* (Fig 9.4)

The site has been the subject of excavations by Ian Stead (Stead 1976) and subsequently by the Humberside Archaeology Unit (briefly noted in Whitwell 1983, 10). Ermine Street divides as it approaches the settlement here and remains have been found along the two arms of the road. Ian Stead's excavations concentrated on an area at the junction and the later work was further east, to the south of the eastern arm of the road as it headed down towards a possible jetty site on the Roman foreshore. This excavation was brought about by proposals to ex-

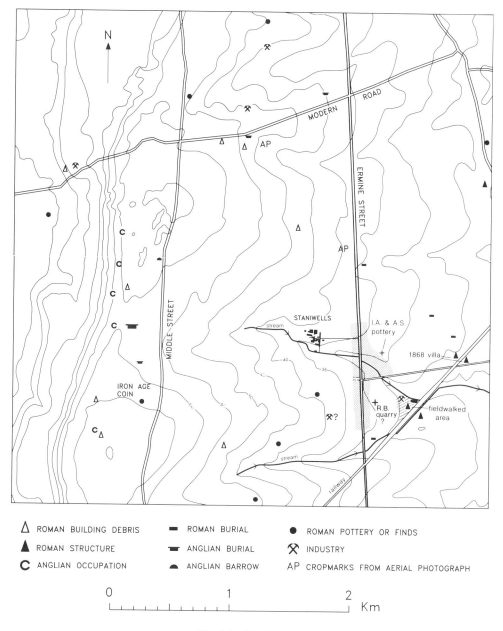

Fig 9.3 *Hibaldstow*

tend Sandhills Quarry and defined the areas of a succession of enclosure ditches which probably belonged to properties fronting on to the eastern arm of Ermine Street, which lay outside the area available for excavation. Though the site has long been known by the extensive scatter of surface finds which include both Iron Age and Romano-British material, there has been no hint of a military installation detectable either from the finds or from the aerial photographs. However the construction of a chicken farm to the north of Composition Lane which lies just outside the scheduled area and is adjacent to the Humber foreshore to the north of the site, revealed a series of coins and 1st century pottery which is likely to have belonged to an early military installation. In order to follow up these chance discoveries the writer instigated further geophysical work to the south of Composition Lane and here a series of small fields or enclosures detected by English Heritage remain undated since fieldwalking has produced only a few indeterminate sherds. This area clearly needs further work in order to determine whether there is any further evidence for military activity on this part of the site.

Old Winteringham has produced no evidence to date of early Anglian settlement and the earliest evidence for post-Roman occupation comes from sites within the medieval and modern village of Winteringham lying a short distance to the north-west of the Roman site.

Roman burials have been noted in the past to the south of Sluice Lane and in the angle formed by Sluice Lane and the road running north-west to Winteringham

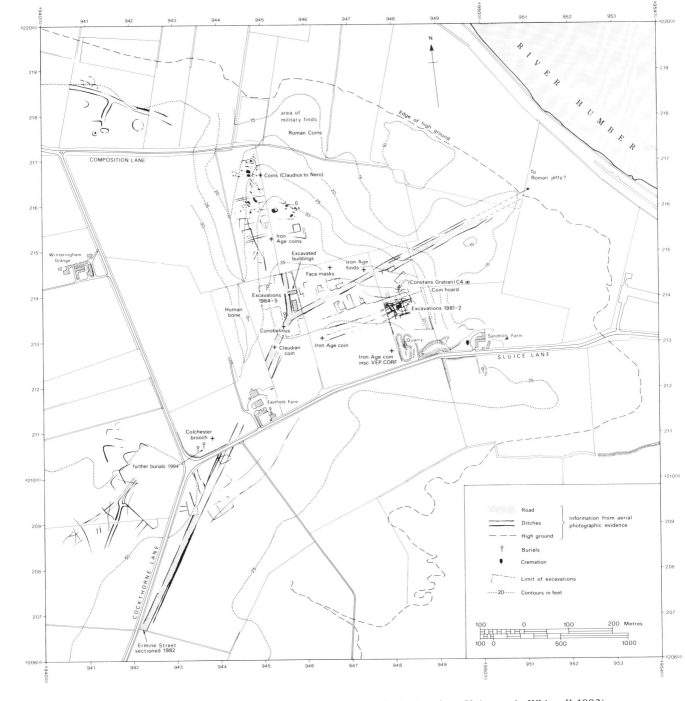

Fig 9.4 *Winteringham (plan by Rob Gillam, Humberside Archaeology Unit – as in Whitwell 1983)*

village. Six further burials were recorded in the latter area in April 1994 by the Humberside Archaeology Unit.

4. *Kirmington* (Fig 9.5)

Kirmington is different from the three sites which have been described above in that it does not lie on the course of a major Roman road. Indeed it lies on the Wolds at some little distance to the west of the probable line of Caistor High Street mentioned above. The site was first

discovered during the construction of a Second World War airfield and since then large collections of finds have been metal detected from the site, over an area of approximately 70 to 80 hectares. Apart from surface finds, the site has the rare distinction of a particularly good record from aerial photographs. The evidence from the air and from the ground has been reviewed in a recent article (Jones & Whitwell 1991). To summarise briefly, there is evidence of an Iron Age settlement here in the form of irregular enclosures which are overlaid by the double ditches of a

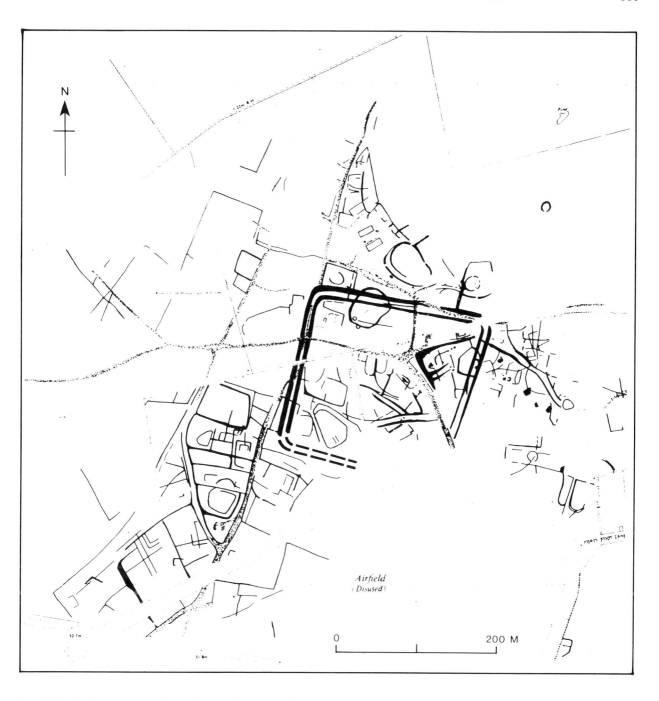

Fig 9.5 Kirmington (reproduced by permission of the Royal Commission on Historic Monuments – based on Jones & Whitwell 1991)

slightly trapezoidal-shaped fort, enclosing an area of approximately 3.4 hectares. This in turn is overlaid by a series of meandering metalled tracks which serve a series of enclosures and rectangular buildings belonging to Roman civilian settlement. Here, as at Owmby, the record of metal-detected Iron Age finds includes coins, brooches and other artefacts. There are also a few sherds of Iron Age pottery which are imprecisely provenanced.

There are very few finds which can be ascribed with certainty to the Roman military phase even though there is clear evidence from the aerial photographs of a fort

enclosure. A little military-type pottery in orange fabric has now been located from recent fieldwork on the site and from early finds housed in Scunthorpe Museum. The Roman civilian finds from the area are many and the coin list continues strongly to the end of the 4th and beginning of the 5th century with coins of the emperors Honorius and Arcadius. The strong coin list at the end of the Roman period at Kirmington stands comparison with those from Old Winteringham and also other late Roman sites adjacent to the Humber at South Ferriby and Deepdale, Barrow (Whitwell 1988). At Kirmington the period from *c* AD 380 onwards is represented by 80–90 coins.

Fieldwalking undertaken by the Humberside Archaeology Unit has covered a large part of the site and confirms the main areas of Roman civilian occupation though adding little to evidence for either pre-Roman or early Roman military occupation. Nor was there any further fieldwalking evidence to support the remarkable series of late Roman and early Anglo-Saxon metalwork which has been found on the site. Some of the more important pieces including zoomorphic late Roman buckles, a *tutulus* brooch, the knobbed terminal of a cruciform brooch, and part of a wrist clasp are noted, with a bibliography by Jones and Whitwell (1991, 60). The medieval and modern village of Kirmington lies a half a mile or so to the east of the Roman settlement, and such hints as there are from the aerial photographs, suggest the possibility of Anglo-Saxon occupation between the two.

The settlement at Kirmington differs in form from the linear arrangement of Owmby and Hibaldstow which focus on Ermine Street. In its more irregular arrangement it is perhaps more akin to the Iron Age and Roman open settlement at Dragonby, near Scunthorpe (Burnham & Wacher 1990, fig 7), with which it is also similar in being served by a minor road. However, though not arranged in a regular grid, the metalled tracks of Kirmington do appear to have been laid out with some semblance of order in having a main crossroads with possible back lanes to the west. From the aerial photographs it is also clear that Kirmington shares with Ixworth in Suffolk the successive phases of an irregular layout of metalled tracks belonging to a civilian settlement superseding the ditches of a fort (Frere & St Joseph 1983, 94–6, pls 52 & 54).

Discussion

All four, or five if we count Dragonby, of the sites mentioned in this article have some evidence of Iron Age occupation. In the case of Owmby it can be said to be extensive, extending to both west and east of Ermine Street as we now know from the results of fieldwork. If we are to take into account and trust the presumed provenance of the many Iron Age coins reported to have come from the site then this was indeed an important settlement and in that respect it is surprising that there is no certain evidence of military activity on the site, although we have mentioned the possibility of military style ditches from the evidence of air photographs.

At Hibaldstow until very recently evidence for Iron Age occupation was completely lacking. It remains for further work to define the extent of the Iron Age site discovered to the east of Ermine Street beside the stream and to decide whether this would have been of a size and importance to warrant suppression by the planting of a fort. Again there is as yet no evidence at all of any such military activity.

Again at Old Winteringham, though the fort had long been searched for, it has eluded all aerial reconnaissance.

It is a sad irony that the discovery of the likely fort site was made in conditions which did not allow any controlled excavation.

At Kirmington as we have seen there is aerial photographic evidence of the Iron Age and Roman military phases of activity on the site, though the photographic evidence for the Iron Age settlement does not suggest a particularly large or important one. However its importance can best be gauged from the fact that it was thought necessary to plant a fort at this point. It should be said that the date of the fort remains untested but in an interpretation of the aerial photographs it seems fairly clear that it overlies the irregular enclosures of the Iron Age and this in turn was superseded by the metalled trackways of the civilian settlement.

Finally it is interesting to draw attention to the fact that the settlements that we have discussed are all without defences. This seems particularly strange in the case of Winteringham which lay immediately adjacent to the Humber and in a particularly vulnerable position. Nevertheless the occupation at Winteringham continued right down to the end of the Roman period. At Kirmington we have some evidence for continuation until the 5th or 6th century. For reasons which are not clear at this stage it was the settlements at Caistor and Horncastle that received late Roman defensive works whereas the sites which would appear on the face of it to be even more vulnerable, being closer to the threats from seaward invasion, were not protected in this way.

Bibliography

Burnham, B C, & Wacher, J, 1990 *The 'small towns' of Roman Britain*

Dudley, H E, 1949 *Early days in North West Lincolnshire*

Everson, P, & Hayes, J T, 1984 Lincolnshire from the air, in *A prospect of Lincolnshire* (ed N Field & A White)

Frere, S, & St Joseph, J K, 1983 *Roman Britain from the air*

Jones, D, & Whitwell, J B, 1991 Survey of the Roman fort and multi-period settlement complex at Kirmington on the Lincolnshire Wolds, *Lincolnshire Hist Archaeol*, 26, 57–62

May, J, 1970 Dragonby: an interim report on excavation of an Iron Age and Romano-British site near Scunthorpe, Lincolnshire, 1964–9, *Antiq J*, 50, 222–245

Price, J, & Wilson, P R (eds), 1988 *Recent research in Roman Yorkshire*, BAR Brit Ser, 193

Smith, R F, 1987 *Roadside settlements in lowland Roman Britain*, BAR Brit Ser, 157

Stead, I M, 1976 *Excavations at Winterton Roman villa and other sites in North Lincolnshire*, Dept Environment Archaeol Rep 9

Whitwell, J B, 1965 Archaeological notes 1964–5, *Lincolnshire Hist Archaeol*, 2, 31–54

——, 1982 *The Coritani: some aspects of the Iron Age tribe and the Roman civitas*, BAR Brit Ser, 99

——, 1983 Old Winteringham, *Lincolnshire Hist Archaeol*, 18, 103

——, 1988 Late Roman settlement on the Humber and Anglian beginnings, in Price & Wilson 1988

——, 1992 *Roman Lincolnshire* (revised edition)

10 When is a town not a town? 'Small towns' on the Nene and Welland in their context

Frances Condron

Introduction

This paper presents an alternative approach to the study of towns and their relations with other settlements. It uses the area around *Durobrivae*, Ashton and Great Casterton to illustrate the argument. The main thrust is that only a relatively small section of the population was involved in acquiring the goods and practices of being Roman; the towns themselves served only a minority – those nearby, and the people of the richest rural settlements. Most people were either not able or had no desire to get involved in the Roman economy, relying more on small, local networks that did not operate through an urban market.

Most research on 'Small Towns' has focussed on the archaeology of the settlements themselves. Accordingly, the three settlements of *Durobrivae*, Ashton, and Great Casterton have been accepted as 'small towns', though with due caution as to their actual functions in the landscape (Burnham & Wacher 1990, chaps 6, 8 and 12). The approach advocated in this paper is to look at the range of settlements in the hinterlands of these small towns in order to assess their economic, and indirectly social and political, impact on the population. It is possible to identify sections of the population that were, at most, only intermittently in contact with a market (this can be seen through the whole of the Roman period), and so not regularly involved in external relations with towns. The emergence of settlements whose inhabitants did not appear to use towns (or at most very infrequently) implies that a sizeable portion of the population of Roman Britain was not involved in the Roman Economy as defined either by Hopkins in 1978 or by Finley in 1973 or AHM Jones in 1974. This decreases ones perception of the importance of towns as focal points across the landscape. It can be suggested that the itinerant merchant played a more integrating role than is generally seen in reconstructions of the Roman Economy. For the later Empire, the larger villas could have acted as focal centres amongst the rural population, as attractive places for the travelling merchants and local producers, though not perhaps as formal markets.

Many recent studies now recognise the inadequacy of the term 'small town' when discussing the 97 sites which have been fitted into this category (though the figure changes as more candidates are offered for consideration). The term covers 'roadside settlements', walled and unwalled sites, 'local centres' (Hingley 1989) – the variation between these sites is vast. The use of the term 'small town' here is taken as a modern label applied by archaeologists to the identified sites, rather than a meaningful description of the settlements themselves.

When looking at relations between towns and rural settlements, villas are the obvious point of comparison. Collingwood (1934, 79), working in the 1920s and '30s, was the first to specify a close link between the town and villa – with villas exchanging their surplus at towns for the luxury goods, cash and specialist services offered at these centres. This basic concept is still held in recent approaches. Thus one often sees the number of villas near to a town cited as an index of its importance as a central place (eg Branigan 1987). This is the idea underpinning more quantitative approaches, such as Central Place Theory, and the construction of Thiessen polygons to give insight into possible territories and areas of influence (eg Hodder 1979). However, such approaches do not always consider variation within small towns as a category. The three 'small towns' considered in this paper illustrate the range covered within the term, and differences in the functions of these places within their landscape.

As with small towns, detailed analyses of villas also reveal a wide diversity of type. For archaeologists, there is no clear point at which one can define a non-villa from a villa site. Smith's work (1978, 117–148) has also highlighted the possibility of 'native' family structures within this most 'Roman' of rural sites, and perhaps the continuity of a socially embedded economy through the whole of the Roman period. But most importantly, there are many sites that do not slot easily into general considerations of town and country relations, notably the small farmsteads and villages. These probably housed the majority of the population, as shown by fieldwalking, aerial photography and other surveying techniques. These sites are usually discussed as part of a hierarchical scheme

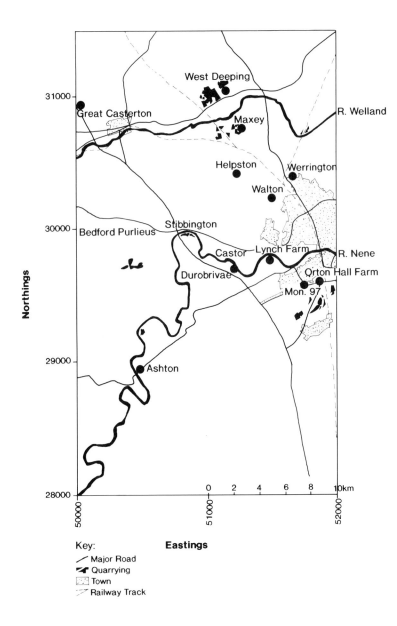

Fig 10.1 *The lower Nene and Welland
valleys*

of rural settlement, with villas at the top, and not often set within the wider context of town and country relations. By glossing over these small sites, or taking them in at second-hand (*via* the villa-estates), the picture of Roman Britain is incomplete. They do not fit easily into general reconstructions of the Roman Economy – non-participation is not an option within Hopkins's (1978) approach, for example.

Taking a more integrated approach allows one to see the full range of sites at work within their landscapes. It is only by looking for relations between settlements within the same area that one can construct a satisfying picture for that part of Roman Britain. This in turn will show the need for a reassessment of current theories on the Roman Economy. The continuity of an embedded element in the economy is a central argument (eg Millett 1990, 165–180). This is generally accepted for the early part of Roman Britain, though somehow society is assumed

to have followed market forces by the later Empire. There are many aspects of later Roman Britain that argue against such a change: multiple ownership of villas is implied by J T Smith's analysis of forms; one can still find people in the countryside not using towns to any degree, even in the 3rd and 4th centuries; overall social fragmentation is hinted at by the decline in the large towns, and although one sees the 'small towns' flourishing, not all can be seen to have taken over the range of services previously available at the larger centres. Although the 3rd and 4th centuries in general saw changes in urban and rural settlement patterns, there was still a strong thread of continuity.

The lower Nene valley is used here to illustrate the benefits of looking at the whole range of sites in an area, rather than concentrating on a specific type. The analysis starts prior to the conquest, and ends around the late 4th to early 5th centuries AD.

The lower Nene valley (Fig 10.1)

Much fieldwork has been carried out in the Nene valley. In particular, Artis excavated many stone structures in the early 19th century (included in Figure 10.11, since very few of these structures were given a date within the Roman period). There are modern surveys undertaken prior to the development of Peterborough New Town (RCHM(E) 1969) and in the lower Welland Valley (Simpson 1966; Pryor *et al* 1985a; 1985b); alongside these can be set major road developments, gravel and sand extraction along the Nene and Welland, and more general finds of sites from the ploughsoil. The area has been well surveyed, and many sites recognised. However, only a few have been uncovered in modern excavations. These include, at the lowest end of the settlement scale, the small, probably single family sites such as Werrington and Monument 97 (Orton Longueville), which provided detailed information on what must have been a common type of settlement. Wild (1976; 1978) has published summaries of settlement development in the lower Nene Valley. Since then, more sites have come to light, particularly those at the lower end of the settlement hierarchy, and they are included in this study. Most of the information on the excavated sites was obtained from the published reports, with extra information kindly given by the excavators (D Mackreth, B Dix). Details on sites in the area generally were obtained from the Cambridgeshire, Leicestershire, Lincolnshire, Northamptonshire and Peterborough Museum SMRs. Tables 10.1 and 10.2 summarise developments on the sites discussed below.

The range of sites around the lower Nene valley is fairly wide – from small-scale, single enclosure settlements showing some continuity from the local Iron Age traditions, through loosely grouped sites visible on aerial photographs to the elaborate stone houses that straddle the Nene in the 3rd and 4th centuries. To illustrate the changes in the landscape, developments have been plotted by century. The Figures show a selection of variables – the term 'site' refers to any concentration of pottery, building rubble, tiles, or dark areas (middens, pits or ditches) that can positively be identified as Roman, and indicate quite intensive use. More details on these sites are not available. The timber structures are those built entirely of timber and other organic materials, and stone structures are those with at least stone foundations, and include those with stone superstructures. Metal working refers to both smelting and smithing.

First century AD settlement (Fig 10.2)

In general, what appears to happen is an initial concentration around the Peterborough area in the 1st century AD. Although it must be admitted that only those sites with detailed dating evidence are being used in the study, the pattern does seem quite striking. These 1st century sites certainly illustrate a hierarchy of sorts. The places

that developed into small towns do have an initial burst of activity – the military presence very near to Great Casterton and *Durobrivae*, and the luxury table wares found at Ashton all point to initial importance.

A glance at a selection of the smaller sites within the study area suggests a broad degree of similarity in respect of material culture showing continuity from the late Iron Age: triangular loom weights, hand-made (later wheel-thrown) coarse pots, evidence for a mixed subsistence economy – cattle, sheep and pig, grain processing from querns – and the drip gullies of the eaves of round houses, which have been found at Werrington (Fig 10.3), Orton Longueville Monument 97 (Fig 10.4) and also at Ashton, as well as picked up undated on aerial photographs from the Nene and Welland. But closer inspection reveals specific differences between them. At Werrington, Period 1 (*c* AD 1–50) (Mackreth 1988) revealed evidence for quite intensive textile production, with many loomweights and sheep outnumbering cattle. Period 2 (*c* AD 50/60 – *c* AD 100) saw a change in emphasis from domestic occupation (though faint traces of posthole structures were found) towards increasing cattle production. The emphasis on poorer joints of meat on the site also reflects some export of animals. Three sherds of samian were found, from Southern and Central Gaul, and these, together with brooches from both periods (five in Period 1, one in Period 2) show some contact with markets. Traces of copper slag and a crucible in Period 1 were interpreted as scraps from itinerant smiths, though other sites of contemporary and later date, as at Maxey (below), housed their own smiths. An unusual sherd of a carinated bowl of a style found at the Longthorpe fortress could indicate a vague military link, though it was unique amongst the site assemblage. Around AD 100 the site was incorporated into a larger field system, with occupation centred elsewhere. So for the 1st century the site indicates some contact with external markets, but with the main emphasis on subsistence.

Excavations at Maxey in 1962–63 (Pryor *et al* 1985b; Fig 10.3) show similarities with Werrington. The site was occupied mainly during AD 50–150, with residual Iron Age sherds. Artefacts recovered were: hand-made and wheel-thrown pottery, clay loomweights, animal bones, daub, and some slag. The pottery forms were mainly storage jars, jars and occasional flagons. Fine wares of the later 1st to early 2nd centuries were used on the site (cordoned bowls, an imitation butt beaker, jars in a pink-orange fabric found also at the forts of Longthorpe, Great Casterton, and native sites such as Moulton Park, Northampton), but in far smaller quantities. Access to local exhange systems is revealed by the range of pots, and the two bronze brooches (one possibly late Iron Age), but the lack of 'Belgic' type forms and even samian again indicates only partial involvement with them. An iron-smelting furnace and probable bronze remelting associated with late Iron Age and early

Table 1   *Finds and dates of occupation of excavated settlements in the Lower Nene and Welland Valleys*

Ticks refer to general information. Occupation shift refers to dates when land use changed from/to general use. Information is for the selection of the excavated sites only, to provide an idea of the variation seen in the materials recovered in the Roman period. Where detailed, the Samian pottery is split into earlier South Gaulish and later forms (hence ticks in S. Gaul but none in All Samian for Lynch Farm), Otherwise, All Samian refers to the recovery of imported terra sigillata *from the site.*

SITE	'Belgic' type pot	Imported E.Ro pot	S. Gaulish Samian	All Samian	Brooch	Pin	C1st/2nd Coins	C3rd Coins	C4th Coins	Start Occup.	End Occup.	Occup. Shift
WERRINGTON	✓			✓	✓				✓	c. 50 BC	c AD 55	c AD 300
MAXEY 1962-63				✓						Mid Iron Age	By late C1st	
MAXEY 1979-81				✓	✓		2	1	2 unworn	Mid Iron Age	c. AD 175 c. AD 325	c. AD 75 c. AD 275
LONGTHORPE FARM 1			✓		✓					Late Iron Age	AD 60	End C2nd
LONGTHORPE FORTRESS		✓	✓		✓		✓			AD 48	AD 62	
MONUMENT 97	✓									c. 100 BC	c. AD 130	c. AD 130
SACREWELL				✓	✓	✓			✓	c. AD 150	c. AD 375	c. AD 375
LYNCH FARM									✓	c. AD 325	c. AD 375	C2nd
ORTON HALL FARM				✓	✓	✓		✓	✓	c. AD 140	end C4th/ early C6th	
HELPSTON									✓	c. AD 125	c. AD 350	
WALTON, N. BRETTON			(✓)	(✓)					✓	C4th?	c. AD 380	pre AD 70 c. AD 175
ASHTON	✓	✓		✓	✓	✓	✓	✓	✓	c. AD 60	c. AD 375	c. AD 125
G. CASTERTON	✓	✓	✓	✓	✓		✓	✓	✓	c. AD 50?	C5th?	c. AD 70
DUROBRIVAE				✓	✓					AD 50	C5th?	c. AD 70
CASTOR				✓					✓	AD 100	end C4th	AD 250 Praetorium
NORMANGATE FIELD				✓	✓	✓	✓	✓	✓	c. AD 70?	end C4th	c. AD 140 c. AD 225

Table 2   *Industrial actiivities and Structures on excavated settlements in the Lower Nene and Weeland Valleys*

Animal ratio refers to the ratio of sheep; cattle; pig, where details were available. These were calculated from the number of fragments, as information on M.N.I.s was not always available. Ticks refer to geneal information.

SITE	Metal Working	Ceramic Production	Animal Ratio	Cemetery	Stone Foundation	Stone Wall	Timber Superstructure	Round Structure	Rectang. Structure	Painted Wall Plaster	Mosaic/Tes Pavemen
WERRINGTON	Itinerant		2:1:✓				✓	✓			
MAXEY 1962-63	Smelting Bronze work						✓				
MAXEY 1979-81	Smelting		Mainly sheep	Informal			✓	✓			
LONGTHORPE FARM 1	(C3rd ✓)	✓									
LONGTHORPE FORTRESS	✓		2:4:1				✓			✓	
MONUMENT 97				✓			✓	✓			
SACREWELL	Smelting				✓				✓	✓	✓
LYNCH FARM	Smelting Smithing		6:35:1 MNI 7:14:2	✓	✓		✓		✓		
ORTON HALL FARM			c. AD 225 x3 cattle		✓		✓		✓		
HELPSTON					✓	✓			✓	✓	✓
WALTON, N. BRETTON			✓:✓:✓		✓		✓		✓		Tesserae found
ASHTON	Smithing Smelting	✓	✓:✓:✓	✓	✓		✓	✓	✓		
G. CASTERTON	Smelting	✓			✓	✓	✓		✓	✓	Baths & Villa
DUROBRIVAE				✓	✓	✓		✓	✓		Mill Hil
CASTOR					✓	✓	✓		✓	✓	
NORMANGATE FIELD	Mainly Smithing	✓		✓	✓	✓	✓	✓	✓	✓	Circular Structures

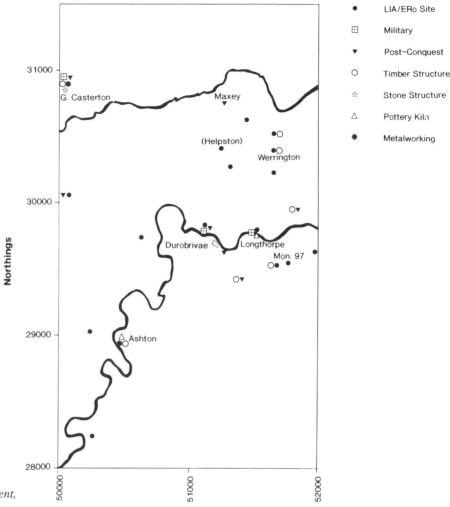

Fig 10.2 *1st century AD settlement,
lower Nene and Welland valleys*

Eastings

Roman finds indicate further the self-sufficiency of the people at Maxey, and the continuity of the later Iron Age tradition of general metalworkers well into the Roman period. This is at the same time as the rise of specialist smithing centres such as Ashton, *Durobrivae*, and probably Kettering (Dix 1987) from the later 1st century AD. Another site at Maxey, excavated in 1979–81 as part of the lower Welland Valley project (Pryor *et al* 1985a and 1985b; Fig 10.3), shows a similar introvert state, with Iron Age traditions of mixed farming continuing well into the Roman period. The continued domination of sheep over cattle well into the 2nd century at Maxey 1979–81 (despite the wet ground which would be better suited to cattle), and the reliance on meat production rather than wool or dairy, all shows a very strong continuity of earlier farming practices (Pryor *et al* 1985a, 219–222). This is more so than at Werrington and Monument 97, where the bones show a shift towards cattle rather than sheep through the Roman period. But both Maxey settlements were capable of supporting a metalworker, with smithing slag found at Maxey 1979–81 (Pryor *et al* 1985a, 180).

At Orton Longueville, Monument 97 (Fig 10.4) shows similar continuity from the late Iron Age through the first hundred years of Roman rule (Dallas 1975). The pre-conquest period saw a move to occupation in a pre-existing enclosure, with three clearly defined round houses and more ephemeral structures. In the mid 1st century AD the enclosure was re-cut, and new timber houses built. The domestic area was moved again around AD 100–140, and part of the enclosure used as a small cemetery. The farmstead was abandoned in the mid 2nd century. Although full details on artefacts recovered from the site were not available, the general conclusions suggest a subsistence economy. But the occurrence of a few pieces of 'Belgic' type pottery on the site indicates access to a higher level of exchange not seen at Werrington.

Another site which needs to be considered is the area under modern Peterborough. Finds were recovered from here from the 19th century, including coins from the 1st to 4th centuries AD, and even earlier (RCHM(E) 1969, 3–4; Cambridgeshire SMR). Pits uncovered in various brickyards indicate quite intensive late Iron Age occupation, and continuity through the whole of the Roman

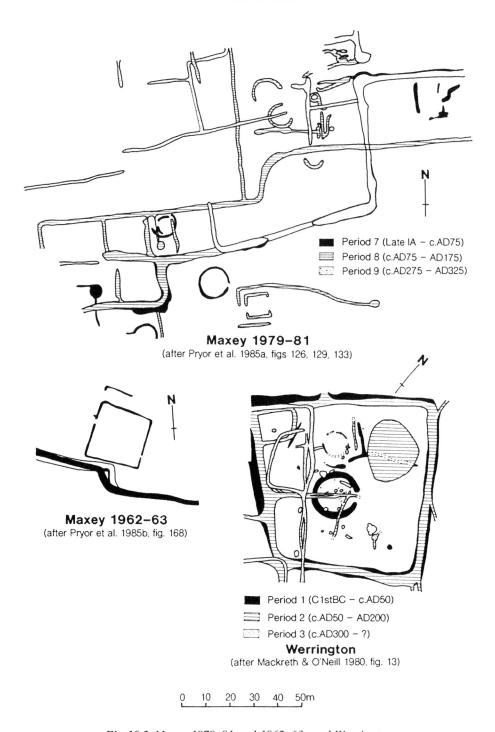

Period 7 (Late IA – c.AD75)
Period 8 (c.AD75 – AD175)
Period 9 (c.AD275 – AD325)

Maxey 1979–81
(after Pryor et al. 1985a, figs 126, 129, 133)

Maxey 1962–63
(after Pryor et al. 1985b, fig. 168)

Period 1 (C1stBC – c.AD50)
Period 2 (c.AD50 – AD200)
Period 3 (c.AD300 – ?)
Werrington
(after Mackreth & O'Neill 1980, fig. 13)

0 10 20 30 40 50m

Fig 10.3 *Maxey 1979–81 and 1962–63; and Werrington*

period. Two pits uncovered in 1910 contained 'Belgic' and pre-Flavian pottery, and coins from the 1st to 4th centuries (RCHM(E) 1969, 4; Cambridgeshire SMR). Unfortunately the lack of detail on these early discoveries makes any interpretation difficult. During the Roman period a large settlement flourished under the modern town, though it is now mainly destroyed.

At the other end of the scale was the legionary fortress at Longthorpe (Frere & St Joseph 1974; Fig 10.5). This supplied its own iron; both smelting and smithing detritus have been found (Todd & Cleland 1976). The legion was supplied *via* the military trade routes, and this is reflected in the artefacts: Lyons ware, amphorae, *terra nigra*, samian, beakers, glass vessels, a wide range of bronze personal and military items, and coins. The animals from the site no doubt reflected extortion: cattle (56%), sheep (29%), pig (14%), and occasional horse, red deer, wild birds, and fish. However, changes on contemporary settlements at the lowest end of the settlement hierarchy are not seen – sites such as Werrington, Maxey

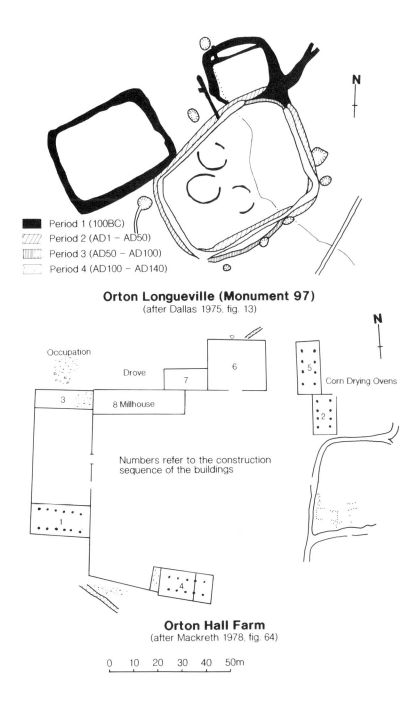

Orton Longueville (Monument 97)
(after Dallas 1975, fig. 13)

Period 1 (100BC)
Period 2 (AD1 – AD50)
Period 3 (AD50 – AD100)
Period 4 (AD100 – AD140)

Occupation

Drove

6

7

5

Corn Drying Ovens

3

8 Millhouse

Numbers refer to the construction
sequence of the buildings

2

1

4

Orton Hall Farm
(after Mackreth 1978, fig. 64)

0   10   20   30   40   50m

Fig 10.4 *Orton Longueville monument 97, and Orton Hall Farm*

and Monument 97 do not appear to suddenly benefit or
suffer from any military supply networks.

Other visible manifestations of the impact of the mili-
tary were the *vici*, at Great Casterton, and also at Ashton,
though little detail on these early settlements is available.
The rubbish pits excavated in the early seasons at Great
Casterton are the only remains found of the *vicus* there
(Corder (ed) 1951, 11–14). The pottery was a mix of late
Iron Age and 'Belgic' styles alongside imported vessels
(South Gaulish samian, Gallo-Belgic wares, *terra nigra*,

and girth beakers, illustrating the military links), giving a
date range from Claudius to the early Flavian period.
Some military presence at Ashton, probably pre-dating
the civilian settlement, was indicated by military bronzes.
R Kenyon's work on the Claudian coins showed them to
be contemporary imitations. These are usually found on
military sites, and presumably also have military origins,
giving further evidence for the military presence on the
site (B Dix, Northamptonshire Archaeology Unit).

So the three 'small towns' within the present study all

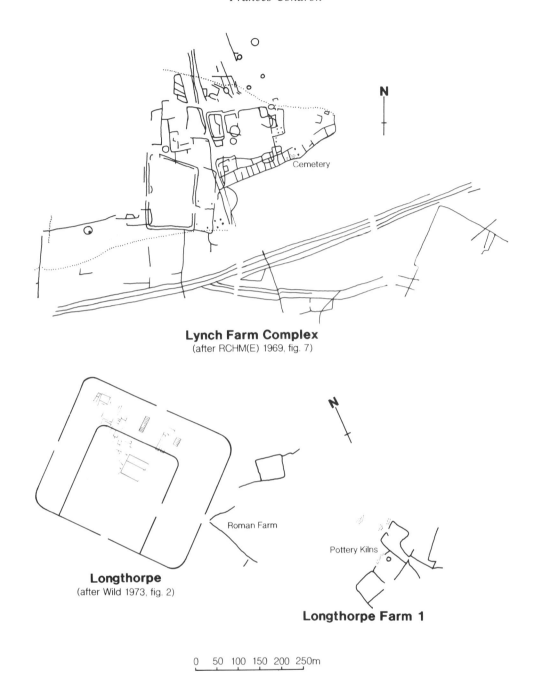

Lynch Farm Complex
(after RCHM(E) 1969, fig. 7)

Longthorpe
(after Wild 1973, fig. 2)

Roman Farm

Pottery Kilns

Longthorpe Farm 1

0   50 100 150 200 250m

Fig 10.5 *Lynch Farm complex; and Longthorpe, legionary fortress, and farm*

had their origins in the 1st century AD, and probably post-dated the conquest. Very little is known of *Durobrivae*, due to the lack of excavation within the walled area. Most information comes from developments in the extra-mural settlement in Normangate Field. Excavations here, particularly in the 1960s and 70s, identified clamps used to produce 'Belgic' influenced pottery in the early 2nd century. This activity could have begun in the later part of the 1st century, as Flavian samian was spread generally around the site (Brown (ed) 1971). Certainly by the early 2nd century areas of Normangate Field had been divided into fairly regular sub-rectangu-

lar enclosures, indicating some element of central control within the community from the beginning.

The pottery assemblage from the main excavations at Ashton does not support evidence for a pre-conquest origin. The ditch in which Hadman found 'Belgic' and imported pottery had been badly disturbed by post medieval quarrying. The sherds in question were in a very poor condition, and their identification as imports is not clear. The six British coins found on the site could also have arrived after the conquest. Only the early brooches (interim report by D Mackreth held at Northamptonshire Archaeology Unit) seem to straddle the Conquest period.

The plots here were organised in the later part of the 1st century and the first structures were timber built; the side roads were probably contemporary with them. The pottery assemblage does indicate that people living at Ashton had advantages over others on rural sites from the start. The range of forms, and the odd imported piece – including imitations of samian, *terra nigra,* Dressel 20 amphorae, and one sherd of a Dechelette 44 amphora, show the ability of the locals to attract relatively luxurious items, even on a small scale. From the beginning iron working was a major activity (Hadman & Upex 1975 and 1977). This need not have been for the surrounding rural population though – one finds metal production on the smallest settlements continuing well into the 2nd century, and other new sites follow this practice into the 3rd and 4th centuries.

Also, the pottery from Ashton does not necessarily support the notion that the settlement acted as a local market centre. The white ware flagons and mortaria that reached the site in the 1st century were from the same production areas (probably from the *Verulamium* region), but the flagons, which were far more numerous, were not reaching Ashton on a regular and even basis. The imported bowls have similar lacunae; these gaps could simply be explained by the demise of one itinerant trader, with no immediate successor. This shows the ability of Ashton to attract such itinerants, but the exchange was on a small scale.

At Great Casterton early Flavian timber buildings were uncovered inside the walled area by Corder (Corder (ed) 1951 and 1961). A small bowl furnace was built in the ruins of one of these buildings. The elaborate stone building (probably the *mansio*), complete with baths, makes a great contrast with contemporary late 1st century structures in this area. The early pot assemblages reveal greater access to Roman items, with Roman forms (and so tastes) well represented from the Flavian period onwards (South Gaulish samian, jars, beakers, platters (Corder (ed) 1961, 39–46)).

The impact of the Roman invasion on the settlement pattern is clearly seen with the military sites, and Ashton, *Durobrivae* and Great Casterton all show superior access to imported and local luxury items relative to surrounding settlements. But evidence for small, rural sites participating in exchange to any degree is limited, and certainly nothing indicates the presence of regular, organised markets or central places.

Second century developments

The second century saw continued occupation of sites, and the emergence of many more, with the Peterborough area no longer dominating the distribution (Fig 10.6).

At Maxey 1979–81 settlement continued through the whole of the century, but there was little to indicate increasing prosperity. The site remained basically 'native', and the people were not buying or trading their way into a Roman lifestyle. The five coins found on the site indicate an effectively coinless economy, centred still on self-sufficiency. Other sites ceased to be occupied. Monument 97 and Werrington were deserted around the middle of the 2nd century; this could simply have resulted from a shift in occupation focus, but it could also indicate the impact of wider forces – a population shift to the Fenland maybe, or the reorganisation of settlements consequent upon the development of the villa estates which become visible in the 3rd and 4th centuries. The vast number of pots represented in the final destruction phase of Monument 97 though is outstanding – over 3,000 sherds, compared with 7,500 from the larger site at Maxey, for the whole of the Roman occupation, showing the variation possible between superficially similar 'native' sites. Nothing else at Monument 97 gave any indication of a more flamboyant lifestyle. The inhabitants here could have obtained the pots from itinerant traders, but presumably they would have required sufficient money to attract the attention of such people.

New rural sites begin to emerge in the 2nd century. At Lynch Farm (Fig 10.5) a new drainage scheme was initiated and recut, though the first actual structures were found in 3rd century contexts. Evidence for a more luxurious level of living is found at Orton Hall Farm. Building debris shows that a relatively elaborate timber building was nearby (fine plaster, but not painted). But again the excavation uncovered only later 3rd and 4th century structures (Mackreth 1978, 210), reflecting a shift in settlement location.

In the 2nd century we get the emergence of structures with at least stone foundations – at Helpston (Fig 10.7) a small simple stone 'cottage' developed into the 3rd and 4th century villa (Challands 1975). In Normangate Field we see the emergence of stone structures, and the development of the various potting and metalworking processes being undertaken in the area. The rise of the lower Nene Valley pottery industry in the 2nd century has been well documented, and its success is illustrated by the swamping of local pottery assemblages from the mid 2nd century onwards.

The small areas excavated in Great Casterton show continued settlement, though the succession of timber structures excavated in 1956 followed different alignments, despite what must have been virtually continuous occupation (Corder (ed) 1961, 34–50). But the small number of coins and small finds, along with the simple nature of the buildings, do not point to any obvious success of the town as an active service centre for a hinterland, although the lack of excavation prevents any firm judgement. Also the erection of the defences around AD 170–180 has to be accounted for; whether local wealth paid for them or they were put up using forced labour or with money from the canton at large, is unknown.

At Ashton the enclosure system was altered in the 2nd century, the ditches being replaced by lines of fences, and simple stone buildings replaced the earlier timber

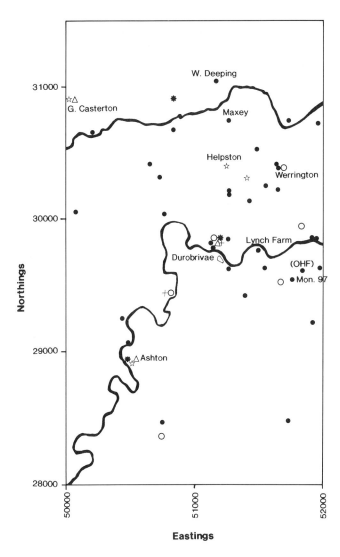

Fig 10.6 *2nd century settlement, lower Nene and Welland valleys*

ones. At no point were there any architectural embellishments. This enclosure system continued in use, effectively along the 2nd century lines, to the end of the settlement's life. By the early 2nd century ironworking, predominantly smithing, was being carried out on a large scale, certainly well in excess of local requirements. This is particularly noteworthy when one considers that both smelting and smithing were being carried out on rural sites in this area through the whole of the Roman period. Possibly the surplus iron was taken by merchants and traded at a distance. Pottery production was taking place at Ashton too – an early 2nd century kiln was found in the former Goods Yard site (badly disturbed by quarrying) but this activity was more probably for the immediate needs of the settlement itself.

The 2nd century then was a period of expansion for *Durobrivae*. The role of Great Casterton in the local economy remains obscure, but a case can be made out for seeing Ashton as having only limited commercial impact on the local population. Certainly settlements at the lower end of the economic spectrum received outside goods to a very small degree.

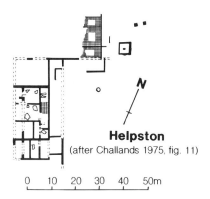

Helpston
(after Challands 1975, fig. 11)

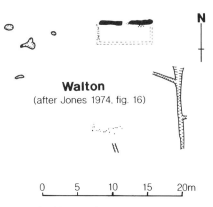

Walton
(after Jones 1974, fig. 16)

Fig 10.7 *Helpston and Walton*

Third century changes

By the 3rd century far more sites are visible in the study area as a whole, particularly in the western half (Fig 10.8). Signs of increasing wealth for some are evident. For example, Lynch Farm, where excavations have uncovered part of the Roman settlement and cemetery and aerial photography has revealed a complex network of ditched enclosures (Jones 1975), shows greater prosperity than the comparable earlier farms such as Werrington and Maxey. The earliest actual structure found here was a small timber building probably of 3rd century date; later in the century better built structures were added, when also a large stone-built fish tank replaced a timber-lined sump. We also have the evolution of elaborate villa houses. Wings were added to the small 'cottage' at Helpston in the 3rd and 4th centuries, and the building was decorated with painted wall plaster (presumably in the 3rd century, the date given to the lime kiln found nearby (Challands 1975, 1976)). To a lesser degree, the people at Walton, North Bretton, invested their success

in their home. This site overlay 1st and 2nd century occupation, but the main complex dated from the late 2nd century, continuing into the 4th. A building, probably an aisled barn, was found, with a concentration of building stone, tesserae, hypocaust and roof tiles. The excavator considered this building to be the main source for this material (Jones 1974). The mixed nature of the farming points towards a mainly subsistence economy – a threshing floor lay to the north of the barn, and querns were found; bones of cattle, sheep, pig and some goat were recovered. However, there were no luxurious small finds (although the excavation was limited in scope). What surplus income there was went into the decoration of the house.

By the late 3rd century a new kind of agricultural settlement was developing. At Orton Hall Farm (summarised by the excavator, Mackreth 1978, 209–228), the central enclosure gradually changed use from a stock yard to an open space enclosed by barns. A lot of grain was being processed on the site: corn drying ovens were built and replaced through the 3rd and 4th centuries, and

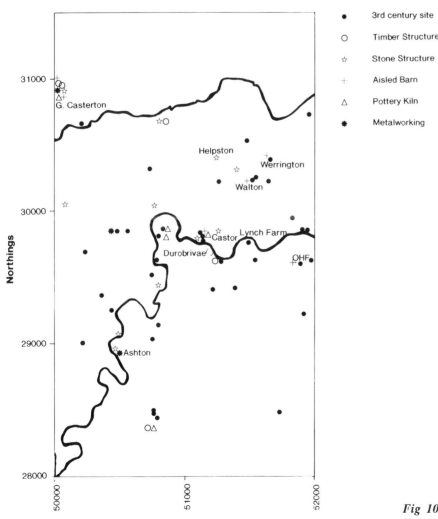

Fig 10.8 3rd century AD settlement, lower Nene and Welland valleys

the capacity of the millhouse (with millstones 90cm in diameter) must have been great. This arable activity was also accompanied by animal husbandry, attested by the many stockyards to the north of the main complex. At the end of Period II (around AD 220–250) there was a threefold increase in the number of cattle kept and processed on site, although this could have been partly in response to some local catastrophe amonst the sheep, as a large pit containing many bones was found (D Mackreth, pers comm). Orton Hall Farm was surely processing a lot of raw produce from the surrounding land but the lack of luxurious pots or small finds, and the basic nature of the buildings (at least one of which was a dwelling house) imply that the people who lived there were dependent on landowners who lived somewhere else – presumably the proprietors of a large villa estate (or just possibly the imperial government).

Ashton continued to prosper through the 3rd century, continuing to produce iron. The enclosure system remained in operation, and the roads saw heavy use (and repair) into the 4th century. The prosperity of *Durobrivae* through the 3rd and well into the later 4th century is well documented, and reflected in the continued success of the pottery industry (and surely also metal and leather working activities). At some point, the large elaborate houses around the town were built, including the vast *praetorium* under Castor village, indicating a scale and concentration of wealth not available in other parts of the lower Nene and Welland valleys. On the evidence we have, Great Casterton did not particularly prosper; the structures uncovered by Corder were not closely packed within the defended area, and the only stone structure in the town (so far identified) was still the *mansio*.

Fourth century developments and decline (Fig 10.9)

The first half of the 4th century saw a continuation of settlement on many sites, and for some unprecedented standards of living. Lynch Farm continued to grow, with a new aisled barn replacing the smaller timber structure. Despite the continued ironworking at *Durobrivae* nearby, iron smithing took place there. One end of the barn was partitioned off as a living area and decorated (red painted plaster walls). To the west a small, square building was erected – interpreted as a Romano-Celtic temple, with a verandah. It was linked to the barn. Lynch Farm implies a site based on self-sufficiency, and like earlier settlements, this included metal tools. The pottery does not show access to a privileged diet – most of the vessels were utilitarian, mainly in local grey wares and colourcoats. There were a few fine wares (decorated beakers, Castor boxes), there were no obvious liquid containers, and the few mortaria were the only concession to a more Romanised diet. The animal bones show both cattle and sheep, with a few pig, horses and dogs and some wild animals (deer). Ages of death for the domestic animals reflected husbandry for meat as well as wool, and the

existence of draft animals. The paddocks and corn drying oven are further proof of a mixed economy. The skeletons from the adjacent cemetery (probably in use from the later 2nd to 4th centuries) indicate the wear and tear of hard working lives (squatting facets on two males, as seen at the Trentholme Drive cemetery, York; four cases of osteo-arthritis, and examples of calcified ligaments; Jones 1975). This site, despite being near *Durobrivae*, does not appear to have regularly taken advantage of the attractions of the town. The few Castor boxes, and the decorated room of the barn reveal a degree of contact with luxuries, though nothing to indicate a need for frequent and sustained visits to the town for trade and other activities.

Maxey 1979–81 was reoccupied from the end of the 3rd century, and deserted by AD 325. Like Lynch Farm, the small finds indicate greater prosperity than the earlier phases, with Castor boxes, beakers and the odd 'hunt' cup being used on the site (Pryor *et al* 1985a, 146–151). The five coins found on the whole of the excavation belong to this phase, but their good condition and small number indicate an effectively coinless settlement. The environmental evidence pointed to an increasing reliance on cereal production, with primary processing taking place off-site. The animal bones (all three Roman phases were treated as one assemblage) show a predominance of sheep rather than cattle, though a few oysters show access to non-local goods (Pryor *et al* 1985a, 214–241).

Orton Hall Farm continued to grow through the 4th century (discussed above), though from AD 375 there was a decline. The Saxon settlement made use of the standing Roman buildings, and this settlement eventually ended in the early 6th century.

The 4th century saw continued prosperity at Helpston, which eventually grew to a house of 21 rooms (Challands 1975). Sacrewell, another elaborate villa house, was first excavated in the 19th century, and then again in 1928, 1963 and 1973. Artis recorded two rooms and the corridor of a villa, with tesselated pavements and much painted wall plaster. Four buildings with pitched stone footings were uncovered in the later excavations. Building 1 had a mortar floor with tiled roof. Fragments of red painted wall plaster were found around Buildings 2 and 3, and a possible malting kiln near Building 4. These outbuildings lay to the east of the main accommodation block, and represent the 'working' side of the villa complex. In the late 4th century these outbuildings were demolished, and replaced by quite extensive ironworking, which included roasting ores and smelting (Challands 1974). A similar change from agriculture to ironworking is seen at Barnack, a few kilometres to the north. The only evidence for consumption patterns at Sacrewell came from surface finds and inadequately recorded excavations. The Cambridgeshire SMR lists the artefacts found there: red and green painted wall plaster, *tegulae, imbrex* and box tiles, samian, Nene Valley coarse wares and colour-coats, shell-gritted ware, cream-ware mortaria, glass (it was not

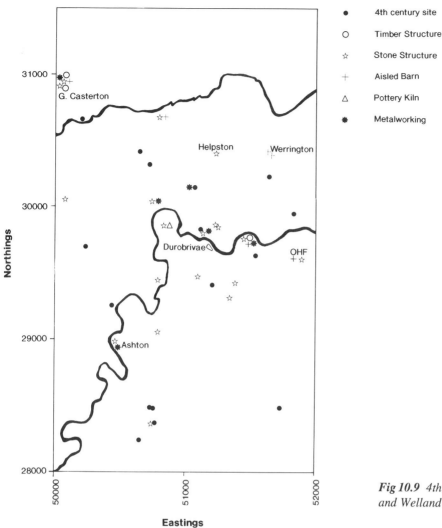

Fig 10.9 *4th century settlement, lower Nene and Welland valleys*

clear whether this was vessel and/or window glass), bronze finger rings, brooches, buckles, bracelets, tweezers, vessel fragments, and 3rd century coins. So alongside the architectural embellishments, the people at Sacrewell were able to acquire a wide range items which would have been available locally.

At *Durobrivae* the extra-mural settlement at Normangate Field contracted through the 4th century. Excavations on the enclosure system showed some ditches silting up from the beginning of the century, but others being maintained for a few more decades, and industrial activity to the late 4th century (Brown (ed) 1971 and 1976). Changes in land use, seen in previous centuries, continued, with the minor road in Normangate Field given over for burial (seen with the mausoleum excavated in 1968, and subsequent finds of less elaborate burials). The *praetorium* under Castor village continued in occupation, though it is not known when it fell out of use. The school of mosaicists based at *Durobrivae*, and the hoard of relatively fine Christian silver reinforce its superiority over the two other 'small towns' (along with its status as a *vicus*). Despite the contraction, *Durobrivae* was a suc-

cessful and outward looking settlement well into the second part of the 4th century; decline only setting in with a vengeance towards the end of the century.

Continuation of a sense of community is seen at Ashton in the creation of the cemetery over old enclosures. But this possibly Christian practice (indicated by the aligned skeletons and lack of grave goods) took place alongside the more pagan use of the far ends of the enclosures for burial, the street fronts still reserved for houses (Watts 1991, 84). Generally, the structures continued to be basic, though the one piece of stonework from the same 4th century well as a circular lead tank could indicate a more pretentious building in the environs. The coin loss pattern at Ashton in the 4th century though could indicate a short period as a market centre. Reece's initial evaluation of the coins (unpublished, copy at Northamptonshire Archaeology Unit) revealed only low levels of bronze issues in the AD 330s, though the 360s were strongly represented, and this trend continued into the 390s. Although coins were being used at Ashton from the 1st century it was not until the second half of the 4th century that coin loss, and so use, was occurring on a regular and concentrated enough basis to reflect fairly intensive trade. However, the latest issues were in good condition, indicating only a short circulation life, and therefore a fairly rapid demise in this burst of economic activity. Ashton continued as a settlement to the late 4th century, though by this time some buildings had fallen into disrepair (Frere 1983, 305–6), and like the other 'small towns' in the area this decline took place some time in the late 4th and probably early 5th centuries.

The 'town' at Great Casterton continued in occupation through the 4th century, and the nearby villa was in use possibly into the 5th century. In the mid 4th century a new wide, shallow, ditch replaced the earlier multiple ditches, and the wall was reinforced with towers. Internally, some buildings continued in use through to the late 4th century (the aisled structure uncovered in 1956). A layer of earth about 6 inches thick was encountered in many of the town excavations, and contained 1st to 3rd century pottery only. The occurrence of the dark earth horizon in many trenches indicates a fairly empty 'town' in the 3rd century, or quite extensive town gardens. This was overlain by a thin layer of iron slag, and excavations in 1958 revealed a robbed-out building of 4th century date, cutting through the slag layer (Corder (ed) 1961, 46–9). The general spreads of iron ore indicate continued ironworking, and the excavator thought local ores were being used. But it need not all be of Roman date since this practice continued in the medieval period, and ore from the great ditch is probably post-Roman. The building encountered in 1958 was on the same alignment as the aisled one uncovered in 1956, perhaps the result of an organised division of the interior of the town. However, the varying orientations seen in the structures underlying the aisled building indicate less organisation within plots (presumably there were such) than seen at Ashton, for example. Continuity of settlement beyond the 4th century is hinted at by the early Anglo-Saxon burials in the late 3rd and 4th century cemetery, and at the extra mural villa the buildings were being made use of long after their destruction by fire around AD 395.

So by the early 4th century there was a wide variety of settlement types in the Nene and Welland valleys. A continuity of more 'native' traditions is seen at Maxey 1979–81, and a similar self-sufficiency at Lynch Farm. At the other end of the scale were rural sites such as Sacrewell and Walton revealing the aspirations of the more fortunate. There are many other unexcavated villas in the study area, and alongside Artis's undated buildings they indicate a substantial and privileged section of society probably showing prosperity well into the 4th century. Metalworking, both smelting and smithing, continued as a rural activity through the whole of the Roman period, despite the specialisation at Ashton and *Durobrivae*. The 4th century saw increasing prosperity in the 'small towns' too, though Great Casterton, despite the defences (and bearing in mind the limited excavations), does not appear to become a market centre at any

time, unlike Ashton. The presence of the *mansio* from the beginning of the settlement seems to argue for a primarily administrative role for this 'small town'.

The lower Nene and Welland valleys in the Roman period: the 'Small Towns' in their context

The three 'small towns' within this area had greater access to Roman material culture, and presumably ideas, from their beginnings, than surrounding settlements. This situation continued into the 3rd century. It is not until the appearance of luxurious rural complexes, the villas, that equivalent standards of living, in many ways superior to those so far identified at Ashton and Great Casterton, were achieved outside the 'small towns'. The cluster of complexes around *Durobrivae* (Fig 10.10) argues for a special relationship between the villas and this site. Presumably they were the main properties of landowners benefiting from the use of woodland and farming areas by people living in and around the town.

The evidence from the smallest settlements in the lower Nene and Welland valleys indicate low levels of involvement in regional exchange. Places such as Werrington and the sites at Maxey show a particularly introverted lifestyle, though Monument 97 illustrates a slightly higher level of access to the local trade network. Lynch Farm in the 3rd and 4th centuries, and the reoccupation at Maxey 1979–81 in the early 4th, show slightly greater affluence, though no obvious regular contact with an urban centre. Subsistence continued to be a basic element in settlements through the whole of the Roman period. Aerial photography (particularly by S Upex, reinforcing the work published by RCHM(E), *A matter of time,* 1960) and fieldwalking data give some impression of the extent to which 'native' traditions continued through the Roman period. Recent photographs of the lower Nene and particularly along the Welland have identified numerous enclosure complexes and fieldwork has confirmed a Roman date for some of them (Fig 10.11). The excavation of such sites, as at Maxey and West Deeping (Simpson 1966, 15–21; Field unpub), reveal these sites to have been self-sufficient. Along the Welland strings of these complexes linked by droveways probably belong to the Roman period, and indicate fairly dense occupation, which surely extended onto the less receptive geologies of the area. This implies a reasonably strong representation of a 'native' lifestyle through the lower Nene and Welland valleys. It is only the larger sites that fit into the concept of a villa-as-farm, with owners/occupiers exchanging fairly substantial surpluses for imported and luxury goods, and strong and regular contacts with traders. Any lower levels of exchange, perhaps based on kinship lines and relied upon in times of stress, do not show up in the archaeological record. If these smallest rural sites were using the 'towns' as markets, then it seems to have been on an irregular basis.

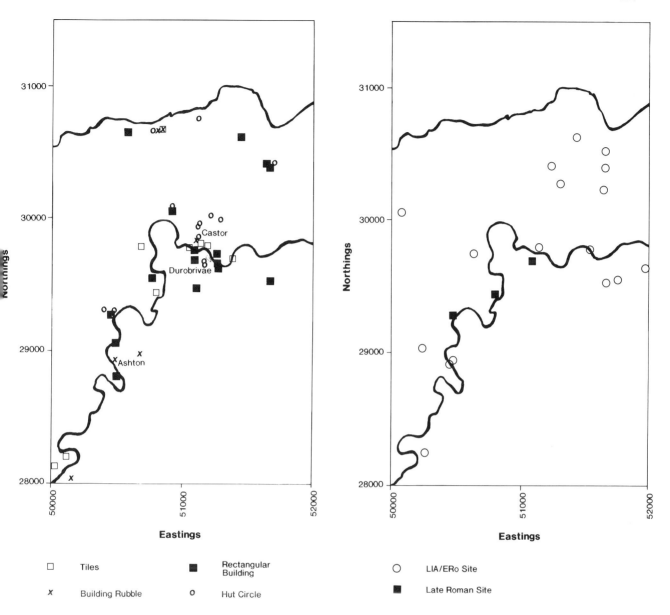

Fig 10.10 *Structures found through aerial photography, lower Nene and Welland valleys*

Fig 10.11 *Early and late Roman sites found through aerial photography, lower Nene and Welland valleys*

The production of pottery was widespread throughout this area, but its sale need not always have been channelled through urban markets. The early pottery assemblages at Ashton imply itinerant traders visiting the site and for the 3rd and 4th centuries, the villas could have acted as minor collection and redistribution centres, as probable customers on an itinerant trader's route.

Metalworking, particularly iron production, was a common industrial practice through the whole of this area, on virtually all levels of sites. Both smelting and smithing occurred on rural sites, as well as smithing at the 'small towns'. Ashton and *Durobrivae* were specialising in the production of ironwork. There is no need to argue for the importation of iron blooms to these sites from areas such as Bedford Purlieus and Stibbington.

Late levels at Ashton produced smelting slag as well as smithing debris, indicating local smelting (B Dix, pers comm). There was also no clear local market for the iron tools – such specialisation presumably produced a surplus, but modern excavations imply that a wide range of rural sites continued to be self-sufficent in iron tools. For *Durobrivae* the urban population could have taken up a lot of custom, but for Ashton a surplus was presumably taken away and traded at a distance, the benefits of these exhanges remaining within the settlement.

In defining whether a 'small town' was acting as a central place or not, one must consider the whole landscape. Rural settlement gives as much information about the degrees of involvement in urban lifestyles as the towns themselves. Using this approach, only *Durobrivae* emerges as a settlement offering a variety of services to the rural population. On present evidence, Great Casterton seems to have been mainly an official centre, the *mansio* and walls pointing towards an interest at provincial level. The excavations, although limited, seem to indicate a relatively stagnant settlement. Ashton did not become a service centre until the later part of the 4th century, this being reflected only in the pattern of coin loss. I argue that the embedded economy continued through the whole of the Roman period. The economy in Britain was never fully monetized (as seen with Maxey for example). There was always a large rural section that did not effectively participate in the market system, continuing a tradition with origins in prehistory.

Acknowledgments

I am deeply indebted to the county archaeologists who gave me free access to the Sites and Monuments Records – Nestor Rooke at Cambridge; the late MD Howe at the Peterborough Museum; Ian George, Lincolnshire County SMR officer; Peter Liddle, Leicestershire Community Archaeologist; Christine Addison, Northamptonshire Archaeology Unit, and Brian Dix, particularly for access to unpublished material on Ashton. Thanks are also due to A Challands, C Dallas, R Jones, D Mackreth, F Pryor, JP Wild, and the Royal Commission on the Historical Monuments of England for their illustrations. I also thank Rob Young, David Mattingly and Alan McWhirr for their advice on drafts of this paper, though the conclusions are of my own doing.

Bibliography

Branigan, K, 1987 *The Catuvellauni*

Brown, A E (ed), 1971 Archaeology in Northamptonshire 1970, *Bull Northamptonshire Fed Archaeol Socs,* 5, 1–44

——, 1976 Archaeology in Northamptonshire 1975, *Northamptonshire Archaeol,* 2, 185–194

Burnham, B C, & Wacher, J, 1990 *The 'small towns' of Roman Britain*

Challands, A, 1974 A Roman industrial site and villa at Sacrewell, *Durobrivae, a review of Nene valley archaeology,* 2, 13–16

——, 1975 The Roman villa at Helpston, *ibid,* 3, 22–3

——, 1976 A Roman lime kiln at Helpston, *ibid,* 4, 22–3

Collingwood, R G, 1934 *Roman Britain* (revised ed)

Corder, P (ed), 1951 *The Roman town and villa at Great Casterton, Rutland*

——, 1961 *The Roman town and villa at Great Casterton, Rutland. Third report for the years 1954–1958*

Dallas, C, 1975 A Belgic Farmstead at Orton Longueville, *Durobrivae, a review of Nene valley archaeology,* 3, 26–7

Dannell, G, 1974 Roman industry in Normangate Field, *ibid,* 2, 7–9

Dix, B, 1987 The Roman settlement at Kettering, Northants: excavations at Kipling Road, 1968 and 1971, *Northamptonshire Archaeol,* 21, 95–108

Field, N (unpub) *Welton to Glentham water pipeline,* Lindsey Archaeological Services (copy held at the Lincolnshire Archaeological Unit)

Finley, M I, 1973 *The ancient economy*

Frere, S S, 1983 Roman Britain in 1982, *Britannia,* 14, 305–6

——, & St Joseph, J K, 1974 The Roman fortress at Longthorpe, *Britannia,* 5, 1–129

Hadman, J, & Upex, S, 1975 The Roman settlement at Ashton near Oundle, *Durobrivae, a review of Nene valley archaeology,* 3, 13–15

——, 1976 Ashton 1976, *ibid,* 5, 6–9

Hingley, R, 1989 *Rural settlement in Roman Britain*

Hodder, I, 1979 The spatial distribution of Romano-British small towns, in *The 'small towns' of Roman Britain* (eds W Rodwell & T Rowley), BAR Brit Ser, 15, 67–74

Hopkins, K, 1978 Economic growth and towns in classical antiquity, in *Towns in societies. Essays in economic history and historical sociology* (eds P Abrams & E A Wrigley), 35–77

Jones, A H M, 1974 *The Roman economy: studies in ancient economic and administrative history* (ed P A Brunt)

Jones, R, 1974 A Roman and Saxon farm at Walton, North Bretton, *Durobrivae, a review of Nene valley archaeology,* 2, 29–31

——, 1975 The Romano-British farmstead and its cemetery at Lynch Farm, near Peterborough, *Northamptonshire Archaeol,* 10, 94–137

Mackreth, D F, 1978 Orton Hall Farm, Peterborough: a Roman and Saxon settlement, in *Studies in the Romano-British villa* (ed M Todd), 209–228

——, 1979 Durobrivae, *Durobrivae, a review of Nene valley archaeology,* 7, 19–21

——, 1988 Excavation of an Iron Age and Roman enclosure at Werrington, Cambs, *Britannia,* 19, 59–152

Millett, M, 1990 *The Romanization of Britain*

Pryor, F, *et al*, 1985a *The Fenland project, No 1: archaeology and environment in the lower Welland Valley,* E Anglian Archaeol, 27, Vol 1

——, 1985b *The Fenland Project, No 1: archaeology and environment in the lower Welland Valley,* E Anglian Archaeol, 27, Vol 2

Rodwell, W, & Rowley, T (eds), 1975 *The 'small towns' of Roman Britain,* BAR Brit Ser, 15

RCHM(E), 1969 *Peterborough New Town. A survey of the antiquities in the areas of development*

Simmons, B B, 1979, The Lincolnshire Car Dyke, *Britannia,* 10, 183–196

Simpson, W G, 1966 Romano-British settlement on the Welland gravels, in *Rural settlement in Roman Britain* (ed A C Thomas), CBA Res Rep 7, 15–25

Smith, J T, 1978, Villas as a key to social structure, in *Studies in the Romano-British villa* (ed M Todd), 149–186

Todd, J, & Cleland, J, 1976 Roman ironworking at Longthorpe, *Durobrivae, a review of Nene valley archaeology,* 4, 19

Watts, D, 1991 *Christians and pagans in Roman Britain*

Wild, J P, 1973a Longthorpe: an essay in continuity, *Durobrivae, a review of Nene valley archaeology,* 1, 7–10

——, 1976 Roman settlement in the lower Nene Valley, *Archaeol J,* 131, 140–70

——, 1978 Villas in the lower Nene Valley, in *Studies in the Romano-British villa* (ed M Todd), 59–70

11 Kelvedon and the fort myth in the development of Roman small towns in Essex

Michael Eddy

Introduction

The Essex village of Kelvedon, identified with the Roman *Canonium,* has been the subject of a substantial programme of rescue/research excavations since 1977. The programme was devised to test a model of settlement development proposed on the basis of evidence from excavations carried out in the late 1960s and early 1970s (Rodwell & Rodwell 1975). A key element in that model was the hypothesised existence of an early Roman fort beneath the present village. The supposed existence of a fort at Kelvedon was taken to explain a dog-leg bend at this point in the otherwise straight London-Colchester road, a feature which had long intrigued both antiquarians and historians.

No structural evidence of a fort of any date was found in the 1977 and later excavations, though a substantial Roman town defence ditch was located together with other features. This additional evidence, both negative and positive, led to a preliminary re-assessment of Kelvedon's development and, more tentatively, of early Roman military sites in Essex (Eddy with Turner 1982). That reassessment was written before the publication of the final report on the pre-1977 excavations (Rodwell, K 1988). In her report, Kirsty Rodwell reviewed the pre-1977 evidence for 'military activity at Kelvedon in the mid 1st century AD ... the most substantial remains ... [being] ... a mid 1st century ditch of characteristically military profile and containing military equipment'. She suggested the existence of a 4ha fort (*op cit*, 135) and expressed this in map form (*ibid*, figs 40 and 98). The fort plan was based on an interpolation from modern topographical features and on the assertion that the 1977 excavations 'failed to locate the [continuation of the military-style] ditch'. A Boudiccan context for the construction of the postulated fort was proposed, based on the comparative numbers of pre-Neronian and Neronian samian sherds and coins (*ibid*, 135).

In fact the 1977 excavations did locate the continuation of the 'military-style ditch', reinterpreted in the interim report as a late Iron Age field boundary (Eddy with Turner 1982, 6).

The existence of an early Roman fort at Kelvedon, Claudian or Boudiccan, has been ruled out in the light of further evidence. This rejection of Kelvedon as a fort site has implications not only for its development as a settlement but also for our understanding of other Roman small towns in Essex and their relation to military affairs in the 1st century AD. I propose here to examine the evidence that gave rise to the postulated fort at Kelvedon and to its subsequent rejection. In large part the claims for a fort at Kelvedon, and for forts elsewhere in Essex, depend on the archaeological perception of the military background within which such hypothesised forts are thought to have operated. In order to understand more fully the reasons for attributing fort status to certain early Roman sites, it is necessary to review the consensus model of early Roman military activity, alternatives to that model, and the status of London within the consensus. I shall then consider the evidence for the Essex forts claimed in various recent surveys of early military activity. This will lead on to a reassessment of Chelmsford and of other 1st century AD military sites in the county.

The evidence from Kelvedon (Fig 11.1)

The 'military-style' ditch at Kelvedon

The archetypal military-style ditch had a V-profile, the point of the V often being replaced by a rectangular slot interpreted either as a deliberately cut 'ankle-breaker' or as a by-product of periodic ditch clearance (a 'shovel cleaning slot'). Such ditches have been attested by archaeology in Roman military contexts and by Roman army handbooks. They were associated both with marching camps and more permanent forts. In the archaeological record the dimensions of the V-shaped ditches are variable, depending on such factors as site geology, projected time of occupancy, imminence of enemy action and type of garrison and/or attacking force. In the case of temporary camps, widths of 4 to 10ft (1.3 to 3m) and depths of 2 to 6ft (0.6 to 1.8m) were common (Collingwood & Richmond 1976, 13). Fort ditches were

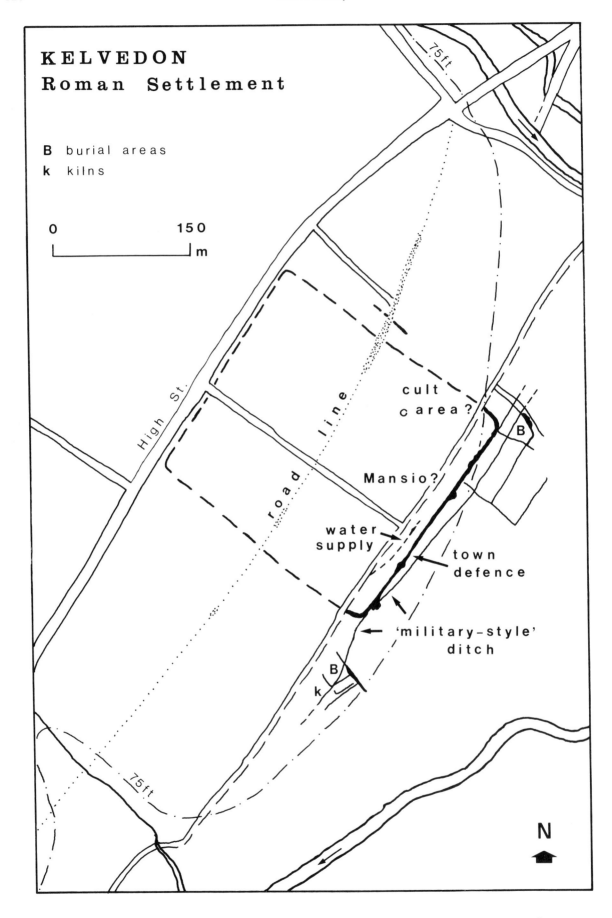

KELVEDON
Roman Settlement

B burial areas
k kilns

0   150
⊢⊣⊣⊣⊢⊣ m

cult
c area?

Mansio?

water
supply

town
defence

'military-style'
ditch

B

k

75ft

High St.

road line

75ft

N

Fig 11.1 Kelvedon, the principal Roman features (based on Rodwell, K 1988, fig 40 with amendments).

usually somewhat wider and deeper, though they could be similar in size to the larger camp ditches.

A ditch of 'military-style' profile was located by Rodwell at Kelvedon and traced for a distance of 84m (Rodwell, K 1988, figs 18 and 19). The south-west end of this ditch had been destroyed by quarrying and erosion, and the north-easterly continuation could not be confirmed at the time. The existence of a 15° deviation in the line of the ditch did not invalidate a military function for it.

Limited trial-trenching by Rodwell failed to locate the continuation of this ditch, and the existence of a gateway to the posulated fort was proposed. A first priority of the 1977 excavations was to examine this possible fort gateway area. The 'military' ditch was relocated but not on the line predicted by Rodwell and Rodwell (1975). It was traced for a further 50m within 1977 Site A. Aerial photography and further excavation allowed the ditch to be traced across country for a total length of some 400m. Its course was gently undulating and the two extremities were lost to quarrying and erosion at one end and in floodplain silts at the other.

The agricultural function of the 'military-style' ditch

If a military function for the ditch is to be maintained, it could be suggested that the ditch formed part of a large fortress of legionary size, the present High Street following the line of the *via principalis* and the north-west side lying under or close to the present London-Colchester railway line. Such a view is difficult to sustain as a fort of such size would have required the total destruction of a substantial native settlement. More decisively, no evidence for Roman military buildings has been recovered within such an hypothesised enclosure.

The ditch line, however, did form a natural limit to both late Iron Age and Roman occupation. It cut across a bend in the River Blackwater, roughly following the division between floodplain and gravel terrace. It isolated an area of river meadow, subject in historic times to flooding, together with a small area of higher and drier land. A ditch on this line would have allowed for easy livestock management with the river Blackwater enclosing the meadow on two sides and the settlement cutting it off on the other.

Beyond the built-up area of Kelvedon the trend of land boundaries is parallel to the excavated ditch and the High Street. This pattern is clearly shown on the Tithe Map. These land boundaries show evidence of a similar degree of sinuosity in their line. At the risk of creating a circular argument, it can be suggested that the present system of rural land boundaries within Kelvedon parish had its origin in late pre-Roman times. Similar early landscapes have been identified at Great Waltham, at Chelmsford, and in south-east Essex (Drury & Rodwell 1980, figs 22 and 23), where the systems are cut obliquely by

Roman roads. In the Kelvedon case the Roman road line was able to follow pre-existing boundaries.

The ditch was less regular in profile than the Rodwells' descriptions would suggest. Eight sections of the ditch were published (Rodwell, K 1988, fig 19), two of which (S19 and S20) were flat-bottomed, 20cm wide at the bottom with vertical or very steep sides until at 30cm from the base they widened out to become an open V in profile. In section S21 the ditch was wider at the bottom and almost U-shaped in profile. In S23 the outer face had been all but removed by a later feature and what survived suggests that it may have been V-shaped with a flat base, like S24 which was the only complete profile recorded. The ditch in S25 is 'Punic' and in S26 the surviving, bottom portion was almost vertically sided.

The ditch had been filled initially with gravel and fine sand (context 173) and later with heavier gravel (172) for part of its length (sections S19 to 521), though in S20 an unnumbered loam is shown between contexts 173 and 172. A loam (context 3) developed over the partially infilled ditch and in S22 filled it entirely, though the ditch was not as deep here as elsewhere along its line. In the area of the battery of kilns 'of military type' (S25 and S26) a loam (unnumbered) is shown between the lowest ditch fill (context 354) and the lowest level of kiln activity (contexts 345 and 353). The impression is that the ditches filled through natural processes with only minimal indications that the fill might have derived from a bank or rampart (context 172 in S21).

The 'military' equipment

No buildings of Roman military plan have been identified within the area of the fort proposed by Rodwell or within the wider Kelvedon village area. The supposedly military kilns are considered by Swan (1984) to be of late Iron Age type.

A small number of military artefacts has, however, been recovered by excavation and as casual finds. The material found prior to 1977 has been published by Rodwell (1988, 57 and 67). The bronze items are: a harness pendant, two pieces of shield binding, a scale of *lorica squamata* (from Rodwell's Area B), a hinge, a repoussé plate, and a harness ring (from Rodwell's Area J and all associated with the military-style ditch). The iron objects are: two poorly provenanced ballista bolts, a 'small socketed spearhead of Roman military type', and another possibly military spearhead (the last two being from Area J). Another scale of *lorica squamata* was recovered in the post-1977 excavations.

The military status of some of these artefacts is clear. The *lorica squamata* and ballista bolts (if the latter are actually from Kelvedon) are Roman and military. What is not clear are the circumstances of loss and, except for the ballista bolts, the whole group need represent the presence of a single soldier.

Despite recent interest in Roman military small finds,

such material is not so closely dated or datable as might be hoped. Scale armour was in use during the Republican and early Imperial period. In Britain scales have been found at Claudian Hod Hill, and at Newstead (dated to between AD 98 and 100). On the continent, scale armour has been found in contexts dated to the second half of the 2nd century. The form of the scales changed over time, and from unit to unit, but the variations are not sufficiently well understood to permit close dating (Robinson 1975, 156). The armour scales and other artefacts of military use from Kelvedon came from secondary fills of features which were of 'military type' or in relatively close proximity to such features. The association of artefacts and an archaeological feature, both 'of military type', is obviously suggestive, and a plausible explanation could be the existence of a fort. However, the suggestion tends to lead towards a circular argument. The ascription of the hypothesised fort to a particular, historically recorded, campaign then follows, based partly on dating evidence of varying precision and partly on a perception of the site's location and function within the consensus model of 1st century Roman military activity. The bulk of the dating evidence is pottery, augmented by rare stratified coins and brooches, relatively crude dating tools for distinguishing between the military events of 43 to 60 AD. Again the argument for the existence of a fort tends to circularity.

The spatial association of military artefacts with the 'military-style' ditch is also suggestive of a functional association. However, the artefacts in question were all recovered from the later fill (context 3) or from a modern intrusion. Where located, the artefacts came from an area barely 7m long or less than 10 per cent of the total length of the ditch excavated by Rodwell.

Early Roman campaigns in south-eastern Britain

To evaluate the circumstances in which forts might have been constructed and military equipment lost, it is necessary to examine the nature of Roman military activity in the south-east generally and in Essex in particular. This military activity can be divided into two types – campaigning and civic administration. The former, as far as Essex is concerned, was restricted to the conquest itself, perhaps the first British revolt of AD 47, and the Boudiccan revolt of AD 60. The original sources for these events comprise the laconic accounts of several classical authors, inscriptions and archaeological material. These have been brought together elsewhere – particularly by Hind (1989) and Webster (1980, 15–31) for the conquest; Rivet (1983) for the first British revolt; and Webster (1993) for the Boudiccan revolt.

The bulk of the literature on 1st century military matters is dominated by attempts to reconcile the disparate and sparse evidence. Much of that literature is of necessity suppositional, based on interpretations both of the archaeological material as well as of the documentary and epigraphic evidence. These attempts are neither valid nor invalid *per se*. They simply represent a series of models or working hypotheses at different levels which are testable to varying degrees in the light of new data accruing mainly from archaeology but also from epigraphy. They are subject to question and revision (Hind 1989, Maxfield 1989 *inter alii*).

The Claudian conquest

The consensus view is that Aulus Plautius landed in Kent, marched parallel to the north Kent coast to defeat the British at the Medway and to cross the Thames in the vicinity of London. From there he brought his troops round to advance into Essex to attack Colchester, the then centre of Catuvellaunian power. One of the clearest expositions, and perhaps the most influential, of the traditional view is given by Collingwood and Myres (1975, 79–80, a reprint of the 2nd edition of 1937). There they argued for three successive waves of troops landing at Richborough, rather than an alternative three-pronged attack on Richborough, Dover, and Lympne. The quantities of men and material required for this invasion plan have been calculated, lending additional credibility to the consensus interpretation (Peddie 1987).

Other interpretations of the scant documentary evidence were proposed in the 19th century, but it was the adoption of Teuber's Medway battle site by such influential scholars as Haverfield, Collingwood, and Richmond that gave greater academic precedence to the Kentish landings. The excavation of possible Roman beachead defences at Richborough and the discovery of the Bredgar coin-hoard gave apparent archaeological confirmation to Teuber's thesis (Hind 1989, 9–11).

Hind has challenged the consensus model on the basis that it does not fit the few geographical details of the campaign known from the documentary sources and that there are now other possible beachead bases, attested by material evidence, which are dated archaeologically to the same period as Richborough. One of these is the excavated site at Fishbourne, near Chichester, and another, known only from finds, is at Fingringhoe in Essex. Hind suggests a landing in the Chichester Harbour area, a dash by Vespasian to support the friendly Dobunni in southern Gloucestershire and a main push east across the Arun and then north to cross the Thames somewhere in the Staines region. From there Aulus Plautius marched on to Colchester *(op cit*, 11–21). A decade earlier Wacher tentatively suggested a secondary landing in the Chichester area, though accepting Richborough as the main landing site (Wacher 1979, 53). Salway (1983, 83) proposed a similar scenario but with an additional third, unidentified landing site to account for the three invasion units described by Cassius Dio.

This is not the place to discuss the various interpretations which the documentary and archaeological evidence for the Claudian campaign may suggest, but certainly the

Chichester area as the main landing is more plausible given the known sailing directions of the invasion force, the stated primary political objective of restoring Verica and the presence of a Claudian supply base in a friendly area. This author's personal preference is for a reworking of Hubner's proposed line of march (Hind 1989, 9), according to which Plautius landed in the Hampshire area and marched inland to the Gloucestershire area to link up with the southern Dobunni. From there the main army group struck eastwards overcoming the native forces probably at the crossing of the Evenlode. Marching east, the Roman forces pushed the Britons across the Lea and awaited Claudius between *Verulamium* and the future site of London. The Romans then crossed 'the River Thames .... where it ..... at flood-tide forms a lake' *(op cit*, 7). It has invariably been assumed that the Thames referred to by Dio was the main east-west stream, but its widening at flood-tide would convert it into an east-west obstacle as well as a north-south one. Such an interpretation of Dio's account seems to solve several of the imponderables of the campaign – such as the apparent lack of a Claudian bridge at London, the absence of any mention of Kent and *Verulamium* by Dio, and the apparently eccentric movements of Vespasian.

A detailed elaboration of this model will have to wait for another occasion but, wherever the invasion force may have landed, the consensus model holds that the main army group, temporarily under the nominal command of Claudius, entered Essex from the south-west. The line of march has been assumed to coincide with the line of the future Roman road (now the A12) from London to Colchester. Considerable research has been devoted to locating material 'proof' for the passage of the invasion force along this route. It has also been assumed that the London-Colchester road possessed strategic value in the early post-conquest decades, an assumption which depends on the early construction of a bridge at London.

The first 'British' revolt

In the surviving account, that by Tacitus, the territory of an unspecified British ally was invaded as Publius Ostorius took over the governorship of the new province. The new governor acted swiftly and decisively, disarming potentially dissident elements and, in a disputed passage, contained 'with camps everything this side of the Trent and Severn' (Rivet 1983, 202). According to Tacitus, the Iceni rose in revolt against these measures. As Rivet *(op cit*, 203–207) points out there are several reasons for thinking that Tacitus attributed the internal revolt to the wrong tribe, and Rivet suggests the Dobunni as the rebel tribe *(ibid*, 206–207). This interpretation seems more plausible and explains the movement of Legio XX from Colchester to Gloucester and the establishment of a *colonia* at the former site to provide a local militia. Such a move would have been most unlikely in the aftermath of a revolt by the Iceni.

The Boudiccan revolt

The revolt of the Iceni in AD 60 was a serious threat to Roman control of Britain. Apart from the infamous behaviour of the Roman soldiery toward Boudicca and her daughters, the Iceni and their southern neighbours, the Trinovantes, were subject to dispossessions and enslavement. According to Tacitus, there was a 'small garrison' at Colchester on the eve of the revolt and this was augmented by a force of 200 inadequately armed troops. This force was surrounded in the temple of Claudius and overcome after a two-day siege. The ninth legion attempted to come to their relief but was routed, all the Roman infantry being massacred. The Roman commander escaped with his cavalry to 'the camp', and the imperial procurator based at an unspecified place fled to Gaul. It is clear that there were hardly any military installations in East Anglia before the rebellion.

The battle which resulted in the defeat of Boudicca is placed in the Mancetter area by Webster (1993, 111–112). Afterwards, we are told that Suetonius concentrated his army, kept it under canvas to finish the campaign and received reinforcements which comprised 8 cohorts and 1000 cavalry, plus 2000 legionaries to make up the losses to the ninth. The auxiliaries went into *new* winter quarters, so there is no doubt that new forts were established now. What we do not know is whether *any*, let alone all, of these were in East Anglia. The scale of losses of the rebellious tribes must have been substantial. The Iceni and Trinovantes would have lost the bulk of their striking power and would have been unlikely to have posed much of a renewed threat, and there must have been an uncertain and more immediately dangerous situation along the western frontier of the province where Suetonius had had to leave unfinished business.

Roman London

Of all the Roman sites in south-east Britain that of London is the key to the consensus model of the conquest and to later events in the two decades after AD 43. London was the hinge point of the supposed line of Roman advance. In that model it was the most westerly point reached before the fall of Colchester. It would have been exposed to counter-attack from the Catuvellauni on the north bank and from their allies on the south. Massive movements of Roman troops and material would have been hindered without an adequate, permanent crossing, while native forces would still have had access to permanent crossings upstream. For the Romans such movements could not have been allowed to depend on the state of the tides or on the vagaries of the wind for naval resupply across the Thames estuary.

The possession and protection of the Thames crossing point required by the consensus model would have been paramount for the Roman commander and would have necessitated at least one bridge and two linked garrisons.

124 *Michael Eddy*

Yet there is no fort known at London until Hadrianic times (Perring *et al* 1991, 109 and 114), and for Tacitus it was simply a settlement of merchants in AD 60 rather than the geographical key to the province. Furthermore, no bridge is known at London until after *c* AD 78, a date based on dendrochronology rather than discarded artefacts (Milne 1985, 47).

While it is inherently dangerous to argue from an absence of evidence, the amount of research effort put into the study of Roman London suggests that this absence of an early bridging point was a real absence. That absence is directly relevant to the course of the conquest campaign, to the subsequent garrisoning of the Essex area, and to the control of the area after the Boudiccan revolt. The absence of a bridge and garrison at London in the first decades of the Roman occupation suggests that the line of the London to Colchester road was not a by-product of the early campaigns, but rather represented a later phase of road construction. The early forts hypothesised along the line of the present A12 would have had little military value, except as police posts, prior to the building of London bridge. After its construction, even police posts would have been unnecessary.

Early Roman forts in Essex (Fig 11.2)

The late 1960s and early 1970s witnessed a substantial increase in the number of early Roman forts claimed for Essex. Frere (1973, fig 2) listed only four Julio-Claudian military sites in the county – the legionary fortress at Colchester, forts at Chelmsford and Great Chesterford, and a possible supply base at Fingringhoe. Webster and Dudley (first edition 1965, 3) included only the legionary fortress at Colchester and the Fingringhoe supply base on their map of Aulus Plautius' advance. In their revised text (1973) they noted the existence of possible forts at Chelmsford and Grays, Thurrock, as well as military activity at Kelvedon.

A survey of early Roman military sites within the territory of the Trinovantes (Essex and adjacent parts of Suffolk and Hertfordshire) proposed a considerable intensification of military construction in the county. Conquest-period forts were claimed at Colchester, Fingringhoe, Kelvedon, Chelmsford, Wickford, Orsett and Tilbury, with possible sites at Braintree, Dunmow, Maldon, Hadleigh, and Mucking. Great Chesterford was attributed to a post-Boudiccan phase (Dunnett 1975, fig 12). In the same year Rodwell surveyed the Roman small towns of the Trinovantes, and stated that 'Chelmsford grew out of a pre-Flavian military base, and other forts were placed alongside several of the major Belgic settlements: at Kelvedon, Great Chesterford and Wickford these have been found in excavation....' He went on to suggest the presence of forts at Coddenham, Suffolk (air photographic evidence); at *Durolitum*, ? Chigwell (no evidence presented); Long Melford, Suffolk (Roman road pattern suggestive of the presence of a fort); Braughing,

Hertfordshire (presence of military bronzes) (Rodwell, W 1975, 93)

In the first county survey of 1st century AD military sites, Drury and Rodwell listed Colchester (legionary), Stanway/Gosbecks, Fingringhoe, Kelvedon, Chelmsford, Wickford, and Great Chesterford as certain or probable and Braintree, Dunmow, and *Durolitum* (? Chigwell) as possible fort sites; along the north bank of the Thames they proposed a possible military function for enclosures at Orsett, Mucking, Gun Hill and Low Street (Tilbury), and Hadleigh and suggested that the existing estuarine settlement of Heybridge was utilised for Roman re-supply. They also brought together finds 'which hint at other sites with a military presence at some time in the 1st century', including a legionary dagger from the River Lea near Waltham Abbey (Drury & Rodwell 1980, 64–5 and fig 20).

In a review of the Roman conquest published in the same year as Drury and Rodwell's county survey, Webster catalogued Colchester, Stanway, Fingringhoe, Kelvedon, Chelmsford, and Great Chesterford as known fort sites and Braintree, Dunmow, Waltham Abbey, and 'near Billericay' as possible sites, though he noted that the last two were unsubstantiated by material evidence of any kind (Webster 1980, 116–7). Fewer sites were given by Johnson (1983, 240) in her study of Roman forts in Britain and Germany – Colchester, Stanway, Kelvedon, Chelmsford, and Great Chesterford. Wacher, in so far as he discussed early forts, took a minimalist view, including only Colchester, Chelmsford, and Great Chesterford on his map of Britain between 43 and 85 AD (Wacher 1978, fig 6).

The *Tabula Imperii Romani* recorded a suspected fort at Great Chesterford (Frere *et al* 1987, 37) and forts at Colchester, Stanway, Fingringhoe, Kelvedon, and Chelmsford (Agache *et al* 1983, 39, 96, 51, 62, and 37). Orsett appeared on the *TIR* map as a fort, though the text made it clear that the symbol should have been altered, as 'what was formerly regarded as a Roman fort proved on excavation to be a defended farmstead of the late Iron Age and Romano-British periods' *(op cit,* 76). Somewhat surprisingly the *TIR* made no mention, under any heading, of Wickford and Heybridge, though both have produced evidence of Roman occupation over a large area.

Jones and Mattingly (1990, 65–66) followed the consensus model of a landing or landings in Kent and dismissed the possibility of a Chichester landing 'since the II legion ... was present at the battle of the Medway'. They saw Richborough as a certain landing site, if too small to accommodate all the invasion force *(op cit,* 66) and, as Roman control was established, it was joined by Fingringhoe, Fishbourne, and Hamworthy as naval supply bases. In their discussion of the garrisoning of Britain, they listed pre-Flavian forts at Colchester, Stanway, Kelvedon, Chelmsford, and Great Chesterford (two) as well as the Fingringhoe naval base.

For the whole of south-east Britain, Webster listed

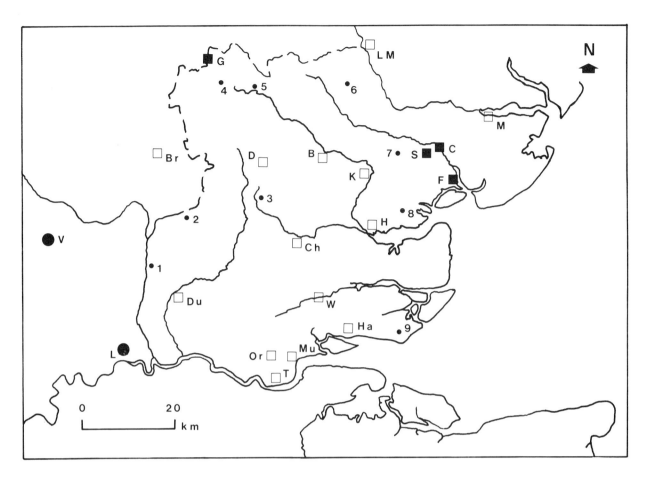

Fig 11.2 Known forts (solid squares), postulated forts now rejected (open squares) and military and quasi-military arte-facts (small, solid dots). Forts - C: Colchester (Camulodunum); F: Fingringhoe; G: Great Chesterford; S: Stanway. Fort and major settlement - V: Verulamium; L: London. Rejected fort sites - B: Braintree; Br: Braughing; Ch: Chelmsford; D: Dunmow; Du: Durolitum (? Chigwell); H: Heybridge/Maldon; Ha: Hadleigh; K: Kelvedon; LM: Long Melford; M: Mistley; Mu: Mucking; Or: Orsett; T: Tilbury (Gun Hill and Low Street); W: Wickford. Military and quasi-military finds: 1: Waltham Abbey; 2: Harlow; 3: High Easter; 4: Saffron Walden; 5: Radwinter; 6: Gestingthorpe; 7: Marks Tey; 8: Tolleshunt D'Arcy; 9: Great Wakering.

137 certain or postulated forts, four legionary bases, five naval supply bases, and two signal stations (1980, 116–121). Wilson (1980, 4) suggested a total of over 240 forts and fortresses from all periods throughout Britain. The basis for Wilson's fort numbers was not explicitly stated but taken at face value the two figures imply that over half the Roman forts in Britain were constructed in the civilian zone and, presumably, mainly within the period AD 43 to 47/8 and around 60.

The expenditure of manpower and time that this scale of construction involved could only have been justified on the grounds that 'the normal Roman practice was to plant a tight network of forts, about a day's march apart, over a newly conquered area to control all the strategic points with the object of preventing hostile elements from gathering together and depriving them of mobility' (Webster 1980, 122). There is a degree of circularity in Webster's statement, for the Roman practice becomes

normal in Britain because a large proportion of the forts which make up the 'normal' pattern are put forward because the perceived norm suggests that they should exist. As Peddie points out, the number of postulated forts would have absorbed all the auxiliary units estimated to have landed in AD 43. 'It is inexplicable that the Roman high command should apparently have been willing, even at a time after the cessation of open hostilities, to fragment their reserves in this logistically expensive way and, by so doing, reduce their ability to respond quickly to a hostile attack ... The network of forts established by Plautius east of the Fosse Way border area was therefore a highly vulnerable method of occupying enemy territory ...'. The weakness of the fort network was shown up by the Roman failure to respond quickly to the Boudiccan revolt in AD 60 (Peddic 1987, 112–3). If such a fort network did exist in the south-east, Peddie's comments are justified.

The Roman forts in Essex reassessed

Of the Roman forts claimed for Essex some have been clearly demonstrated to have been false identifications, particularly the group of small, rectangular enclosures along the Thames. The enclosures at Mucking and Orsett have been shown to be pre-Roman (Toller 1980); those at Tilbury are dated to the late Iron Age/Roman transition and, like the unexcavated Hadleigh enclosure, are most closely paralleled by the Mucking and Orsett enclosures. The presence of possible forts beneath Roman small towns is based on the supposition that forts were constructed at communication nodes. There is no structural evidence for forts at Braintree, Dunmow, Heybridge/Maldon, or Mistley. The site of *Durolitum* has yet to be definitively located, and at none of the postulated locations has unequivocal material evidence of a fort been produced (Eddy with Turner 1982, 22–25).

Wickford has been proposed as a possible pre-Flavian fort site (Drury & Rodwell 1980, 65), and the possibility was admitted by the writer (Eddy with Turner 1982, 24). Since then Wickenden (1988, 239–241) has published a list of the 'military bronzes' from Wickford, where a length of 'military-style ditch' was located by Warwick Rodwell in rescue excavations undertaken between 1965 and 1971. As with so much 'military' material, the military ascription is far from certain, and a number of later pieces are included. Of the coins listed, sixteen are definitely pre-conquest compared with twelve Claudian to Vespasianic coins. If all or some of the Claudian coins are included with the pre-conquest examples, the pattern is surely more suggestive of a native trading site than of a fort. Publication of the report on the excavations is in preparation, and until the report appears the military status of Wickford should be considered to be as uncertain as that claimed for Kelvedon.

The Roman fort at Chelmsford

The presence of an early Roman (Boudiccan) fort at Chelmsford has been proposed on the basis of a length of excavated ditch and military artefacts. The Roman place-name, *Caesaromagus,* has also given rise to speculation about the site's status. The 'military' equipment listed from Chelmsford was recovered from throughout the town area, with six examples each on the *mansio* and 'frontage' (postulated fort) sites and seven from the temple site (Wickenden 1988, 235–237). As with the Kelvedon military equipment some is of dubious military association, and some post-dates the suggested fort.

The structural evidence for 1st century military activity comprised two ditches (contexts 245 and 218 (Drury 1988, 52–56)). In an early interim, Drury (1975, 163) suggested that context 245 represented a military work compound which acted as a base for the military advisers who helped to create *Caesaromagus* shortly after the conquest. In the final report, context 245 was discussed

under the title of 'the 'military' ditch', though the only evidence for its military association was its early pottery (Claudio-Neronian, with the secondary fills being post-Boudiccan). Context 245 in part followed the pre-existing late Iron Age field pattern, in part the newly constructed Roman road. There is nothing, however, to suggest that this ditch was anything other than a adaptation of existing land divisions to new, post-conquest circumstances.

Context 218 (Phase IVA in the interim, Period IV.4 in the final report) 'clearly formed part of a fort, of .. unknown extent. A gateway was excavated, the metalled gap through the rampart being flanked on the north by a pair of postholes'. The southern side had been destroyed by later features (Drury 1975, 159). In the final report, only this 'ditch and rampart ... seems (*sic*) unequivocally military' and they were seen as representing a reduction in size of a larger fort which straddled the main London-Colchester road in the two sub-periods stratified between contexts 245 and 218 (Drury 1988, 128). The larger fort was put forward as the 'most probable explanation' for the Period IV.4 'fort' ditch overlying existing Roman roadside ditches. Context 218 was comparable in shape to, though somewhat larger than, the supposed fort ditch at Kelvedon. In size, the ditch was comparable to 'the bottom of the average range for Flavian fort ditches', while the rampart behind it was similar in width to the average for early Roman military ramparts. The gateway was reconstructed as a double portal on the basis of the spread of gravel metalling inside the gateway, and parallels at the Lunt and Brough were quoted (*op cit*, 56).

However, this reconstruction requires the distance between the butt ends of the ditch at the gateway to be some 5m apart. Only one butt end, the northern, is known. The gap between the two butt ends could be as little as 3m. The gate could then be reconstructed as a single gate between 4 and 5m wide, in keeping with a field gate to admit a cart. The spread of gravel metalling to the northern side of the gateway is not necessarily of significance as it may reflect the continued use of the land according to pre-Roman boundaries. The presence of layers of sand within the postulated rampart was explained by the excavator as the importation of river sands from the Chelmer basin to provide a free-draining base for the rampart. The importation of sand and its archaeological survival in layers around the edges of an enclosure can also be explained in an agricultural context.

Rather than a military presence at Chelmsford, it is possible to argue on the basis of the excavated evidence that the construction of the Roman road in *c* AD 60/65 led only to a limited change of existing land-use in the area. As Drury (*ibid*, 126) points out, urban development did not begin at Chelmsford until *c* AD 120. If the presence of a fort in the 1st century is less certain than had been thought, this reopens the question of why the place gained the imperial honorific of *Caesaromagus*.

The use of the name in the 1st century is, of course, an

assumption based on the presence of Claudius at or near Colchester in AD 43. It is unlikely that the imperial title would have been associated with a purely speculative venture such as Chelmsford seems to have been before *c* AD 120. A more plausible context for the imperial place-name might be found in the urbanization of the province promoted by Hadrian, in Britain in AD 121/122. A Hadrianic attribution would still allow sufficient time for *Caesaromagus* to enter the Antonine Itinerary. It would also give expression to three layers of meaning to Roman/Trinovantian relations, rather than the two identified by Wacher (1974, 196) − a reminder of Trinovantian/Roman friendship at the time of Caesar, a reminder of Rome's liberation of the Trinovantes from the Catuvellauni, and a confirmation of the relationship between Rome and the Trinovantes. The status of Chelmsford as a possible *civitas* capital still remains unclear but if a 1st century military origin is abandoned it becomes less of an oddity among Roman small towns in Essex and in Britain.

Colchester and Great Chesterford

Of all the candidates for Roman forts that have been proposed within or just beyond the modern county boundaries of Essex, the group of military works at Colchester is the most firmly founded both on historical and archaeological grounds. The presence of two Roman forts at Great Chesterford is well attested by aerial photographic evidence. The details of Colchester and Great Chesterford's Roman military past will not be discussed here. Recent excavations and other fieldwork at Colchester have been published or are in the process of being published by the Colchester Archaeological Trust, and summaries by Crummy (1977) and Wacher (1974, 104−120), among others, are available. The current state of our knowledge of Great Chesterford is reviewed by Burnham and Wacher (1990, 138−142).

The military complex at Colchester − the legionary fortress, the Stanway fort, and the presumed naval supply depot at Fingringhoe are, with the two phases of military construction at Great Chesterford, the only unequivocal military bases known in Essex.

Conclusion

Maxfield (1986) and Millett (1990) have pointed out the suppositional basis for much of our interpretations of the Roman conquest and its immediate aftermath, while Hind (1989) has challenged the consensus strategy of the invasion itself. Within Essex, forts of the invasion period have been claimed on the basis that the consensus model requires forts to exist in an area which was supposedly the primary objective of the conquest and a main theatre of later operations. Under the consensus forts are further assumed to have been placed at nodal points in the landscape, such as road junctions and river crossings. As small towns or villages grew up at such points, forts were expected to exist beneath them. However, despite several decades of intensive fieldwork within the county and beyond, remarkably little firm evidence for forts has been found either under small towns or in the countryside. Even some of the firmest excavation evidence, like that from Kelvedon and Chelmsford, will not withstand critical examination and reinterpretation.

In a number of cases, some authors have substituted the term 'military activity' for the concept of a specially constructed fort. 'Military activity' is so broad a concept as to be meaningless and often relies on the presence of artefacts of minimal military application. The circumstances of loss of artefacts with possible military affinities needs to be known, or at least suggested, before they can be taken as representative of real military activity. The identification of camps or forts on the basis of short lengths of ditch of supposedly 'military style' is similarly misleading. The structural evidence required to confirm the existence of a fort or camp should include evidence of internal structures and not be limited to the defences alone.

Accepting that the structural evidence for a fort at Chelmsford is not as certain as has been claimed adds weight to Millett's view (1990, 40−60) that forts were constructed in response to factors of supply of forward units and political control of conquered or allied territory.

The Colchester complex had a dual function, providing an entry point for military supplies at Fingringhoe and an administrative and policing base for the allied Iceni and 'liberated' Trinovantes. Great Chesterford, at the junction of Icenian, Trinovantian, and Catuvellaunian territories provided a similar function. It also stood close to the Icknield Way and the Fens and could control access to and from Icenian territory, as well as providing protection to supply columns moving into the territory of the Corieltauvi.

The limited number of known forts in Essex argues against a Roman military basis for urban development. Kelvedon seems to have developed into a Roman small town from an existing late Iron Age settlement, and most of the other small towns of Roman Essex seem to have done likewise. Only Chelmsford and Dunmow seem to have developed on virgin sites. Official stimulus, in the early 2nd century rather than the mid 1st, may explain Chelmsford's growth, while Dunmow seems to have grown up in response to a need for a small market centre between Braintree and Braughing arising from post-conquest changes in economic conditions.

Acknowledgements
Numerous people have contributed directly and indirectly to my views on the Roman occupation of Essex. My former colleagues at Essex County Council provided lively criticism and helpful comment, while John Peter Wild at Manchester lent a patient ear and a keen mind.

Warwick and Kirsty Rodwell and Paul Drury have provided the essential high-quality field data for many of the sites under consideration and without their efforts Roman Essex would be less well known. Any errors of commission or omission are mine.

Bibliography

Agache, R, *et al*, 1983 *Tabula Imperii Romani. Condate-Glevum-Londinium-Lutetia*, British Academy

Burnham, B C, & Wacher, J S, 1990 *The 'small towns' of Roman Britain*

Collingwood, R G, & Myres, J N L, 1975 *Roman Britain and the English settlements* (reprint of 2nd ed rev, 1937)

——, & Richmond, I, 1976 *The archaeology of Roman Britain* (2nd ed rev 1969)

Crummy, P, 1977 Colchester, fortress and colonia, *Britannia*, 8, 65–107

Drury, P J, 1975 Roman Chelmsford–*Caesaromagus*, in *The 'small towns' of Roman Britain* (eds W Rodwell & T Rowley), BAR Brit Ser, 15, 159–173

——, 1988 *The mansio and other sites in the south-eastern sector of Caesaromagus*, Chelmsford Archaeol Trust Rep 3.1, CBA Res Rep 66

——, & Rodwell, W, 1980 Settlement in the later Iron Age and Roman periods, in *Archaeology in Essex to AD 1500* (ed D G Buckley), CBA Res Rep 34

Dunnett, R, 1975 *The Trinovantes*

Eddy, M R, with Turner, C, 1982 *Kelvedon: the origins and development of a Roman small town*, Essex County Council Occasional Paper 3

Frere, S S, 1973 *Britannia . A history of Roman Britain* (first published 1967)

——, Rivet, A L F, & Sitwell, N H H, 1987 *Tabula Imperii Romani. Britannia Septentrionalis*, British Academy

Grant, M (trans), 1972 *Tacitus. The annals of imperial Rome*

Hind, J G F, 1989 The invasion of Britain in AD 43–an alternative strategy for Aulus Plautius, *Britannia*, 20, 1–21

Johnson, A, 1983 *Roman forts of the 1st and 2nd centuries AD in Britain and the German provinces*

Jones, G D B, & Mattingly, D, 1990 *An atlas of Roman Britain*

Maxfield, V A, 1986 Pre-Flavian forts and their garrisons, *Britannia*, 17, 59–72

——, 1989 Conquest and aftermath, in *Research on Roman Britain 1960–89* (ed M Todd), Britannia Monograph Series 11, 19–29

Milne, G, 1985 *The port of Roman London*

Millett, M, 1990 *The Romanization of Britain: a essay in archaeological interpretation*

Peddie, J, 1987 *Invasion. The Roman invasion of Britain in the year AD 43 and the events leading to their occupation of the West country*

Perring, D, & Roskams, S, with Allen, P, 1991 *Early development of Roman London west of the Walbrook, The Archaeology of London*, 2, CBA Res Rep 70

Rivet, A L F, 1983 The first Icenian revolt, in *Rome and her northern provinces* (eds B R Hartley & J S Wacher), 202–207

Robinson, J R, 1975 *The armour of imperial Rome*

Rodwell, K, 1988 *The prehistoric and Roman settlement at Kelvedon, Essex*, Chelmsford Archaeol Trust Rep 6, CBA Res Rep 63

Rodwell, W, 1975 Trinovantian towns and their setting, in *The 'small towns' of Roman Britain* (eds W Rodwell & T Rowley), BAR Brit Ser 15, 85–101

——, & Rodwell, K, 1975 Kelvedon, *Curr Archaeol*, 45, 25–30

Salway, P, 1981 *Roman Britain*

Swan, V G, 1984 *The pottery kilns of Roman Britain*, RCHM(E) Suppl Ser 5

Todd, M (ed), 1989 *Research on Roman Britain 1960–89*, Britannia Monogr Ser 11

Toller, H S, 1980 An interim report on the excavation of the Orsett 'Cock' enclosure, Essex: 1976–79, *Britannia*, 11, 35–42

Wacher, J, 1974 *The towns of Roman Britain*

——, 1978 *Roman Britain*

——, 1979 *The coming of Rome*

Webster, G, 1980 *The Roman invasion of Britain*

——, 1993 *Boudica: the British revolt against Rome AD 60*

—— & Dudley, D R, 1980 *The Roman conquest of Britain AD 43–57* (first published 1965)

Wickenden, N J, 1988 Some military bronzes from the Trinovantian civitas, in *Military equipment and the identity of Roman soldiers* (ed J C Coulson), Proc 4th Roman Military Equipment Conference, Brit Archaeol Rep Int Ser, 394, 234–256

Wilson, R, 1980 *Roman forts: an illustrated introduction to the garrison posts of Roman Britain*

12   New thoughts on town defences in the western territory of Catuvellauni

Charmian Woodfield

'John Farmar tolde me that theer appere certen ruines or diches of a castelle at Towcestre. Enquire farther of this.' Leland, *Itineraries*, I.

The genesis of this paper lay in the preparation for publication of a quarter of a century's work by various hands on the defences of Towcester, Northamptonshire (Woodfield, C 1992). There it is concluded that 'it now seems incontrovertible that the central area of the town, which had by now developed in long road-side ribbons (RCHM 1982, 151), was given unusually substantial defences with a coeval stone wall and bank, about AD 170–75, enclosing an area of *c* 11.75 hectares.' Towcester thus appears anomalous in relation to the general run of smaller Roman fortified towns in Britain. Frere (1987, 150, 239–243, modifying earlier statements in 1965, 138: 1984(a), 63, 71) suggested that many (but not all) towns had a two stage sequence in their defences; an earthwork circuit of 180–185 or a little later, and added masonry walls 'before the reign of Probus 276–282', the walls of London being 'exceptionally early' at AD 180. At Towcester there is only one stage, and the defences as a whole antedate the suggested first stage of this scheme by as much as a decade. Towcester is also anomalous in that its circuit does not enclose 'all or a large area of the town' as stated to be the norm by Salway (1984, 264) and Frere (1987, 240).

This paper will suggest that Towcester does not in fact stand alone, but that there are parallels for the archaeology of its defences in defended towns which lie along the line of the western Catuvellaunian borders in the later years of the 2nd century AD (Fig 12.1).

1. The defences and status of Towcester
(Figs 12.2, 12.3 and 12.4)

The archaeological position in this town was unusual in that there was, for once, adequate dating evidence for the bank and wall, and at least four recorded sections, at sites A, Ci/Cii, Civ, and D which told basically the same structural and dating story, certainly as concerned the coeval wall and bank. The primary ditches were more problematical due to later, 4th century, recuts and also to

recuts probably of the Norman period, further complicated by the defensive works of Prince Rupert of Bavaria in the Civil War, but twin ditches at least now seem reasonably certain.

The defensive zone at Towcester, from the back of the 2nd century rampart to the outer edge of the 2nd century counterscarp bank, is as much as 60m wide (Fig 12.3, and recording of the counterscarp bank by the writer) and appears to have run over a length of some 1.5 kms. Its construction must have caused much damage to the fabric of the town, cutting its way apparently through a minimum of some eight major road frontages (the Brackley Road on Fig 12.2 being the Roman road to King's Sutton). The defences would have done little to defend the mass of the civilian population living in their suburban ribbon development and some people may actually have been moved out of the defended area: one must assume that they were the equivalent of the nuclear bunker of modern times, designed to defend the machinery of state, that is administration, supplies, communications, taxes, and perhaps on occasion the military.

The bank width of some 12 m is that of an unusually large rampart, but the town wall width at *c* 3m is only a little over average size (Fig 12.3). Despite being dug away by recuts, there were indications of a multiple ditch system of the 2nd century. This involved shallow ditches some 6 to 7 + m wide occurring in the wide area in front of the wall and inside the counterscarp bank. The inner and outer ditches are well attested, but there is no evidence either way for an intermediate ditch. There are parallels at Exeter where the second ditch is some 25m out from the wall (pers comm C Henderson), and at Chelmsford, where there is an inner wider ditch 5m across and two smaller outer ditches (Allen, P 1988, 458), both defences dating from the later 2nd century, Chelmsford probably between AD 160–175.

Identifiable activity within this defensive zone seems to have shortly come to an end at Towcester, but not before a rich pit dating to pre- *c* AD 175 from a well-to-

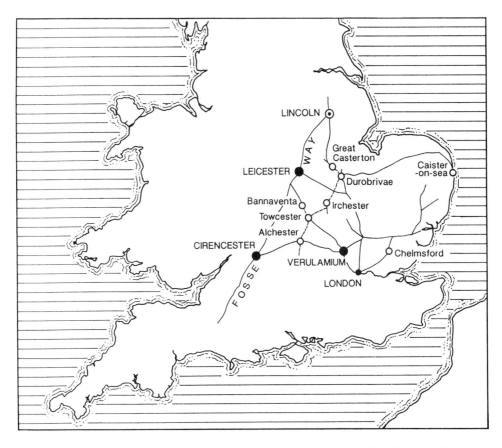

Fig 12.1 Map of relevant area of lowland Roman Britain (after Woodfield, C 1992)

do household had been dug through the tail of the rampart at the north-eastern corner (Site C, feature 10, Figs 12.2, 12.3 and 12.4). It is this pit, recorded by the writer in 1976, with its estimated 74 coarse ware and 50 samian vessels, which has been a crucial element in dating these defences.

The impressive nature of the fortifications raises the question of the status of the town (presumably that of a *pagus* centre).

Fig 12.2 indicates the present state of knowledge on the location of these defences, showing where excavation and recording have taken place, although it does not include an evaluation carried out in 1992 immediately south of Site A (Audouy, M & Webster, M C 1992). Fig 12.2 also includes the best attested fragments of stone buildings that are known. All Towcester excavations produce flue tile, including sometimes hollow box voussoirs, from heated buildings, and two have produced tesserae, suggesting that many substantial buildings must have existed.

Although little is known in detail of these buildings, the wealth of the town in architectural terms is hinted at by the apparently 2nd century architectural masonry recovered from both inside and outside the defended area (Woodfield, P 1978, 71–73, 77, 81–82, 85, figs 2, 4 and 5, and 1981, fig 3, no 1) (Fig 12.10 this paper). There is also material recovered by the writer from the elaborate,

presumably public, bath building, perhaps the *mansio*, known under the parish church (Frere 1984 (b), 300; and Fig 12.2). In addition an apparently pentagonal stone temple or other public building was recorded near the junction of the Watling Street and Alchester roads (Lambrick 1980, fig 4, 44–45) and in 1991 a circular stone structure was briefly seen on site Civ, both indicated on Fig 12.2. There is the well-known Towcester head, from a presumably large-scale funerary monument resembling the Igeler Säule, in the British Museum (Zahn 1968; Toynbee 1962, fig 52). Recent work on the alabastron (an alabaster, or more accurately, banded stalagmite, flask) from Towcester in Northampton Museum (Woodfield 1994, fig 29) shows it to be connected with the worship of Isis (Boon 1982, 848; Wild 1981, 91–2) and a temple or shrine is to be expected. Imported finds further support these indications of wealth particularly from the Flavian period (Parry & Woodfield forthcoming), and the Antonine period produced, *inter alia*, particularly fine vessel glass (Price 1980, 63, figs 14, 15 and 16: Allen, D 1992, fig 12), indicative of wealthy households. It should be noted that the construction of the defences seems to have been accompanied by a cut-off in occupation activity in the town, but not in the suburbs, where the sharp decline seems to occur some half century later (Lambrick 1980, 45, 59; Brown & Alexander 1982, 29; Woodfield, C 1992, 59; Brown & Woodfield 1983, 52).

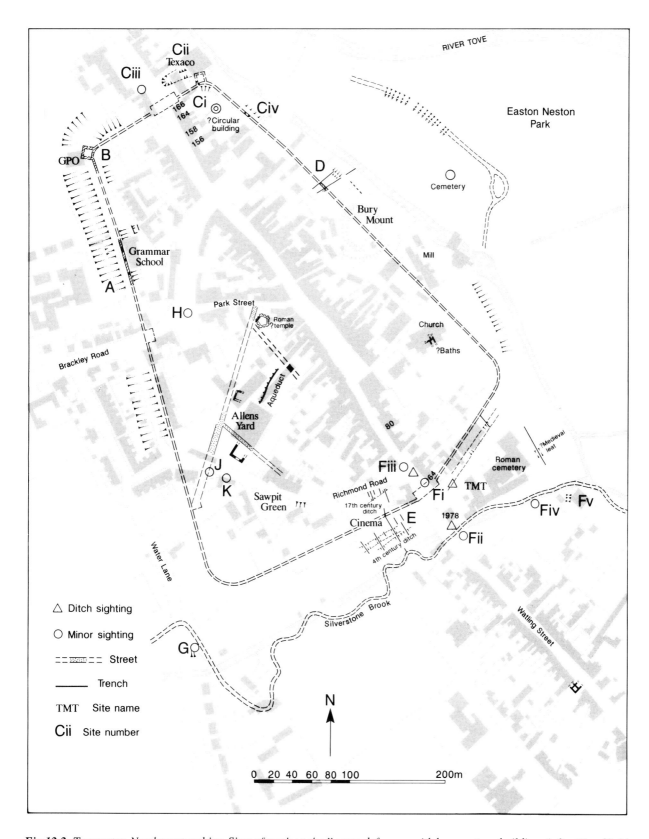

Fig 12.2 *Towcester, Northamptonshire. Sites of work on the Roman defences, with known stone buildings (after Woodfield, C 1992)*

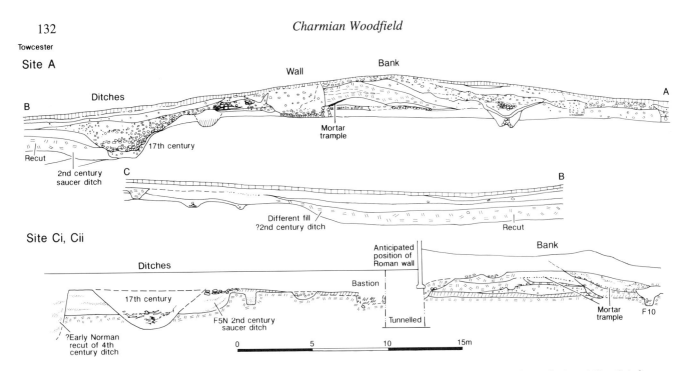

Fig 12.3 *Towcester, Northamptonshire. Sections through the defences, Site A (after Brown & Alexander) and Site C (after Woodfield, C 1992)*

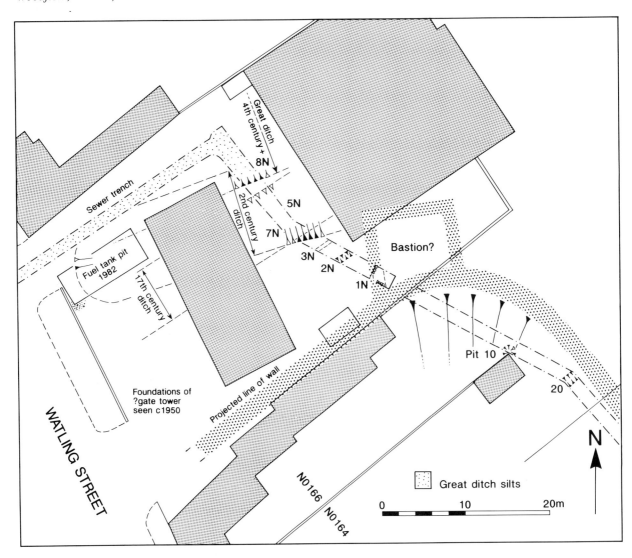

Fig 12.4 *Towcester, Northamptonshire. Plan of NE corner of defences, Sites Ci and Cii (after Woodfield, C 1992)*

Re-evaluation of Towcester Site A: the Grammar School

Site A (Fig 12.3) was excavated in 1954 by John Alexander, and later published by A E Brown (Brown & Alexander 1982). The conclusion drawn in that paper that the wall and bank were very probably part of the same operation and dated from the 170s is now confirmed, the trace lines of mortar/builders' trample in the bank being now paralleled in recorded sections at Sites C and D. There are however now some re-interpretations, agreed in discussion with A E Brown, for the eastern, deeper, part of ditch 5b is now taken to be the remains of a 2nd century wet, shallow, saucer-shaped ditch. The 1982 paper also suggested 'alternatively more than one ditch may have been dug now' (*ibid*, 28), this suggestion being based on a hint in the original records of a different fill at the outer, western end of the wide ditch, indicating that another 2nd century ditch probably existed. This suggestion seems to have been confirmed by the recent, 1992, evaluation, where much of the shallow outer 2nd century ditch survived recutting. The presence of 'individual periods of use' of the ditch was noted in 1992 but the dates given for the pottery, which has been re-examined by the writer, run too late (Audouy & Webster 1992, 5, 6 and fig 3). The Roman pottery in fact appears to start in the mid 1st century and to cut off in the later 2nd century.

Towcester, Site Ci and ii (Figs 12.3 and 12.4; recorded by C Woodfield in 1976)

This is fully discussed in Woodfield, C (1992), but is included here as it gives the profile of the inner early defensive ditch (feature 5N), paralleled at Alchester (Fig 12.5), the saucer profile being in fact a common form for defensive ditches in marshy conditions. The back garden latrine pit, feature 10, is also shown. The position of this, cutting a cobble and limestone surface (11) which clearly post-dated the construction of the main bank, provides the principal dating evidence for that work of *c* AD 170–175.

Preliminary bank and an alteration of plan? (Sites A, Ci and Civ, Figs 12.2 and 12.3)

There was a hint of an early, but also Antonine, bank at Towcester, which could have formed part of a small scale unfinished defensive earthwork (Woodfield, C 1992, 20–4), but this remains inconclusive. It could still be part of the construction of the main defences, a primary bank arising from casting ditch material behind the area scheduled for the construction of the wall (thus obviating the need to carry material round a partly built wall; Jarrett 1965, 57), the anomalies observed being part of some working platform (Woodfield, C 1992, fig 3, and Fig 12.3 this paper for Ci section).

The addition of Towcester to the list of towns with late Roman bastions is also noteworthy.

Dating. A date in the 170s is attested on both Site A and Site C.

2. Late 2nd century banks and stone walls in towns along the western boundary of the Catuvellaunian territory (for details, Table 12.1)

The date of *c* AD 170–5 implies the walling of Towcester possibly a decade or two before London (Maloney & Hobley 1983, 96). This apparent anomaly however appears to be repeated in a line running across country in a south-west/north-east direction from Alchester, through Towcester, probably Irchester, and Water Newton, with an outlier at Great Casterton, that is along the line of the apparent western Catuvellaunian boundary (Fig 12.1). Great Casterton seems likely to be an 'outpost', or rather perhaps a back stop, to this line, and *Bannaventa*, the history of whose defences remains confused, may be. These fortifications would appear to protect the Akeman (Alchester), Watling (Towcester) and Ermine (Water Newton and Great Casterton) Streets, but Irchester does not protect a major known road. A re-examination of the evidence for these towns suggests that they had wide late 2nd century defensive zones with coeval stone walls and banks, and multiple ditch systems with the outer ditch 25m – 30m from the wall. An account of their defences is given below.

a) Alchester (Fig 12.5)

Structure. The excavator stated that 'The town defences consisted of a dump rampart of gravel and sand tips faced by a stone wall. Wall and rampart body were of one build only, since the mortar construction levels immediately behind the wall faded without break into the main bulk of the rampart' (Young 1975, fig 2 and 139). (Three separate mortar levels are, in fact, shown, as broken thick black lines, on Fig 12.5, this paper.)

Dating. Antonine samian was found both below and in the rampart, and an Oxford mortarium of not later than *c* AD 150–60. A date in the second half of the 2nd century, but not later than *c* 150–160, was supported by the coarse pottery, the fact of 'the total absence of pottery of any later date' being commented on (*ibid*, 148, 150).

b) Irchester (Fig 12.6)

The resemblance to the Towcester dimensions is of interest, but Irchester's contemporary internal angle towers (Knight 1967, fig 3) are not apparently paralleled there, but seem likely to have been at Alchester (Young 1975, 154).

Charmian Woodfield

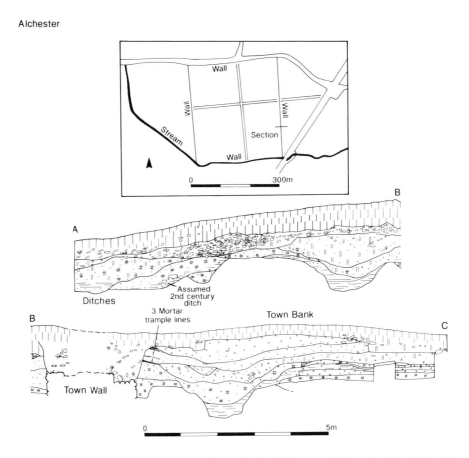

Alchester

Fig 12.5 *Alchester, Oxfordshire. Section through the defences, and location plan (after Young)*

Irchester

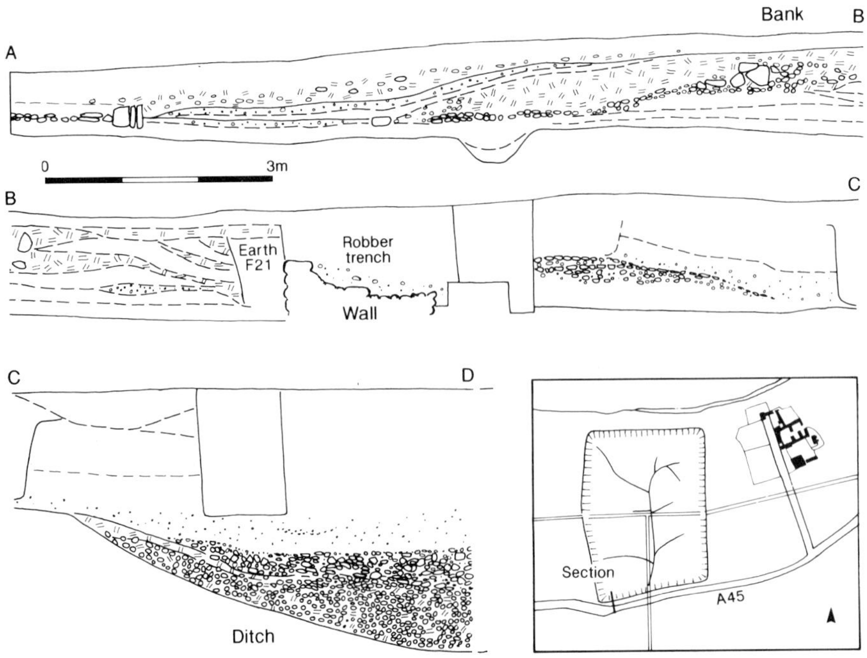

Fig 12.6 *Irchester, Northamptonshire. Section through the defences (after Knight) looking E, and location plan. F.21 does not appear on the W face*

Structure. Wall and Bank (Knight 1967). The evidence for the contemporaneity or otherwise of the wall and bank is contradictory on opposing sections of Knight's trench. The section published of the cut (Fig 12.6), thought by the excavator to show the insertion of the wall, does not in fact reach the bottom of the wall, and may well just be the archaeological trench clipping part of the construction trench (0.53m to 0.76m wide as recorded) for some feature added to the back of the wall (*cf* Towcester, Bury Mount (Woodfield, C 1992, figs 3 and 6) or indeed another internal tower as at the south-west corner of Irchester (Knight 1967, fig 3)), or perhaps conversely some sort of exploratory robbing trench, with its sterile earth fill. There is no plan for the extent or shape of this cut. It might also have been a 'working space', as occurs on the Quadrant 10 section at Towcester, Site A (Brown & Alexander 1982, fig 3).

On the opposite section, 1.85m away, the 'construction trench' was 'no more than half an inch wide', and was clearly barely apparent, giving at first the impression 'that wall and bank were contemporary' (*ibid*, 109–110). This section certainly looks more like a contemporary wall being constructed against the trimmed front of a partially constructed bank, the half-inch gap representing normal slump. The evidence certainly does not prove the later insertion of a wall.

The absence of mortar trample through the surviving bank, 0.74m high, could be because the wall was constructed when the bank was higher than now surviving (the height of the lowest mortar trample at Towcester, Site Ci, is some half dozen centimetres greater, Fig 12.3). In addition the stone core of the bank seems more likely to have accompanied a rubble stone wall, and there is further copious stone rubble on the berm, directly on the later 2nd century ground surface (*ibid*, 110), sealed apparently by the same metalling as was noted on the back of the earth rampart. The tips of 'light limestone rubble' and 'large limestone blocks' in the rampart seem most likely to have been stonemason's waste (*ibid*, 108).

Ditch System. The double (or perhaps treble, if recutting destroyed a third inner ditch) ditch system seems probably to have been of the late 2nd century, modified in the late 3rd or earlier 4th, but again there is no proof of date (Hall & Nickerson 1967, fig 2; Knight 1967, fig 4). The outer ditch occurred some 25m out from the wall, a very similar position to that suggested at Towcester.

Dating. Knight dated the bank to *c* AD 150–200, but the lack of Nene Valley colour-coated ware in it, thought in 1967 to suggest a date before 200, must now imply a date some two or three decades earlier. Discussion with pottery colleagues (in particular Pauline Marney of the Milton Keynes Archaeological Unit) suggests a date for the seventeen vessels illustrated from the bank (Knight 1967, fig 10, 36–51, and 54) of *c* AD 160 – *c* 180. The apparent loss of the samian from both the 1967 sites is unfortunate.

The lack of any published Roman pottery from the Hall and Nickerson ditches makes it difficult to be specific. The outer of these two ditches, 'sterile' for Hall and Nickerson, produced 'late second to fourth century' pottery for Windell (1984, 36) but the one published fragment of a shelly storage jar (No 45, fig 12) is unhelpful, and its context, 107, seems in any case likely to be from a later recut. Clearly all that can be said is that part of the ditch system must be contemporary with the bank and/or wall, and that a multiple ditch system in the late 2nd century is the most likely.

c) Chesterton (Durobrivae) (Fig 12.7)

The work in 1957 has not been published, and the pottery and detailed site records seem not to be available from English Heritage but some of Ernest Greenfield's sections were drawn up for publication by the Department of the Environment. The 1957 section (Fig 12.7) was cut through part of the rampart, the wall, berm, and a small section of a late, wide, wet defensive ditch. The excavator stated that the 'pottery under the ramp' (town bank) 'deposited after the erection of the wall base, dated both to the second century' (Greenfield 1958, 139). The back of the largely clay bank was bounded, and in part overlaid, by metalling, here known to be an intra-mural road continuing in use well beyond the initial construction, and remetalled some half dozen times. The bank itself was interleaved with mortary builders' trample, and there is no sign of any cut-back or construction trench for insertion, and the wall and bank are indisputably coeval (pers comm D F Mackreth). Additionally there is a rubble apron on the berm overlying a primary occupation level which extended beneath the bank and which produced coins of Trajan and Vespasian from under the tail of the bank and the adjacent industrial area to the rear.

The ditch section shows that feature filled with rubble from the wall collapse, confirming a late date. The drawn section shows a slight W-profile and other suggestions of earlier cut-away features. A ditch with a berm of some 5m is not impossible in the 2nd century scheme. By analogy a double ditch system would be expected at that period.

3. Early stone walls and coeval banks in adjacent territory (Fig 12.1 and Table 12.1)

The apparent existence of this defensive line prompted a consideration of the defences of adjacent walled towns, firstly to the south-east. However the evidence for Godmanchester, on Ermine Street, does not suggest a wall and bank of this date (Crickmore 1984, 114). The evidence is poor to non-existent at *Magiovinium* on Watling Street (Wilson (ed) 1970, 289) but what dating evidence there is for its defences, relating mainly to the

Chesterton/Durobrivae

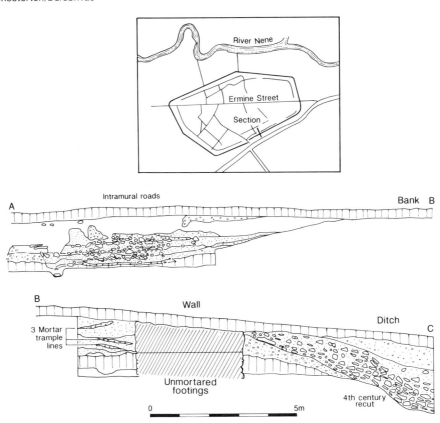

Fig 12.7 *Chesterton/Durobrivae, Cambridgeshire. Section through the defences and location plan (after Greenfield)*

ditch, suggests a late date for that feature and although a stone wall seems to have been recorded, it is undated and unpublished (wall/gate footings of some 2 to 2.15m wide being recorded by P Tilson in a GPO trench in 1969, (pers comm Hedley Pengelly, who holds the drawn section)). The section was recorded in the south-west verge of Watling Street (see Woodfield, C 1977, fig 2, opposite the final 't' of 'Street'). Two sherds, not apparently later than the 2nd century, were recovered from the bank.

However, some ten Roman and nine English miles north-west of Chesterton/*Durobrivae*, on Ermine Street, here presumably in Corieltauvian territory, a different picture presents itself.

a) *Gt Casterton* (Fig 12.8)

Structure. The question of the footings of the wall needs to be examined in some detail, as the excavators' conclusion that the bank and wall were of one date has been called in question. Todd (1991, 40) has suggested 'The published sections ... suggest that an earlier rampart has been cut back to receive a stone wall.'

However, the section of wall referred to here (Corder (ed) 1951, fig 3) (Fig 12.8 this paper) is an anomalous section out of twelve (this is the one cut in 1950, *vide*

supra; seven more were cut in 1951–2, another in 1953 (*idem* 1954, 1, 3, and fig 1, pl IV) and three more in 1955 (*idem* 1961, 24, 26 and fig 8, fig 5, and pl VIIa)). Fig 12.8 this paper shows nine of these trenches.

In all other cases 'the wall was built upon a thick layer of brown soil which overlay the natural stratum of decaying limestone' which 'as always' contained 'sherds from the pre-wall occupation up to *c* AD 180' (*idem* 1961, 24 and fig 8).

In addition not only are there two clear instances illustrated of builders' stone chippings and mortar lying directly on that ubiquitous pre *c* 180 brown clayey surface on the berm in front of the wall (*idem* 1954, pl IV, *idem* 1961, 24 and fig 8) but in one instance the chippings also occur below the rampart (*idem* 1961, 26, pl VIIa). The conclusion that the wall and bank are indeed of one build seems inescapable.

The anomaly in the footings for the wall in the 1950 section (Fig 12.8) is that they overlie a thin (± 0.1m thick) 'clean spread' of clay and stone, here exceptionally intervening between the ubiquitous brown primary clay/occupation layer on limestone. In the other eleven sections the wall is either built directly on, or inserted shallowly into, this layer. This clean material found overlying the clay/occupation level, stretching along the berm and underlying the wall, was said to have come from

Great Casterton

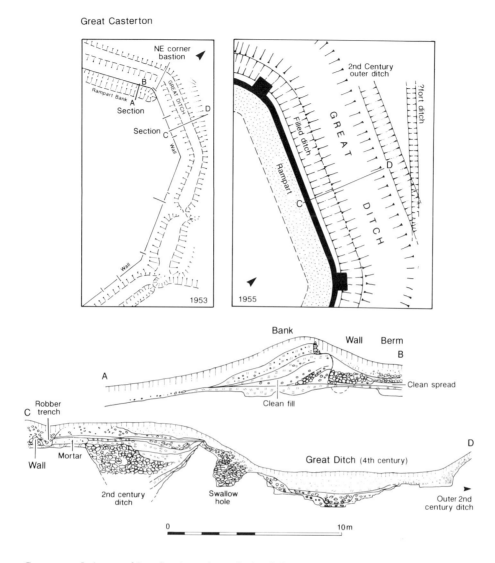

Fig 12.8 Great Casterton, Leicestershire. Sections through the defences and plan of N angle of town and location plan (after Corder & Webster)

spill from the material from the original ditch excavation, as it was being carried southwards to form the clean tips in the early stages of the rampart. Whereas a query might arise on a single section with this configuration, there seems no cogent reason to disagree with Corder and Webster's assessment in view of all the other evidence, and indeed the problem of why the wall was not taken through this loose layer to the substantial clay level below remains, whether the wall was contemporary with the bank or added to it.

Dating. An examination of the published pottery relevant to the dating of the rampart (*idem* 1951, 8–14, figs 4 and 5, *idem* 1954, 7–10, fig 2) confirms Gillam's opinion of a date in 'the decade AD 170–180' for the construction of the defences (*idem* 1954, 3).

In view of the evidence at Great Casterton, attention is called to the possible position of *Bannaventa*, in the same position relative to Towcester as Great Casterton

is to Chesterton/*Durobrivae*, 11 English miles north-west of Towcester. *Bannaventa* is the smallest of this group of towns.

b) *Bannaventa* (Fig 12.9)

Structure. There was much denudation and disturbance on this site, making interpretation difficult. Dix and Taylor (1988, 304) state that the wall's course remained unclear and emphasize that their interpretation of the defensive sequence is uncertain. There are, in fact, difficulties in accepting their hypothesis that a 10m long strip of mortar (not seen elsewhere on the circuit) (*ibid* fig 3 and Fig 12.9 this paper), only 0.15m deep but as much as 3.66m wide, the base of which is higher than the base of the rampart by some 0.25m and apparently sitting in loam, with no trace of the normally unmortared footings of these structures – can really represent a late 3rd century town wall. An additional problem is that the wall is said

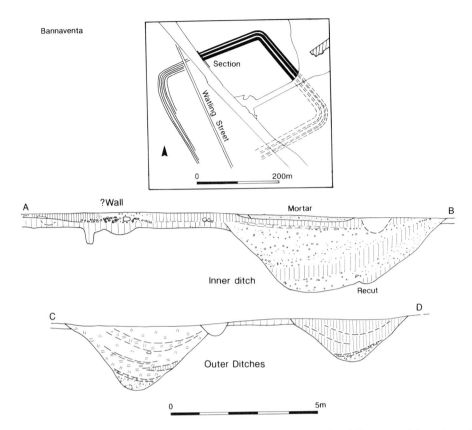

Fig 12.9 Whilton Lodge/Bannaventa, Northamptonshire. Section through the defences and location plan (after Dix &
Taylor).

to be deliberately placed over a filled-in ditch (the illustrated pottery from which in fact could be largely later 4th century, *ibid* fig 7). It is also said that none of the sections across the inner ditch contained evidence of strengthening or underpinning. All this would appear to present the builders with much unnecessary labour and avoidable structural problems, and this writer prefers the alternative view that the stone recorded as 'base of rampart' is the disturbed remains of the footings of a wall at least some 2.5m in width fronting the rampart (*ibid* 304, fig 3, and Fig 12.9 this paper). It seems more likely that the thin mortary strip over the ditch in Fig 12.3, which incidentally contained early Saxon pottery, could be a late levelling off from the clearance of masonry buildings, perhaps for agricultural purposes. Part of a Roman small module turned stone column shaft (Fig 12.10, No 6) was found at *Bannaventa* during a fieldwalking exercise by the Upper Nene Archaeological Society, too late for inclusion in the catalogue of Roman masonry from Northamptonshire (Woodfield, P 1978) but drawn by him and reported to the Northamptonshire SMR. This find indicates that at least some buildings of substance must have existed at *Bannaventa, pace* p 338 of the 1988 report. (The mortar could, of course, have simply come from the demolition of the adjacent wall).

There seems no reason why the original defences might

not have consisted of a later 2nd century stone wall and contemporary bank, with a triple ditch system as suspected at Great Casterton, and suggested at Irchester. It is probable that at a later period the two outer ditches may have been recut, or they may merely have silted up, 4th century pottery accumulating over 2nd century sherds. There are certainly suggestions in the profile as drawn that the outer ditch was recut (or even cut) in a later period, though no detail is given. The internal ditch, however, showed every sign in its profile of having been recut (ie ibid Fig 3 and 12.9 this paper) but with the dating evidence apparently coming from over two metres of undifferentiated fill it is not possible to say when.

What was found cannot prove or disprove the hypothesis of a contemporary bank and stone wall, and the question remains open.

Dating. Samian and the coarse wares coming from the rampart suggested a date in the late 2nd century. The inner ditch was thought to be late 2nd for it was thought that the late 2nd century rampart was made from its material and it cut two ovens producing mid to late 2nd century finds, but the pottery of its fill, which was over 2m deep, was treated as one. This fill contained material from the late 1st century onwards to material that could

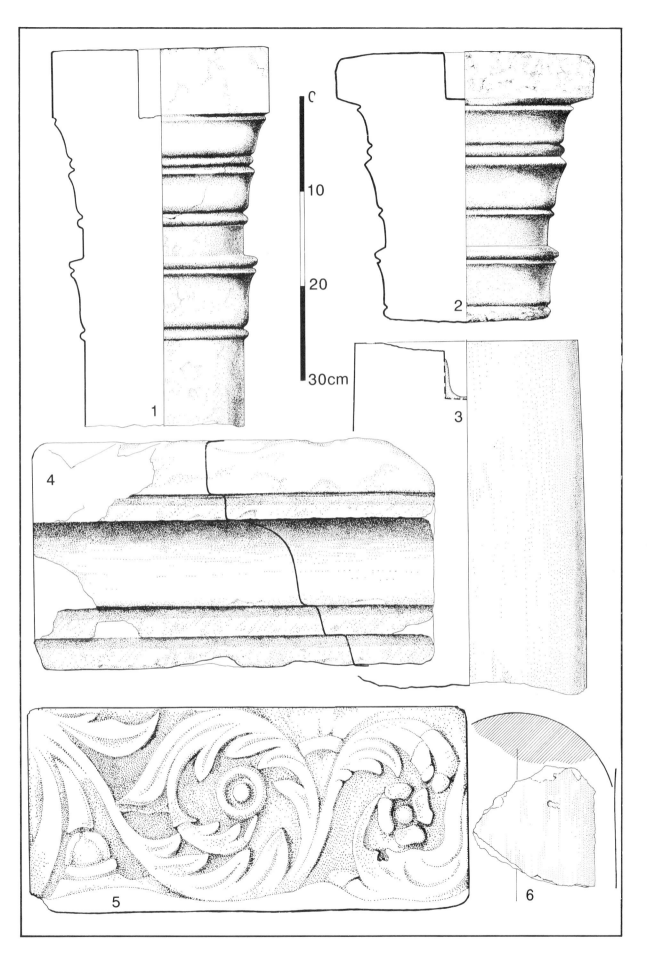

Fig 12.10 *Roman architectural stonework from Northamptonshire. Nos 1, 3–5 Towcester, 2 probably Towcester, 6 Bannaventa (after Woodfield, P 1978)*

be late 4th (Dix & Taylor 1988, 302, 305, 307; and fig 7, particularly 31, 32 and 33, a BB1 flanged bowl and fish dish, and an Oxford C45).

The middle ditch cut a 2nd century oven. The published pottery was not separated as to depth of fill where it occurred, or indeed from that of the outer ditch. The combined pottery for these two ditches is 2nd to 4th century, though a piece of Antonine samian was recorded from the outer ditch (*ibid*, 309).

The outer ditch 'appeared' to cut an earlier ditch which contained pottery dating at the least to the later 3rd to early 4th centuries (no further details either of pottery or stratigraphy). This may of course well date a recut of this ditch, not its orginal cutting. The evidence is not sufficiently precise for the dating problems to be solved.

4. Similarities in the defences of this group of towns (Table 12.1)

The width of the walls is as much as 3m at Towcester, Irchester, and Chesterton/*Durobrivae* (though it also occurs at 2.5m in the first two of these towns). Widths of 2.5m are recorded at Alchester, *Bannaventa* and Great Casterton. Bank widths are greatest again at Towcester and Irchester (some 12m) with *Durobrivae* a little behind at ± 10m. There is then a gap to the ± 7m at Great Casterton and 5–6m at Alchester. *Bannaventa* may well also have occurred in this last band (mimimum 4.8m). The suggestion is that Towcester, Irchester and *Durobrivae* may just have had some sort of senior status. At all these sites (except at *Bannaventa* where the evidence did not survive) the bank seems to have been similarly built up behind the wall as the construction of the latter advanced.

Berms are more variable, as one would expect as they relate as much to topography, geology and the water table as defensive formulae. They are also not so much a matter of labour and cost, though they might be a matter of status as they widen the defensive zone. With the uncertainties of ditch dating and the problems of recutting they are also difficult to determine. The berm certainly seems to have been widest at Towcester, at up to 13.5m (though it fell within the lower range on some Towcester sites). Between 3 to 7m seems to be the normal range for the other towns, though Irchester may have exceeded this.

As for the width of the defensive zone, a double, or perhaps even treble, ditch system of this date is strongly suggested at Great Casterton, the base of the outer ditch, thought to have been 2nd century, being 31.7m out from the front of the wall. A wide 2nd century defensive zone is also known at Towcester (Site A), the equivalent measurement to a postulated position for the outer ditch being some 29m, and the 1992 evaluation seems to have picked up a 7m wide outer ditch in the expected place. The equivalent measurement at the south-west corner of the Irchester defences is some 24.5m, the outer ditch being probably

of this date, and recut later. Nothing is known about any outer ditch system at Alchester or Chesterton, and the outer ditch at *Bannaventa* seems anomalous at a width of 1.5m, and in any case is likely to be of later date.

If one were to advance the hypothesis of a standard 2nd century ditch width of some 5–7m, particularly the inner ditch of a multiple system, this would include Towcester, Irchester, Alchester and *Bannaventa*, all inner ditches (but the date of the Irchester inner ditch is uncertain though thought to be early). It would also include the middle ditches at Great Casterton and *Bannaventa* (the *Bannaventa* date being tentatively 2nd century). Possible third ditches at Great Casterton (6.1m) and Irchester (4.2m) (the last probably of this date, later recut) suggest that a triple ditch system was also possible. It is not known whether the outer ditch at Towcester represents a second or a third ditch but the amount of space available suggests the first alternative. It has been already noted that the outer ditch at Exeter was also some 25m out from the wall and that a triple ditch system of this date is known at Chelmsford. All this does seem finally to dispose of the old inevitability of the narrow 2nd century defensive ditch zone model.

In general the evidence suggests, even though through a glass darkly, a wide defensive zone with generally standardised ditch widths for this group of towns, with, more clearly, coeval stone walls and banks, perhaps on a larger scale for Towcester, Irchester and *Durobrivae*, with further hints that the work may have been planned at some regional centre, presumably to meet some regional threat.

The late Roman period
It is of interest to note that defensive planning in the area appears to have taken a less unified form towards the end of the Roman period. Towcester, Chesterton/*Durobrivae* and Great Casterton were, however, all provided with bastions and wide ditches at some time later in the 4th century. Alchester, Irchester and probably *Bannaventa* are likely simply to have had their, or some of their, ditches recut, but whether at the same period in the 4th century as each other, or indeed the first group referred to above, is not clear.

5. The possible context for these defences: late Antonine fires

That there were fires in certain Romano – British towns at various points in the 2nd century is well-known – London 150–60, *Verulamium* 155–60 or a little later, and Wroxeter forum *c* 169. These are usually regarded, perhaps too readily, as accidental. But in the area under consideration there is good evidence for a series of late Antonine fires, mostly in villas, which might imply serious disturbances or unrest of some kind (Woodfield, C 1989, 264, fig 2). At Stanton Low, Milton Keynes, the villa was destroyed by fire in the late Antonine period, as was the first stone-founded villa at neighbouring

Table 12.1 Dimensions of defensive systems of towns discussed in this paper

ALCHESTER (defended area, *c*10 ha, *c*25 acres)

DIMENSIONS for 2nd century defences. Wall and bank contemporary.

Wall footings width	2.4m	to	2.5m
Dump rampart width	5m	to	6m
Berm width	5m	to	5.8m
Saucer-shaped ditch	7m wide (p 140) 0.8 deep max. Wet.		

OVERALL WIDTH   Some 21m+

No information on possible outer ditches or counterscarp.

TOWCESTER (defended area *c*11.75 ha *c*29 acres)

DIMENSIONS for 2nd century defences. Wall and bank contemporary

Wall footings width	2.5m	to	3m
Dump rampart width (with? 'metalling')	11m	to	?12m
Berm width	*c*6.25m	to	*c*13.5m
Saucer shaped ditch	*c*5.5m	to	+8.0m *c*1m to *c*1.8m deep. Wet. (Outer ditch sectioned 1992, width *c*7m, depth 1m min.)
Counterscarp bank	*c*12m	to	13m

OVERALL WIDTH ±60m

IRCHESTER (defended area *c* 8 ha, *c* 20 acres)

DIMENSIONS

Wall width (Knight 1967)	2.45m	to 3.05, coursed rubble facing.
Bank width (Knight 1967) (with 'metalling')	12.2m	

Berm width (Hall & Nickerson 1967 13.7m to 15.25m (assuming inner ditch is late). If an inner 2nd century ditch existed but was later cut away, min. width of berm would be 7.6m. Either width certainly would imply a stone wall.

Double ditch system, assumed later 2nd century (inner ditch assumed not of this date):

2 dish shaped, both (Hall & Nickerson 1967)	5.03m wide	1.7m deep	Siting discrepancy with Windell due to 4th cent. recut.
middle (Windell 1984)	2.2m wide	1.0m deep	
outer (Windell 1984)	4.2m wide	1.5m deep	'W' of profile recut? (Windell 1984, F 103, Fig 9).

OVERALL WIDTH Some 40m wide overall (but no surviving counterscarp bank).

(The 14.3m wide ditch recorded during a watching brief 'under difficult conditions' (Knight 1967, Fig 4, 107), apparently in the same area as the triple ditches, is thought to be a sighting of the internal face of the inner ditch, a false bottom in that ditch, and the external cut for the middle ditch, these two cuts being some 13m apart. The disturbance between (Windell 1984, fig 8) was probably then interpreted as continuous ditch fill, particularly if there was not time to clean the smear in a machine cut trench. David Windell agrees with this hypothesis (pers comm)).

CHESTERTON/*DUROBRIVAE* (defended area *c*18 ha, *c*44.5 acres)

DIMENSIONS

Wall width	2.9m
Bank width (with rear 'metalling', here an intra-mural road *c*3.6m wide, irregular edges).	10.0m ±
Berm width	Unknown to 2nd century ditch, but in excess of *c*3.5m (3.2m to late ditch)
Ditch	(Min width *c*2m. Min depth *c*1.0m.) The incomplete drawn section is that of the late 26–28m wide ditch.
	There are slight hints of possible earlier cuts.

OVERALL WIDTH, 2nd century and 4th – from back of rampart some 40m minimum without counterscarp bank.

Table 12.1 continued

GREAT CASTERTON (defended area *c*7.2 ha, *c*17.75 acres)

DIMENSIONS for 2nd century defences. NB on rock.

Wall footings width	*c*2.45m	erected direct on earlier occupation (clay-over-limestone)
Dump rampart width	*c*7m ± (north)	
Berm width (with builders' trample)	2 to 3m ± to V-ditch	
(Berm to 4th cent ditch	8.25m	(5.20m from bastion front))
V-ditch ? 2nd cent width	6.4m	min depth 2.9m
2nd cent outer width	6.1m	depth 1.7m
		base 31.7m out from front wall
		2nd cent ditches not recut.

Probably three 2nd cent ditches?, 1 possibly obliterated by Great Ditch? (otherwise 27.45m gap between the two 2nd cent ditches.)

(4th cent ditch width	18.3m	depth	3.35m)
(4th cent counterscarp	7.6m minimum)		
OVERALL WIDTH	45.11m		

with outer 2nd cent ditch but no information on 2nd cent counterscarp.

BANNAVENTA (defended area *c*4 – 4.5 ha, *c*10–11 acres)

DIMENSIONS for 2nd century defences, based on Dix & Taylor 1988, fig 3 and Fig 12.9 this paper

Wall footings width	2.5m (width of stone band on Fig 12.3)	
Dump rampart width loam and gravel	4.8m minimum (if 'metalling' is assumed to be part of bank)	
Berm width perhaps	4.8m (but inner face of original ditch cut away).	
Inner ditch	*c*5 to 6m wide (on hypothetical reconstruction of earlier form, see residual ditch bottom on NW face of section).	depth 2.2m
(Later inner ditch	*c*7.5m wide, as recut	2.6m deep)
Middle ditch	5.3m wide	2.13m deep
Outer ditch?	4. m wide	1.5 deep
OVERALL WIDTH. Some 30m ±		

Bancroft (before 170 according to the samian) and the clay-walled proto-villa at Wood Corner (again on samian evidence *c* 170) (Zeepvat 1987, 68; Woodfield, C 1987, 55: pers comm Hedley Pengelly).

The villa at Piddington, South Northants, was also destroyed by fire at this time (Friendship Taylor & Woodfield 1981, 202, and fig 1), as also the villa at Easton Maudit (Bozeat) six miles to the north-east (pers comm Marc Line and David Mallows and examination of the structures and pottery by the writer). The villa buildings at Cosgrove, South Northants 'fell into disuse in the late 2nd century and were demolished' (Quinnell *et al* 1991, 4) the causes of this in so heavily ploughed a site being uncertain. At the nearby villa at Mileoak, Towcester, there were destruction levels with burnt timbers, rubble, and 'burnt material' and here the desertion is dated to the later Antonine period, but thought to be pre AD 170 (Green & Draper 1978, 28, 41), and there was additionally a post 150, pre-200, fire at the Wood Burcote villa also near Towcester, which it is thought may relate to this series, (pers comm Roy Turland). The samian, including stamps, gave a date of late Antonine, post *c* 160, for the fire – I am grateful to Hedley Pengelly and Brenda Dickinson for this information. In Towcester itself, the pottery from a pit in the south-west of the later walled town, with much burnt daub and nails was dated by the samian to the late Antonine (but post AD 160) period (Lambrick 1980, 75). Late Antonine coin hoards of the 170s and early 180s in the area may well suggest unrest (Woodfield, C 1989, fig 2). Additionally a widespread pre-defences fire is known at Alchester (Iliffe 1929, 111, fig 4; and 1932).

To this can be added the villa at Great Weldon, in east Northants, the ash from the conflagration producing Antonine samian with a date range of AD 150–180 (Smith *et al* 1988–9, 28).

This may help to explain why an analysis of pottery reaching north Buckinghamshire showed so many changes in the pottery industry in the late 2nd century in the areas of the Upper Nene and *Verulamium*, where production of fine grey and oxidised wares disappears or their distribution declines, to be replaced by pottery from the Ouse and its tributaries from expanded native-derived shelly and grogged industries, perhaps representing a reaction against *Romanitas* as well as a cheaper product (Woodfield, C 1987, fig A; Johnston 1969, 76.) Further, at Fulmer and Hedgerley in south Buckinghamshire, whose products reach this area, production ceases suddenly *c* 170 (Corder 1943, 158, Oakley *et al* 1937, 256.) No decline in mortaria from the Oxford area was however apparent.

The question of late Antonine fires has been discussed elsewhere (Rodwell 1975, 85–101). Here reference is made to several small towns and rural sites suffering disastrous fires in the closing years of the 2nd century in Essex, these being linked to the construction of defences at Chelmsford and Wickford. Drury refers to the Antonine fire deposits at these two towns as containing human bone, and states that the samian suggests a date of *c*150 to 180 for them (Drury 1984, 29–30).

It is worth noting also that the forum of Caister by Norwich was completely destroyed by fire post 160 (Frere 1971, 3, 9). A good deal of reconstruction of villas in Suffolk occurs at this time although fires are not specifically known and the records are in most cases inadequate. Certainly the small towns of Pakenham and Hacheston have produced no evidence for fires of this date (pers comm Judith Plouviez). Further work in this area might clarify the position, and if Caister by Yarmouth is now interestingly to be thought of as an early Saxon Shore fort of the late 2nd or early 3rd century to parallel Brancaster and Reculver (pers comm David Gurney) then reasons for its construction need to be sought. It has to be admitted that there is not much evidence for comparable destruction between Essex and the south-east Midlands at this period, except possibly for a fire at the villa at Gadebridge, Herts, where burnt painted wall plaster was recovered from late 2nd – early 3rd century contexts in a well, and there were signs of burning on standing walls, later refurbished (Neal 1974, 27, 29 and pers comm). Additionally the period 8 house at Gorhambury, Herts, was so severely damaged by fire in *c* 175 that radical rebuilding was required (Neal *et al* 1990, 44–48 and 57–60).

6. Discussion

In the early stages of preparing this paper Wales was considered as a possible source of trouble, given the evidence for destruction at Wroxeter, but continued occupation by the army in fair strength in the second half of the 2nd century (Frere 1987, 146) would really make this an unlikely trigger for our line of defended towns on the western Catuvellaunian border. Similarly, the defences in the north of the province appear to have been effectively held in the sixties and seventies of the 2nd century (Salway 1984, 202–3). Therefore if one is looking for raiding as the cause of town fortification, then a contagion spreading from the south-east might be a rather better possibility, given the fires in Essex and also the new fort at Caister by Yarmouth. An incursion by the Chauci as a preliminary to their attack on north-east Gaul in the early 170s is possible (Hartley 1983, 93). There remains the difficulty of the geographical gap in the evidence for destruction mentioned above and the puzzling failure to defend such places as Canterbury at this time. So another possibility might be a purely internal revolt, perhaps by the peasantry, which threatened the security of the roads and the official traffic they carried.

That the perception of a military threat could lead to the construction of defences can be clearly demonstrated by the case of Alcester, where an earthwork defence was constructed to enclose a previously uninhabited area, defended by the river and marshland, adjacent to the town *c* 200–220 AD (pers comm Jeremy Evans). The massive damage inflicted on a town like Towcester, with some half kilometre of prime frontages wiped out by the construction of a 60m wide circuit, and much loss of back land, looks more likely to be due to a compelling desire for protection than a wish to impress. It should also be noted that the new defences at Chelmsford were levelled within the first twenty years of the 3rd century, and Kelvedon in the same period; also the defences of Wickford were not completed (Crickmore 1984), all factors which suggest a short lived crisis (Frere 1984(a), 69).

With the obviously relevant *coloniae* and cantonal capitals – Lincoln, Leicester, Cirencester and *Verulamium* – considerations of status may have come into play as well. Whether there was a decision to defend them at precisely the same time as this group of small towns is not clear given the imprecision of the dating evidence (Woodfield, C 1992, 60 for a discussion of this), although most were given defences at some point in the later 2nd century. The intention to have contemporary walls and banks may always have been present; the larger size of some of these towns meant that their defences show greater structural and chronological complexity, with wall and bank construction falling out of step.

There can be little real doubt of the involvement of the *civitas* and of the provincial governor in the decision to erect these defences though the date is likely to be too early for imperial permission to have been required (Frere 1984(a)). In this context the question of the highly anomalous percentages of BB1 in Towcester at the time of their erection and possibly for a decade or two afterwards may be significant (Woodfield, C 1992, 36 and Brown & Woodfield 1983, 79). The walling of certain towns in the south, eg Chichester, Dorchester, Silchester and Winchester is accompanied by a surge of BB1 to proportions of some 25% (pers comm Malcolm Lyne). Might

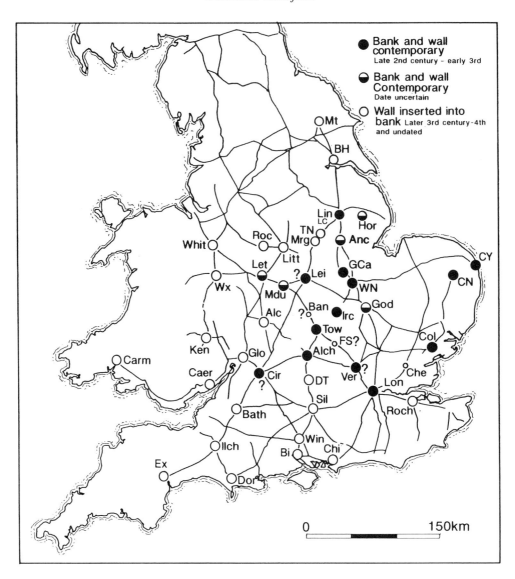

Fig 12.11 *The eastern concentration of late 2nd/early 3rd century defences with contemporary banks and walls*

KEY *to Fig 12.11 (after Crickmore 1984).*

The insertion of walls into legionary fortress defences is here ignored, as are towns with late walls only, and where the evidence is uninterpretable. Cirencester and *Verulamium* are included provisionally because they both have stone gates and interval towers and may have been partially walled at the given date. At Leicester the wall and bank seem to be contemporary in part. *Bannaventa* remains open to interpretation.

Alc	Alcester	Dor	Dorchester, Dorset	Mdu	*Manduessedum*
Alch	Alchester	Ex	Exeter	Mrg	*Margidunum*
Anc	Ancaster	FS	Fenny Stratford	Mt	Malton
BH	Brough-on-Humber	Glo	Gloucester	Roc	Rocester
Ban	*Bannaventa*	God	Godmanchester	Roch	Rochester
Bi	Bitterne	GCa	Great Casterton	Sil	Silchester
CN	Caistor-by-Norwich (St Edmund)	Hor	Horncastle	TN	Thorpe by Newark
CY	Caister-by-Yarmouth (on-Sea)	Ilch	Ilchester	Tow	Towcester
Caer	Caerwent	Irc	Irchester	Ver	*Verulamium*
Carm	Carmarthen	Ken	Kenchester	WN	Water Newton
Che	Chelmsford	Lei	Leicester	Whit	Whitchurch
Cir	Cirencester	Let	*Letocetum* (Wall)	Win	Winchester
Chi	Chichester	LinLC	Lincoln, Lower *colonia*	Wx	Wroxeter
Col	Colchester	Litt	Littlechester		
DT	Dorchester-on-Thames	Lon	London		

this suggest the presence of detachments of military engineers, with the military's known high use of this cheap and serviceable ware? At Towcester BB1 was 22% of a deposit of *c* 170–175AD in a latrine pit cutting the new rampart at the north-east corner of the defences. The normal percentage at that date in the locality, but outside the town, is about 3% or less.

It may also be presumed that the army would be present to man the walls in an emergency wherever possible. In this context recent study, initiated by the writer, of the heart-shaped military pendant from Towcester now in the British Museum (BM 1882 6–21, 147) has shown it to be of mid or late 2nd/early 3rd century date and probably used as part of the trappings of the cavalry (Oldenstein 1976, 124–7; McCarthy 1990, 122, fig 109, no 51; Woodfield forthcoming, fig 5). (The writer is grateful to Cathy Johns for making this object available and to Glenys Lloyd – Morgan for the identification).

7. Conclusion

The old 2nd century narrow defensive-ditch zone model, and likewise the model of the 2nd century earthen bank refaced with stone in the later 3rd century, are here questioned, and a date of *c* AD165 to *c* 175, but centering on *c* 170, is advanced for this particular group of towns, with defences featuring a stone wall (Figs 12.1 and 12.11).

The Towcester defences are put forward not as an unacceptable curiosity standing on their own but as part of a planned defensive line protecting towns important presumably not only locally as administrative centres but also for the road network to the central, and indeed further afield to the northern and western, parts of the province (Fig 12.11). The towns discussed here lay along the western marches of Catuvellaunian territory, and their defences seem likely to have been brought into being by serious trouble in the region, for an examination of the records of destruction in an area some 17 km square, lying between the Watling Street and the Upper Nene, produces an abnormal number of fires centring on *c* AD 170. No such fires are known from Leicestershire (pers comm Richard Pollard), perhaps implying a geographically restricted crisis. The source of these fires may perhaps be looked for locally, or as coming from an area of south-eastern Britain, particularly perhaps the area of modern Essex, where there is a similar record, and an abnormal number of earthwork defences (Crickmore 1984, fig on p 13). It looks as if what happened in the 160s/170s was alarming enough to make vulnerability clear (and perhaps affected the villas, the expense of whose construction may have been a contributory cause, more than the towns), but did not seriously affect the economy, since in the immediate area of Towcester the villas are rebuilt and the town's suburbs appear to thrive, but both run into trouble in the Severan period.

The evidence for a defensive scheme on the postulated model is strong at Towcester and Great Casterton

and clear at Alchester. A similar situation is likely at Chesterton/*Durobrivae* and Irchester. *Bannaventa* is a possibility. It seems likely that these stone walled towns preceded the widespread urban earthwork defences and are the immediate predecessors for that activity, not the successors.

The theory of central control in the erection of Romano-British town defences has been recently questioned by Millett – 'Variability, inconsistent with central control is the keyword' (Millett 1990, 139) but it may well be that we should be looking for regional (in the geographical sense, not that of the *civitates* necessarily) patterns of control, related to regional problems. These may require the back-up of the governor, but need not mean a concerted province wide programme.

Acknowledgements
Thanks are due to Ernest Black, George Boon, Paul Booth, Tony Brown, Maggi Darling, Jeremy Evans, David Gurney, Martin Henig, Chris Henderson, Mike Jarrett, Don Mackreth, Pauline Marney, Rosalind Niblett, Hedley Pengelly, Judith Plouviez, Richard Pollard, Richard Reece, Warwick Rodwell, Bob Rutland, Paul Sealey, Linda Viner, John Wacher, Nick Wickenden and David Windell, who all provided valuable information. The illustrations are the work of David Williams, MAAIS, except for Fig 12.10, which is the work of Paul Woodfield, ARIBA.

Bibliography
Allen, D, 1992 *The glass*, in Woodfield, C, 1992
Allen, P, 1988 In Frere, S S, Roman Britain in 1987, East Anglia, *Britannia*, 19, 458
Audouy, M, & Webster, M C, 1992 *An archaeological evaluation at Sponne School, Towcester*, Northants Archaeology Unit, Contracts Section
Boon, G, 1982 Roman alabaster jars from Trier and Cologne, *Bull Board Celtic Stud*, 19(4), 847–9
Brown, A E, Orr, C, & Woodfield P, 1981 The Stowe charter – a revision and some implications, *Northamptonshire Archaeol*, 16, 136–147
——, & Alexander, J A, 1982 Excavations at Towcester 1954: the Grammar School site, *Northants Archaeol*, 17, 24–59
——, & Woodfield, C, 1983 Excavations at Towcester, Northamptonshire: the Alchester Road suburb, *Northamptonshire Archaeol*, 18, 43–140
Corder, P, 1943 The Roman pottery made at Fulmer, *Rec Buckinghamshire*, 14.3, 153–187
—— (ed), 1951 *The Roman town and villa at Great Casterton, Rutland*, University of Nottingham
——, 1954 *The Roman town and villa at Great Casterton, Rutland, second interim report*, University of Nottingham
——, 1961 *The Roman town and villa at Great Casterton, Rutland, third report*, University of Nottingham
Crickmore, J, 1984 *Romano-British urban defences*, BAR Brit Ser 126

Dix, B, & Taylor, S, 1988 Excavations at *Bannaventa* (Whilton Lodge Northants), 1970–1971, *Britannia*, 19, 299–339

Drury, P J, 1984 The temple of Claudius at Colchester reconsidered, *Britannia*, 15, 7–50

Frere, S S, 1965 Town defences in Roman Britain, *Antiquity*, 9, 137–39

——, 1971 The forum and baths at Caistor by Norwich, *Britannia*, 2, 1–26

——, 1984 (a) Romano – British urban defences in earthwork, *Britannia*, 15, 63–74

——, 1984 (b) Roman Britain in 1983. I, Sites explored. 5. The Midlands, *Britannia*, 15, 290–305

——, 1987 *Britannia, a history of Roman Britain*

Friendship-Taylor, R M & D E, & Woodfield, C & P, 1981 Piddington Roman villa, in Archaeology in Northants 1980 (ed A E Brown), *Northamptonshire Archaeol*, 16, 202

Green, C, & Draper, J, 1978 The Mileoak Roman villa, Handley, Towcester, Northamptonshire. Report on the excavations of 1955 and 1956, *Northamptonshire Archaeol*, 13, 28–67

Greenfield, E, 1958 Note in Roman Britain in 1957, The Midlands, *J Roman Stud*, 48, 139

Hall, D N & Nickerson, N, 1967 Excavations at Irchester, 1962–3, I, *Archaeol J*, 124, 65–99

Hartley, B R, 1983 The enclosure of Romano British towns in the second century AD, in *Rome and her northern provinces* (eds B Hartley & J Wacher), 84–95

Iliffe, J H, 1929 Excavations at Alchester, 1927, *Antiq J*, 9.2, 105–136

——, 1932 Excavations at Alchester, 1928, *Antiq J*, 12.1, 35–67

Jarrett, M, 1965 Town defences in Roman Britain, *Antiquity*, 39, 57–9, 137, 227

Johnston, D E, 1969 Romano – British pottery kilns near Northampton, *Antiq J*, 49, 75–97

Knight, J K, 1967 Excavations at the Roman town of Irchester, II, 1962–3, *Archaeol J*, 124, 100–128

Lambrick, G, 1980 Excavations in Park Street, Towcester, *Northamptonshire Archaeol*, 15, 35–118

Maloney J, & Hobley, B (eds), 1983 *Roman urban defences in the West*, CBA Res Rep 51

McCarthy, M R, 1990 A Roman, Anglian and medieval site at Blackfriars Street, Carlisle, *Cumberland and Westmorland Antiq Archaeol Soc Research Ser*, 4

Millett, M, 1990 *The Romanisation of Britain*

Neal, D S, 1974 *The excavation of the Roman villa in Gadebridge Park, Hemel Hempstead 1963–8*, Soc Antiq Res Rep 31

——, Wardle, A & Hunn, J, 1990 Excavation of the Iron Age, Roman and Medieval Settlement at Gorhambury, St Albans, *Engl Heritage Archaeol Rep*, 1

Oakley, K P, Vulliamy, C E, Rouse C, Cottrill, F, 1937 The excavation of a Romano British pottery kiln site near Hedgerley, *Rec Buckinghamshire*, 13, 252–280

Oldenstein, J, 1976 *Bericht der Römisch-Germanischen Kommission*, 57, 49–284

Price, J, 1980 *The glass*, in Lambrick, G, 1980, 63–68

Quinnell, H, *et al*, 1991 The villa and temple at Cosgrove, Northamptonshire, *Northamptonshire Archaeol*, 23, 4–66

Rodwell, B, 1975 Trinovantian towns and their setting, in *The 'small towns' of Roman Britain* (eds W Rodwell and T Rowley), BAR Brit Ser, 15, 85–101

RCHM 1982 *An inventory of archaeological sites in South West Northamptonshire, IV*

Salway, P, 1984 *Roman Britain*

Smith, D J, Hird, L, & Dix, B, 1988–9 The Roman villa at Great Weldon, Northamptonshire, *Northamptonshire Archaeol*, 22, 23–68

Sunderland, J R, & Webb, M (eds) 1994 *Towcester, the story of an English country town: a celebration of two thousand years of history*

Todd, M, 1991 *The Coritani*

Toynbee, J M C, 1962 *Art in Roman Britain*

Wild, R A, 1981 *Water in the cultic worship of Isis and Serapis*

Wilson, D R (ed), 1970 Roman Britain in 1969: The Midlands, *Britannia*, 1, 289

Windell, D, 1984 Irchester Roman town, excavations 1981–82, *Northamptonshire Archaeol*, 19, 31–51

Woodfield, C, 1977 A Roman military site at Magiovinium? *Rec Buckinghamshire*, 20.3, 384–399

——, 1987 Wood Corner, in *Roman Milton Keynes* (ed D Mynard), 52–60, Bucks Archaeol Soc Monograph 1 (author's unaltered copy at Society of Antiquaries and Haverfield libraries)

——, 1989 A Roman site at Stanton Low, on the Great Ouse, Buckinghamshire, *Archaeol J*, 146, 135–278

——, 1992 The defences of Towcester, Northamptonshire, *Northamptonshire Archaeol*, 24, 13–66

——, 1994 Prehistoric and Roman Towcester, in Sunderland J R, & Webb, M (eds) 1994, 1–51

Woodfield, P, 1978 Roman architectural masonry from Northamptonshire, *Northamptonshire Archaeol*, 13, 67–86

——, 1981 The carved stones, in Brown, Orr & Woodfield, 1981, 141–147

Young, C, 1975 The defences of Roman Alchester, *Oxoniensia*, 40, 136–170

Zahn, E, 1968 Die Igeler Saüle bei Trier, *Rhein Kunststätten*, 38

Zeepvat, R J, 1987 Bancroft villa, in *Roman Milton Keynes* (ed D Mynard), Bucks Archaeol Soc Monograph 1, 60–79

13   Durobrivae, Chesterton, Cambridgeshire

D F Mackreth

Durobrivae tends to be a popular example of a small town; it lies in open country, parts of it show well on aerial photographs, two treasures come from there, it has a satisfying relationship with the perceived Roman infrastructure, major rural buildings and, of course, the pottery industry. Its very size, however, leads to difficulties and also a confusion of name. The town runs for some three kilometres along Ermine Street and has a giant suburb over the bridge in what is generally called Normangate Field. It was the latter, coupled with the great building under the village, which led early antiquaries to call the site Castor, hence 'Castor Ware' for the local colour-coated pottery, but it was concentration on military origins which gave rise to its being called Water Newton. The site lies in the parishes of Chesterton and Water Newton south-west of the river and Ailsworth and Castor across that. The walled town is in Chesterton parish and, following usual rules, that should be the English name of the site.

Wacher included the town in his *The towns of Roman Britain* (Wacher 1975, 408–410); its size and suburbs, and other indications suggested to him that it may have become a *civitas*. Further thinking, however, has removed the site from this category by implication, as *Durobrivae* is included, under the title of 'Potential Cities', in *The 'small towns' of Roman Britain* (Burnham & Wacher 1990, 81–91) where, incidentally, the reader will find a host of useful statistics. The same arguments are advanced about its possible late Roman status and the conclusion is: 'Taken cumulatively, this archaeological evidence sets Water Newton apart from all other minor towns studied in this volume'. This being so, Chesterton should be the last place to cite as a typical example of a small town, but any attempt to place it in a context is bound to end up by clutching at straws.

The name of the site, *Durobrivae*, has been deduced from the Antonine Itinerary and the Ravenna Cosmography, and is confirmed by a *dipinto* (Guide, p 3, GWA 158) and mortaria stamps (Wild 1974, 147). The name means 'bridges-fort' (Rivet & Smith 1979) and the plural seems to be definitely applicable to the bridge element alone. The aerial views of the fort site in Water

Newton parish (eg, St Joseph 1953, pl IX, 1), in the centre of Figure 13.1, provides the fort, but it was not in isolation. Down river is the Longthorpe fortress (Frere & St Joseph 1974) which had, arguably, a fort opposite it in what are now called Ferry Meadows, the site disappearing when the lakes there were made (Wild 1974, 145, fig 1) and Figure 13.1 reveals some highly suggestive cropmarks in Normangate Field immediately east of the junction of King Street with Ermine Street. Taking the northern boundary to be where Splash Dyke is now, the dimensions of the enclosure are almost exactly the same as those of the fort south of the river. Pairing of forts on either side of a river is a necessary precaution in 'difficult' terrain and a fortress with up to three attendant forts emphasises the strength of the Roman army here; it would be a foolishness to find a separate event for each of these real and potential military sites. These units should have been brigaded together to form a fighting force beyond the needs of a plain policing role.

In modern terms, these military installations control the junction of the A47 with the A1, the equivalents of Ermine Street and the Fen Causeway. There are two foci: the river crossing at *Durobrivae* and the other more or less below the major loops in the river. The latter occupies a good defensible position much closer to the end of the Fen Causeway which itself may have divided into two on Whittlesey island, the known branch running north and another, unevidenced, running west to cross the river at Horsey Toll. A sword from the island could even indicate a further military site, now lost in the brick pits there (Howe 1978, fig 14). The events attached to Boudicca's insurrection reveal the purpose of the army group (Frere & St Joseph 1974, 38–39) and, with the suppression of that, the need for it came to an end. The natural advantages of the town site would have given rise to civilian occupation, but whether it was associated with a fort maintained beyond the closing down of the Longthorpe fortress can only be guessed at. There has been no modern excavation within the walled area save for two trenches across the defences (Taylor 1958, 139). All that survives of the records is part of a written text,

148

D F Mackreth

Fig 13.1 Durobrivae

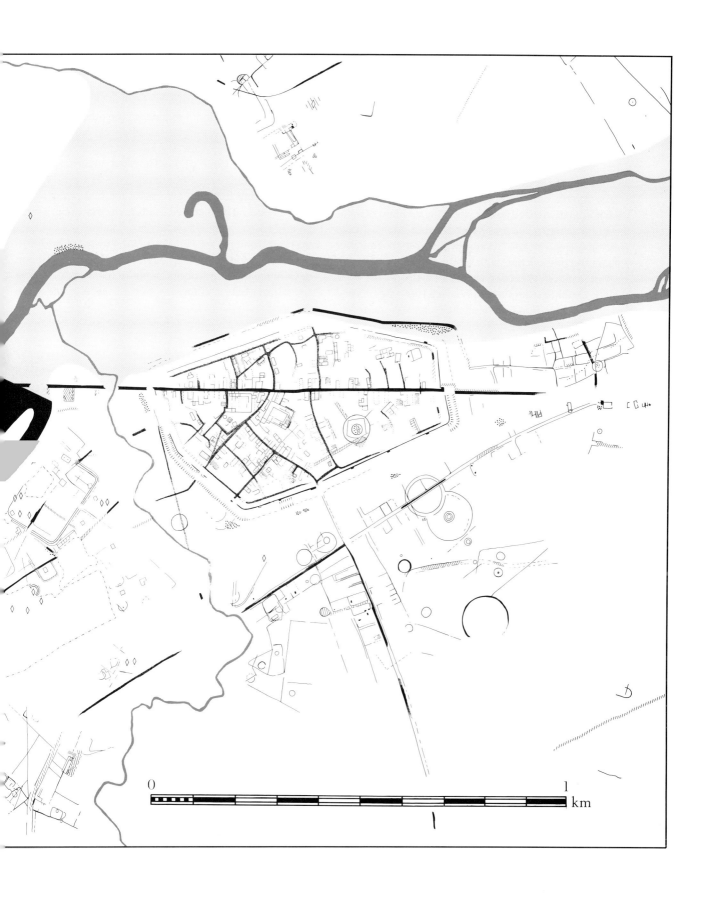

0   1
km

a section and a few sherds, the bulk of the pottery being lost along with the original field notes.

Detailed knowledge of the site derives almost exclusively from air photographs, and Figure 13.1 was compiled from over a thousand. The chief sources were the collections of the Cambridge University Committee for Air Photography, the National Archaeological Survey and the collection built up by Dr S G Upex with the support of the Nene Valley Research Committee. Two major inhumation cemeteries have been omitted, the stippling marks areas of burials recorded by Artis (1828, pl 23) and in Ernest Greenfield's surviving records.

For convenience sake, the site south of the river has been notionally slewed so that Normangate Field remains the north suburb, but the Water Newton fort is in the west suburb and the road running away from the Irchester gate passes through the south suburb. A plain plotting of air photographs makes the plan diffuse with only the roads to tie it together (Burnham & Wacher 1990, figs 18 and 20). Adding the flood plain of the Nene and the minor tributaries gives a greater cohesion to the whole (Fig 13.1). The chief tributaries are Splash Dyke looping round Normangate Field and under Mill Hill, and Billing Brook dividing the west suburb from the walled town. The extent of the flood plain is based upon the 1948 floods which themselves were used to define the flood plain in modern planning terms. The floor of the present valley, based on findings in the excavations carried out in Orton Meadows (to be published), is probably a relatively uniform half a metre above the Roman equivalent. This means that the bulk of whatever is Roman under the silt does not show, but the knowledge that this is so serves to emphasise the prominence of the causeway carrying Ermine Street to the bridge.

The river was tidal up to the site of the town until modern times and such an aid to boats journeying to and from the Wash must have been a factor in the development of the town, especially as moving goods in bulk was so much cheaper by water than by road (Jones 1964, 871–872; Greene 1986, fig 14; Peacock 1982, 159). The walled area sits on a slight ridge between the river and lower ground to its south which is more defensible than an equivalent area in Normangate Field or where the Water Newton fort lies. The chief roads are obvious, but only Ermine Street and King Street are known outside the town. The one running south clearly went to Irchester, but like the further course of the southern bypass road, its course is obscure. The road running east out of Normangate Field should join the Fen Causeway, but its line is unknown; the great bank running through the field at the top of Love's Hill is a medieval headland only.

The overall plan obviously lacks any regularly conceived layout, except in the south suburb where elements of a regular 'toft and croft' layout can be seen along the bypass and Irchester road; perhaps their relatively uncomplicated appearance is a mark of their ultimate failure. In Normangate Field, apart from the end-on houses

along Ermine Street, there is little trace of coherent planning, even the faintly orthogonal arrangement around the suspected fort is very limited. Somewhere in this suburb lies the major building illustrated by Artis who fails to identify it on any plan (Artis 1828, pls 26(4), 32). The layout to the east is based upon two roads springing from a branch road running from the bridge. One has a prominent metalled *agger* not evident in the other which runs up to, and is basically aligned on, the great building under Castor village (Fig 13.2; Burnham & Wacher 1990, fig 21; RCHM(E) 1969, pl 3). The west suburb, once the features related to the fort are removed, is formless and, even allowing for the giant gravel pit, had probably always been so. The metalled roads in the east suburb were possibly associated with wharves or landing stages along the river frontage. Any others running up to the bridge to the west would have been subject to flooding. Ribbon development along Ermine Street runs towards London for at least half a kilometre, and for at least the same distance along King Street.

In the town, air photographs show the west half fairly well, but the eastern area is more elusive (eg, Burnham & Wacher 1990, fig 19). The London and Irchester gates were offset and the Lincoln gate was probably so. Enough square projections from the town wall are known for their disposition to be guessed at. They were probably external towers rather than bastions. Inside is an intramural road, most of the internal roads running out to this. The only other distinctive road element is the crude orthogonal layout south of the road running between the two major buildings which itself continues beyond the defences indicating that it was there before: the faintest of marks suggesting a towered gate are so elusive that they are better ignored. The road points to a major approach from the west before the defences were built, and the bypass, with its suburb and a road from there to Ermine Street were probably in existence when they were begun. The cumulative evidence of air photographs shows that the interior of the town was packed with buildings: this was no show place subsidised by wealthy landowners, although one building had Alwalton Marble veneer and it, or another, had a hypocaust (Artis 1828, pl 26 (1 and 2)).

One of the major buildings has a small *tempelbezirk* attached, approached by a metalled branch road from the south-west. There may be another sacred area inside the pentagonal walled area in the large ring ditch away to the south-east. The Christian 'treasure' came from this end of the town.

The excavations in Normangate Field are unpublished. Most were designed to find out about the pottery industry and all, in terms of the size of the site, were pitifully small. Hence we are likely to learn little of the development and dating of the site. Ernest Greenfield's excavations at the junction of the southern bypass road with Ermine Street found little significantly earlier than the early second century.[1] In default of pottery or coins, the only class of material which has been gathered from the whole site is brooches, it is true mainly from Normangate Field, but the whole at over a hundred is as representative a collection as those from major Roman towns. Fewer than 3% could go back to before the arrival of the Roman army, about 10% represent time the Longthorpe fortress was occupied, another 15% or so belong to the later 1st century and the earliest years of the 2nd century. Allowing for a few doubtful cases, the residue of at least 60 to 70% belongs to purely 2nd century into early 3rd century occupation; thereafter, brooches cease to be useful. This spectrum contrasts with those from ordinary urbanised sites which show a decline in the 2nd century, the bulk being earlier than 100/125. This conclusion may have something to say about the general growth of the town.

Most towns were a response to the needs of the local population. The larger they are, the more successful at fulfilling these needs they presumably were, but at times there is the suspicion that there may have been functions other than those of a plain local service centre, and this applies to *Durobrivae*. Larger towns were uniformly *civitates* or higher in status from their foundation. This was clearly not the case with *Durobrivae* and why, in any case, should the largest town of its 'type' be here anyway? The pottery industry cannot be the sole reason as potters as such were low in the social scale, but an overview of the industry may provide some food for thought.

Everyone knows of the colour-coated, barbotine-decorated, Nene Valley beakers (Guide, figs 3 and 4), rouletted Castor boxes (Guide, fig 7, 89), even the painted and bossed extravaganzas (Guide, fig 7, 74, 78, 85; fig 8, 97, 98), but few understand that these exported items formed only a small percentage of the production at any time. The Nene Valley industry was large and important, but its chief market was always the Fens where its plainer, utilitarian products (Guide, fig 3,11; fig 2, 15–21; fig 4, 40–43; fig 7, 75–77, 83, 85, 87, 88) enjoyed a virtual monopoly (Hartley & Hartley 1970, 167). All the evidence shows that the industry only really begins to expand after 150 and had assumed its dominating role by 200. This matches the dating suggested by the brooches and both should reflect a general increase in population and prosperity in the town. The relationship of this expansion to the development of the Fens (Salway 1970, 9; Hartley & Hartley above) seems inescapable.

We know nothing of other industries in the town and suburbs, but there must have been others as potting alone could never have sustained a settlement half the size of *Durobrivae*. To the west, in Bedford Purlieus (Artis 1828, pl 1) and beyond lay a major iron-producing industry and rescue work has identified at Laxton Lodge, Wakerley, an important smelting centre (Jackson & Tylecote 1988, 279), its debris running for hundreds of metres along the minor stream there (*ibid*, 288). Given the right circumstances, here is an opportunity to test a basic hypothesis: smelting took place close to the source

of the ironstone, production of finished goods could have been anywhere. The huge transport costs of carting bulky raw materials over even a modest distance are not to be contemplated. Traces of ironworking in Normangate Field are known (Wilson 1963, 135), but nothing like enough debris to represent hundreds of tons of blooms being turned into implements or fittings for carts and buildings. The field survey carried out many years ago by David Hall and his associates in the old Soke of Peterborough revealed a lacuna in the settlement pattern to the north-west of *Durobrivae*. It is so marked that new discoveries are unlikely to eradicate it completely. The soils are not particularly inferior and it is tempting to see here an area of woodland reserved for producing the fuel needed for major iron-smelting and for the town.

If the two largest non-organic local industries cannot be used to explain the size of the town, one will need to look elsewhere. There are strong grounds for thinking that pottery once it had left its immediate marketing area and because it was so cheap, travelled in small quantities on the back of a main trade (Fulford 1977, 58; Greene 1986 162–163) or formed part of a cash cargo on a return trip. Either way, the area where the greatest quantity of finds is made, outside a radius of, say 15–25 kilometres (Peacock 1982, 156), probably represents the chief focus of trade carried out with the area producing the pottery. This automatically means the Fens and it should not be chance that one of the largest groups of kilns known is at Stanground, on the banks of the Nene as it flowed in Roman times (Evans 1979), suggesting a move by some potters closer to their main market (Greene 1986, 165).

Had *Durobrivae* lain in almost any other stretch of countryside, there would have been some mild curiosity over what could have created such a marked bias in the marketing area. But *Durobrivae* lies, to all intents and purposes, on the Fen edge and is the largest town close to any part of the Fens, its 'rivals' being *Lindum, Ratae, Verulamium* and *Venta Icenorum*. The lack of villas in the Fens would normally be taken as a sign that the area was not rich and its material culture is unimpressive (Simmons 1979, 187). The land was, and is, highly productive and its produce would have needed marketing. In the lands south-east of the Fosse Way one can perceive a network of 'small towns' making the longest journey into a market from a farm a matter of relative convenience. But a look at Burnham and Wacher's distribution (1990, fig 1) of what they accept as 'small towns' shows that north of Cambridge, east of the A1 and south of Horncastle there is only one town as such: *Durobrivae*. The sites at Bourne and Sawtry may have been no larger and more complex than say, Sapperton or Ashton while the true character of the enigmatic site at Stonea may only emerge with its full publication (Jackson & Potter, forthcoming).

The predominant view of the status of the Fens in the Roman period is that they formed an imperial estate, possibly originating from lands bequeathed in

Prasutagus's will (Salway 1970, 10; Applebaum 1972, 31–2; Frere 1987, 267–270). An important factor in determining to whom the Fens may have belonged is the presence of features which only a major authority could have commanded: the major droves-cum-canals (Phillips 1970, Maps K, L), the Midfendic (Simmons 1979) and the Car Dyke, the last being the crux. The work is not continuous. The section north of Billinghay, and possibly north of the Slea is an old natural water-course (*ibid*, 1979, 185, fig 3) and there is no proven course south of the old Nene (Evans 1979) until the famous Cambridgeshire Car Dyke is reached. The Car Dyke appears where the uplands shade imperceptibly into the Fens, hence the isolated appearance of the section near Cambridge. North of that a natural boundary may have been provided by the old West River and the like (Clarke 1949, fig 9) as far as the land of meres where RIB 230 may be a survivor of a series in this sector.

Despite all the evidence, there is a persistent belief that it had been a canal (Frere 1987, 267–268, 273, Index). The prime requirement of a canal is a level bed: the Car Dyke does not have one (Simmons 1979, 190; Pryor 1978). Any system of locks, and not one is evidenced, needs a natural water supply to its highest point: the section between the Welland and Nene does not have one and none which could have been diverted to serve in its place. A canal requires that the barges or boats have an unimpeded run, not earth causeways across it (Simmons 1979, 189–190).

Simmons has addressed the question of the Car Dyke's function: it is one of two drainage channels, the other being the Midfendic (Simmons 1979, 192–196, figs 3, 6 and 7). The Cat's Water is the equivalent of the Midfendic between the Nene and Welland, its Roman date guaranteed by the way the Roman Fen Causeway deflects in its course to cross it. The only stream, however, which the Car Dyke captures in this section is Werrington Brook, hardly an adequate reason for the massive scale of the Dyke which is maintained wherever it appears, even at Eye where it could have been reduced without being any less of a drain. The form of the Dyke has not been perfectly fixed, but the Cambridge section has a bank on each side (Clarke 1949, pl 16), and this is repeated in the stretch near Whitepost Farm at Eye, but with a suggestion of a berm between each bank and Dyke. Simmons reconstructs the Dyke in Lincolnshire as having banks rising directly from the edges of the Dyke (Simmons 1979, fig 5). The upland bank would prevent surface water from being collected, therefore the Dyke would only have collected ground water efficiently. The great care, however, to ensure that the earthwork was both formidable and visible recalls the equally impressive Vallum and a vaguely similar function may have applied to both: they separated one kind of jurisdiction from another (Frere 1987, 119). In the case of the Car Dyke, it would mark the formal boundary of a tract belonging to the *patrimonium* in the Fens.

To return to the pottery industry, one would normally assume that the people in the Fens would have drawn their supplies from the nearest convenient points, but there may have been a constraint on supply, if the Fens had been run from a central point. The very size of *Durobrivae* suggests that it had been the general *entrepot* for Fenland produce, and it would seem to follow that this explains the dominance of the pottery industry and that any central administration may have been based there as well. However, a central administration need not have been where the goods were handled, all it need have done is to have issued orders for others to carry out.

One of the curious features of *Durobrivae* is the presence of five large semi-rural buildings around it, at least four of which are villas[2] (Artis 1828, pls 1, 16–22, 33, 34, 35; RCHM(E) 1969, 17(18), fig 6; 25–26, fig 11). The occasional town with a villa just outside its walls is not uncommon – Cirencester, Leicester and Great Casterton – but there is an excessive number here. Of the two south of the river, one is ordinary, the other is unknown today. The two villas north of the river are much larger, one in Ailsworth parish apparently having reserved land around it, and the other on Mill Hill, Castor (Fig 13.1, top left), has a fine view over the walled town.

The fifth site, also with a good view over *Durobrivae*, is of an entirely different order: Fig 13.2. It lies under Castor village and is, consequently, difficult to appreciate, but remains of its walls, now becoming very eroded, can be seen sticking out into the lanes round the north side of the church. Modern excavations have been very limited, the best evidence for the building being that recorded by Artis (1828, pls 2–8, 10–13, 26(3)). The basic plan is of a main court lying at the foot of two terraces, each about 16 ft (5m) high, the structures on the second embracing the first. Artis's outline plan (*ibid*, pl 13) suffers from a distortion only discovered when the original of Fig 13.2 was prepared some years ago. Much is conjecture in the overall layout, but rescue work next to the school found a wall almost exactly where one was proposed on the south-east side of the main court.[3] The bath-house excavated by the late Charles Green (Green & Dallas 1987, 118–128, fig 6) is shown in the area of the courtyard, but had almost certainly been demolished by the time that the one excavated by Artis was built (Artis 1828, pl 6). Remains of stone buildings lining the road leading to this complex were found when new playing fields were laid out across its line in 1990.[4]

The whole is truly palatial in size, the overall site measuring 902ft (275m) by 400ft (122m), but the scale of the structures on the top terrace only really emerges when the left-hand wing is considered. It had a single room not less than 79ft (24m) long and 29.5ft (9m) wide inside all heated by a full hypocaust. The height of the room could hardly have been less than *c* 30ft (9.14m) and, when 16.5ft (5m) for the terrace is added and a minimum of another 16.5ft (5m) for the gable, the whole wing would have been no less than 63ft (19.2m) high.

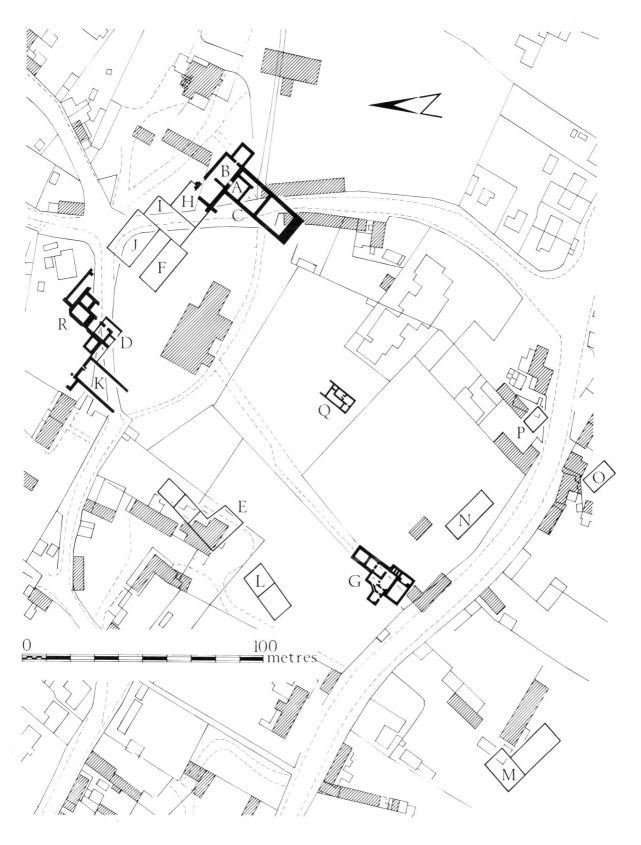

Fig 13.2 *Castor village, plan showing the remains of the Roman building around the church. Structural elements A-H are those so lettered by Artis on his Plate XIII, J-R are those which he left undesignated, or have been added to the plan since his time.*

These dimensions coupled with wall thicknesses of a yard or more, do not belong to an ordinary villa, let alone a guild for pottery traders (Wild 1974, 165). The central element on the top terrace can be reconstructed as a great hall, Artis's mosaic in the churchyard (Artis 1828, pl 7) probably came from his structure 'F' (*ibid*, pl 13) which might have been a room set in the front of the upper terrace. As for Lewis's 'temple' (Lewis 1966, 61, 97, fig 58), he ignored the continuations of the side walls shown by Artis (1828, pl 11, 2) and failed to realise that the structure was integral with the overall plan, possibly because Artis put his 'A' on his plate 13 in the wrong place. The room is, in fact, the end room of the right-hand wing and is at first-terrace level. The building is poorly dated: the bath-house in the court seems to have come to an end before the 4th century and the one group of pottery sealed by the building on the terraces is better suited to *c* 300 than before.

This type of plan is recognisably that of a *palatium*, the word 'palace' in modern English is not an adequate substitute. Examples can be quoted from London (Marsden 1975), Cologne (*ibid*, fig 30) and Dura-Europos (Boëthius and Ward-Perkins 1970, 451, fig 167). Most have a main hall in a range looking out over a terrace to an open view and, as it happens, all three are on river banks, but then they are in proper urban settings. Fishbourne also conforms in the sense that the 'Audience Chamber' is on the main axis and raised on a terrace (Cunliffe 1971, figs 24 and 25). Of course, many villas have a large central room set behind a colonnade, but it is the difference in scale (cf Rivet 1958, fig 8) which places Castor with these other, acknowledged, buildings of special character. But if there was a *palatium*, whose *officium* was it intended to serve? The holder should have had a very high status and his presence effectively within *Durobrivae* should have been related to a function served by the town and its immediate region. Normally, one would associate such a dwelling with a governor and it is just possible that the intended user was the governor of the suggested short-lived province of *Caesariensis* : there is no guarantee that he would have shared London with the Vicar and no evidence that there was any major function attached to Lincoln (Frere 1987, 198–199, 331).[5] On the other hand he may have been military, the place of his residence related to local resources, but this is a dangerous road to follow and surely it would be pushing things too far for the chief *procurator rei privatae* to have had such an establishment? Whoever it was, the chances would be that residence would have been periodic. If there had been an intimate relationship with elements of the 'central government' of the empire, one might expect the overall site of *Durobrivae* to mirror rather closely the fortunes of that: only excavation will tell (Esmonde Cleary 1989, 73–75, 138–141).

All excavations at *Durobrivae* have been relatively small and none has dealt with the core of the site. Con-traction in one part of one suburb may not be a proper image of the whole. A trench across the southern defences showed that the rampart and wall were raised together possibly late in the 2nd century (Taylor 1958, 139). A second trench laid out over part of the Irchester gate (*ibid*) seems not to have shown that it was offset as the air photographs, almost all taken much later, so clearly show.

It is many a year since C E Stevens (1937, 199) suggested that *Durobrivae* became a *civitas* and a recent summary of discussions concluded that all the signs were that *Durobrivae* should be set aside from the general class of small towns (Burnham & Wacher 1990, 90–91), which means that the town is in a kind of limbo: not regular enough to be an accepted member of one class, and too large and elaborate to be a member of a lesser breed. By the 4th century at least, a *saltus* like the Fens would have been part of the *res privata* and run by a *procurator rei privatae* (Jones 1964, 788) who would have had his court to which barristers were accredited (*ibid*, 485–486), and that would have had to have been in a place of no lower status than a *civitas*.

The two treasures found here are well known and one is famous as the earliest known Christian hoard or treasure in the Empire. Its possible significance can lead to much speculation, but only one deduction is considered here. The 'votive' leaves have holes which means that they were fixed to a structure and, as the collection has a basic functional unity, that should have been a church. The high walled dish, the flagon and the two handled cup all fit easily into a liturgical framework and the other bowls or drinking cups also suit. By the end of the 4th century, one would have expected a church inside a *civitas* and a bishop. The treasure could even be a mark of the growing prosperity of the community: liturgical equipment should have been consecrated and, as such, probably not melted down when replaced by more magnificent gear, but hidden within consecrated ground, probably within the church itself.

A new look at the site after many years does nothing to diminish its interest. It is a pity that relentless ploughing continues to bring more of the site to the surface within the extensive scheduled areas. Without a change in management, the bulk of the site under this supposed protection will be destroyed without any other record than a few air photographs and a disproportionately small amount of excavation.

Notes

1. J R Perrin who has prepared the pottery report on the material from Ernest Greenfield's sites, very kindly gave me the gist of his findings.
2. The supposed villa (RCHM(E) 1969, 17 (17), fig 5) lying west of the well known Ailsworth villa is marked by a major scatter of Bronze Age flints and a complete absence of Roman material.

3. The excavation was carried out by Mr I Meadows and I am very grateful to him for the information. The wall was later than an inhumation burial with hobnails in its footwear.

4. Only a limited amount of salvage work was possible, but there were all the signs of a regularly laid out scheme lining the approach road. I am, again, very grateful to Mr Ian Meadows both for the information and for showing me the site.

5. I am indebted to Mark Hassall for the suggestion, although he may not be quite as sanguine about it as I would like to be.

Bibliography

Applebaum, S, 1972 Roman Britain, in *The agrarian history of England and Wales, Vol I (ii), AD43–1042* (ed HPR Finberg), 3–277

Artis, E T, 1828 *The Durobrivae of Antoninus identified and illustrated in a series of plates exhibiting the excavated remains of that Roman station, in the vicinity of Castor, Northamptonshire*

Boëthius, A, and Ward-Perkins, J B, 1970 *Etruscan and Roman architecture*

Burnham, B C , & Wacher, J, 1990 *The 'small towns' of Roman Britain*

Clarke, J G D, 1949 Report on the excavations on the Cambridgeshire Car Dyke, 1947, *Antiq J*, 29, 145–163

Cunliffe, B, 1971 *Excavations at Fishbourne 1961–1969*, Soc Antiq Res Rep 26, Vol 1

Esmonde Cleary, A S, 1989 *The ending of Roman Britain*

Evans, R, 1979 The early courses of the River Nene, *Durobrivae, a review of Nene Valley archaeology*, 7, 8–10

Frere, S S, 1987 *Britannia, a history of Roman Britain*, 3rd ed

——, and St Joseph, J K, 1974 The Roman fortress at Longthorpe, *Britannia*, 5, 1–129

Fulford, M, 1977 Pottery and Britain's foreign trade in the later Roman period, in *Pottery and early commerce* (ed DPS Peacock), 35–84

Green C & I, & Dallas, C, 1987 Excavations at Castor, Cambridgeshire, in 1957–8 and 1973, *Northamptonshire Archaeol*, 21, 109–148

Greene, K, 1986 *The archaeology of the Roman economy*

Guide *Roman pottery from the Nene Valley: a guide*, M D Howe, J R Perrin & D F Mackreth, Peterborough, nd

Hartley, K F, & B R, 1970 Pottery in the Romano-British Fenland, in *The Fenland in Roman times* (ed C W Phillips), 165–169

Howe, M, 1978 From the Museum, *Durobrivae, a review of Nene Valley archaeology*, 6, 21–23

Jackson, D A, & Tylecote, R F, 1988 Two new Romano-British iron-working sites in Northamptonshire – a new type of furnace? *Britannia*, 19, 275–298

Jones, A H M, 1964 *The later Roman Empire, 284–602, a social, economic and administrative survey*

Lewis, M J T, 1966 *Temples in Roman Britain*

Marsden, P, 1975 The excavation of a Roman palace site in London, 1961–1972, *Trans London Middlesex Archaeol Soc*, 26, 1–102

Peacock, D P S, 1977 *Pottery and early commerce*

——, 1982 *Pottery in the Roman world: an ethnoarchaeological approach*

Phillips, C W, (ed), 1970 *The Fenland in Roman times: studies of a major area of peasant colonization with a gazetteer covering all known sites and finds*, Roy Geogr Soc Res Ser, 5

Pryor, F A, 1978 The Car Dyke, *Durobrivae, a review of Nene valley archaeology*, 6, 24–25

Rivet, A L F, 1958 Town and country in Roman Britain

——, & Smith, C, 1979 *The place-names of Roman Britain*

RCHM(E), 1969 *Peterborough New Town, a survey of the antiquities in the areas of development*

St Joseph, J K, 1953 Air reconnaissance of Southern Britain, *J Roman Stud*, 43, 81–97

Salway, P, 1970 The Roman Fenland, in *The Fenland in Roman times* (ed C W Phillips), 1–21

Simmons, B B, 1979 The Lincolnshire Car Dyke: navigation or drainage? *Britannia*, 10, 183–196

Stevens, C E, 1937 Gildas and the Civitates of Britain, *Eng Hist Rev*, 52, 193–203

Taylor, M V (ed), 1958 Roman Britain in 1957, I. Sites explored, *J Roman Stud*, 48, 130–155

Wacher, J, 1975 *The towns of Roman Britain*

Wild, J P, 1974 Roman settlement in the Lower Nene Valley, *Archaeol J*, 131, 140–170

Wilson, D R (ed), 1963 Roman Britain in 1962, I. Sites explored, *J Roman Stud*, 53, 125–159

14 Sapperton

Brian Simmons

Introduction

Sapperton lies on the Upper Lincolnshire Limestone in a shallow dry valley, typical of this sort of terrain. A spread of alluvium has washed down the slopes of the hills, to east and west, over many years; Roman Sapperton was sited in the bottom of the valley on the alluvium (Fig 14.1A). At the base of the dip slope, and immediately to the west of the site, a series of springs, now more or less dry because of the recent lowering of the water-table, was once the source of the River Glen. In wet weather, nonetheless, the springs become active and rapidly flood the site. The same occurrence was true in Roman times, but, perhaps, with greater frequency; there is evidence from the excavations for this phenomenon, as will be seen later in the paper.

The valley in which Sapperton lies gives its name to a Roman road, known locally as Long Hollow, which connects King Street (also called Mareham Lane), at a point slightly to the north of Bourne, with Ermine Street a mile (1.4 km) to the south of Ancaster (Fig 14.2) (Margary 1973, 232–3). Long Hollow plays a significant part in the understanding of Sapperton, as, too, does a previously unrecorded east-west Roman road which crossed Long Hollow within the town itself (Fig 14.1B).

Very little was known of Roman Sapperton before the 1920s and nothing survives above ground (Phillips 1934, 179). Indeed, the modern village of Sapperton is situated half a mile or so (800m) to the north-east of the site of the Roman town, and, like many of the villages in this part of Lincolnshire, is greatly reduced from its medieval size, now not much more than a hamlet. Present day Sapperton is concerned only with farming, mainly arable and sheep, and, in this sense, its economy has probably changed little over many centuries. The subsistence of Roman Sapperton may well have been based on a similar lifestyle. From the field survey, conducted before excavation commenced, it was evident that there was a relatively extensive spread of Roman material on the surface, indicating, perhaps, something more than a minor native settlement. The spread of surface debris, and other artefacts, extended for about half a mile (800m) on a north-south axis, but was contained within a rela-

tively narrow strip, no more than about 50 yards (45m) wide. This linear development was alongside the boundary common to the former parishes of Sapperton and Humby. A further discrete area of surface finds lay some 100 yards (90m) to the east of the first, linear remains; no relationship was determined between these two separate areas during the course of the work described here. The results of the fieldwork suggest that the Roman town of Sapperton covered 10 acres (4 ha), more or less.

To the north of Roman Sapperton, at a distance of about seven miles (11.5km), lies the Roman walled town of Ancaster (Todd 1981), perhaps of a similar size to Sapperton when the extramural buildings of Ancaster are taken into consideration. About eight miles (12.5km) to the south is Bourne. Bourne poses an enigma in Roman terms as very little of an urban nature can be adduced from the many chance finds which have been discovered there over many years. The nature of Roman Bourne, and its importance, are discussed elsewhere (Simmons, forthcoming). Nevertheless, Bourne, or a site to the north, Stainfield (not illustrated), could qualify for inclusion in a list of small Roman towns. East of Sapperton, commencing at a distance of almost seven miles (c 11 km), are the silt fens of Lincolnshire, a huge expanse abounding in Roman settlements, but without any candidate for the same list of Roman towns. On the other hand, six miles (9km) to the west, a more likely choice for a small town is Saltersford (Whitwell 1970, 64–5). Thus, to north, south and west Sapperton could be equidistant, or nearly so, from other Roman small towns. The closer proximity of the sea, then compared to now, could have played a part in the prosperity of the town (see Fig 14.2, and Simmons 1980, 56–73). In the vicinity of Sapperton were several villas. Haceby had been excavated long ago (de la Bere 1935, 67, 72), but two other villa sites were discovered as the direct result of fieldwork. One, in the parish of Ropsley and Humby, is not so likely as a second within the parish of Braceby and Sapperton . This second one, lying about 300m to the east of the town, was notable for its three ploughed-out mosaics. Other scatters of Roman pottery and building materials, within a mile or two of Sapperton, also suggest smaller scale

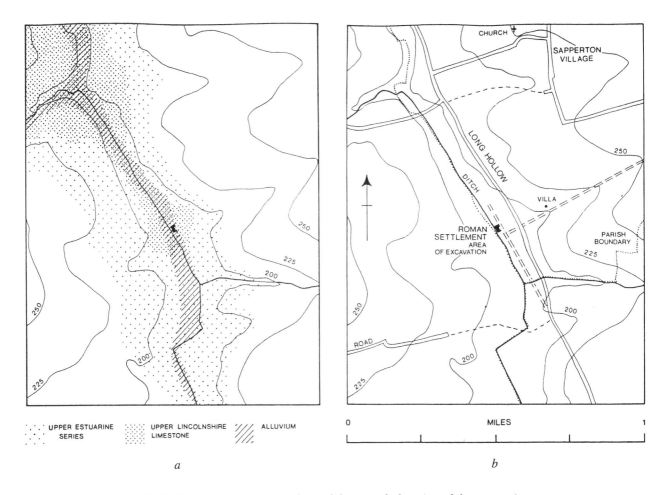

Fig 14.1 *Sapperton: a, the geology of the area; b, location of the excavations*

establishments (Fig 14.2). In this way, a picture emerges of the possible interdependence of small towns, villas and native settlements, each with the other.

But there had been land use and probable settlement in the valley prior to a Romano-British presence. The field survey, already mentioned, demonstrated that several periods were represented: finds of prehistoric flints and other stone implements (from Mesolithic to Iron Age) suggested, by their abundance, more than a passing interest in the region in the millennia prior to the Roman one. A mile to the south, at Hanby, was an early Saxon site (not shown), evinced from the fairly numerous sherds which were retrieved during the same fieldwalking programme. It was also during this programme that research was completed into establishing the line of the Roman road going from Sapperton into the Fens (Simmons 1975, 75–8). It is unfortunate that time did not allow for a western extension of this road to be established, apart from a short length probably going into Leicestershire.

Mention should be made of the first documented reference to Sapperton, which is in the Domesday Book, 1086/7 (Foster & Longley 1976, 17, 88). The place-name means 'the place of the soapmakers' (Ekwall 1960, 404). However, there may be an earlier reference to Roman

Sapperton contained in the Antonine Itinerary, that of the place-name *Causennae* or *Causennis* (Rodwell 1975, 87–8; Rivet & Smith 1979, 305). Scholars, in the past, have suggested that the best candidate for this reference is Ancaster, although the mileages given in the itinerary conflict with the actual. More recently, doubt has been cast on the validity of Ancaster being the *Causennae* of Roman times. Better argument would suggest that either Sapperton or Saltersford qualifies for the place-name.

Reasons for the excavations

During the fieldwalking programme it was evident that damage was being done to the buried remains of substantial Roman walls and other structures. This damage was caused by three agencies: the over-enthusiastic activities of a local treasure hunter, deep ploughing, and the removal of large quantities of stone from the surface of the field. Holes dug by the metal-detector user reached depths of two feet (60 cm) or more and, in one case, the treasure hunter had removed part of a hedge; in so doing, a buried wall was badly damaged. At the same time, or nearly so, the farmer had deep ploughed the field bringing to the surface many tons of dressed stone which were

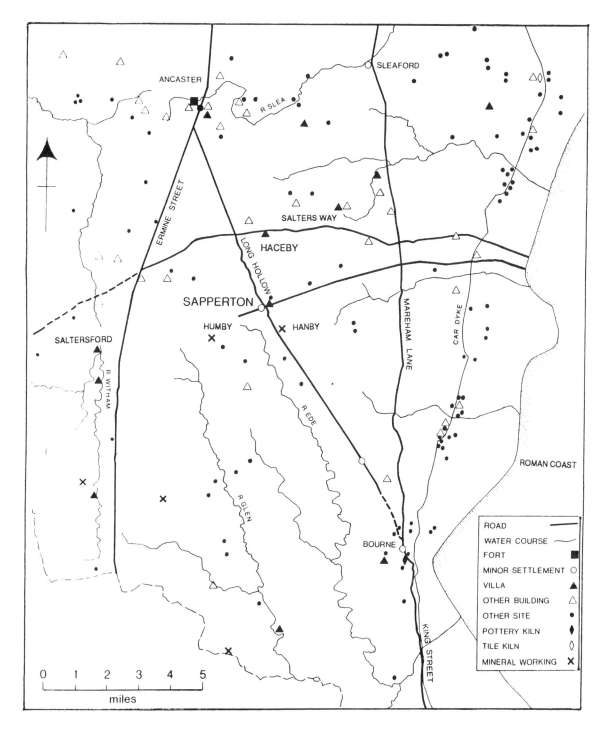

Fig 14.2 Roman settlement around Sapperton

then carted off the field, thus reducing the level of this part of the field sufficiently to ensure that succeeding ploughings dug slightly deeper into the stone walls, again bringing more stone to the surface which was subsequently taken off the field. This cycle might have continued indefinitely had not the farmer been acquainted with information regarding the origin of the stones which he was so diligently removing. Fortunately, the practice has now ceased.

These three causes of damage were enough to convince the Department of the Environment (now English Heritage) to finance, modestly, a trial excavation. Coincidentally, an American university (the University of Evansville, Indiana) was interested in extending its academic programme to include archaeology at its British campus at Harlaxton, Grantham. For this reason, undergraduates helped on the excavations for that first year, and, eventually, season by season, until 1988, with one

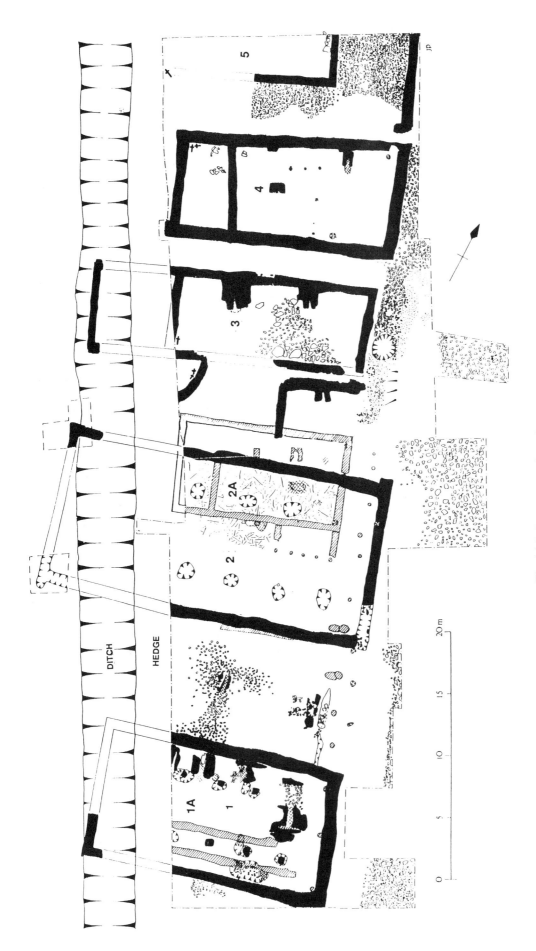

Fig 14.3 Sapperton: plan of excavations

or two breaks. Other help was forthcoming from various M S C schemes, schools, from the landowner, the late Sir Oliver Welby (the help was continued by Sir Bruno Welby), and particularly the farmer, Mr Alan Limb.

The excavations were, of necessity, conducted as training for the students, by and large. Consequently, progress was slow but amply rewarding. In the early days, there was little difficulty in testifying to the extent of damage caused by deep ploughing. Scars left by chisel ploughs were noted in numerous places, and, in one instance, a chisel plough was found broken and deeply embedded in a wall. Freshly ripped out stone was also an indication of the destruction which these implements make to archaeological levels.

The excavations

The main part of the excavation (Fig 14.3) was opened up piece by piece through succeeding seasons, not the most satisfactory method. The scheme presented here is to deal with the earliest phase first and work forward, chronologically; this scheme does not coincide with the major report, which is forthcoming (in *East Anglian Archaeology*). Only Buildings 1 and 2 were totally excavated

Phase 1 – Iron Age activity

The evidence for this phase is by inference only. Although there was a reasonably large amount of Iron Age pottery, two coins and three brooches, it was all residual, much of it from either the quarry pits, or the later post pits used for the large aisled building (Building 2). As there had already been Iron Age pottery found on the surface of the field, some of it stamped and rouletted (Elsdon 1975, 26–7, 74, 92), and in some quantity, it must be assumed that there was an Iron Age settlement close by, but in what location has yet to be identified. There were certainly no structures in the excavation which could readily be ascribed to this period.

Phase II – Roman quarry pits and Roman road (not illustrated)

As has been stated previously, the geology of the area is predominantly limestone; in the valley where the Roman town is situated there is a thickness of alluvial soil. This was not the earliest Roman ground level; serious flooding had taken place in the late 3rd century AD which tended to heighten the platform on which the later structures were built, aided by a contemporary and deliberate raising of that platform. Between the early alluvium and the top of the solid limestone is, and was, a variable thickness of cornbrash, not unlike gravel. Into the cornbrash had been dug quarry pits of differing dimensions and depths; an average area of quarry pit (at its surface) might be of the order of 10–15 sq m, and an average depth of one metre, but caution would have to be exercised when considering these measurements. Cornbrash is loose, difficult to excavate, archaeologically, and now weathers rapidly, as, presumably it did in the Roman period. The resultant holes are amorphous in shape and probably bear little relationship to their original characters. As far as could be judged, the quarry pits were on only one side – the west – of the early road.

The purpose for extracting the cornbrash was not easy to decide. However, the road immediately to the east of the earliest buildings, and lying partly beneath, and therefore destroyed by the later buildings, may well have been the recipient of the cornbrash in order to complete the construction of an *agger*. The surface of this road appeared to have been finished with concrete; the tell-tale 'skim' of wet concrete was observed. If so, then this was a rare use of concrete in Roman Britain. The constituent parts for the manufacture of concrete – sand, lime cement, ballast and water – are, of course, all easily obtained locally.

Dating the construction of linear features, such as roads, is a hazardous proposition, for usually few buried artefacts remain to give clues. The fact that the latest buildings had destroyed the use of this road, gives, at least, some idea of a time after which the road was not in use, perhaps AD 300 . Equally, if the other end of the time scale is considered, then there is a slight indication of a date after which the road was made, namely the mid-40s AD when Ermine Street was first in use (Long Hollow connects King Street with Ermine Street and would, thus, have to post-date the construction of those two roads). Somewhere between 45 and 300, however, is not good enough. A second, and marginally tighter date could be obtained by considering, particularly, the frontages (ie the eastern walls) of the penultimate buildings beneath 1 and 2, and Buildings 3, 4 and 5. These buildings appear to respect the line of the road and could, therefore, be contemporary with, or after the making of the road; a tentative date for the construction of these buildings is mid-3rd century. On the other hand, what slender dating information was forthcoming from below the *agger* suggests a late 1st century date, perhaps Agricolan, for the construction of the road.

Phase III – filled quarry pits, and plough marks (not illustrated)

The filling of the quarry pits was completed by about AD 100 – perhaps later rather than earlier, as the buildings which followed were of early 2nd century date; the pits appeared to have been eventually and deliberately filled to create an even surface for the first buildings on the site. A Claudian coin and some scraps of pottery, together with the slow, natural accumulation of humus, gave an indication of a period when the pits were subject to accidental silting and debris. Almost dramatically, this random filling was completed by the organised dumping of many tons of iron slag across this part of the site. The derivation of the iron slag is not known and it can only be concluded that it came from fairly close at hand, from a substantial iron-making furnace, or furnaces, whose provenance or provenances have yet to be discovered.

Once the iron slag was in position, a plough, or large rake, was used to level the site. It is hardly conceivable that the plough marks, which were relatively well preserved, could have been left from agricultural pursuits; commercial crops, presumably, would not have thrived too well on a diet of iron slag.

Phase IV – the first building period (not illustrated)

All that remained of these buildings were robbed foundation trenches; their dimensions were not obtainable from the meagre remains available for study. However, like the better preserved buildings of the later 3rd century, these flimsy remains appeared to be aligned onto the 'concrete' road, maybe confirming that the date of the construction of the road was early. Nothing else survived of the first buildings – no floors, hearths or furnaces, nothing to indicate the use to which these structures were put, nor, indeed, their dimensions.

Phase V – the second building period (not illustrated)

As in Phase IV, the second building period was represented by robbed trenches, and again, as in the earliest period, floors and any possible internal structures had not survived. However, the robbed walls in Phase V were of the classic text book 'ghost' wall variety. These walls, two in number and at right angles to each other, were located beneath Building 2 more or less in the centre of the area of that building. A possible date of destruction of the second building period is early to mid-3rd century.

Phase VI – the third building period (shown as hatched lines on Fig 14.3)

Of all the buildings excavated at Sapperton, the structure directly beneath Building 2 was the most rewarding. For this reason this building will be described first and, for ease of reference, will be called Building 2A.

Building 2A

The entire plan of Building 2A was not recovered as the south-west corner was obscured by a hedge; permission was not sought from the farmer to destroy the hedge. Nevertheless, sufficient of the walls was uncovered to be reasonably certain of the overall outside dimensions, which were 14.7m by 7.8m; it fronted onto the 'concrete' road. The building was divided into two unequal parts by a partition wall; the rear, western room was without doubt the living area – the smaller of the two – while the front was the workshop area.

To take the living area first, this had a well made plaster floor and the walls had been rendered with painted plaster, some of which survived *in situ*, while part of the remainder was recovered from the destruction layers of the building. Midway along the partition wall was a doorway with a step down of about 25 cm onto the earthen floor of the workshop. An interesting feature of the doorway was that a small posthole was uncovered on the living-room side on the south jamb of the door. The posthole suggested an arrangement for a pivot on which the door swung.

In the workshop there had been several hearths and furnaces, only one of which will be dealt with here. This hearth was L-shaped with flues at either end of the L. In the flues were discovered several pieces of coal which were analysed by the Scientific Department of the National Coal Board (now British Coal). Their findings were that the coal could have originated in the coalfields of Northumberland, Durham or Yorkshire on the one hand, and the coalfields of Warwickshire, Leicestershire/South Derbyshire or Nottinghamshire/North Derbyshire on the other. This only leaves Lancashire, the Forest of Dean and Kent of the English coalfields not accounted for. The only conclusion to be drawn from this information is that the furnace was fired by coal which had come from some distance thereby establishing trade links with somewhere. The nearest coalfield to Sapperton is the one in Leicestershire, which is also the shallowest in the country. Consequently, this is the coal which could most easily be mined or opencasted, in Roman terms, perhaps an obvious choice.

The destruction of Building 2A occurred towards the end of the 3rd century. Levelling of the walls had been made to almost one metre above Roman ground level and the ensuing void had been filled with stone, thus creating a platform. The infill was nearly all good quality, undressed building material. In this rubble fill were many artefacts amongst which were the crude figure of a Romano-Celtic god made of the local limestone, and a complete quern-set, the bottom stone of which had been broken in antiquity, no doubt a minor disaster in its day.

Attached to the eastern end of the southern wall was an annexe, two walls of which, the east and west, were made of limestone, while the southern wall was made, presumably, by utilising the five postholes which were spaced more or less equidistantly on this side. The fourth wall was, of course, that common to both buildings. The purpose of the annexe is not clear, but it could well have been a store for the workshop, although there was no obvious doorway connecting the two.

Generally, all the walls of Building 2A were constructed of local, undressed limestone, *c* 80cm wide and with rubble infill; there were slight traces of mortar which was badly weathered.

Building 1A

At the southern end of the excavated area shown on Fig 14.3 were the foundations of two parallel walls which have been attributed to the same phase as Building 2A. This attribution was done only on the basis of the similar, but not wholly convincing, dating evidence which was recovered from beneath them, and the fact that the more southerly of the two walls appeared to have a common frontage with the better preserved Building 2A and Buildings 3,4 and 5. If the two walls were associated their function with one another is unclear. Equally, if their roles were separate what those roles were is also unclear. Both the method of construction and width of the walls compare with those of Building 2.

Buildings 3, 4 and 5

Two general points can be made in regard to these buildings. Firstly, most of the records of the excavations for this part of the site were destroyed in an arsonist's fire; the arsonist was not apprehended. Secondly, only the most recent layers were excavated for the reason that the University of Evansville changed its teaching policy at this time.

In broad terms, it can be seen that the three buildings have the same frontage alignments as Building 2A and possibly 1A. Two of them, 3 and 4, have partition walls like that of Building 2A and are of the type known as strip buildings, as all the complete buildings excavated at Sapperton have been. But there the similarities end. In thickness of wall, in overall size of structure, and in the ratio of length to breadth (especially in the case of Buildings 3 and 4) all vary. It is likely that the purposes of use varied, too, although little survived except for the shallowest of stone filled foundation trenches, some parts of stone floors, and the vestiges of hearths and furnaces.

In detail, Building 3 had a curved wall attached to its southern wall towards the western end. As in the southwestern corner of Building 2A, some of the curved wall was concealed by the western boundary hedge of the field. It is assumed that the curved wall was part of a semicircular attachment to Building 3. There was no discernible floor to the structure but it held a grisly secret, the graves of three babies; the remains of two other babies were close by. Also externally to this building, outside its eastern wall, was a shallow well. Associated with the well were four postholes making a square in plan, assumed to be the remains of a cover for the well. The well itself was curious in that it was only 1.5m deep and had been deliberately filled, perhaps by AD 300 . Its fill was of clean clay, homogeneous in character, unlike the usual mixed silt and organic material recovered from most wells. The well had the appearance of being meticulously cleaned before being deliberately filled. The only finds from it were a broken tile and a piece of bone. However, in the crevices included in the stone lining of the well were nine coins, one of which was a silver blank; the eight inscribed coins were of the late 3rd century.

Internally, Building 3 had two surviving hearths, both of which were badly preserved and, thus, indeterminate in character.

Little can be added to the comments already made concerning Buildings 4 and 5.

Phase VII – postholes in the 'concrete' road

At a time between the abandonment of Buildings 1A and 2A and the construction of Buildings 1 and 2, a row of posts was erected towards the centre of the concrete road. This construction virtually destroyed the use of the road as a means of transport, except for pedestrians. The need for a fence in this position is obscure, unless it was as a rudimentary means of defence. With the exception of two double postholes – one inside Building 2 and the other to the south of the same building – the postholes were between 30 and 50 cm in diameter and, on average, 70 cm deep. The two double postholes were somewhat larger with the rear (ie the western) holes being suggestive of wooden buttressing. There was some evidence to suppose that the posts had been removed deliberately, possibly immediately prior to the commencement of the erection of Buildings 1 and 2.

Phase VIII – the final buildings

Both Buildings 1 and 2, the final structures on the site, were aisled but still of the traditional strip building type. Of the two, Building 1 was the smaller at 21m by 11.2m, against 27.2m by 13.8m of Building 2, both sets of measurements being overall. The thickness of the walls was similar, on average 1m but with variations within each wall. Depth of foundations also differed. When the 'concrete' road had been used as a base, the depth of foundations was minimal, no more than 10 cm. In other places, where unstable conditions had been encountered, for example above the filled in quarry pits, the construction trenches were sometimes a metre or more in depth, with the stone foundations being made, on occasions, in herring-bone fashion, presumably for strength. There were times, nonetheless, when precautions of this nature were ignored and subsidence had occurred allowing part of a wall to sag. An extreme example of such subsidence had happened on the northern wall of Building 1, towards the north-east corner.

Comparing the method of construction of the aisles, one building with another, is of note. In Building 1, stone stylobates had been made, square socketed at the top and possibly made in this way to receive the tenon of a wooden post. The shape of the stylobates was of truncated square-section pyramids but no two were alike in dimensions. Post pits had been dug, relatively shallow at no more than 75 cm, which had then been packed with limestone. Onto these post pits had been placed the stylobates; eight post pits were recorded with six stylobates still *in situ;* two were found in the hedge bottom and had clearly been recently damaged and brought to the surface by deep ploughing. Although the complete plan of Building 1 was recovered that portion of it under the hedge was left unexcavated; undoubtedly, there are more stylobates still awaiting discovery in this area, but, on the other hand, a partition wall cannot be excluded. Because there is a fundamental problem with the geometry of this building (the south-east corner is grossly out of square), the prediction of where the missing stylobates lie causes difficulty. In themselves, the stylobates form a regular pattern; consistently, from centre to centre, they are 3m apart and 2.3m from their nearest walls except for the short, end walls. Here, the distances from stylobate to wall vary, making the unknown part of the building, beneath the hedge, difficult to interpret. It should be noted that the south-west corner of Building 1 was recovered during commercial ditch cleaning; its north-west counterpart had not survived the 18th century ditch cutting.

Post pits and stylobates had also been used to create the aisles in Building 2, but in quite a different manner. Here, the post pits were usually much deeper and of greater diameter, the exceptions being where use had been made of the angle, presumably for strength, at the south-east corner of Building 2A, and two postholes within the stonework of the eastern wall. These latter postholes gave the clue as to the fabric of Building 2; the posts went through a possible cill wall which may have been continued upwards by half-timbering. Only one stylobate survived *in situ* in Building 2 and that by chance. The south-western stylobate, the one closest to the hedge, had been protected by a greater depth of topsoil. This stylobate was crude in construction, merely being four stones which had been roughly dressed to accept a (wooden) post of about 30cm diameter, and placed on top of a post pit. In this location, also, was the sole hint of a floor, again surviving because of the depth of topsoil. The floor, or perhaps its foundation, was made of pieces of limestone laid on edge but at an angle, in the manner of herringbone work; the stones for the aisle had been laid in one direction, while those for the nave were in another. From this arrangement the width of the aisle could be worked out with some certainty at 2.8m, which measurement coincided with the assumed centres of the post pits. Taking these centres as authentic, the distance between stylobates in an east-west direction was, thus, almost exactly 4m. As in the other buildings described above, that part of Building 2 obscured by the hedge was not excavated. However, beyond the hedge and ditch both corners of this building were located, the north-west one with its foundations still intact while the south-west corner was represented by ghost walls. In plan, measurements and general internal arrangements, Building 2 is not unlike a structure from Ickleton, Cambridgeshire (*J Brit Archaeol Ass*, 4, 1849, 356–78; this reference is taken from Smith 1963, fig 4).

No other superstructure of Building 2 remained but, after its abandonment and final collapse, weather, and probably a rising water-table, together with floods from the spring line, a few metres to the west, created a gully (not illustrated) which ran through the length of the building on its northern side. The gully issued into a large, sealed pothole in the later of the two roads (the cobbled road – yet to be described), the contents of which included several coins and other artefacts, no doubt waterborne when the gully was active, and representing the final date of destruction of Building 2. Included in the assemblage was a coin of Arcadius (AD 383–408). It seems likely that Building 2 might have survived into the 5th century after which it, and the Roman town of Sapperton, ceased to exist. With the exception of a doubtful structure in the corner of Building 3, a shallow pit, perhaps – but no more than that – a putative *grubenhaus*, there was nothing to suggest post-Roman occupation, and certainly nothing of an artifactual nature.

Furnaces, hearths and the cobbled road

A courtyard between Buildings 1 and 2 is ascribed to this final phase at Sapperton as, too, is the cobbled road. In the courtyard was a well constructed furnace, clay lined and in the shape of a thin channel, its walls being, on average, 30cm apart and about the same in height. The true purpose of the furnace is not known, but it had clearly been subjected to intense heat. It had the properties of being similar to a runnel for conducting molten iron.

In Building 1 several hearths survived in one state of preservation or another. Towards the eastern end of the building was a T-shaped kiln of the type sometimes described as a corn-drying kiln. Ranged on the inside of the northern wall were three identical hearths, or as near identical as can be judged. The central one of the three was more intact than the others, with its two stone walls complete at foundation level, with a stokehole pit retaining some reddened ash. The overall dimensions of this hearth were 2m long and 1.8m wide. Associated with the stokehole were potsherds, not unlike briquetage – and yet not exactly of this kind – sheep bones and potash. Was this the home of the soapmakers whose memory is recalled in the place-name of Sapperton? The ingredients for making soap, anciently, were potash, sheep or goat tallow and salt. There was a link between the Roman coast and Sapperton (see above, p 157) but whether salterns were active at this time is not known.

A cobbled road replaced the 'concrete' road in the early 4th century when the property boundaries of Buildings 1 and 2 were extended eastwards by 3m or so. The surface of the road was laid on the slight slope of the *agger* of the 'concrete' road and, in so doing, finally destroyed any possible use of the earlier of the two roads.

Discussion

The siting of the Roman town of Sapperton in the bottom of a shallow valley, subject to flooding was a question which was not easily answered when the fieldwork and excavations commenced. It appeared to be pointless to build a town in such an apparently non-salubrious setting unless other factors were at work. After all, the slopes leading to the valley afforded drier land and better positions.

Equally, why it was necessary in the 4th century to destroy what, on the face of it, had been a perfectly good road – the 'concrete' one – to replace it with an inferior surface a short distance away was something of a conundrum. Instead of destroying the 'concrete' road to gain a larger building plot, the more obvious choice appeared to be to extend westwards rather than to the east.

Both questions could be resolved by looking beyond the curtilage of the town. On either flank of the valley were villas whose boundaries could have contained whatever land the townspeople had in mind to develop. Indeed, the western parish boundary of Sapperton, defined by a ditch and hedge, is of some interest in this respect. Towards the end of the 18th century its position had been moved a short distance eastwards. Originally, it had respected the western backs of all the excavated buildings. For reasons which are unclear, in the 1780s the boundary was altered in such a way as to move the ditch and hedge, cutting through the foundations of the buildings. A former line of the ditch was excavated at the rear of Building 2 showing that the earlier ditch was a metre or two to the west of the rear wall. To confirm the antiquity, or otherwise, of the boundary a tree count was made in the hedge. Consistently, where it was known that the hedge was in its original place, the tree count showed many species; where the hedge had been moved, the tree count was only two. Although this is not offered as conclusive evidence for a common property boundary between villa and town, and, therefore, a point beyond which the town was unable to expand, it would satisfy the reasons why the expansion occurred eastwards and why the town was in the valley; the villa owners on either hillside may have been dominant, negating any pos-

sibility of plebeian development on their land. Equally, it should not be overlooked that the origins of Sapperton were possibly at that moment when communications, trade and urban development were growing at about the time of Hadrian. The empty, linear areas on either side of the road might have been attractive for the purpose of such settlement, soon to be the small town of Sapperton, and when the economic advantages being experienced at the beginning of the 2nd century could have been utilised.

Bibliography

de la Bere, R, 1935 Archaeology from the air, *The Lincolnshire Magazine*, 2, No 3

Ekwall, E, 1960 *The concise Oxford dictionary of English place-names*, 4th ed

Elsdon, S M, 1975 *Stamped Iron Age pottery*, BAR Brit Ser, 10

Foster, C W, & Longley, T, 1976 *The Lincolnshire Domesday and the Lindsey Survey*

Margary, I D, 1973 *Roman roads in Britain*, 3rd ed

Phillips, C W, 1934 The present state of archaeology in Lincolnshire, *Archaeol J*, 91, 97–187

Rivet, A L F, & Smith, C, 1979 *The place-names of Roman Britain*

Rodwell, W, 1975 Milestones, civic territories and the Antonine Itinerary, *Britannia*, 6, 76–101

Salway, P, 1981 *Roman Britain*

Simmons, B B, 1975 *The Lincolnshire Fens and Fen edge north of Bourne* (unpublished M A thesis, University of Leicester)

——, 1980 Iron Age and Roman coasts around the wash, in *Archaeology and coastal change* (ed F H Thompson), Soc Antiquaries London Occas Pap, n ser, 1, 56–73

——, forthcoming *Bourne in the Roman period*

Smith, J T, 1963 Romano-British aisled houses, *Archaeol J*, 120, 1–30

Todd, M, 1981 *The Roman town of Ancaster, Lincolnshire: the excavations of 1955–1971*

Whitwell, J B, 1970 *Roman Lincolnshire*

15   Sandy

Michael Dawson

Introduction

Roman occupation of the site at Sandy, Bedfordshire, has been recognised since at least the 17th century, when finds from Chesterfield were recorded by John Aubrey (Aubrey 1668–1671). More finds were made in the 19th century during the construction of the Great Northern Railway, and later when a branch line to Potton was laid; by the beginning of the 20th century, sufficient evidence had been recovered to confirm the presence of Iron Age, Roman and Saxon burials. By the mid 1970s excavation on the southern side of Chesterfield (Johnston 1974, 37), and finds made during grave digging in the municipal cemetery, had begun to focus attention on the location of the settlement area.

In the years since Johnston's work, more Roman material has been found in the cemetery, mostly from the excavation of modern graves, and some artefacts were collected by the cemetery keeper, H Gurney. Unfortunately his collection was dispersed following his death.

In 1987, human skull fragments were found during the excavation of a modern grave in the municipal cemetery and brought to the attention of Sandy Town Council. The discovery led to an archaeological assessment which revealed the presence of extensive Roman stratigraphy. Full scale excavation was subsequently undertaken to clear the cemetery of its Roman remains and this took place over three seasons in 1989, 1990, and 1991.

Interpretation of the early evidence prior to the more recent excavations was undertaken by Johnston, who was equivocal as to whether Sandy constituted a small Roman town or a larger village (Johnston 1974, 35, 51). Johnston, however, drawing on the evidence of chance small finds, suggested an economic model for Sandy as a centre of *consumption and redistribution* (Johnston 1974, fig 15). More recently, Millett (1990, 135 table 6.5) has included Sandy in his list of Roman small towns which owe their origins to a late pre-Roman Iron Age settlement, yet Sandy was not included in the small towns discussed by Burnham and Wacher (1990). The purpose of this paper is to reassess the status of Sandy and to attempt to place it in its landscape context.

Extent of settlement

The focus of the Roman site is an embayment of the Greensand ridge, where most of the archaeological finds have been made. It is on a bend in the Roman road from Baldock to Godmanchester where this road turns northeast through a low saddle of the Greensand ridge before crossing the clay vale occupied by Waterloo Farm and Woodbury Low Farm in the parishes of Tempsford and Roxton. The extent of the Roman settlement at Sandy has not been established with certainty; to the south the furthest structural remains are those excavated by Johnston at the Bungalow site (Fig 15.1, 13; Johnston 1974, fig 2). A small assessment (Dawson & Moore 1993) further south still, in land parcel 207–210, found only ditches, but topsoil finds of pottery, including Nene Valley colour coats and amphorae as well as animal bones suggest this was possibly just beyond the structural limit of the town. Aerial photographs show a pale linear parchmark crossing Chesterfield, and together with 19th century descriptions of allotment owners quarrying away gravel, they confirm the line of the Baldock road south of Galley Hill (Fig 15.1). Even further south, a recent aerial photograph has the parallel ditches of the agger of the road as it passes south of the main railway line at Biggleswade. Finds made from the late 17th century onwards in Chesterfield (Fig 15.1, 10), including the cemetery and allotment gardens to the north, probably indicate the main area of settlement. Where the line of the Roman road turns northwards, close to the modern cemetery boundary, it follows the line now known as Hazells Hedges. The recent excavations have shown that the presence of a stream, flowing from the east into the Ivel in the late Iron Age, which may have been influential in the change of the road line. On the north bank of this stream were extensive structural remains and a secondary road.

The northern limit of the settlement is less easy to establish. The quarrying away of Tower Hill (Fig 15.1, 11) and the discovery of extensive evidence of Roman activity there (Johnston 1974, fig 4) is difficult to assess, but this area probably did form part of the settlement. Of considerable interest are the sections used by Johnston to locate the line of the *Viatores* route 225 (Johnston 1964). The route itself has been discredited (Simco 1984, fig 68 (d)) yet the evidence of gravel metalled road surfaces recovered from the sections remains to be accounted for. In fact these sections probably identify the course of shorter secondary roads within the settlement similar to those excavated in the 1989–91 seasons. These may therefore extend the area of settlement possibly as far north as the Fire Station (Fig 15.1, 4). Watching briefs in the town in Bedford Road (Fig 15.1, 2) and Stonecroft (Fig 15.1, 5) have produced no Roman evidence, although two human burials in the Avenue (Fig 15.1, 3) and finds from All Saints Church (Fig 15.1, 6) suggest that the settlement may stretch along the east bank of the Ivel. The recovery of finds in 1981 (Dix & Aird 1983, 2) located Roman settlement at Engayne Avenue (Fig 15.1, 1), one kilometre north of Chesterfield, but the lack of finds from the intervening area suggests this is a separate rural site, perhaps an outlying farm.

Despite the degradation of recent quarrying and 18th and 19th century work on the Ivel navigation (Cooke 1990) some evidence has been recovered from the western side of the settlement. In 1989 a single boxwood comb, dated to the Roman period (Fig 15.4) was found in the silt of a Roman ditch and this seems to indicate the northern limit of an extensive area of Iron Age and Roman activity along the west bank of the Ivel. From this area, known as Warren Villas, waterlogged remains found in ditch fills of the 1st century BC indicate settlement was limited by the flood plain to the first gravel terrace and the same must apply to Roman Sandy on the eastern bank. On the eastern side of Roman Sandy the steep slope of the Greensand ridge probably limited the settlement and only two coin finds have been recorded from Swaden (Fig 15.1, 12).

If all the disparate evidence is drawn together the extent of the settlement at Sandy may be no greater than the 10ha of the embayment in the Greensand ridge. But this assumes a settlement concentrated in one location, whereas the discovery of artefacts across a wide area may point to a more dispersed settlement with clusters of dwellings and some ribbon development along the river bank and roads. This dispersal of settlement is far from unique as the evidence from Baldock, Hertfordshire (Burleigh forthcoming) and Frilford, Berkshire (Hingley 1989, fig 62 c) shows.

The Iron Age landscape

The proximity of Sandy to the Ivel and the line of the Roman road identified by St Joseph (Simco 1984, 65), running westwards towards Bedford, suggests a ford or bridge nearby and therefore that the road junction and river crossing were especially influential in the origination of the settlement. However these were not the only factors.

The evidence of late Iron Age and early Roman activity along the Ivel and Ouse valleys, although dominated by cropmark sites (Fig 15.2) in the main, seems to indicate that Iron Age rural settlement was made up of small farms. These were possibly single family units, comprising an occupation area enclosed in some cases within a ditch and bank. Many, such a Mill Farm (HER 302) and Cople (HER 1480) had limited field systems and only a few sites occupy more than 6ha. Evidence from rescue projects is providing more detail but often from sites which have been only partially excavated. The span of occupation of these sites shows considerable variety. At one Iron Age farm site, at Stagsden (Dawson forthcoming), occupied from the late Iron Age to the 2nd century AD, structures were relocated within the same settlement in the mid 1st century. In contrast, a similar site west of Stagsden seems only to have been occupied in the Roman period. At Warren Villas quarry, south of Sandy, settlement dated from the late Iron Age probably to the late Roman period on a site that was on the gravel terrace immediately above the flood plain of the River Ivel in the 1st century BC (Robinson 1992, 200–201). At Wyboston (Tebbut 1957), another settlement which was established on the gravel terrace in the late Iron Age may have been abandoned for 60 years after flooding before being reoccupied in the early Roman period. The expansion of agriculture into more marginal areas, more extensive ground clearance and increasingly intense agricultural exploitation in the late Iron Age could have been responsible for raising the water table; this is suggested by the discovery of mould board plough marks in the gravels of the flood plain. The plough marks, dating to the 1st century BC, have been found with waterlogged environmental material in them which indicates cultivation in very damp conditions (Robinson 1992, 203 & Table 19.1). In the same area the waterlogged silts of ditches highlight the problems not only of seasonal flooding but of more permanent inundation.

Continuous activity at many of these settlements into the late Roman period has yet to be demonstrated conclusively. At two sites, Norse Road (TL 100515) and Warren Villas (TL 185470), late Nene valley colour coat and shell tempered pottery suggest activity at the end of the 4th century. At Warren Villas the coin series ends with issues of Valentinian (AD 383) but the site has yet to be fully analysed.

At Norse Road a complex picture is emerging. The site was occupied in the early Iron Age within a single ditched enclosure. Subsequently, occupation may have ceased before re-occupation in the late Iron Age, but in a slightly different location. A pattern of abandonment and re-occupation may account for a series of enclosures on the same site.

A second major trend recognised in south-eastern Britain in the 1st century BC and later is the agglomeration of settlements and the growth of local centres (Fulford 1992, 23–38; Hingley 1989, 76–77). There is only limited evidence for this in the Ouse valley. In particular the

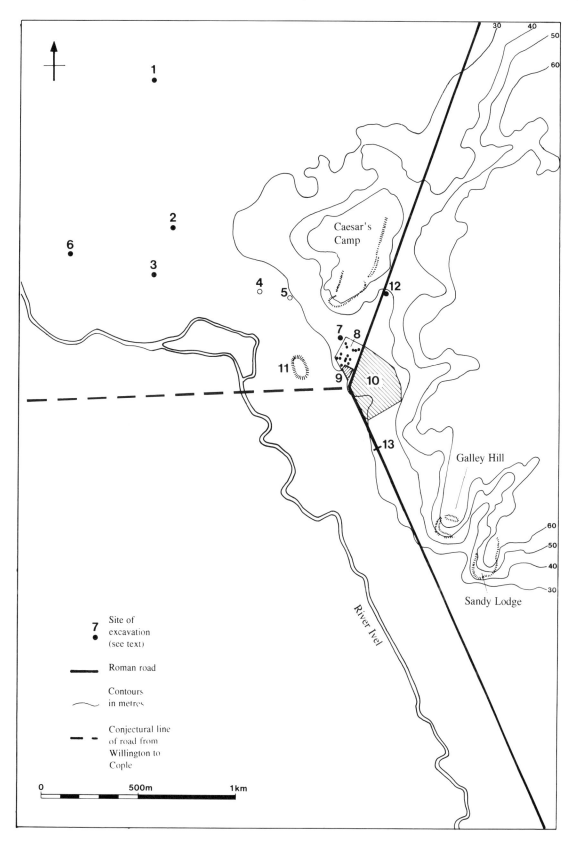

Fig 15.1 The archaeology of Roman Sandy.

Key. 1. *Location of Roman remains in Engayne Avenue (Dix & Aird 1983);* **2.** *Location of the watching brief at Bedford Road;* **3.** *Location of burials in The Avenue;* **4.** *Section through the Roman road at the Fire Station (Johnston 1974, fig 1);* **5.** *Location of the watching brief at Stonecroft;* **6.** *Location of All Saints Church where Roman burials were recovered (Johnston 1974, fig 1);* **7.** *Section through the Roman road in the cemetery keeper's garden;* **8.** *Sandy cemetery showing the distribution of finds;* **9.** *Site of excavations by BCCAS 1987–1990;* **10.** *Chesterfield;* **11.** *Tower Hill;* **12.** *Swaden;* **13.** *Location of excavations at the Bungalow (Johnston 1974, fig 1).*

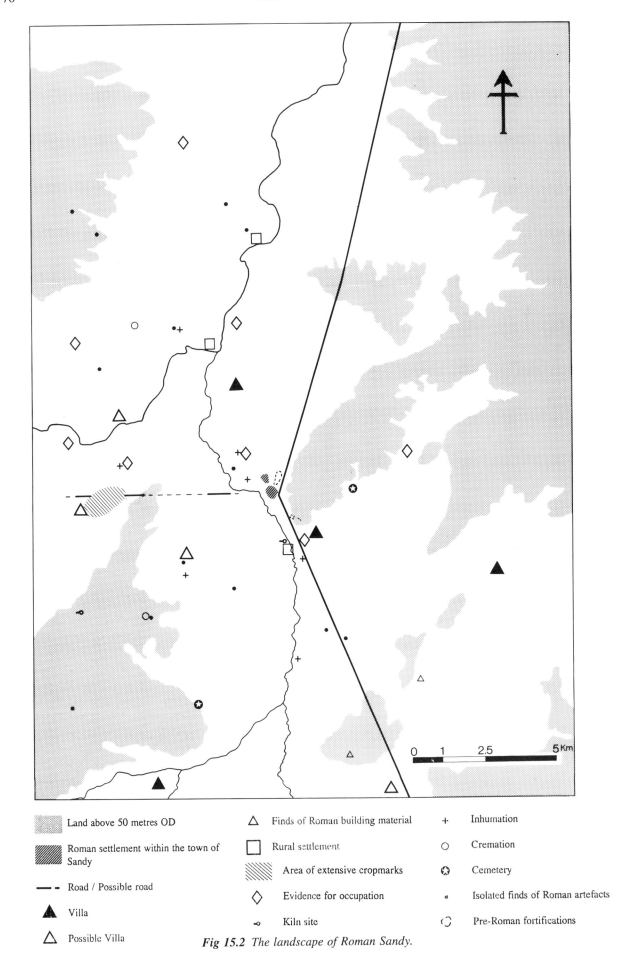

Fig 15.2 The landscape of Roman Sandy.

Land above 50 metres OD

Roman settlement within the town of Sandy

— — Road / Possible road

▲ Villa

△ Possible Villa

△ Finds of Roman building material

☐ Rural settlement

Area of extensive cropmarks

◇ Evidence for occupation

Kiln site

+ Inhumation

○ Cremation

✪ Cemetery

Isolated finds of Roman artefacts

◌ Pre-Roman fortifications

cropmark complex at Willington combines the route of a Roman road with a series of enclosures and probable habitation sites spread over more than a kilometre (Simco 1984, figs 63, 64). Not all sites, however, follow this pattern. At Salford a palisaded settlement with fourteen round house sites and several four-post structures may have been abandoned by the late 1st century AD. This site was first occupied at the end of the Bronze Age and although pottery of the middle Iron Age predominates there are three 1st century AD cremations and three small groups of samian and Roman coarse wares. In contrast to settlement agglomeration the evidence from Salford seems to indicate episodes of occupation of only some of the house sites. At another Iron Age site, the ditched enclosure at Willington (Pinder 1986, 22–40), no date closer than the Iron Age could be adduced from the excavated pottery assemblage, although it too seems to have been abandoned by the Roman period.

Thus the transition period around the Roman invasion appears to be one of increasing pressure on the landscape, and although there is a tendency towards the growth of hamlets and small villages, this may be tempered by a pattern of settlement which is still subject to the periodic abandonment of sites.

A pre-Roman site at Sandy

The site now commonly referred to as 'Roman Sandy' could have originated with a late Iron Age site which underwent a slight shift to cluster about the road line. Settlement evidence local to the Sandy site has been examined in the past through limited excavation and ground survey. On the Greensand ridge above the Roman site are three Iron Age ditched enclosures (Fig 15.1). Caesar's Camp, enclosing seven acres has been described as a Belgic hillfort (Hawkes & Dunning 1930, 258), whilst Galley Hill, a smaller rectangular enclosure, has been referred to as a promontory fort, and Sandy Lodge as an unfinished promontory fort (Dyer 1971, 9). No archaeological excavation has taken place at either Galley Hill or Caesar's Camp. Several small trenches were excavated at Sandy Lodge (Dyer 1971), revealing a stone revetted entrance. Finds were restricted to early Iron Age pottery. At Caesar's Camp, the few surface finds that have been recorded are similarly restricted to early Iron Age sherds. There is thus no firm evidence to suggest continuity of settlement between the enclosures and the Roman site.

Lower down the slopes of the Greensand ridge, in the area of Chesterfield itself, artefacts recovered from the cemetery, in particular a late Iron Age pottery assemblage including a large near complete pedestal urn of a type Thompson has called Category A (Thompson 1982, 33ff), suggest activity in this area in the late Iron Age. A partially surviving drip gulley of a round house discovered in 1987 (Fig 15.3) may be firmer evidence of a pre-Roman settlement but as more of such buildings are shown

to exist in the Roman period we cannot be certain. Iron Age coins from the 1989 excavation have an early bias with seven LX examples including three late 1st century coins of Tasciovanus and two of Cunobelinus (*c*AD10–40) (C Haselgrove *ex litt*). A single section cut through the Roman road at The Bungalow revealed a pit, hearths and a recut ditch which contained 'Belgic' pottery suggesting therefore some re-adjustment with the construction of the road.

Roman settlement

As with many other Roman small towns in the vicinity of a road junction and river crossing, the growth of Sandy probably accelerated in the late 1st and early 2nd centuries AD. Of particular importance to Sandy is the date of the construction of the road for this probably marks the inception of the Roman settlement. Dr Haselgove suggests that two coins of Cunobelinus (classic A M207, M251), from his Colchester mint, may have been in circulation with the Roman army, as two Claudian copies were recovered during the same season of excavation (Davies *ex litt*). Such early military activity no doubt relates to the construction of the road. Excavation along the road line has taken place. In 1954 at The Bungalow site Johnston excavated a section through a gravel surface which, sealing a pit and ditch containing pre-Domitianic samian and Belgic pottery, was dated to the mid 1st century. Further north observations made during construction of a gas pipeline at Tempsford aerodrome show only that the road there did not have a metalled surface. Lastly sections cut through the road at Godmanchester, Pinfold Lane (Burnham & Wacher 1990, 125), date the construction to the 1st century AD.

The lack of settlement dislocation or destruction horizons, despite military action during the conquest period, implies continuity in the pattern of rural settlement in this area, establishing that the origins of Sandy lie in the context of an established Iron Age landscape. However a more dynamic role for the settlement at Sandy was proposed by Bigmore who interpreted cropmarks in the landscape north of Biggleswade as evidence of centuriation and by implication evidence of deliberate settlement or reorganisation. His theory is built upon aerial photographic evidence in the area between Biggleswade and Sandy (Bigmore 1979, fig 3), yet extensive excavations within this area, at Warren Villas, and assessment work at Broom have shown many of the cropmark ditches to originate in the Iron Age and that aerial photographs in this area under-represent archaeological features by a factor as high as ten.

The recent excavations at Sandy covered an area of *c* 2000m. The excavations comprised four trenches from 1987 on, including a small evaluation in 1987/88 (Fig 15.1, 9; Fig 15.3). The site was found to be preserved beneath approximately 1.20m of colluvial soil build-up which had accumulated from the early medieval period

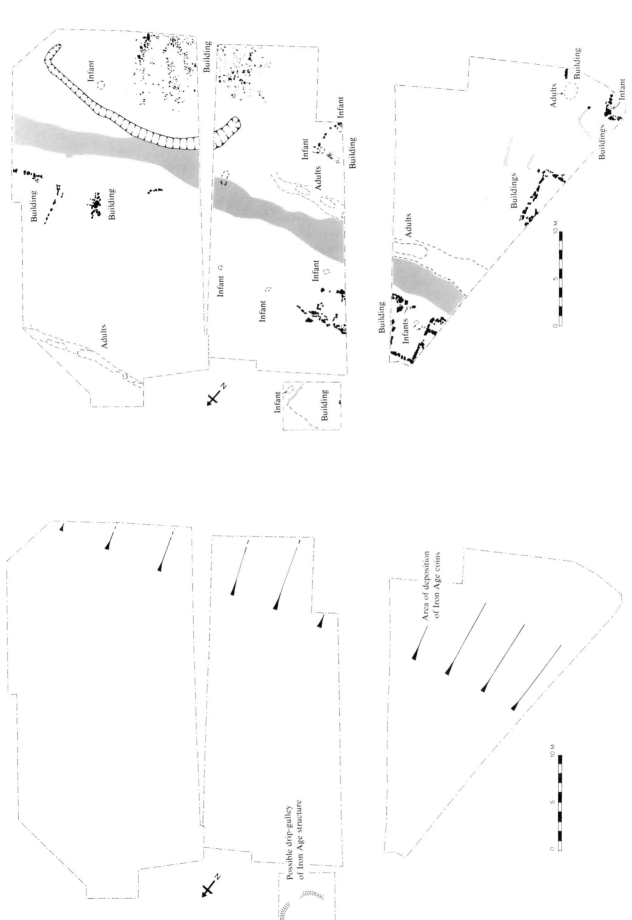

Fig 15.3 Left: pre-Roman Sandy; right, Roman Sandy in the 4th century. Excavations 1987–90.

onwards. The recovery of large quantities of non-ceramic and ceramic finds from this horizon suggests that some of it derived from the erosion of Roman structural remains further upslope to the east. The site sloped gently from north-east to south-west, dipping more steeply on the south side into the bed of a watercourse. Preservation of structural, cultural and environmental evidence was good in the neutral soils and the colluvial cover had preserved the latest horizons from later damage from 19th century market gardening. Structurally, the excavation revealed the line of a roadway, subsidiary to the main road to Godmanchester. The gravelled road curved across the site from east to west (Fig 15.3), and had probably been in use throughout the Roman occupation of Sandy. On the south side of the road an early watercourse silted up during the late 1st or early 2nd century AD and was later built upon. On the north side a sequence of structures had been built directly on pasture land.

The line of the gravel roadway had been repeatedly resurfaced and lateral drainage ditches cleared and renewed throughout its use. On the north-west side, the series of structures consisted mostly of timber framed, single celled, thatched or shingled dwellings with only two possible multiple celled examples. In these dwellings use had been made of blocks of local coarse sandstone to make dwarf foundation walls on which timber frames had been constructed. The best preserved buildings date to the late Roman period but they are preceded by other earlier post-built structures. On the southern side of the road, beneath a final phase of buildings represented by at least four structures, was an area of industrial waste. This had been thrown into the dry or sluggish course of an earlier stream and included iron slag as well as copper alloy waste with fragments of broken moulds, one with copper alloy still inside. Although the limited area of the recent excavations sheds no light on the pos-

sible expansion and contraction of the whole settlement area, later Roman developments in Sandy are evident in the changed layout of buildings and the appearance of burials amongst the buildings. Structural changes in the form of the building techniques also appear to have undergone some evolution. In the early period house structures based on post-built frames or founded on wall plates or sleeper beams, laid into the sand or old ground surface, are replaced in the later phase by timber-framed buildings whose foundations are dwarf stone walls or stone pads.

The settlement was evidently subject to some zoning, particularly in the case of blacksmithing, which seems to have endured for a considerable time without a change in location. Some areas that were occupied by houses remained in similar use throughout the period but in other areas significant changes of use took place. The slow running stream south of the road was gradually filled in, with a mixture of butchery waste and industrial ash, until houses were ultimately built over it in the 4th century. Perhaps most striking of all is the appearance of burials in the settlement area. Placed between the structures and alongside the road were single burials exhibiting a wide range of body position whilst three groups of multiple inhumations were placed in an open space between the road and houses. The latter were in a soil horizon which had built up above the silts and ash of the filled in stream bed. A third group of burials comprised several graves laid out in a row at the rear of houses in the north-west of the site (Fig 15.3). Preliminary identification of pottery accessory vessels and stratigraphy indicates that the burials were being placed in the 4th century and probably whilst the buildings were standing as no burial encroaches upon any of the structural remains.

Religion has always figured prominently in discussions of Sandy (Johnston 1974, 51; Simco 1984, 59) and although excavation has failed to find evidence of a for-

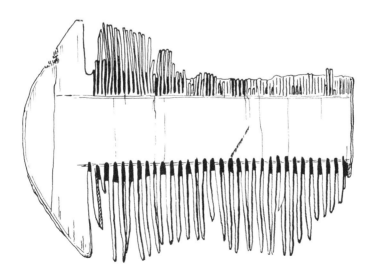

Fig 15.4 Sandy: Boxwood comb from Warren Villas Quarry (full size).

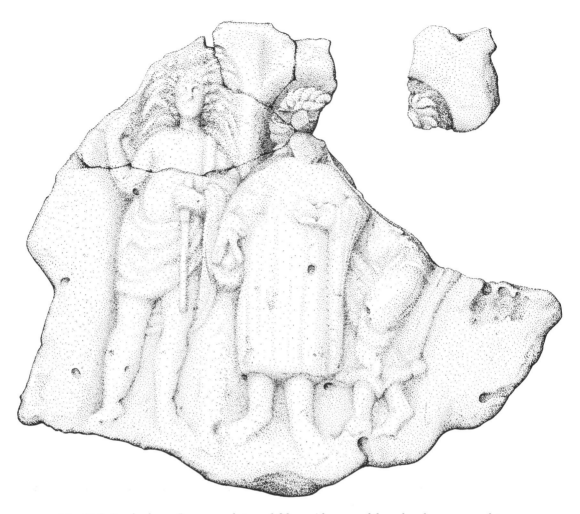

Fig 15.5 Sandy: large Roman sculpture, 1.20m, wide, carved from local coarse sandstone.

mal temple site artefact finds continue to suggest a religious focus. Previous finds from Sandy have included
two hoards; one containing bronze vessels (Kennett 1969a
& b), the second, ironwork (Manning 1964 & 1972),
both of which were attributed to religious practice. During the recent excavations a votive sculpture depicting
three full length figures in relief was discovered (Fig
15.5). The main fragment of the commission is 1.16m ×
.76m and is carved from local sandstone. The partially
nude figure on the left with narrow drape worn in Greek
fashion may be a Venus or nymph; but equally could be
a Celtic deity. The attendant figures on the sculpture may
be *genii* and seem to be dressed in everyday clothes to
integrate otherwise Roman inconography into a scene
where local character is expressed by the central partici-
pant. A date span from the late 1st century to the late 3rd
or 4th century has been proposed (Appleton & Dawson
forthcoming).

Even though much of the religious evidence is from
the Roman period there is now a firmer indication that
Sandy also had a religious focus in the Iron Age. In the
primary silts of the stream bed on the southern side of

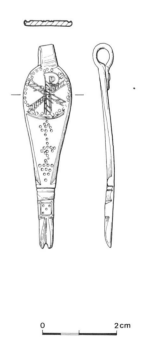

*Fig 15.6 Sandy: small copper alloy cosmetic implement
inscribed with Chi Rho (full size).*

the recent excavations were nearly 30 Iron Age coins, all bronze except for a gold half stater of Tasciovanus. That these were recovered concentrated in such a location suggests ritual disposal in a water-filled hollow.

Lastly the influence of pagan ritual drawn from the two hoards and the sculpture must be set alongside the small cosmetic implement with a Chi Rho inscribed on the terminal (Fig 15.6). This has been assigned a late 4th century date on the basis of the design of the Chi-Rho (Watts 1991). The context from which it came indicates that it has been ploughed out of a deposit east of the recent excavations.

Developments in the landscape

The extent to which Sandy's development may have been influenced by the late Iron Age movement towards larger nucleated settlement has been suggested above. In economic terms this presupposes an indigenous population which would have provided a new market for Roman trade (Burnham & Wacher 1990). In addition to religious aspects artefacts recovered from excavations continue to suggest that Sandy may have assumed the role of a market centre. The variety of objects present at Sandy include several exotics which may represent trade but could equally well be chance losses alongside a major road, in particular, a single ivory panel from a small casket probably originating in northern Italy. It depicts a male arm with a cloak billowing over the elbow behind part of a Hyrsus suggesting that the subject is Bacchus (M Henig *ex litt* 1989). Similarly, an oculist's stamp (Simco 1984, 54) inscribed Gaius Valerius Amandus and Gaius Valerius Valentinus had been taken to suggest that some individuals, involved in trade at Sandy, possessed citizenship. In the very short term the influx of soldiers or trade along the new highway could have been influential in establishing a settlement based on commerce. The coin list for the 1987–1989 excavation (J A Davies *ex litt*) allows some preliminary comparisons. In the first instance there is a steady coin loss right through to the end of Roman Britain with reduced loss in periods VIIb (AD 180–93) and XIIIa (AD 294–330) in common with other Romano-British sites. Secondly there are possibly two dispersed coin hoards, one from the mid 280s, and a second from the 3rd/4th century. But unrestricted economic development is not a universally accepted model for early town growth (Millett 1990, Finlay 1985). Along with the other rural habitation sites, in particular Warren Villas, it is clear that the early growth of Sandy was contemporary with the appearance of a kiln possibly used to produce white ware flagons and more certainly vessels with a grey and orange sandy fabric (Slowikowski & Dawson forthcoming) and this may be the first evidence that Sandy acted as a market for producers in the surrounding area. However the consistent contrast between the presence of coins at Sandy and the paucity of them on non-villa rural sites must be addressed before Sandy

can be accepted as the centre of a local monetised economy. Already the influence of the Iron Age settlement pattern has been shown to be important in the location of Sandy, and religion, services associated with the river crossing such as a ferry, blacksmithing or stabling are all activities evident at Sandy that are not necessarily dependent upon trade.

In other large towns, such as *Verulamium*, development has been linked to the growth of villas in the surrounding countryside. Recent work in the Ouse, Ivel, and Flit valleys has established the presence of more substantial farm estates than were recognised in recent publications (Simco 1984, Map E). Whilst it is premature to attempt any detailed analysis of the economic relationships maintained between them and Sandy it is equally clear that Sandy did not stand apart from developments in the region, as the settlement is the nearest point on the road system for many of the villa farms.

Within a ten mile radius of Sandy are villas at Eyworth, Shefford, Furzenhall (Johnston 1959), Astwick, Newnham (Simco 1984, 97), Great Barford, Cople and Melchbourne, all of which are located on lighter brickearth soils usually found above gravel deposits. In the Nene and Welland valleys (Wild 1978, 62; Pryor & French 1985, 309) population migration into the newly drained Fens, following the construction of the Car Dyke in the reign of Hadrian, may have led to depopulation which allowed the development of villa estates.

In the middle Ouse valley there is insufficient evidence to identify any common factor in the 2nd century which may have influenced the development of villas but soil type and location seem particularly important. It remains unclear whether villas developed as a result of their owners' ability to exploit the market assumed to exist at Sandy or whether other factors were responsible.

Excavation has taken place at the villas of Newnham Marina, Bletsoe and Kempston Church End. At Newnham a Belgic phase was recorded but it was unlike Gorhambury or Stanwick (Neal 1989 and 1992), not the predecessor of the later villa (Simco, pers comm). At Kempston Church End part of a pitched stone foundation was perhaps the remains of a circular building, possibly a round house of similar design to that at Stanwick (cf Neal 1989, fig 5). At Bletsoe the villa was untouched by excavations which concentrated on the 4th century cemetery.

Conclusion

The excavated remains at Sandy, in particular the evidence of agricultural activity (quern stones, iron tools and the predominance of spelt grain), the recognition that in only a few buildings was stone used, none of which was likely to have been deliberately quarried, and the dispersed settlement pattern is sufficient basis to question Johnston's proposed model for economic activity at Sandy.

Although at a preliminary stage, an alternative model

should involve a more prominent role for the pre-existing Iron Age population for whom the focus at Sandy was at least partially religious. In addition the road network, developed soon after the invasion, provided economic and cultural stimulus sufficient to encourage the growth of the Roman period settlement, but this need not necessarily indicate the development of a free market (Millett 1990, 168; Esmonde Cleary 1992). Throughout the Roman period Sandy appears to have remained an agricultural centre which was also involved in providing facilities for travellers along the highway. The redistribution of goods, such as pottery, need not necessarily have taken place through Sandy, nor need Sandy be seen as a general market. Instead goods brought to Sandy may have been specifically to service its function as roadside settlement. It is possible that Sandy was the site of a *mansio*; there is however no evidence for this despite the fact that the site is nearly midway between Baldock and Godmanchester.

The demise of Roman Sandy is evident in the lack of artefacts by which to date structures later than the late 4th or early 5th centuries. Structurally the latest features on the site are two ditches which whilst respecting the line of the road were dug through the remains of buildings flanking it. At the east end of the site a line of postholes crossed the road. These were dug from a shallow soil horizon which had formed above the road surface. Together these features suggest a reversion to agricultural use for at least part of the settlement. Elsewhere in the Sandy area pottery of 5th century date has been recovered (Kennet 1970). This may indicate the arrival of Saxon settlers bringing with them the rite of cremation in contrast to the inhumations found amongst the Roman period settlement.

Bibliography

Aubrey, J, 1668–71 *Monumenta Britannica*

Bigmore, P, 1979 *The Bedfordshire and Huntingdonshire landscape*

Burnham, B, & Wacher, J 1990 *The 'small towns' of Roman Britain*

Cooke, M, 1990 The Ivel Navigation and its bridges *Bedfordshire Magazine*, 22 (175), 289–294

Dawson, M, & Moore, C, 1993 *Archaeological assessment (stables) at 8 Stratford Road, Sandy, Bedfordshire*, Bedfordshire County Council

Dix, B, & Aird, P, 1983 Second century pottery from Sandy, Bedfordshire, *Bedfordshire Archaeol*, 16, 2–7

Duncan, H B, 1988 Roman boxwood comb, *Roman Finds Group Newsl*, 1

Dyer, J, 1971 Excavations at Sandy Lodge, Bedfordshire, *Bedfordshire Archaeol J*, 6, 9–17

Esmonde Cleary, A S, 1992 Small towns past and future, *Britannia*, 23, 341–344

Finlay, M I, 1985 *The ancient economy*

Fulford, M, 1992 Iron Age to Roman: a period of radical change on the gravels, in *Developing landscapes of lowland Britain* (eds M Fulford & E Nichols), Soc Antiqs Occ Pap 14, 23–38

Hawkes, C F C, & Dunning, G, 1930 The Belgae of Gaul and Britain, *Archaeol J*, 87, 150–335

Hingley, R, 1989 *Rural settlement in Roman Britain*

Johnston, D, 1959 Furzenhall Farm excavations, provisional report, unpub Bedford Museum Coll Acc No 1992/110

——, 1964 Contributions to: The Viatores, *Roman roads in the South East Midlands*

——, 1974 The Roman settlement at Sandy, Bedfordshire, *Bedfordshire Archaeol J*, 9, 35–55

——, 1975 Sandy, in *The 'small towns' of Roman Britain* (eds W Rodwell & T Rowley), Brit Archaeol Rep, 15, 225–31

Kennett, D, 1969a A Roman bronze bowl from Sandy, *Bedfordshire Archaeol J*, 6, 4

——, 1969b Late Roman bronze vessel hoards in Britain, *Jahrbuch des Romisch-Germanischen Zentralmuseums Mainz*, 16, 123–48

——, 1970 Pottery and other finds from the Anglo-Saxon cemetery at Sandy, Bedfordshire, *Medieval Archaeol*, 14, 17–34

Manning, W H, 1964 A Roman hoard of ironwork from Sandy, Bedfordshire, *Bedfordshire Archaeol J*, 2, 50–7

——, 1972 Ironwork hoards in Iron Age and Roman Britain, *Britannia*, 3, 224–250

Millett, M, 1990 *The Romanisation of Britain*

Neal, D S, 1989 The Stanwick villa, Northants: an interim report of the excavations of 1984–88, *Britannia*, 20, 149–61

——, Wardle, A, & Hunn, J 1990 *Excavation of the Iron Age, Roman and medieval settlement at Gorhambury, St Albans*, Engl Heritage Archaeol Rep 14

Pinder, A, 1986 Excavations at Willington, 1984, Part II, Iron Age and Roman periods, *Bedfordshire Archaeol*, 17, 22–42

Pryor, F, & French, C, 1985 The Fenland Project, No 1: archaeology and environment in the Lower Welland Valley, 2 vols, *E Anglian Archaeol Rep*, 27

Robinson, M, 1992 Environment, archaeology and alluvium on the river gravels of the South Midlands, in *Alluvial archaeology in Britain* (eds S Needham & M G Macklin), Oxbow Monogr 27, 197–209

Simco, A, 1984 *Survey of Bedfordshire. The Roman period*

Slowikowski, A, & Dawson, M, (forthcoming 1994) A Romano-British kiln at Warren Villas Quarry, *J Roman Pot Stud*

Tebbutt, C F, 1957 A Belgic and Roman farm at Wyboston, Bedfordshire, *Proc Cambridge Antiq Soc*, 50, 75–84

Thompson, I, 1982 *Grog tempered 'Belgic' pottery of southern eastern England*, BAR Brit Ser, 108 (i)

Watts, D, 1991 *Christians and pagans in Roman Britain*

Wild, J P, 1978 Villas in the Lower Nene valley, in *Studies in the Romano-British villa* (ed M Todd), 59–69

16   The plan of Romano-British Baldock, Hertfordshire

Gilbert Burleigh

Introduction

Baldock is well-known as a regionally important late Iron Age settlement which developed into a Romano-British small town (Stead & Rigby 1986). Further extensive excavations since Dr I Stead's campaign (1968–1972), and a number of large-scale geophysical surveys, over the last fifteen years, have added very considerably to our knowledge of this settlement (Burnham & Wacher 1990, 281–88; Burleigh *et al*, forthcoming).

The maximum area occupied by the Romano-British settlement was probably around 100–120 acres (40–48 hectares) by the 2nd century AD; contracting to perhaps as little as 70 acres (28 hectares) by the 4th century. Dr Stead's major excavations and trial trenching examined an area in total of about 5 acres (2 hectares), and geophysical surveys by the Ancient Monuments Laboratory in 1970 and 1979 covered areas totalling approximately 29.3 acres (11.87 hectares).

Major and minor excavations since 1978 under the direction of the author have examined about a further 8 acres (3.24 hectares), making the total excavated area at Baldock approximately 14.66 acres (5.93 hectares), including the excavations of W P Westell and E S Applebaum in the 1920s and 1930s, and those of Dr J Moss-Eccardt in 1968. In addition, further extensive geophysical surveys have been carried out by the Ancient Monuments Laboratory since 1990, covering about another 31.4 acres (12.71 hectares), including most of Walls Field and the other Scheduled Area of Bakers Close. The exceptionally well-preserved remains on the latter area revealed impressively clear information as parch-marks during the drought conditions in the summer of 1990.

The total geophysical survey area therefore adds up to about 60.75 acres (24.6 hectares), of which 8.8 acres (3.56 hectares) have been excavated. A further 5.86 acres (2.37 hectares) of excavations have occurred on areas not subjected to geophysical survey. Thus, the total area of archaeological investigation stood at approximately 66.6 acres (26.97 hectares) at the end of 1992. Set against a settlement area of about 120 acres (48 hectares), this must make Baldock one of the best studied Romano-British settlements of its type.

Apart from Bakers Close, most of the area to the west of the Clothall Road (A507) is built over by the medieval and modern town, and so may only be examined in relatively small parcels. Indeed, on the eastern side of the ancient settlement, the majority of Upper Walls Common is now built over, so preventing much more information coming from there; the exception being the remaining 6 acres (2.43 hectares) largely occupied by a length of the Icknield Way and other roads, together with a number of enclosures and part of a very extensive cemetery. This area is also due to disappear under housing development soon but not before further excavations take place.

Figure 16.1 shows all the available information about the plan of the settlement up to the end of 1992. The sources are all the excavation and observation records, the results of the geophysical surveys, and plotting from aerial photographs. Figure 16.2 is a diagrammatic interpretation of what we know of the pre-Roman settlement plan. Likewise Figure 16.3 is an interpretation of the Romano-British town plan.

Full interpretation and discussion must wait until the final publication of the more recent excavations and surveys occurs. A programme of post-excavation work is well under way and making good progress. This programme is supported by English Heritage, North Hertfordshire District Council, Hertfordshire County Council, and a number of developers. Publication will be in the form of five monographs; four of these will be devoted to the excavations of several complete and partial cemeteries, and the last volume to the settlement itself. The first report is expected to be published in 1995 and the next two reports in the following year.

The Pre-Roman settlement (Fig 16.2)

The settlement developed from at least the beginning of the 1st century BC near the source of the river Ivel, which flows north to join the Ouse. It is also at the intersection of a number of prehistoric tracks linking it with settlements at Sandy, Braughing, Welwyn and *Verulamium*; routes which meet the Icknield Way at Baldock. It has

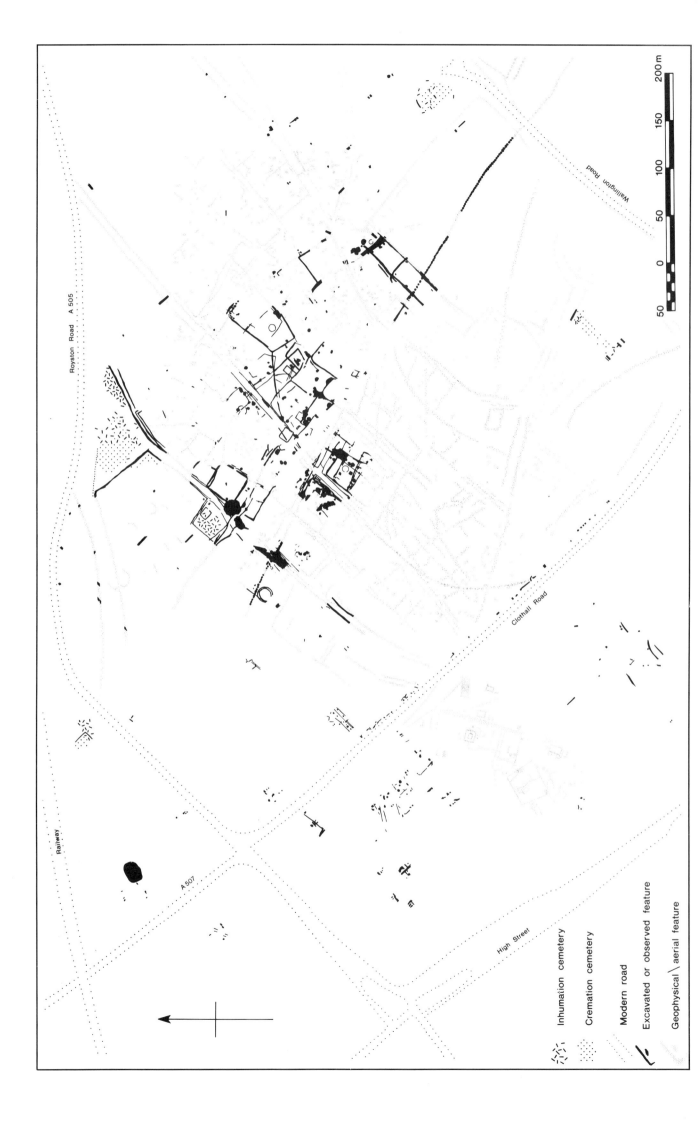

Railway

Royston Road   A 505

Wallington Road

Clothall Road

A 507

High Street

200 m
150
100
50
0
50

Inhumation cemetery

Cremation cemetery

Modern road

Excavated or observed feature

Geophysical \ aerial feature

been suggested that the settlement may have been significant enough to enable it to be classified as a minor *oppidum* (Cunliffe 1991, 145). This is more fully discussed by the present author elsewhere (Burleigh 1995).

The Iron Age settlement area was delimited on its eastern side by a string of burial enclosures and cemeteries sited along a low SE-NW ridge; including a 33m square enclosure which contained a 'chieftain's' burial with a bronze-bound wooden bucket, fragments of iron mail, and pig skeletons. This ridge and the use to which it was put were defined to the west by a pit alignment (1). This seems to have marked the eastern limit of the settlement in the earlier 1st century BC. However, by the decades immediately before the Roman Conquest, the settlement appears to have breached this pit alignment, and to have encroached onto the burial zone. On the west, the settlement was again defined by burials, including a wealthy 'chieftain's' burial, although far fewer than on the east, and not including any known cemeteries.

The trackways and cemeteries together delimit the extent and boundaries of the nucleated settlement, roughly in the shape of a triangle. The picture which is emerging of the late Iron Age settlement is that although it covered much of the same area as the later small town, perhaps 50–70 acres (20–28 hectares), occupation and structures were far less dense; suggesting an agglomeration of enclosed farmsteads separated by paddocks, fields, and tracks.

Although the settlement area does not appear to have been defended in a conventional sense, the track which enters the settlement from the south-eastern, Braughing, direction was bisected in a number of places by banks and ditches (2); as if there was some attempt to control traffic entering the settlement from that direction. Indeed, similar short lengths of multiple banks and ditches seem to define a twelve kilometre square territory for the *oppidum* to the east of the Baldock settlement itself (Burleigh 1995).

Other features to be noted on Figure 16.2 include a double semicircular ditched feature which may prove to be a later Bronze Age settlement enclosure (3); and other lengths of pit alignment (4), including one recently tentatively identified from aerial photographs, which may have helped to define an original late Iron Age settlement area (5). The enclosures dated to the late Iron Age on Figure 16.2 reflect where of necessity the major archaeological excavations have taken place; which is why an attempt has been made to indicate the core of the early settlement from dated finds, pits, ditches, and other features known from smaller-scale work.

Buildings dated to the pre-Roman period are rare so far. This is probably due to a combination of factors, such as the effects of intensive later Romano-British activity within the same enclosures, coupled with the destructive effects of medieval and modern ploughing on the shallow topsoil; as well as the fact that the original buildings themselves were constructed of highly per-

ishable materials on very slight foundations. In addition, no major excavations have yet occurred in the presumed centre of the late Iron Age settlement.

One small circular building, only 5m in diameter, has been identified. It lay at one end of a ditched, open-ended, enclosure, 120m long by 20m wide, situated at the south-eastern extremity of the core settlement. On the outside of this structure were a number of cremation burials, and it has been provisionally interpreted as a shrine or mortuary house (6).

The Romano-British settlement (Fig 16.3)

The first thing that strikes one about the plan of the post-Conquest settlement is the remarkable appearance of continuity with its predecessor, suggesting that the descendants of the Iron Age settlers were carrying on much the same life-style except under Roman administration, and with the benefits of imported consumer products, and, to some extent, improved building techniques.

All of the tracks through the settlement were still in use, except now improved with metalling and drainage ditches; and many new internal roads were built to serve the increasing number of enclosures and buildings with their occupants. The elements of a rough grid system are apparent, indicating some town planning.

All the earlier cemeteries continued in use, and new ones developed, including three in the late Roman period, constructed in former settlement areas, apparently as the town contracted. New burial rites did develop but alongside the continuation of earlier practices. The positions of the cemeteries defined the town limits since there were no defences or other major boundary features.

Many of the pre-Roman ditched enclosures continued in use, and others were constructed. There was an increase in the number of buildings erected, as well as in the sophistication of building techniques, styles and materials. Nevertheless, round houses were still being constructed at least as late as the 3rd century, and the superstructure of most buildings was composed of timber and clay, although some buildings had tiled roofs. Some buildings were given more secure foundations consisting of flint and chalk rubble, especially where the footings passed over earlier ground disturbances, but the majority of structures were erected directly on the solid chalk bedrock. There is no good local building stone. However, there were large numbers of shallow (up to *c* 2.25m deep) quarries, presumably to extract chalk for building purposes.

That the population of the settlement was increasing in size can be inferred from the increase in buildings, enclosures and roads. This is reflected in the greater numbers of burials in the pre-existing cemeteries, and in the development of new cemeteries.

The foundations of a small Romano-Celtic temple survive on the west side of the town, associated with a number of enclosures, and other buildings. A large en-

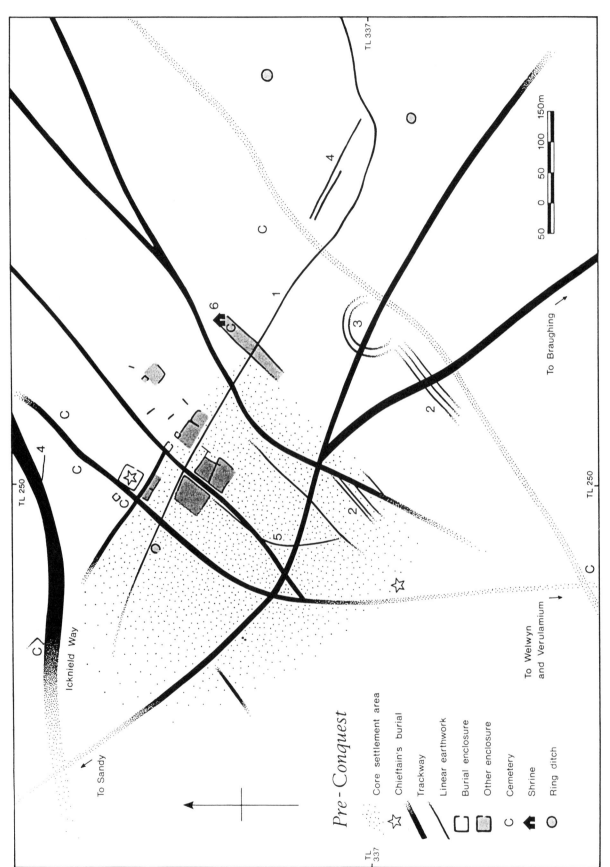

Pre-Conquest

Core settlement area
☆ Chieftain's burial
Trackway
Linear earthwork
Burial enclosure
Other enclosure
C Cemetery
Shrine
Ring ditch

Icknield Way

To Sandy

To Welwyn
and Verulamium

To Braughing

TL 250

TL 337

Fig 16.2 Pre-Conquest Baldock

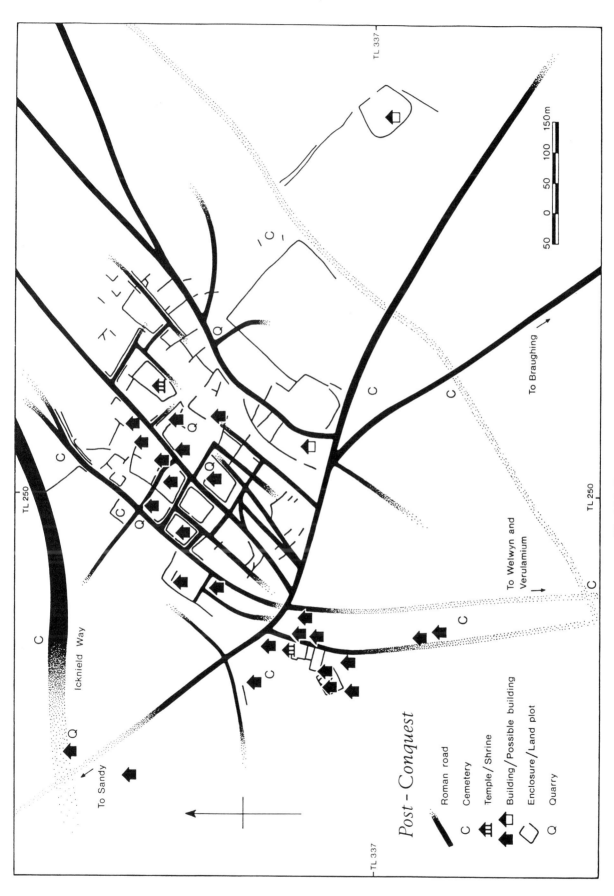

Fig 16.3 Post-Conquest Baldock

closure on the eastern side of the town contained a number of pits and wells which produced a considerable quantity of votive objects, including model axes, a spear, and an antler; an iron rattle; a small fragment of bronze apparently from a large statue; and a remarkable collection of 44 iron spearheads, 33 of them in one feature (Stead & Rigby 1986, 86). The enclosure ditch and the features in which the ritual objects were found may be dated to the 3rd – 4th century AD. The only building identified within this enclosure was a small round house, but in a relatively unsophisticated native settlement such as Baldock there seems little reason why this should not have been the site of a shrine. Besides an infant burial near the round house, which may not be significant, there was a single late Roman adult inhumation found in a grave dug in the vicinity of the pits which produced the majority of the votive objects at the northern end of the enclosure; this may be more significant.

Future fieldwork

Within a few years it is intended to construct a bypass to one side of Baldock, and a planning application for an eastern route has been submitted at the time of writing. However, it is possible that a northern route will eventually be the preferred option. Whichever alternative is chosen, a substantial amount of known archaeology will be affected, including several LPRIA and Romano-British farmsteads, roads and land boundaries. A bypass development will therefore provide an opportunity for the examination of areas peripheral to the main settlement itself.

In addition, there is a possibility that a large part of the Scheduled Area of Walls Field will be converted into a recreation field. Sooner or later this may include the provision of sports facilities which would involve ground disturbance. In this instance, if Scheduled Monument Consent is granted, in time there may be further opportunities to investigate the core of the settlement.

Acknowledgements

I am grateful to Jane Read for drawing the plans and to Mark Stevenson for background research and support. I would also like to express my gratitude to Andrew David and the staff of the Ancient Monuments Laboratory for allowing the use of the excellent results of their geophysical surveys.

Bibliography

Burleigh, G R, *et al*, forthcoming *Excavations at Baldock, Hertfordshire, 1978–1989*, forthcoming monograph series, North Hertfordshire District Council

——, 1995 A late Iron Age *oppidum* at Baldock, in *The archaeology of the Chilterns* (ed R Holgate), Luton Museum

Burnham, B C, & Wacher, J, 1990 *The 'small towns' of Roman Britain*

Cunliffe, B, 1991 *Iron Age communities in Britain*, 3rd ed

Stead, I M, & Rigby, V, 1986 *Baldock: the excavation of a Roman and pre-Roman settlement, 1968–1972*, Britannia Monograph Series 7

17   Secondary urban centres in Gaul

Anthony King

Introduction

Many secondary centres in Gaul are large and highly developed by Romano-British standards. Mandeure, Belfort (*Epamanduodurum*) covered an area of at least 150 ha and boasted a large and imposing theatre (see Fig 17.1 for location map). Mâlain, Côte-d'Or (*Mediolanum*) perhaps covered 200 ha, if peripheral villas are included (Mangin and Tassaux 1992, 478). Lausanne, Switzerland (*Lousonna*) was equally large (Fig 17.2). It was a roadside settlement that has been the focus of considerable archaeological attention (Kaenel 1977; Paunier *et al* 1989), which can help to sketch in chronological and other details. In origin, the settlement emerged in the Augustan or just pre-Augustan period alongside the important road link between Italy and the Middle Rhine area that ran across the Great St Bernard Pass and through the Swiss lowland valley. It was also on the side of Lac Léman, and there is evidence for a lakeside port facility. The town plan shows a rudimentary forum, a building interpreted as a basilica, a dominant Romano-Celtic temple and extensive housing and workshop remains. There are also several pottery kilns. The position of the town was very favourable for both trading, industrial and population growth, and it may legitimately be asked what status this settlement had in terms of urban hierarchy. Was it actually a 'small' town, or did it gain the urban elements necessary to elevate it to more than a local centre? This is an important question in relation to Gallic towns to which we will return.

Mâlain, like Lausanne and many other such towns, had evidence for industrial or craft production. The excavated part of Mâlain consists of a street fringed with strip buildings, many of which have cellars behind them, and signs of enamel working and other industries (Roussel 1979; *Gallia Informations* 1987–1988, 2, 12–14). Small towns clearly grew in part because of this type of production. Many specialised in certain industries, eg Lezoux and Rheinzabern on fine pottery (Bémont & Jacob 1986, 138–44), Tournai on stone (Amand 1984), Blond, Haute-Vienne, on tin (Desbordes & Lacotte 1987), and probably gained a wider than local reputation because of this. For most such towns, the urban nucleus itself served as a focus for industrial activity on its periphery, as has been very well documented at Rheinzabern, or in the immediate hinterland. The market function of the town and the road system combined to concentrate the initial stages of the product distribution system onto the small towns. This had led Mangin (1985) and Whittaker (1990, 116–17) and to suggest that small towns were productive centres, whereas large towns, ie the *civitas* capitals, etc, were parasitical on them, in that the wealth created in the small towns (*vici*) drained to the large towns, where wealthy houses with mosaics, etc, tend to be found. There is some truth in this, since inscriptions to *negotiatores* are predominantly found in the larger towns, eg Lyon, Mainz. However, this hypothesis ignores the vagaries of excavation in the larger towns which have tended to stick to urban nuclei where the public buildings predominate, not their peripheries where industrial production would have been located. Where investigations have taken place in peripheral areas, eg in Cologne (Hellenkemper 1980, 70, Beil 2), Trier (Huld-Zetsche 1993) and Augst (Laur-Belart 1991, 166ff), clear signs of intensive industrial production are found. It is likely that many of the larger towns served as industrial foci just as many small towns did, and indeed by virtue of their greater size and status, could command greater industrial throughput than most small towns. The wealth in the larger towns could thus have been locally generated, not derived simply from neighbouring small towns and the countryside. The relationship, therefore, between smaller and larger towns was more complex than Mangin's and Whittaker's hypothesis suggests, and we will need to bring in aspects apart from economics.

Oppida, religion and secondary centres

The sort of industrial specialisation alluded to above is also found at one of the most famous of Gallo-Roman small towns, *Alesia* (Fig 17.3), where bronze-working hearths, crucibles and moulds, all mainly from one part of the town, reflect considerable activity (Mangin 1981). *Alesia* is important to us for another reason, namely its previous incarnation as an Iron Age hill fort and the site

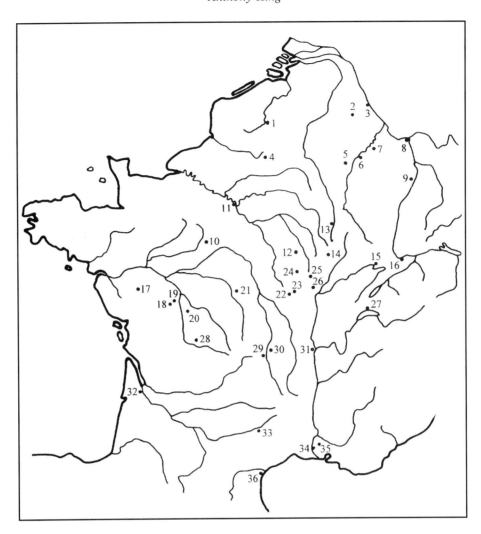

Fig 17.1 *Map of Gaul showing towns and cities mentioned in the text.*

*Key: **1**, Tournai; **2**, Aachen; **3**, Cologne; **4**, Ribemont; **5**, Titelberg; **6**, Trier; **7**, Wederath; **8**, Mainz; **9**, Rheinzabern; **10**, Verdes; **11**, Paris; **12**, Vertault; **13**, Grand; **14**, Langres; **15**, Mandeure; **16**, Augst; **17**, Faye-l'Abbesse; **18**, Vendeuvre-du-Poitou; **19**, Naintré-Vieux-Poitiers; **20**, Antigny; **21**, Bourges; **22**, Mont-Beuvray; **23**, Autun; **24**; Alesia; **25**, Mâlain; **26**, Nuits-St Georges; **27**, Lausanne; **28**, Blond; **29**, Gergovia; **30**, Lezoux; **31**, Lyon; **32**, Bordeaux; **33**, La Graufesenque; **34**, Arles; **35**, Glanum; **36**, Narbonne.*

of Vercingetorix's defeat in 52 BC (Le Gall 1985, 10ff). Most of the Gallo-Roman remains date from the late 1st century AD onwards, however (Bénard & Mangin 1985), and the question has to be posed as to how and why the town became established. It is by no means alone in being an *oppidum* with subsequent occupation – it is sufficient to mention Bourges (*Avaricum*; see Dumasy 1992, 442–3), Langres (*Andematunnum Lingonum*) and Mont Beuvray (*Bibracte*). In the case of the last-mentioned site, there seems to be a peaceful continuity into the Roman period, until considerations of civic prestige and commerce led to abandonment in favour of the more accessible new town of *Augustodunum*. Other secondary centres also had hill fort origins, such as the Titelberg, Luxemburg (Metzler 1984), or Vertault, Côte-d'Or (*Vertillum*). But why establish a town at *Alesia*? It was the site of a major defeat and must have suffered enormous disruption at the time of Caesar's siege. It should

have been regarded as an inauspicious place, especially to the new generation of Gallic aristocracy busy taking up a Romanised life-style (King 1990a, 64–6). Two possible lines of explanation suggest themselves for the emergence of *Alesia* as a Roman town. Firstly, the countryside around is broken and not very fertile. The hill fort itself is in a fine position for settlement, however, and, given the evidence for industrial working, could have acted as a magnet for co-operative craft production.

Perhaps equally, if not more important, is the religious factor. It is well-known that hill forts, both in Britain and Gaul, often had an element of religious continuity from the Iron Age to the Roman period. A good Gallic example is *Gergovia*, where the site apparently dwindled to a small group of temples and associated structures (Brogan & Desforges 1940). At *Alesia* there are several temples, and although continuity from the Iron Age is not proven, the cults are essentially Celtic in ori-

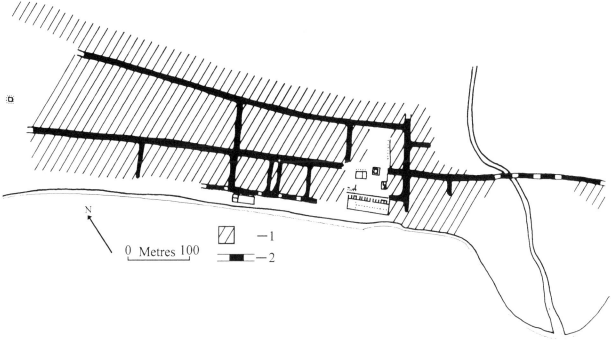

Fig 17.2 *Lausanne (after Paunier et al 1989).*

Key: *1 area of occupation; 2, inferred road*

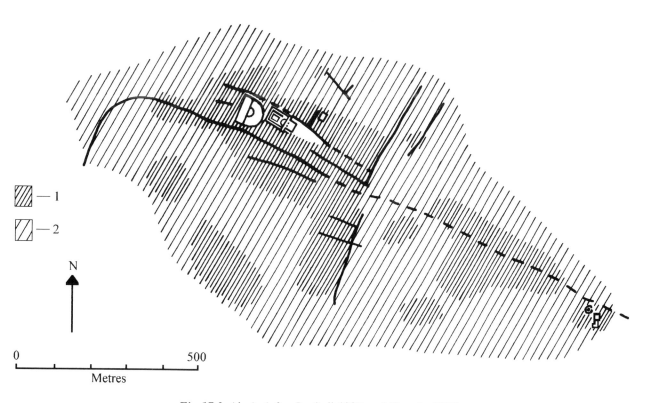

Fig 17.3 *Alesia (after Le Gall 1985 and Mangin 1981).*

Key: *1, area of dense occupation; 2, area of slight occupation*

gin. An outlying shrine to Apollo Moritasgus has evidence of being a healing sanctuary with origins in the 1st century BC (Espérandieu 1910/1916). The temple in the centre of the Roman town is more surprising – it appears to have links with the Capitoline Triad, but around the temple are large concentrations of pottery offering groups that are much more Romano-Celtic in character (Le Gall & Sénéchal 1974). Since the earliest material dates to the late Iron Age, it is possible that the site was an Iron Age shrine that became Romanised in part during an early phase of development, that also included the theatre and the organisation of the streets. Other finds point to the importance of the town in religious terms; reliefs of Epona, a local cult (Oaks 1986), also a possible *celicnon* in the form of a two-storey portico associated with Ucuetis (a deity only attested at *Alesia*), and the famous Gaulish language inscription mentioning Ucuetis and *Alesia* (Olivier 1992). A plausible hypothesis, therefore, is that the *oppidum* saw initial post-conquest development primarily in terms of religious continuity, intended to preserve the sanctity of the site in the aftermath of the military trauma of 52 BC. Subsequently, perhaps several decades after the conquest, local economic factors led to the rise of *Alesia* as a secondary centre, eventually attaining an area of 80 ha, with many of the appurtenances of a small *civitas* capital.

In archaeological and urban planning terms, any sacred site established prior to the growth of a town should manifest itself both in the phasing and stratigraphy, and in its spatial relations with other features such as roads and buildings. Chronologically, many temple sites are relatively very early compared with other building activity, as exemplified by the early date of *Alesia's* shrine to Apollo Moritasgus. They are often the earliest monumental structures to be built, and can display precocious evidence for Romanisation. At Ribemont, Somme, for example, the temple itself was reorganised along Romanised lines in the Augustan period, prior to the setting up of the other parts of the rural sanctuary (Cadoux 1984a).

As far as spatial disposition is concerned, it is notable that many towns, both large and small, have clusters of Romano-Celtic temples. The most famous is the Altbachtal site on the margins of the gridded street area of Trier (Gose 1972), but smaller groups occur in other towns, such as Antigny, Vienne (Fig 17.4; Fauduet 193, 33; Richard 1992), or in Britain, Silchester (Boon 1974, 152ff) and Springhead (Harker 1980). At many sites it is clear that the street layout respects the siting of the temples, which, when combined with the chronological evidence for pre-Roman or very early post-conquest establishment of the religious focus, as at Trier and Antigny, indicates the primacy of the shrines in determining the topographical layout and growth of the town. Other factors, too, were obviously as important, notably the prior existence of an Iron Age (usually high-status) settlement or a Roman military establishment, but the religious factor has tended to be overlooked by archaeologists, and needs a higher profile in interpretations of urban origins.

The religious factor brings us to a related and overlapping class of secondary centre in Gaul, the rural sanctuary. Many of these sites are as large as most small towns and have urbanistic elements to them, such as a monumental focus, often with a theatre and baths, housing and aspects of a regular layout (cf Braemer 1973). Some develop as non-religious foci too, especially if they are capable of attracting the trading and industrial elements already discussed, such as at Naintré-Vieux-Poitiers (*Vetus Pictavis*: Olivier & Fritsch 1982) where there are pottery kilns not far from the theatre and inscribed standing stone, or Nuits-St Georges, Côte-d'Or, where an extensive trading post emerged alongside the major routeway and large Romano-Celtic temple, equivalent in size to the well-known 'Temple of Janus' at Autun (Planson 1976; Horne & King 1980, 443, fig 17.3.2).

A few rural sanctuaries develop as populous religious towns in their own right, particularly if they have important pilgrimage cults, which in the main were those connected with healing. A prime example is Grand (*Aquae Granni*? or *Andesina*?: Frézouls 1982), a sanctuary in an out-of-the-way location distant from major routeways, where a cult of Apollo Grannus, which may have received the imperial patronage of Constantine, gave rise to a flourishing town for pilgrims wishing to be healed by dreams in the ritual of 'incubation'. Aachen (*Aquae Granni*?) is also a healing shrine to Grannus, with medicinal baths (Cüppers *et al* 1982). Here, too, a town grew up around the sanctuary, possibly not unlike that at Bath (*Aquae Sulis*). In western Gaul, some of the rural sanctuaries were successful in providing nuclei for rudimentary towns, and this may also have been due to the religious significance of the site (eg Vendeuvre-du-Poitou: Fig 17.5; Nicolini 1976; Dumasy & Fincker 1992, 303, fig 8). A feature of many rural sanctuaries is their pre-Roman religious origins, well-demonstrated by recent excavations at Ribemont (Cadoux 1984b), and suspected elsewhere on the basis of artefactual evidence, such as at Faye-l'Abbesse, Deux-Sèvres (Horne & King 1980, 409–10). Mangin and Tassaux (1992, 468) have doubted that much of the religious evidence antedates the Caesarian conquest, but this is probably due more to the late tectonisation of Gaulish religious sites (King 1990b), rather than the exclusively post-conquest establishment of the sanctuaries. Another important feature of the rural sanctuaries is their early monumentalisation in stone during the Julio-Claudian period, which Picard (1976) has seen as a deliberate policy of providing Romanised foci in a rural landscape, to act as *pagus* centres. If this is correct, the successful development of the policy would presumably have seen the growth of true urban centres around the sanctuaries, as of course did in fact occur in a significant number of cases. Picard termed the rural sanctuaries *conciliabula*, without any real direct evidence for the ancient usage of this term.

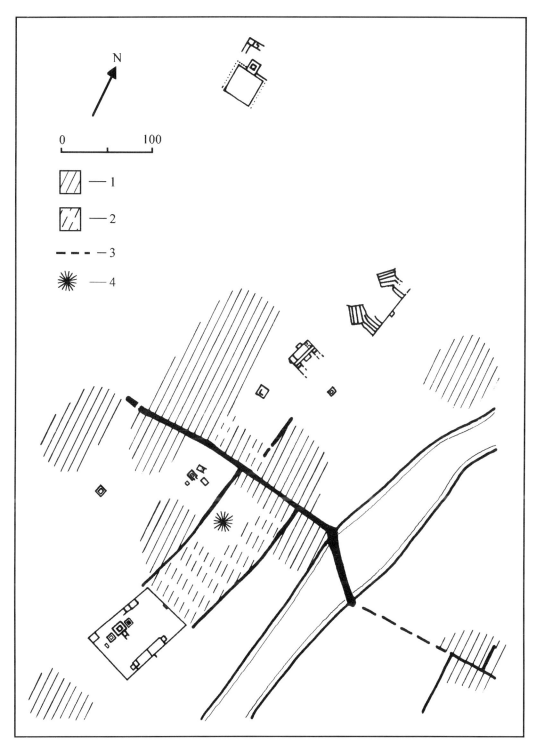

Fig 17.4 *Antigny (after Richard 1992).*

Key: 1, area of occupation; 2, inferred area of occupation; 3, inferred road; 4, possible site of forum

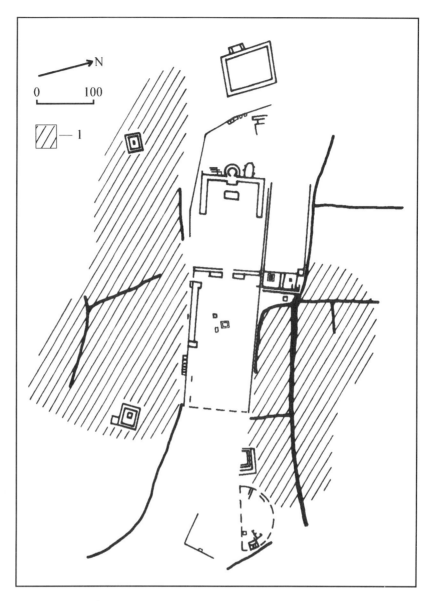

Fig 17.5 *Vendeuvre-du-Poitou (after Dumasy & Fincker 1992, fig 8).*

Key: 1, area of occupation (habitations, inns, etc)

Economic zonation and Gallic secondary centres

Discussion of this aspect of urban studies inevitably re-
volves around the question of why some sites developed
into small towns while others did not. After all, many
important road junctions did not have roadside settlements, many rural sanctuaries remained as temple sites
and nothing more, and most hill forts did not continue
into the Roman period in any significant way. Some
planned centres failed to develop into population centres, such as Verdes, Loir-et Cher, where the forum,
basilica and baths were laid out as a nucleus that never,
apparently attracted a large population (Provost 1988,
105–10). The answer to the question probably comes
down to issues of population density, economic development and the positioning of the larger towns. For Gaul,

these matters are of some interest, since general considerations of the economy show that development was not
even, with the west and north remaining predominantly
rural, and the south and to a lesser extent, the east, being
more highly developed and more urbanised.

One of the reasons for this zonation was the existence
of two communication corridors from the Mediterranean
coast, one from Narbonne across the Carcassonne Gap
to Bordeaux and the west coast, the other up the Rhône/
Saône valley and eastern Gaul to the Rhineland and Britain. Both encouraged trade and production along their
margins, but the former saw its *floruit* in the late Iron
Age to the Julio-Claudian period (Roman 1983; Cunliffe
1988, 81–6), before substantial secondary town development had taken place. The eastern corridor was more
important, and indeed grew in importance as the army

became well-established on the Rhine frontier and in Britain, thus encouraging the development of military supply routes that ran, in some cases, from the Mediterranean coast northwards (Middleton 1979; 1980; 1983; King 1990a, 115–6; Bekker-Nielsen 1984, fig 3.1). Civilian trade probably grew from largely military origins to become self-sustaining as Romanisation proceeded apace in 1st century Gaul and Germany, and secondary centres such as La Graufesenque, Lezoux and *Alesia*, as well as the larger towns, could thrive on the demand for their products that emanated, in the main, from markets further north. These secondary centres were often, as in the case of the three just mentioned, not on major routes, but accessible to them. Presumably they were near the materials necessary for their manufacturing industries, and the cost of transporting the finished products was less than for bringing the raw materials to the sites. It is notable in the case of a specialised manufacture such as samian ware that the vast majority of the kiln centres were within easy reach of the eastern communications corridor or the large towns on it that could provide a nodal market. Samian ware was made elsewhere in Gaul, such as in Poitou (Bémont & Jacob 1986, 130–6), but never achieved success on the scale of the major producers. The relevant raw materials were also fairly widely dispersed (cf Duhamel 1975), but as might be expected, it seems that a realisable demand was necessary to stimulate samian production, which only happened along the main economic corridors.

Bekker-Nielsen (1984, fig 4.1; 1989, 24–32) has also suggested that the small towns in central and eastern Gaul grew in stature because of the long distance between the larger towns and the need for intermediate markets. This is a classic central-place theory explanation, similar to that invoked by Hodder and Hassall (1971) for the development of Water Newton. Bekker-Nielsen (1984, 55) also observed that many of these Gallic small towns acquired the trappings of the larger towns, such as *fora*, basilicas, possible *curiae*, theatres, baths, etc. He termed them intermediate towns, though from a British perspective we would happily regard many of them as *civitas* capitals if judged from the archaeological remains alone.

A relevant issue in the discussion of the size of towns is the parameter of population density. It is possible that the devastation of the conquest period resulted in a low population during the decades immediately following, relative to potential pre-industrial carrying capacity. Caesar's account gives both direct and indirect indications of population loss due to death or enslavement, for instance the case of the Helvetii, apparently numbering 368,000 at the start of their migration, of which only 110,000 survived to be resettled (*BG* 1.29). Although most of Gaul never suffered depredations of its population on this scale, it is very likely that a significant proportion of the (male) population did not survive the wars. When towns started to be established in the Augustan period, much of the interior of Gaul probably only needed

sparsely-scattered major centres to provide effective administration and services, with the result that the inter-centre distance in most of the Three Gauls is in excess of 55km, and for the rural (ie upper) parts of Aquitania, Lugdunensis and Belgica, exceeded 100km (Bekker-Nielsen 1989, 25–6). Population growth during the early Empire almost certainly occurred, despite being very difficult to prove directly, so that it may have peaked in the range 11–12 million for the whole of Gaul and Germania (see Ferdière 1988, I, 86, and King 1990a, 107–8 for further discussion). Of course, population growth in itself would not necessarily bring about growth in the number and size of urban centres. A predominantly rural population could have remained largely self-sufficient, except for such factors as the payment of taxes and the cultural stimulus provided by the rapid acceptance of Romanisation by the defeated Gallic elite. These factors required access from the countryside to the facilities provided by primary and secondary urban centres. In this way the hypothesis can be advanced that small towns grew in size as intermediate centres because of the long distances between the *civitas* capitals in many parts of Gaul. Rural sanctuaries also served a similar function, and, as we have seen, grew into towns in their own right in some cases.

In theory, continued population growth should lead to the so-called' small' towns becoming large enough to rival the fully-constituted primary centres, and ultimately to the sub-division of *civitates* to create more administrative centres from the secondary agglomerations. Interestingly, however, the only region of Gaul where this actually occurred was in Aquitania, where the region of Novempopulania south of the Garonne had four cities in the early 1st century AD, but by the time of the Notitia Dignitatum had thirteen (Bekker-Nielsen 1989, 43). For historical and ethnic reasons (see Caesar, *BG* 1–1; Mangin & Tassaux 1992, 478), this region seems to have been predisposed to tolerate subdivision of larger *civitates*, whereas in most of the rest of Gaul administrative areas retained their original extent, with the result that many 'small' towns had the urbanistic features of the 'large' towns, but not the juridical status of a primary centre.

'Small' and 'large' towns

The size of Gallic secondary towns seems to suggest that there is a continuum in urban form, from simple village-like road settlements like Wederath (*Belginum*: Haffner 1970), through to sites like *Alesia* with many urban features. The more sizeable of these 'small' towns grade into the more formally planned towns that had municipal rather than lesser status in the juridical hierarchy of Roman administration. Towns could, of course, be elevated in status without appreciable change to their physical appearance. A telling example in this respect is *Glanum*, Bouches-du-Rhône (Rivet 1988, 198–200), where there is a theatre, an important sanctuary, a forum, basilica, baths, monumental arch, imposing mausoleum, etc. *Glanum* started life as a relatively lowly settlement, only marked out by its religious focus. However, urbanisation along Hellenistic/Roman but also partly Celtic lines was rapid and by the 1st century AD the town was awarded the *ius Latii* (Pliny, *NH*, 3.4.5). It had made it into the upper reaches of the urban hierarchy and the townsfolk had access to Roman citizenship. It was a town in a favoured position economically which also showed a propensity to Romanisation, both factors which helped its elevation in status. Despite this, however, the town was always regarded as being within the territory of the colony at Arles.

The problem that *Glanum* poses for us is that it is only the survival of a relevant historical document that informs us of the town's position in the urban hierarchy. Archaeologically it is the same as both the precocious *vici* further north, and the lesser colonies and *civitas* capitals. The mixture of Roman administrative terms with archaeological reality is not a happy one, and it is probably best for archaeologists to put aside Roman legal definitions of towns, and to devise a scheme of ranking by the presence and absence of urban criteria. Goudineau (1980, 387–9) has done this for the larger towns in Gaul, although his scheme has not been published in detail and in fact includes legal status as a factor (Fig 17.6). His criteria include area (of the town, its cemeteries and its territory), monumental features (walls, gates, arches, public buildings, aqueducts, houses), industry (workshop evidence, dispersal of products), epigraphy (number of inscriptions, level of evergetism, distribution of citizens to other towns, number of slaves, etc) and status (type of statute, level of citizenship, position as provincial or inter-provincial centre). Bekker-Nielsen (1984, 55, fig 2.7) has also gone a certain way in this direction with his criteria of *fora*, basilicas and *curiae*. To this could be added sculpture, inscriptions, temples, funerary monuments, other monumental appurtenances, baths, gridded layouts, total area, etc. Although there is room for much debate over the nature of the criteria and their relative weighting, and how to account for the variable extent of archaeological investigation in each town, a scheme of this sort would go a long way to objectifying comparative studies between regions and provinces, and would allow us to test suggestions about urban development with greater clarity.

To conclude, the evidence from Gaul seems to steer research in a different direction from that apparent in Britain at the present time. I am conscious of having ignored the smaller settlements, for which the Gallic evidence is poor compared with Britain, and which would be regarded as villages. Larger secondary centres, by contrast, are better known, and, as we have seen, were generally larger, founded earlier and had very different sequences of development (especially in the late Roman period). Despite this, settlements in both Britain and Gaul were established within the Roman cultural *koiné* and its

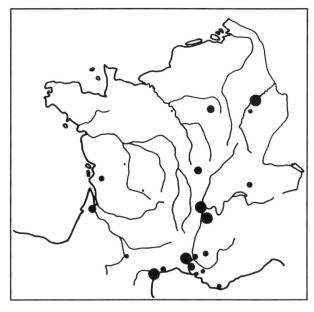

Fig 17.6 *Goudineau's ranking of major towns in Gaul, omitting Marseille and the Rhineland (after Goudineau 1980, fig 325). The size of the circles indicates the rankings in general terms. The actual rank order is: 1, Lyon; 2, Narbonne; 3, Nîmes; 4, Trier, Vienne; 6, Arles; 7, Bordeaux, Autun; 9, Reims; 10, Vaison; 11, Saintes, Avenches; 13, Béziers, Orange; 15, Fréjus; 16, Aix, Metz, Toulouse; 19, Poitiers, Limoges, Paris*

expression of civilisation as being encapsulated in urban form. It should be possible to compare provinces using a system of urban criteria, in order to judge how far and to what extent urbanisation was the norm, was successful, and, of crucial importance for study of the smaller secondary centres, how far down the settlement hierarchy Roman ideas of urban form penetrated.

Bibliography

Petit and Mangin 1994a and 1994b were published too recently to be used for this article, but the references are included here because of the importance of these new volumes for the study of secondary urban centres.

Amand, M, 1984 L'industrie, la taille et le commerce de la pierre dans le basin du Tournaisis à l'époque romaine, *Rev Nord*, 66, 209–19

Bekker-Nielsen, T, 1984 *Bydannelse i det romerske Gallien*, Aarhus

——, 1989 *The geography of power: studies in the urbanization of north-west Europe*

Bémont, C, & Jacob, J-P, 1986 *La terre sigillée gallo-romaine*, Paris

Bénard, J, & Mangin, M, 1985 Les étapes de la romanisation d'une agglomération indigène du Centre-Est des Gaules: l'exemple d'Alésia, in *Les débuts de l'urbanisation en Gaule et dans les provinces voisines* (ed R Bédon & P Augin) (Caesarodunum 20), Paris, 103–15

Boon, G C, 1974 *Silchester, the Roman town of Calleva*

Braemer, F, 1973 Recherches sur l'implantation des sanctuaires dans la Gaule romaine, in *Pour une géographie sacrée de l'Occident romaine* (ed R Chevallier) (Caesarodunum 8), Tours, 144–55

Brogan, O, & Desforges, E, 1940 Gergovia, *Archaeol J*, 97, 1–36

Cadoux, J-L, 1984a Le sanctuaire gallo-romain de Ribemont-sur-Ancre (Somme): état de recherches en 1983, *Rev Nord*, 66, 125–45

——, 1984b L'ossuaire gaulois de Ribemont-sur-Ancre (Somme). Premières observations, premières questions, *Gallia*, 42, 53–78

Chevallier, R (ed), 1976 *Le vicus gallo-romain* (Caesarodunum 11), Paris

Cunliffe, B W, 1988 *Greeks, Romans and barbarians: spheres of interaction*

Cüppers, H, *et al*, 1982 *Aquae Granni: Beiträge zur Archäologie von Aachen*, Cologne/Bonn

Desbordes, J M, & Lacotte, R, 1987 Du vicus gallo-romain au village médiéval: l'exemple de Blotomagus/Blond (Haute-Vienne), in *Les mines et la métallurgie en Gaule et dans les provinces voisines* (ed R Chevallier) (Caesarodunum 22), Paris, 291–6

Duhamel, P, 1975 Les ateliers céramiques de la Gaule romaine, *Dossiers Hist Archéol*, 9, 12–20

Dumasy, F, 1992 Agglomérations et cité: l'exemple des Bituriges Cubi, in Maurin 1992, 439–60

——, & Fincker, M, 1992 Les édifices de spectacle, in Maurin 1992, 293–321

Espérandieu, E, 1910/1916 Fouilles de la Croix Saint-Charles au Mont Auxois, *Mém Comm Antiq Côte-d'Or*, 15, 255–80; 16, 41–68

Fauduet, I, 1993 *Les temples de tradition celtique en Gaule romaine*, Paris

Ferdière, A, 1988 *Les campagnes en Gaule romaine*, 2 vols, Paris

Frézouls, E (ed), 1982 *Les villes antiques de la France. Belgique 1, Amiens, Beauvais, Grand, Metz*, Strasbourg

Gose, E, 1972 *Der gallo-römische Tempelbezirk im Altbachtal zu Trier*, Mainz

Goudineau, C, 1980 Les villes de la paix romaine, in *Histoire de la France urbaine. I, La ville antique* (ed G Duby), Paris, 233–391

Haffner, A, 1970 Belginum: eine keltisch-römische Siedlung an der Ausoniusstrasse, *Kurtrierisches Jahrbuch*, 10, 203–22

Harker, S, 1980 Springhead: a brief re-appraisal, in Rodwell 1980, 285–8

Hellenkemper, H, 1980 Wohnviertel und öffentliche Bauzonen, *Führer zu vor-und frühgeschichtliche Denkmälern, 37, Köln I: enführende Aufsätze*, Mainz, 67–76

Hodder, I, & Hassall, M, 1971 The non-random spacing of Romano-British walled towns, *Man*, ser 2, 6, 391–407

Horne, P D, & King, A C, 1980 Romano-Celtic temples in continental Europe: a gazetteer of those with known plans, in Rodwell 1980, 369–555

Huld-Zetsche, I, 1993 *Trierer Reliefsigillata Werkstatt II*, Bonn

Kaenel, G, 1977 *Lousonna: la promenade archéologique de Vidy* (Guides archéol Suisse 9), Lausanne

King, A C, 1990a *Roman Gaul and Germany*

——, 1990b The emergence of Romano-Celtic religion, in *The early Roman Empire in the West* (ed T F Blagg & M Millett), 220–41

Laur-Belart, R, 1991 *Guide d'Augusta Raurica*, 5th ed, Basel

Le Gall, J, 1985 *Alésia* (Guides archéol France 5), Paris

——, & Sénéchal, R, 1974 Dépôts d'offrandes auprès du principal temple d'Alésia, *Comptes Rendus Acad Inscriptions Belles-Lettres*, 207–15

Mangin, M, 1981 *Un quartier de commerçants et d'artisans d'Alésia*, Paris

——, 1985 Artisanat et commerce dans les agglomérations secondaires du centre-est de la Gaule sous l'Empire, in *L'Origine des richesses dépensées dans la ville antique* (ed P Leveau), Aix-en-Provence, 113–31

——, & Tassaux, F, 1992 Les agglomérations secondaires de l'Aquitaine romaine, in Maurin 1992, 461–96

Maurin, L (ed), 1992 *Villes et agglomérations urbaines antiques du Sud-ouest de la Gaule* (Aquitania Suppl 6), Bordeaux

Metzler, J, 1984 Das treverischen Oppidum auf dem Titelberg (Luxemburg), in *Trier, Augustusstadt der Treverer*, Mainz, 68–78

Middleton, P, 1979 Army supply in Roman Gaul: an hypothesis for Roman Britain, in *Invasion and response: the case of Roman Britain* (ed B Burnham & H Johnson), BAR Brit Ser, 73, 81–97

——, 1980 La Graufesenque: a question of marketing, *Athenaeum*, 58, 186–91

——, 1983 The Roman army and long-distance trade, in *Trade and famine in classical antiquity* (eds P Garnsey & C Whittaker), 75–83

Nicolini, G, 1976 Les sanctuaires ruraux de Poitou-Charente: quelques exemples d'implantation et de structure interne, in Chevallier 1976, 256–72

Oaks, L, 1986 The goddess Epona: concepts of sovreignty in a changing landscape, in *Pagan gods and shrines of the Roman Empire* (eds M Henig & A King), Oxford Univ Committee for Archaeol Monogr 8

Olivier, A, 1992 Les chapiteaux à consoles du 'celicnon' d'Ucuetis à Alesia, *Rev Archéol Est Centre-Est*, 43, 307–27

——, & Fritsch, R, 1982 Le vicus de Vieux-Poitiers, *Archéol*, 163, 52–61

Paunier, D, *et al*, 1989 Le vicus gallo-romain de Lousonna-Vidy, *Cahiers Archéol Romande* 42 (Lousonna 7), Lausanne

Petit, J-P, & Mangin, M (eds), 1994a *Les agglomérations secondaires: la Gaule belgique, les Germanies et l'Occident romain*, Paris

——, 1994b *Atlas des agglomérations secondaires de la Gaule belgique et des Germanies*, Paris

Picard, G-C, 1976 *Vicus* et *Conciliabulum*, in Chevallier 1976, 47–9

Planson, E, 1976 Le vicus des Bolards, Nuits St-Georges (Côte-d'Or), in Chevallier 1976, 148–56

Provost, M, 1988 *Carte archéologique de la Gaule: le Loir-et-Cher, 41*, Paris

Richard, C, 1992 Antigny (Vienne), in Maurin 1992, 22–4

Rivet, A L, 1988 *Gallia Narbonensis: southern Gaul in Roman times*

Rodwell, W (ed), 1980 *Temples, churches and religion: recent research in Roman Britain*, BAR Brit Ser, 77

Roman, Y, 1983 *De Narbonne à Bordeaux: un axe économique au Ier siècle avant J-C*, Lyon

Roussel, L (ed), 1979 *Mâlain-Mediolanum 1968–1978: le mobilier,* Besançon

Whittaker, C R, 1990 The consumer city revisited: the *vicus* and the city, *J Roman Archaeol*, 3, 110–18.

Wightman, E, 1976 Le vicus dans le contexte de l'administration et de la société gallo-romaine: quelques réflexions, in Chevallier 1976, 59–64

——, 1985 *Gallia Belgica*

18   Small towns of the Ubii and Cugerni/Baetasii civitates (Lower Germany)

Michael Gechter

This survey deals only with the *vici* within the territory of the cities of *Colonia Claudia Ara Agrippinensis* (CCAA) (Cologne) and *Colonia Ulpia Traiana* (CUT) (Xanten) (Fig 18.1). The city territories were identical to those of the civitates of the Ubii, the Cugerni and Baetasii. The *civitates* of the Sunucci, in the area of present-day Aix-la-Chapelle and those of the Batavii, Texuandri, Cannefates and Frisiavones in present-day Holland are not discussed.

The landscape

The province of Lower Germany – Germania Inferior – was the northernmost province of the *Imperium Romanum* on the continent. Geomorphologically it is characterised by the valleys and the delta of the Rhine and the Meuse. In the south, it included the northern part of the central Rhine valley north of the mouth of the Vinxt stream and to the west, the northern foothills of the Eifel mountains. In the area of Bonn, the Rhine valley widens gradually into the Lower Rhine basin, which extends to the mouth of the river Erft in the north. The basin is bordered by the Bergisches Land in the east and by the Ville ridge and the Eifel foothills in the west. West of this basin between Rhine and Meuse lie fertile loess plains. North of the mouth of the River Erft, the lowlands of the Lower Rhine extend to the present German-Dutch border, merging with the Meuse lowlands in the west, and the Westphalian lowlands in the east. To the north-west, in present-day Holland, the lowlands are adjoined by the Rhine-Meuse marshes which extend to the North Sea. North of the marshland lies the east Dutch Geest and in south, the Meuse lowland. The Westphalian and the Meuse lowlands were interspersed with numerous bogs. Thus traffic could only move north and south along the rivers Rhine and Meuse.

The Roman occupation

In pre-Roman times this region between Meuse and Rhine was inhabited by a Germanic population whose material culture exhibits a strong Celtic influence. As Caesar re- corded, this was the homeland of the Eburones. The Menapii lived north of this area in the Meuse-Rhine delta. The Sugambrii were settled east of the Rhine.

In 53 BC Caesar invaded Eburonian territory, de- stroyed their army, plundered their land and sold the inhabitants as slaves. The Roman troops then withdrew from the Rhine into the hinterland, into modern France. Troops were first stationed on the Rhine in 16 BC. From the Claudian period onwards, Roman forts remained on the same sites for nearly 300 years.

Roman roads

Before the Romans could transfer their troops to the Rhine, the newly conquered territory had to be integrated to the existing Gallic road system. A road was built from Lyon to the Channel coast near Boulogne-sur-Mer. Near Rheims a road branched off to Trier. A third road led *via* Besançon to the Upper Rhine. The newly-built road sys- tem of the Lower Rhine was connected to that of Gaul *via* Trier and the Upper Rhine. The *limes* road ran along the Rhine *via* Mainz-Koblenz-Bonn-Cologne-Xanten- Nijmegen to the mouth of the river. Another important road led from Trier through the Eifel mountains to Co- logne. This joined the Cologne-Rheims road at Zülpich. A similiar road to that in the Rhine valley ran north- south through the Meuse valley, parallel to the river, as far as Nijmegen. The only important east-west route was that from Cologne *via* Jülich-Heerlen-Maastricht- Tongeren-Bavai to Boulogne-sur-Mer.

The civitates

Civitas Ubiorum

In the middle of the 1st century BC, the Ubii migrated from their homelands in the upper Wetterau into the ter- ritory abandoned by the Eburones. Their oldest settle- ment was Bonn, where there is evidence for a native Germanic settlement dating to about 40 BC. Pottery simi- lar to that in Bonn has also been found in Neuss. It is possible that Ubian settlements were founded in the area

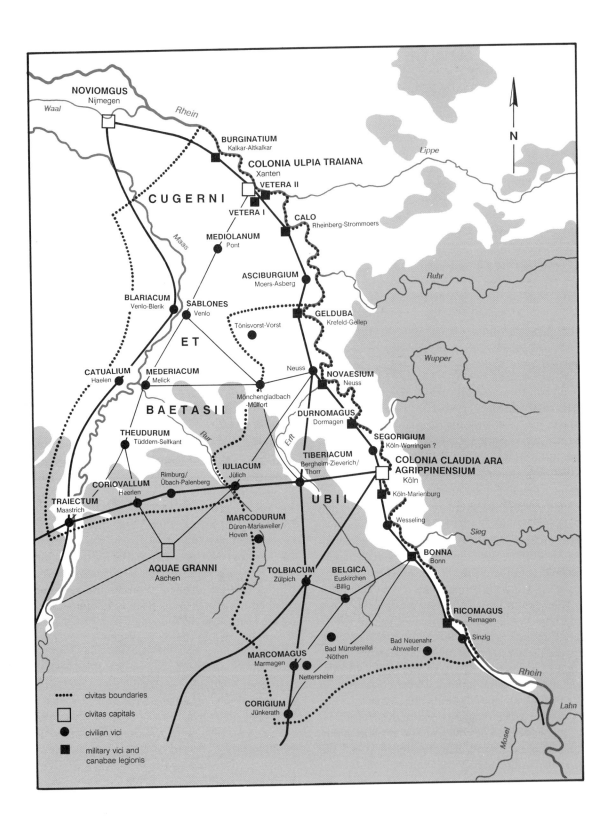

Fig 18.1 *Small towns of the Ubii and Cugerni/Baetasii.*

of Remagen and Dormagen. Cologne was finally established as the capital of Ubii in the middle of the last
decade BC. The tribal territory, later the territory of the
CCAA, was bordered in the east by the Rhine and in the
south by the Vinxt stream, whose name originates from
ad fines. Further south, Jünkerath-*Corigium* was also
included in the Ubian territory. In the west, the rivers
Inde, Rur and Niers formed the boundary. In the north
the boundary ran in a line from Krefeld to the Rhine
(Rüger 1968, 82; von Petrikovits 1980, 112–18).

Civitas Cugerni et Baetasii

This dual *civitas* with its capital at Xanten (CUT) lay to
the north-west of the Ubian territory. Its boundaries followed the Rhine in the east and extended north almost as
far as Kalkar. In the west, it was bordered by the neighbouring *Provincia Belgica*, which lay on the left bank of
the Meuse. It is not known how far its boundary extended
beyond the Cologne-Heerlen-Maastricht road in the south.
In the south, the territory of the *civitas* included parts of
the loess plains but in the north included only the sand
and loam areas.

The population was similarly heterogeneous. It can
be assumed that a proportion of the pre-Roman population – the Eburones and Menapii – still existed; nonetheless Tiberius settled the Sugambrii, originally from east
of the Rhine, in this area in about 8 BC. The latter are
known as Cugernii and are possibly responsible for the
Elbe-Germanic influence present in the grave goods of
the first half of the 1st century AD. The Baetasii on the
other hand seem to originate from a branch of the
Eburones or Menapii (Rüger 1968, 86–7, 96–9; von
Petrikovits 1980, 112–18: pers comm C Bridger).

Small towns

Small towns or *vici* are defined in negative terms, being
Roman settlements which are neither *coloniae*, nor
municipia. They are of lower status and undefined in
legal terms. They are dependent upon higher ranking
towns, in our case the CCAA or CUT. Representatives
of the *coloniae* were responsible for administration within
the *vici*.

Vici in Lower Germany from the 1st to the 3rd century, and here I include the *canabae legionis* and the
settlements at the auxiliary forts as they functioned similarly, differ from the *coloniae* and *municipia* in the following ways:

– The settlements have no regular street plan, having
   gradually grown up along a road, which is usually
   lined on both sides with buildings. In the 3rd century the settlements contract in size.
– The settlement is not delimited by a boundary wall.
– Often there is no definite town centre.
– The boundaries between the settlement area and the

cemeteries fluctuate. In small towns the dead were
buried along the exit-roads, but also within the settlements, behind the houses.

In the 2nd century industrial processes using fire were
confined to the lee side of the settlement, as was also the
case in the *coloniae*. At this time, the richer settlements
assumed an urban appearance, by building public baths
or a forum/temple etc. However, the small towns in Lower
Germany do not show the same degree of urbanity as the
vici in Upper Germany and Belgica. The *vici* are very
simple in structure and are basically trading and commercial centres. Public buildings such as baths, theatres,
a forum/basilica etc, common in the neighbouring provinces, are absent here.

In the following catalogue of sites, the *vici* are classified according to their location. It is also possible to
group them as follows according to criteria established
for Gaul by A Grenier in 1931:

1   Villages with religious and economic functions situ-
    ated on a road. The larger of our *vici* can be classi-
    fied in this group, such as the *canabae legionis*,
    settlements on crossroads and at river crossings.
    Independent manufacturing areas develop very
    quickly in such small towns with potteries and tileries,
    stonemasons, workshops etc. They supplied the lo-
    cal market. There was often a *beneficiarius* post in
    such *vici*. Smaller cult shrines were probably present.

2   Former native centres, now Romanised. The former
    civitas capital of the Ubii (Bonn) falls into this cat-
    egory.

3   Small market-towns whose economic basis consists
    of handicrafts and trade, situated on a road. The
    majority of the settlements belong to this category
    and differ only in size from those in the first group.

4   Small agricultural hamlets. The settlement of
    Tönisvorst-Vorst can be placed in this group, but,
    unfortunately nothing much is known of the settle-
    ment itself.

5   Industrial settlements. Outlying potteries, mining and
    smelting settlements belong to this category. The
    products were traded at markets in other *vici*.

6   Cult centres. The larger cult-centres with temples
    and shrines, which lie isolated in the countryside
    take on a specific settlement role. The priests and
    their servants would have lived in or near the cult
    centre. Similarly, inns to accommodate the worship-
    pers and stonemasons' workshops must have been
    located nearby. The large cult centre of the *matronae
    Aufaniae* in Bonn is excluded from this category, as
    it was of regional importance and attracted worship-
    pers from all over the province.

The place names of *vici* are attested either in historical sources (Tacitus, the Antonine Itinerary and the *Tabula*

Peutingeriana) or in inscriptions and their sites are archaeologically substantiated, as in the case of *Tolbiacum* and *Juliacum*. In other cases, only the name of the *vicus* is known, as with *Segorigium*. In an inscription from the *vicus* Nettersheim the place name has unfortunately been erased. A further interesting example is the *vicus Lucretius*, named in three inscriptions from the municipal area of Cologne. This would seem to indicate that an urban ward could be regarded as a separate *vicus*.

The original military function of the road network played an important role in the development of settlements in the territories of CCAA and CUT. *Vici* developed from the early military posts at bridges, eg Mönchengladbach-Mülfort. However, it is very noticeable that the bridges on the *limes* road which cross the tributaries of the Rhine did not attract settlements. In the case of the bridges at the mouth of the Vinxt stream, the boundary with Upper Germany, over the Gumme near Bonn and over the Erft river near Neuss, the settlements developed several kilometres distant from them.

Settlements on rivers played an important role as ports. Here it was possible to load goods directly from the road onto ships. It appears that both banks of the river were settled at crossing points (bridges, fords and ferries). Examples of such opposed settlements, mostly established in the 2nd century are Rimburg, Jülich and Maastricht. It is also interesting to note that the *vici* along the parallel roads in the Meuse valley developed opposite one another. A ferry connecting the settlements on opposite banks of the river can be assumed for Venlo/Blerik and Melick/Haelen.

A further factor which encouraged settlement was the building of fortified granaries in the 2nd century, to house produce paid in tax eg Mönchengladbach-Mülfort. Such central granaries had a positive influence on the economic strength of a settlement, as the farmers were bound to bring in their produce once a year.

The continuing occupation of the settlements outside the auxiliary forts of Moers-Asberg and Dormagen after the departure of the military is most informative. This clearly shows that these settlements provided important services for the farmsteads of the surrounding countryside and thus continued to exist after the departure of the garrison.

The buildings in the *vici* were mostly of the strip house type. In addition inns for the accommodation of travellers are known. Ground plans of other types of buildings have only been recovered in Heerlen and Bonn. These particular *vici* cannot really be classified in any of the above groups. Bonn was not only the former *civitas* capital of the Ubii, but also a *canabae legionis* and at the same time an important regional cult centre, where administrative officers and traders from CCAA, and even the *legatus legionis* of Strasbourg, made dedications. Heerlen is remarkable for its large public baths. This is the only example in Lower Germany of a phenomenon familiar in Gaul: people of influence trying to give their native *vici*

an urban appearance by donating public buildings. Heerlen provides the only example of this kind of urbanity in a small town in Lower Germany.

As a result of the economic decline and the climatic deterioration towards the end of the 2nd century, farming on the sand and loam soils became unviable. The agricultural infrastructure in the countryside broke down; the *vici* here became superfluous and were abandoned or were not rebuilt after the Frankish attacks in 275 AD. Even CUT was affected. In contrast, the *vici* in the loess areas were unaffected since farming continued to be viable. The economic basis remained sound and these *vici* continued into the 5th century; most were fortified in the 4th century (van Buren 1955; Galsterer 1992; Gechter 1992; Grenier 1931; Kunow 1988, 1989, 1992; von Petrikovits 1977, 1980; Sommer 1992).

In the gazetteer below D signifies Germany and NL The Netherlands.

Canabae legionis

Bonna – Bonn (D)

From the Claudian period onwards the *canabae legionis* developed south of the legionary fortress at Bonn. The settlement extended north-south along the *limes* road.

In the 1st century the buildings were wooden: in the 2nd and 3rd centuries they were half-timbered structures on stone foundations. These were mainly strip houses. However, nearer to the legionary fortress superior housecomplexes were built in stone, eg an atrium house. A *beneficiarius* station was situated here. A cult centre lay directly south of the fortress. At the beginning of the 3rd century a forum/temple was built. A second cult centre lies under the present day minster. In the mid-2nd century a large temple dedicated to the *matrones Aufaniae* was built. The temple drew worshippers from all over the province.

The soldiers buried their dead along the *limes* road in the immediate vicinity of the fortress; in the *canabae legionis* the civilians buried their dead behind their houses. In the 2nd century an industrial area grew up further south along the *limes* road where industrial processes using fire (the manufacture of pottery, tiles and smoked meat) were relocated. After the Frankish attacks in 275 AD the *canabae legionis* were not rebuilt (M Gechter in Horn 1987, 364–72; *idem*, 1989; *Antonine Itinerary*, 250, 254, 3; 370, 7; *Peutinger Table*, II, 6).

Apud aram Ubiorum – Cologne (D)

Despite the present lack of evidence, *canabae legionis* must have existed in Cologne from 14 to 25 AD, during the short occupation of the double legionary fortress. It was probably situated south of the Ubian *oppidum*, in the area later occupied by the naval base at Cologne-Alteburg (H G Hellenkemper in Horn 1987, 459–61; B Päffgen, in press).

Novaesium – Neuss (D)

The *canabae legionis* of the fortress at Neuss are only documented for the period from Claudius to Domitian. The settlement was much smaller than that at Bonn, but similarly included potteries, tile and smoke kilns. Certain structures have produced evidence of several building phases, first in wood, followed by rebuilding in stone. With the transfer of the legion to Xanten-*Vetera* II at the end of the 1st century, the stone buildings of the *canabae legionis* were abandoned and later demolished (G Müller in Horn 1987, 580–88; Chantraine *et al* 1984, 81–6).

Vetera I – Xanten (D)

According to Tacitus, the *canabae legionis* of *Vetera castra* near Xanten had already developed into a proper *municipium* with a large population by 69 AD. The half-timbered buildings were destroyed with the fortress during the Batavian revolt (M Gechter in Romer 1987, 619–25; Tacitus *Histories*, IV, 22).

Auxiliary vici

Rigomagus-Remagen (D)

The *vicus* at Remagen lay south of the fort on the *limes* road. In the earlier phase the buildings were half-timbered, and were partly replaced in stone at a later date. The vicus's potteries supplied the civilian population and the troops. A *beneficiarius* station was situated here. After the assault on the fort in 275 AD the settlement was abandoned (H H Wegner in Cüppers 1990, 529–31; *Peutinger Table*, II 5).

Köln-Marienburg (D)

A *vicus* at the naval base of the Rhine fleet, which lies some 3 km south of the CCAA, is unknown (M Oschmann in Horn 1987, 516–19).

Durnomagus – Dormagen (D)

The fort and the *vicus* at Dormagen both lie on a side channel of the Rhine. The *limes* road ran between the embankment and the *vicus*. The remains of half-timbered houses, a Mithraeum and a *beneficiarius* station are all that is known of it. This *vicus* appears to have continued in existence into the 4th century, after the abandonment of the fort around 200 AD (G Muller in Horn 1987, 516–19; Gechter 1989, 74–6; *Antonine Itinerary*, 254, 5).

Burungum

This fort is known from the Antonine Itinerary, but the site has not yet been located (*Antonine Itinerary*, 255, 1).

Novaesium – Neuss (D)

The *vicus* was established after 100 AD on the same site as the former *canabae legionis* and extended north of the auxiliary fort on both sides of the *limes* road. Exca-vations have revealed half-timbered buildings. The discovery of a *fossa sanguinis* of the Cybele cult, dating to the 3rd century, is particularly remarkable. Neither the fort nor the *vicus* appear to have been rebuilt after 275 AD (G Muller in Horn 1987, 585; H G Horn, *ibid*, 588; *Antonine Itinerary*, 255, 2; 370, 5; *Peutinger Table*, II, 5).

Gelduba – Krefeld-Gellep (D)

The *vicus* lay in a half circle around the cavalry fort. The settlement included public baths, large warehouses and a large market hall interspersed with houses. A cult site with a Mithraeum and ritual shafts was situated southwest of the fort. The *vicus* originated in the Flavian period and was extended in stone in the 2nd century. It was not rebuilt after 275 AD (C Reichmann in Horn 1987, 534; *Antonine Itinerary*, 255.3).

Asciburgium – Moers-Asberg (D)

The *vicus* lay south of the fort on both sides of the *limes* road. The buildings consisted of half-timbered strip-houses lining the road. *Beneficiarii* were stationed here. Two pottery kilns of Claudian date were established in the settlement. It was founded in the Augustan period. After the abandonment of the fort in the Flavian period, it continued to exist, although reduced in size, until the end of 2nd century when it too was abandoned (T Bechert in Horn 1987, 565; *Peutinger Table*, II, 5).

Calo – Rheinberg-Strommoers (D)

In 1974 the remains of a settlement with half-timbered buildings and wells were discovered near Strommoers. It may well be the site of the hitherto unlocated fort of *Calo*, known only from the Antonine Itinerary. A *vicus* is unknown (source material unpublished; *Antonine Itinerary*, 255, 4; 370, 4).

Burginatium – Kalkar-Altkalkar (D)

Only the approximate site of the *vicus* is known. It is presumed to lie on both sides of the *limes* road to the north-west of the fort, which was founded in the Claudian period. A 3rd century dedication to Mithras is known (M Gechter in Horn 1987, 452; *Antonine Itinerary*, 256, 2; 370, 1; *Peutinger Table*, II 4/5).

Settlements at crossroads

Tolbiacum – Zülpich (D)

From the mid 1st century onwards, the site developed at an important nodal point where several major roads linked Bonn, Cologne and Neuss with Trier and Rheims. The settlement of the *vicani Tolbiacenses* was administered by the CCAA. It was situated on the Mühlenberg, west of the crossroads, where a dedication to the *deae Quadrubiae* stood. The settlement is mentioned by name for the first time by Tacitus, in the year 69 AD. In the 2nd century, a *beneficiarius* station was located here.

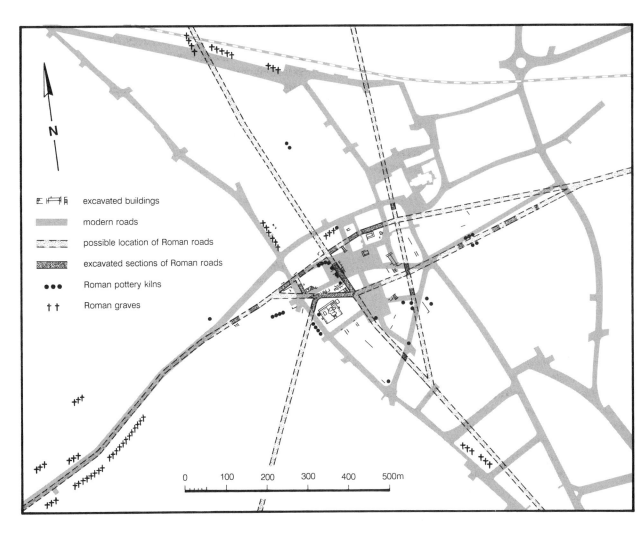

Fig 18.2. Coriovallum – Heerlen: settlement in the 2nd century, after W A van Es (shading indicates modern roads).

The public baths are the only buildings to have been excavated. They were built in the late 2nd century and continued in use until the 4th century. A cult centre lay south of *Tolbiacum*, near the village of Hoven, where the *matrones Albiahenae* and the *dea Sunuxal* were venerated. This *vicus* which was 6 ha in extent was destroyed in the Germanic invasion of 275 AD, but later rebuilt on a smaller scale and fortified (M Gechter in Horn 1987, 650–53; *Antonine Itinerary*, 373, 4; Tacitus, *Histories*, IV, 79).

Tiberiacum – Bergheim-Zieverich/Thorr (D)
This settlement is known only from the Antonine Itinerary. It is probably located at the crossroads of the Heerlen-Cologne and Trier-Neuss roads, as suggested by surface finds (Hagen 1931, 204–6; *Antonine Itinerary*, 375, 8).

Coriovallum – Heerlen (Fig 18.2) (NL)
This *vicus*, which lies on the crossroads of Aachen-Xanten and Cologne-Bavai roads was founded in the Augustan period. It experienced economic prosperity at the end of the 1st century; potteries were established, which continued in production until the end of the 2nd century. This prosperity was manifested in the building of large public baths, covering an area of some 2500 sq m. This is very unusual for a settlement of 10–15 ha in Lower Germany. *Coriovallum* was possibly the headquarters for the administration of the Baetasii. The *vicus* was administered by the city officials from the CUT. In the 4th century the settlement was fortified (van Es 1981, 147–50; *Antonine Itinerary*, 355, 7; 378, 6; *Peutinger Table*, II, 5).

Settlements at river crossings

Traiectum-Maastricht (NL)
The vicus of *Traiectum ad Mosam* developed at the crossing of the main Cologne-Bavai road over the Meuse at the beginning of the1st century. A river port was also established. In the 2nd century the *vicus* was rebuilt in stone and public baths constructed. In the 2nd and 3rd centuries a *vicus* developed on the west bank of the Meuse

– the present -day Wijk. Together the settlements were some 15 ha in extent. The settlement became important in the late Roman period, when it was fortified (van Es 1981, 145–6; Dijkmann 1992, 367–8).

Corigium – Jünkerath (D)

This, the southernmost *vicus* on Ubian territory, was the centre of the *pagus* of the Talliates. The settlement developed in the course on the 1st century on the Trier-Cologne road, around a bridge over the River Kyll. It consisted of strip houses with arcades fronting the road. The width of the house fronts was *c*10 m; the depth of the buildings as much as 24 m. Ironworking took place in the settlement. After 275 AD the *vicus* was rebuilt and fortified (Cüppers 1990 403–5; *Antonine Itinerary*, 373, 1; *Peutinger Table*, II 6).

Iuliacum – Jülich (D)

Jülich lay in Ubian territory, east of the river Rur. This *vicus* developed in the Augustan/Tiberian period on the important main road from Bavai to Cologne. The place name is verified by the find of a dedication to Jupiter, dating to the early 2nd century. Stone buildings were usual from the Flavian period onwards. The *vicus* was 10 ha in size. No complete ground plans of buildings are available from Jülich, as the medieval and post-medieval towns have destroyed much of the settlement. A *beneficiarius* station was situated here. There is evidence for a bakery, the working of copper alloys, shoemaking and textile production as well as the working of horn and bone. A small pottery and tile manufactory, dating to the lst century, was situated to the north of the settlement. Later, a potters' quarter developed to the south-east of the *vicus*. At the beginning of the 4th century Jülich was fortified.

On the opposite side of the river, in the territory of the Sunucci, a settlement developed between the roads to Aix-la-Chapelle and Heerlen. An aerial photograph shows buildings of the strip house type (CB Rüger in Horn 1987, 447–50; Perse 1992, 353–58; *Antonine Itinerary*, 375, 7; 378, 7; *Peutinger Table*, II, 5).

Rimburg (NL) – *Übach-Palenberg Schloss Rimburg* (D)

The present town of Rimburg lies in Holland; the castle on the other side of the river in Germany. The Roman settlement lay on both banks of the river Wurm on the Bavai-Cologne road. It developed around tne bridge in the Augustan period. The buildings are of the strip house type. A tavern has been located on a square. Evidence of a potters' quarter beginning in the 3rd century, a shoemaker's workshop and the maufacture of copper alloys has been found. The settlement continued into the 4th century; a fortification is unknown (Hagen 1931, 214; van Es 1981, 157–58).

Mönchengladbach – Mülfort (D)

Mülfort lies on the east bank of the river Niers, where it is crossed by the Neuss-Melik road. It is a typical roadside settlement, which probably developed from a military post of the Augustan period, as indicated by a soldier's grave of this date. In the 2nd century, the settlement extended for some 600 m along the road, covering some 11 ha. The houses were fronted by arcades. Pottery and tiles were made within the settlement. In the mid 2nd century a fortified granary was built in wood and replaced in stone in the 3rd century. The *vicus* was not rebuilt after 275 AD. On the opposite bank of the river was a similar, but smaller settlement on Baetasian territory (D von Detten in Horn 1987, 554–7; *idem* 1991, 54–5; M Gechter, *Stadtgeschichte Mönchengladbach*, in press).

Small settlements on major roads

Marcomagus – Marmagen (D)

The site is named in the Antonine Itinerary and the Peutinger Map. It lies at the junction of the Trier-Cologne and Trier-Bonn roads. Archaeologically, nothing is known of it (*Antonine Itinerary*, 373, 2; *Peutinger Table*, II, 6).

Belgica – Euskirchen-Billig (D) (Fig 18.3)

The Roman settlement lies near the present day village of Billig, at the junction of the roads from Zülpich, Bonn and Cologne to Trier. *Beneficiarii* appear to have been stationed there since the Flavian period. The settlement is triangular in form; some 20 building complexes have been documented. They are mostly of the well known strip house type, 5–15m wide and 20–35 m long. The fronts of the buildings are taken up by shops facing the road. Four square buildings, probably taverns with an upper storey, were situated at the crossroads. A market place has also been identified. The *vicus* covered some 10 ha. Dedications and cult statues suggest that temples to Jupiter, Diana, Mithras and several *Matronae* must have existed. The settlement continued into the 5th/6th century. The site does not appear to have been fortified (C B Ruger in Horn 1987, 422–5; *Antonine Itinerary*, 373, 3).

Theudurum – Selfkant-Tüddern (D)

This settlement is known from the Antonine Itinerary and is usually equated with Tüddern, which lies on the Heerlen-Xanten road. The site covers an area of roughly 9 ha (*Antonine Itinerary*, 375, 5).

Mederiacum – Melick (NL)

This *vicus*, which is situated on the Heerlen-Xanten road, is named in the Antonine Itinerary and may be associated with Melick (*Antonine Itinerary*, 355, 4).

Sablones

This *vicus* is known only from the Antonine Itinerary,

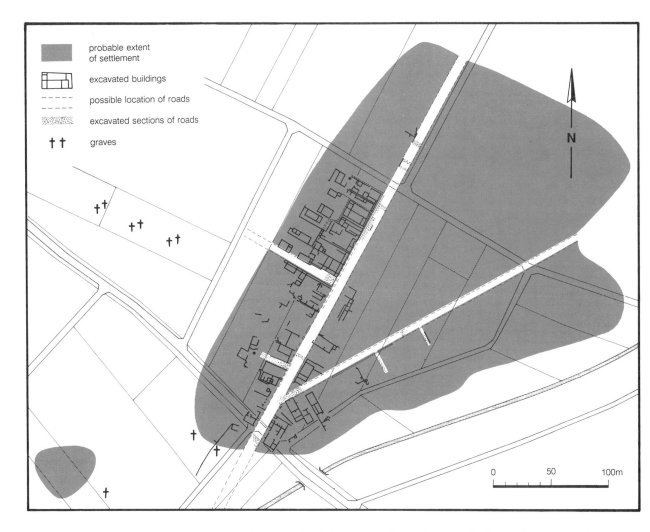

Fig 18.3 *Belgica: Euskirchen – Billing; settlement in the 2nd century, after H G Horn (shading indicates probable area of settlement).*

where it is described as lying on the Heerlen-Xanten road. It may possibly be associated with settlement remains found at Venlo (van Es 1981, 158; *Antonine Itinerary*, 355, 3).

Mediolanum
This settlement on the Heerlen-Xanten road is similarly only known from the Antonine Itinerary. It may be identical with the present day settlement of Pont (*Antonine Itinerary*, 375, 2).

Feresne
In the Peutinger Map, the settlement is situated on the Maastricht-Nijmegen road. The exact site remains unknown (*Peutinger Table*, II, 5).

Catualium – Haelen (NL)
This site is also marked in the Peutinger Map on the Maastricht-Nijmegen road and probably lies under the present settlement at Haelen (Rüger 1968, 40: van Es 1981, 157; *Peutinger Table*, II, 4).

Blariacum – Venlo-Blerik (NL)
This settlement on the Maastricht-Nijmegen road is shown on the Peutinger Map. It may possibly have been sited opposite Sablones, which is presumed to be situated near Venlo (van Es 1981, 158; *Peutinger Table*, II, 4).

Wesseling (D)
The site lies at the junction of the *limes* road and the road from *Belgica vicus*. Settlement remains have yet to be found, but the presence of large cemeteries and dedications to the *Iunones* and the *matronae Afliae* indicate the existence of a settlement some 5 ha in size, in the 2nd and 3rd centuries (Horn 1987, 617–8).

Segorigium – Cologne-Worringen (D)
The *vicus* is known only from a dedication by the *vicani Segorigiensis* (CIL XIII, 8518) (Rüger 1968, 81).

Novaesium – Neuss (D)
The *vicus*, which lies beneath the medieval town of Neuss, was founded in the Tiberian period. It was built on both sides of the *limes* road. The settlement was extended and

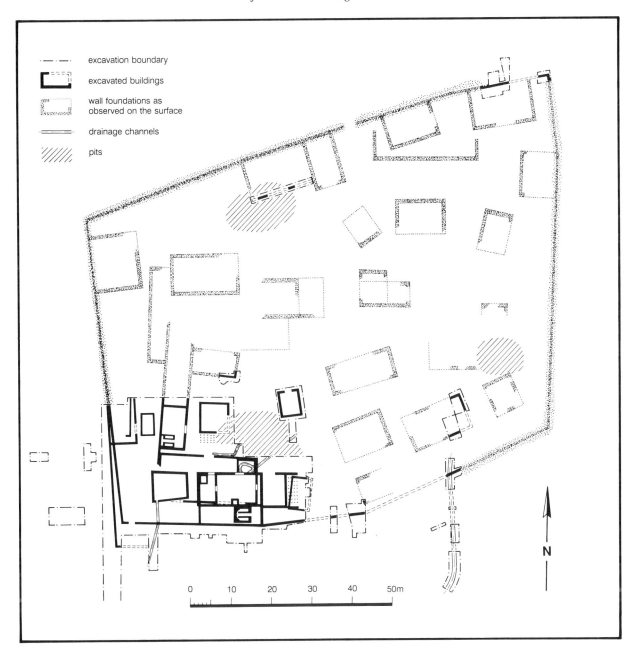

Legend
- — · — excavation boundary
- excavated buildings
- wall foundations as observed on the surface
- drainage channels
- pits

0 10 20 30 40 50m

N

Fig 18.4 Bad Neuenahr – Ahrweiler : industrial settlement in the 2nd/3rd century, after H Cüppers.

reconstructed in stone during the Flavian period and covered some 12 ha. Several buildings with hypocaust heating dating to the 2nd/3rd centuries have been found. The site was possibly fortified in the late Roman period (G Muller in Horn 1987, 586).

Rural settlements

Tönisvorst-Vorst (D)
A large Roman cemetery dating from the Tiberian to the Antonine periods has recently been excavated near Vorst. The settlement belonging to the cemetery has not yet been located. An analysis of the cremated bone indicates that in the 2nd century the settlement must have included more than four households. At the end of the 2nd century the site was abandoned (C Bridger, unpublished PhD thesis, Bonn 1992).

Industrial settlements

Sinzig (D)
Sinzig is a pottery manufacturing centre south of the river Ahr. It was situated at the mouth of the river between the Rhine and the *limes* road. Settlement remains are unknown but four pottery kilns and one tile kiln have been excavated. The pottery dates to the 1st and 2nd centuries. Potters from Trier tried to produce *terra sigillata* here in the middle of the 2nd century. This was soon

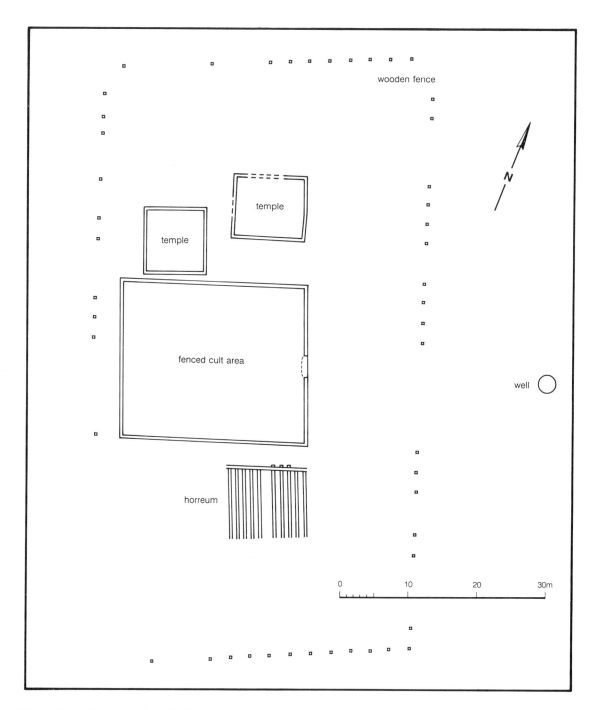

Fig 18.5 *Bad Munstereifel – Nöthen: religious settlement in the first half of the 2nd century, after H G Horn.*

abandoned as the quality of the local clay was too poor (H H Wegner in Cüppers 1990, 554–5).

Bad Neuenahr-Ahrweiler (D) (Fig 18.4)
In 1959 a small settlement was discovered in the hills south of the Ahr valley, in which iron ore was smelted. The settlement was enclosed by a wall. The buildings were simple rectangular half-timbered structures built on stone foundations. A furnace was also excavated. Slag

heaps were spread throughout the area. The settlement dates from the 1st to the 4th century (H H Wegner in Horn 1987, 326; Kleemann 1971, 34,77).

Religious settlements

Bad Münstereifel-Nöthen (D) (Fig 18.5)
This small settlement, situated at the top of a hill, originally included three temples and a granary dating to the

mid 1st century. The area was enclosed by a wooden fence. One temple was enlarged in the second half of the 2nd century. Here the *matrones Vacallinehae* were venerated. The dedicatees came from the local neighbourhood. It is not known whether accommodation for the priest or an inn lie outside the enclosed temple area; this is likely to be the case. In the 4th century the complex was rebuilt in stone. Four cult-buildings were constructed, including a Romano-Gallic temple and a basilica. The complex was destroyed at the end of the 4th century (Horn 1987, 342–5).

Bonna – Bonn (D)
For the religious settlement at Bonn see above.

Marcodurum – Düren-Mariaweiler/Hoven (D)
The Ubian settlement of *Marcodurum*, mentioned by Tacitus (*Histories*, IV, 28) has long been associated with a Roman settlement on the west bank of the Rur, between Mariaweiler and Hoven. Only surface finds are known from this site, including the ornamented stone door frame of a temple entrance. The large numbers of metal finds from this unexcavated site indicate the presence of a native settlement. Late Celtic coins and the ornamented door frame suggest that this may be the site of an Ubian settlement with a cult centre dating to the beginning of the 1st century (finds unpublished; Hagen 1931, 241).

Nettersheim (D)
The cult centre of the *matrones Aufaniae* was situated on high ground between two streams, the Urft and the Schleif. Three cult buildings lay within an enclosure. An inscription names the donors as the inhabitants of the neighbouring *vicus*, whose name remains unknown. Only one building in this *vicus* has as yet been excavated. Nearby, a *beneficiarius* post was situated on the main Cologne-Trier road. The *vicus* dates from the 2nd to the 4th century (Horn 1987, 571–4).

Acknowledgements
The text was translated by Jennifer Göbel.

Bibliography

Antonine Itinerary A Reise, *Das Rheinische Germanien in der antiken Literatur*, Leipzig, 1892 (reprint 1969, XIII, 99–113)

van Buren, AE, 1955 *Vicus*, in *Paulys Realencyclopädie der Classischen Altertumswissenschaft*, 2090–4.

Chantraine, H, *et al*, 1984 *Das römische Neuss*

Cüppers, H, 1990 *Die Römer in Rheinland – Pfalz*

v Detten, D, 1991 *Arch in Deutschland*, 1

Dijkmann, W, 1992 Funde aus Maastricht in *Spurensicherung. Archäologische Denkmalpflege in der Euregio Maas – Rhein*, Ausst Katalog Aachen. Kunst u Altertum am Rhein 136 (Mainz), 367f

v Es, WA, 1981 *De Romeinen in Nederland*

Galsterer, B H, 1992 Romanisation und ein heimische Tradition, in *Die römische Stadt im 2 Jahrhundert n Chr*, 377–89

Gechter, M, 1989 *Castra Bonnensi*

——, 1989 *Arch Rheinland*, 74–6

——, 1992 Das Städische Umland in Niedergermanien im 2 Jahrhundert n Chr, in *Die römische Stadt im 2 Jahrhundert n Chr*, 153–61

Grenier A, 1931 *Manuel d'archéologie gallo-romaine II*, 695 ff

Hagen, J, 1931 *Römerstrassen.*

Horn, H G, 1987 *Die Römer in Nordrhein-Westfalen*

Kleemann, O, 1971 *Vor-und Frügeschichte des Kreises Ahrweiler*

Kunow, J, 1988 Zentrale Orte in der Germania Inferior, *Arch Korrespondenzbl*, 18, 55–67

——, 1989 Strukturen im Raum, *Arch Korrespondenzbl*, 19, 377–90

——, 1992 Zentralität und Urbanität in der Germania Inferior des 2 Jahrhunderts n Chr, in *Die römische Stadt im 2 Jahrhundert n Chr*, 142–52

Perse, M. 1992 Stadarchäologie in Jülich, in *Spurensicherung* (as above, under Dijkmann 1992), 353 f

v Petrikovits, H, 1977 *Kleinstadte und nichtstädtische Siedlungen im Nordwesten des römischen Reiches, das Dorf der Eisenzeit und des frühen Mittelalters*, 86–134

——, 1980 in *Rheinische Gesichte* 1,1, 118–24

Peutinger Table K Miller, *Die Peutinger Tafel*, 1887 (reprint 1961)

Rüger, C B, 1968 *Germania Inferior*

Schalles, H J, v Hesberg, H, Zanker, P, 1992 *Die römische Stadt im 2 Jahrhundert*

Sommer, S, 1992 Die Städischen Siedlungen im rechtsrheinischen Obergermanien, in *Die römische Stadt im 2 Jahrhundert n Chr*, 119–41

19   Small towns: then, now – and then?

John Wacher

Modern urban archaeology, with some minor exceptions, began in the 1940s, largely due to the work of the Luftwaffe. Unfortunately, or perhaps fortunately for the inhabitants, it normally bombed the most important centres of industry or communication, or antiquity (the so-called Baedeker raids), which usually corresponded with the chartered towns or *civitas* capitals, such as Canterbury, Exeter and London. For those interested in the small towns, and they were then very few, only Bath was as severely treated. Consequently when archaeologists awoke to the fact that there was a golden opportunity, the like of which had never occurred before and might never occur again, it was to the major towns that attention was turned, beginning with Canterbury in 1944 (Williams 1947).[1] Also, as yet, many small towns were still greenfield sites or under only moderate ploughing and continued to slumber undisturbed until in 1950, Nottingham University began its annual summer school for extra-mural students at Great Casterton (subsequently published: Corder 1951, 1954, 1961; Todd 1968) Among the tutors was Graham Webster, who may properly be called the father of small town archaeology, and who went on to explore a number of sites in the Midlands, such as Wall, Kenchester and Chesterton-on-Fosse. But even then it was often only the defences which were examined, since it was thought simplistically that they could tell most about the history of a town's development, and in many cases they still survived as standing earthworks.

But by then also, other things were beginning to happen to the English countryside. New arterial roads and motorways, some planned before the war, suddenly became realities, as at Water Newton, Catterick and Springhead.[2] Large new suburbs and housing estates began to proliferate, as at Alcester (Mahany forthcoming: Booth 1980). Moreover, not satisfied with the destruction wrought by the Luftwaffe, developers started pulling down town centres for rebuilding, while the most serious threat to many small towns was the ploughing, with attached government grants, of more and more grassland with ever-deepening ploughs. The latter was insidious and it was some time before archaeologists realised

just how much damage was being done; but often by then it was too late.

As a result, interest in small town archaeology was gradually aroused and a fair amount has since been saved. We shall never know, though, how much was lost and there are still occasional horror stories, such as the wholesale destruction of a large part of Whilton Lodge.[3] The introduction of management agreements by the old Ancient Monuments Board of the Department of the Environment, whereby farmers were paid not to plough specified sites helped a little. But invariably the areas so designated are minimal and often cover no more than the interior and fortifications of a settlement, such as Chesterton-on-Fosse, and completely exclude any suburbs or cemeteries.

What then is known? Of the larger examples, we have a tolerable knowledge of Corbridge, Water Newton and Kenchester, mainly from aerial photographs.[4] The defences of the first remain somewhat elusive; nor do we know how the military establishments functioned in relation to the town. Corbridge is the only known case so far in Britain, apart from London, where there is a close conjunction between military and civil. Carlisle and Ilchester still remain largely unexplored internally, although modest amounts of information have recently been recovered from the former (McCarthy 1984, 65–74). Ilchester has produced some interesting suburbs and cemeteries (Leach 1982; Burrow 1984, 21–2).

With the minor fortified towns, our knowledge is patchy. Alchester, Godmanchester, Catterick and Wanborough possess recognisable plans and histories of development;[5] but the defences of the latter remain a puzzle. Extra-mural areas have been extensively explored at Towcester, Braughing, Alcester and Ilchester,[6] but less is known of the internal arrangements, while the fortifications of Dorchester-on-Thames and Great Casterton have been reasonably well documented (Frere 1962, 114–49; 1985, 91–174; Corder 1951–61; Todd 1968).

Sites with specialised functions have tended to be of greater interest and have therefore received more attention. The religious establishments at Bath have long been famous, although little is known about the defences and other areas in the town (Cunliffe 1969; 1976, 1–32; 1979; Cunliffe & Davenport 1985). Other similar religious centres at Nettleton, Springhead, Wycomb and Frilford have been more generally covered (summaries in Burnham & Wacher 1990, chap 9), mainly because they are not encumbered by modern towns. Industrial centres, such as Charterhouse, Droitwich, Mancetter and Wilderspool have yielded a great deal of information which is sometimes of variable quality and not always evenly distributed over the sites (*ibid*, chap 10). Among the number of uncategorised and undefended sites, Ashton, Baldock, Camerton, Sapperton, Tiddington and Hibaldstow are probably the best known in terms of plan and development (*ibid*, chap 12, and this volume).

Some 50 small towns have so far been identified in Britain. It can, therefore, be claimed that of this number only about 20 have been extensively investigated. For the remainder our knowledge ranges from moderate to virtually nothing, as at Buxton and Willoughby. But it must also be admitted that as a class, it is often extremely difficult to extract evidence from small towns by excavation, even when they are still open fields, for a number of reasons.

Many of the vernacular buildings in small towns were often of an ephemeral character, leaving little trace of floors or foundations. The former frequently only survive for the early levels, while the overall depth of stratified deposits is not great when compared with major towns. When combined with the deep ploughing of open field sites, the result is the virtual total removal of the latest, and probably most significant, layers. In addition, haphazard stone robbing, following ploughing, has more often than not removed even the indications of wall trenches. Consequently, of all classes of Romano-British monuments, small towns are the most difficult to interpret and least clearly understood.

But the frequent inability to find buildings on some sites may have other causes. At some, such as Wall, Mancetter (Burnham & Wacher 1990, 276, 259), Caistor (Lincs) and Horncastle (*ibid*, 240–45), there is an almost total lack of masonry buildings contemporary with the defences, and it may also be true of others. It is likely that many of these fortified enclosures situated on main roads were *burgi*, as Webster has shown, and similar to a number of late road stations in northern Gaul and Germany (Webster 1971, 38–45). Thus the enclosures were probably purely military in origin. It is not known if or when units of the field armies were deployed in Britain in the 4th century. Catterick seems to have been partly converted to hold a cavalry unit after 370 (Wacher 1971, 171) but elsewhere there are no convincing signs of any mobile field units. But the first need for such a unit, especially if operating widely, was a secure base for food, equipment, spare horses and fodder. Are we therefore looking in vain for permanent buildings in these enclosures? There was certainly a return to timber construction in some Saxon Shore forts (Cunliffe 1975, 65–8)

while tents were still known, as Vegetius makes clear. Moreover, horses do not have to be kept under cover, although some form of protection for fodder would be required. At over a thousand cubic metres of modern compressed hay for a single troop of thirty or so horses[7] this would represent a sizeable stack for a complete regiment. But it would leave little archaeological trace. So there is a problem here which needs to be addressed in the future.

Others also abound. Undoubtedly though the most pressing need is preservation of what is left from ploughing or development. It should not be beyond the wit of English Heritage to negotiate terms through the Ministry of Agriculture to include such sites in the set-aside policy for farmers, thus preserving them from continued ploughing. But even here some kind of site management would be required to prevent the growth of scrub or trees, or erosion by stock.

In general terms, it now seems clear that the origins of most small towns lay in Iron Age settlements or in the *vici* attached to sometime forts, or in a combination of both. But proof and more detailed information is needed of many individual examples, as well as the mechanics by which an Iron Age village or farm, or a *vicus*, became a small town.

Although many sites are best known for their defences, more information is still required about them, although in many cases the poor state of survival does not help. Very few gates have been excavated, Chesterton-on-Fosse, Kenchester, Great Chesterford and Godmanchester providing the few planned examples.[8] The distribution of interval towers seems very erratic, as it does with major towns; many such as Wall, Mancetter and Catterick appear to have none, yet Great Casterton is equipped at the angles, as is Ancaster, where the unusual fan-shaped towers are reminiscent of the eastern Danube frontier (Todd 1981, 29–35; for the Danubian examples Mócsy 1974, 108). Refinement in the dating of fortifications is everywhere required, although this introduces a factor not confined to small towns alone.

Closely related to the problems of defences are those concerning the physical expansion or contraction of a settlement. From what little information that is available, it is clear that considerable changes can be expected to have occurred in settlement density and land use in the peripheral areas of small towns. These will, of course, reflect social and economic variations.

Streets could profitably be examined in greater detail not, as they often are at present, by cutting sections across them, but by stripping lengths, especially at junctions, where it will be possible to test the oft-repeated supposition that 'the street system developed piecemeal'. Moreover, street surfaces can sometimes be related to the construction of defences, with a corresponding change occurring in the aggregate used, as at Brough-on-Humber and Cirencester.[9]

In most small towns there must have been official, or

quasi-official, buildings, such as *mansiones*, *mutationes*, granaries, stores-buildings for collecting taxes in kind, and residences for the different kinds of *regionarii*, who are attested by inscriptions at all too few sites. *Mansiones* can be identified with some confidence, but the remainder represent many difficulties of interpretation, even when possible candidates have been discovered.

One remarkable factor, hitherto almost unnoticed, and common to many towns throughout Britain, both major and minor, was an almost universal architectural revolution, when timber gave way to masonry for domestic and commercial buildings in the late 2nd and 3rd centuries. What social or economic changes are concealed here? It probably has little to do with the longevity of timber-framed or half-timbered buildings which is often quoted as no more than 25 years. Properly constructed and maintained, these, as well as cob and other clay-based structures, can survive for several hundred years, as indeed many still do today from the Middle Ages. Was it because the demand for stone for public buildings had been satisfied, leaving the quarries with surplus capacity, before the onset of major defensive schemes must once again have absorbed all that they could produce?

Small towns, with their lower building densities, also provide splendid opportunities for the study of property boundaries, such as have been observed at Hibaldstow, Baldock and Ashton among others.[10] These would amply repay a more comprehensive study as would also the means by which water supplies were provided. Very few small towns had aqueducts which, given their fairly common occurrence in the major towns, is surprising and illuminates the sharp difference in basic amenities enjoyed by the two classes of site.

Another question which needs an answer is why there was so much metallurgical activity in almost all small towns, far beyond, so it would seem, the needs of the local community. Again this is something of a contrast with major towns, and may reflect local service areas more accurately. It also reflects on the argument that most of the population would have been engaged in agriculture and the production of food, even on a mixed farm. Periods of intense activity are interspersed with lulls when little or nothing needs, or can be, done.

Looking to the future, and apart from the prime need of preservation, what is wanted is a coordinated and systematic study, perhaps sponsored by a national society or other body, of a type already suggested by the present writer elsewhere (Burnham & Wacher 1990, 321). Then perhaps we shall begin to understand the place which this very varied class of monument occupied in the scheme of things in Roman Britain.

Notes

1. For a review of these earliest excavations in their context see Frere 1984, 29–46
2. The dual carriageway of the A1 skirts the south-western side of the walled enclosure at Water Newton (Frere & St Joseph 1983, 172), while the new line of the A1 at Catterick Bridge cuts through the middle of the small town. Springhead is similarly bisected (Burnham & Wacher 1990, 59)
3. A large part of the interior was stripped to the subsoil before excavations could take place: *Britannia* 3 (1972), 325; 4 (1973), 296
4. Convenient summaries for most of the sites mentioned in the text can be found in Burnham & Wacher 1990. See also Bishop & Dore 1988 for Corbridge; Mackreth 1979 and this volume for Water Newton; Wilmott 1980, 117–33 for Kenchester
5. Alchester: Burnham & Wacher 1990, 98; Godmanchester: Green, 1975, 197; Catterick: Wacher 1971, 167–74; Wilson, Jones & Evans (eds) 1984; Wanborough: Phillips & Walters 1977, 223–7; Anderson & Wacher 1980, 115–26
6. Towcester: Brown, Woodfield & Mynard 1983, 43–140; Woodfield 1994; Braughing: Partridge 1975; Alcester: Mahany forthcoming; Booth 1980; Ilchester: Leach 1982; Burrow 1984, 21–2
7. Information from Miss Shirley Renowden, Old Mill Stables, Lelant, Cornwall
8. Chesterton: *J Roman Stud*, 52, 1962, 171; Kenchester: Heys & Thomas 1959, 100–116; Great Chesterford: Brinson 1963, 76; *Britannia* 12, 1981, 350; Godmanchester: Green 1975, 204
9. Brough: Wacher 1969, 55–6; a similar change was also observed in the streets of Cirencester. Although this has not yet been fully published, it can be observed in the illustrated section: Wacher & McWhirr 1982, fig 6.
10. Hibaldstow: Smith, 1987, 189–98; Baldock: Stead & Rigby 1986; Ashton: Dix 1983, 18–20; *Britannia*, 6, 1975, 253; 8, 1977, 399; 9, 1978, 442; 10, 1979, 302; 12, 1981, 341; 14, 1983, 305–6; 15, 1984, 300–1; 16, 1985, 288; 17, 397

Bibliography

Anderson, A S, & Wacher, J, 1980 Excavations at Wanborough, Wiltshire: an interim report, *Britannia,* 11, 115–26

Bishop, M C, & Dore, J N, 1988 *Corbridge: excavations in the Roman fort and town 1947–1980*

Booth, P, 1980 *Roman Alcester*

Brinson, J G S, 1963 Great Chesterford, in Romano-British Essex (ed M R Hull), *Victoria County Hist Essex,* Vol 3, 72–88

Brown, A E, Woodfield, C, & Mynard, D C, 1983 Excavations at Towcester, Northamptonshire: the Alchester Road suburb, *Northamptonshire Archaeol,* 18, 43–140

Burnham, B C, & Wacher, J, 1990 *The 'small towns' of Roman Britain*

Burrow, I, 1984 Ilchester, Northover and Limington Road, in Somerset Archaeology 1982 (eds I Burrow, S Minnitt & B Murless), *Somerset Archaeol Natur Hist Soc,* 127 (1982), 21–2

Butler, R M (ed), 1971 *Soldier and civilian in Roman Yorkshire*

Corder, P, 1951 *The Roman town and villa at Great Casterton; 1st interim report*

——, 1954 *The Roman town and villa at Great Casterton: 2nd interim report*

——, 1961 *The Roman town and villa at Great Casterton: 3rd interim report*

Cunliffe, B W, 1969 *Roman Bath*, Soc Antiq Res Rep 24

——, 1975 *Excavations at Portchester, Vol 1*, Soc Antiq Res Rep 32

——, 1976 The Roman baths at Bath: excavations 1969–75, *Britannia*, 7, 1–32

—— (ed), 1979 *Excavations in Bath 1950–75*

——, & Davenport, P, 1985 *The temple of Sulis Minerva at Bath, Vol 1: the site*, Oxford Comm Archaeol Monogr 7

Dix, B, 1983, Ashton Roman town, *South Midlands Archaeol*, 13 (1983), 18–20

Frere, S S, 1962 Excavations at Dorchester-on-Thames 1962, *Archaeol J*, 119, 114–49

——, 1984 Canterbury: the post-war excavations, *Archaeol Cantiana*, 100, 29–46

——, 1985 Excavations at Dorchester-on-Thames 1963, *Archaeol J*, 141, 91–174

——, & St Joseph, J K S, 1983 *Roman Britain from the air*

Green, H J M, 1975 Roman Godmanchester, in *The 'small towns' of Roman Britain* (eds W Rodwell & T Rowley), BAR Brit Ser, 15, 183–210

Heys, F G, & Thomas, M J, 1959 Excavation on the defences of the Romano-British town of Kenchester, *Trans Woolhope Natur Fld Club Herefordshire*, 36 (1958), 100–116

Leach, P, 1982 *Ilchester, vol I: excavations 1974–1975*

Mackreth, D, 1979 Durobrivae, *Durobrivae, a review of Nene valley archaeology*, 7, 19–21

McCarthy, M R, 1984 Roman Carlisle, in *Settlement and society in the Roman North* (eds P R Wilson, R F J Jones, & D M Evans), 65–74

Mahany, C, forthcoming *Roman Alcester*

Mócsy, A, 1974 *Pannonia and Upper Moesia*

Partridge, C, 1975 Braughing, in *The 'small towns' of Roman Britain* (eds W Rodwell & T Rowley), BAR Brit Ser, 15, 139–57

Phillips, B, & Walters, B, 1977 A *mansio* at Lower Wanborough, Wiltshire, *Britannia*, 8, 223–7

Smith, R F, 1987 *Roadside settlements in lowland Roman Britain*, BAR Brit Ser, 157

Stead, I M, & Rigby, V, 1986 *Baldock: the excavation of a Roman and pre-Roman settlement, 1968–1972*

Todd, M, 1968 *The Roman fort at Great Casterton, Rutland: excavations in 1960 and 1962*

——, 1981 *The Roman town at Ancaster, Lincolnshire*

Wacher, J, 1969 *Excavations at Brough on Humber 1958–1961*, Soc Antiq Res Rep 25

——, 1971 Yorkshire towns in the fourth century, in *Soldier and civilian in Roman Yorkshire* (ed R M Butler), 165–77

——, & McWhirr, A, 1982 *Cirencester excavations I: early Roman occupation at Cirencester*

Webster, G, 1971 A Roman system of fortified posts along Watling Street, Britain, in *Roman frontier studies 1967* (ed S Applebaum), 38–45

Williams, A, 1947 *Roman Canterbury, No 2*

Wilmott, A, 1980 Kenchester (Magnis): a reconsideration, *Trans Woolhope Natur Fld Club, Herefordshire*, 43, 117–33

Wilson, P R, 1984 Recent work at Catterick, in *Settlement and society in the Roman North* (eds P R Wilson, R F J Jones & D M Evans)

Woodfield, C, 1994 The defences of Towcester, Northamptonshire, *Northamptonshire Archaeol*, 13, 67–86